HUGH S. JOHNSON AND THE NEW DEAL

HUGH S. JOHNSON
AND THE NEW DEAL

JOHN KENNEDY OHL

NORTHERN ILLINOIS UNIVERSITY PRESS

DEKALB, ILLINOIS

1985

Library of Congress Cataloging in Publication Data

Ohl, John Kennedy, 1942–
  Hugh S. Johnson and the New Deal.

  Bibliography: p.
  Includes index.
  1. Johnson, Hugh S. (Hugh Samuel), 1882–1942.
2. New Deal, 1933–1939. 3. United States—History—
1933–1945. 4. Politicians—United States—Biography.
5. United States. National Recovery Administration—
Officials and employees—Biography. I. Title.
E748.J35O37 1985   973.917'092'4   85-10456
ISBN 0-87580-110-2

Excerpts from *The Blue Eagle from Egg to Earth* by Hugh S. Johnson.
Copyright 1935 by Doubleday & Company, Inc. Reprinted by permission of
Doubleday & Company, Inc.

The following memoirs from the Columbia Oral History Collection are
copyright by The Trustees of Columbia University in the City of New York
and are used by permission. Dates of copyright are: 1972: Chester C. Davis,
William H. Davis, Julius Emspak, Gardner Jackson, Marvin Jones, Gerard
Swope; 1975: James B. Carey, Jerome N. Frank, Ernest Gross, Milton Handler,
James M. Landis, Eugene Meyer, M. L. Wilson; 1976: Frances Perkins, Henry A.
Wallace; 1980: James P. Warburg; 1984: Charles E. Wyzanski.

For Maria, whose encouragement made this book possible

CONTENTS

PREFACE

IN THE summer of 1933 the United States was mired in the worst depression in its history. Many factories lay idle, and over one-fourth of the work force was jobless. Millions of others were working only for a pittance. Responding to the desperate pleas of business and labor for action, Congress, in June 1933, passed the National Industrial Recovery Act, a twofold measure designed to speed recovery and cure economic ills through industrial self-government and public works spending. Harking back to World War I, when business and government had cooperated through the War Industries Board to mobilize industry behind the war effort, the program for industrial self-government was based on the assumption that businessmen, coordinated and assisted by the federal government, could bring about economic recovery and social progress. During the next two years industrial self-government, as implemented by the National Recovery Administration, was at the center stage of President Franklin D. Roosevelt's New Deal. Under the aegis of NRA, more than 500 industries drew up fair trade codes governing business and labor practices, and for a brief time many believed that NRA was leading the nation into a new age of prosperity and industrial harmony. Before long, however, a wide gap developed between the promise and the reality of industrial self-government, turning NRA into a major arena of conflict. When the Supreme Court declared NRA unconstitutional in 1935, the agency had few mourners.

More than any other individual, Hugh S. Johnson was the architect of the depression-inspired experiment in industrial self-government. A veteran of the WIB and a man possessing an encyclopedic knowledge of American industry, he was a vital advocate of industrial self-government within the Roosevelt circle in the spring of 1933. Then, as head of NRA from 1933 to 1934, he directed its implementation. In the process he became, next to the president, the most visible of the early New Dealers. Johnson's prominence as a New Deal–era figure continued after the demise of NRA, when he became a syndicated newspaper columnist whose pungent opinions on domestic and foreign policy kept him in the national limelight.

The primary purpose of this book is to examine Johnson's role as an exponent of industrial self-government in the early New Deal years. It is my intention to show that as NRA administrator he had a significant impact on the American political economy during that critical period and, through a recounting of his activities, to illuminate the limitations of industrial self-government as a managerial tool for achieving stability and progress in twentieth-century America. I have not, however, restricted my study to Johnson's NRA tenure. I also describe his pre–NRA career, for it was marked by varied experiences and accomplishments in both the military and business that readied him for his NRA stint. In this respect, Johnson personifies the emergence of industrial self-government and its transmission, from the mobilization of 1917–1918 to the recovery effort of 1933. In addition, I describe Johnson's post–NRA career, because his growing estrangement from the New Deal and Roosevelt reflects many of the personal and ideological factors that shaped the opposition to the president and his policies in the late 1930s and early 1940s.

I would like to express my gratitude to a number of individuals for their help in the preparation of this book. More than two decades ago, Professor Ralph F. de Bedts of Old Dominion University began researching Johnson's career. He secured what was left of Johnson's private papers, the bulk of which were destroyed in a storm, from Johnson's secretary and interviewed some of Johnson's surviving family members and acquaintances. Later he turned his attention to another project and most graciously permitted me to use the Johnson material he had put together. I also have benefitted from the assistance of my fellow historians who have offered advice and encouragement, and it was my good fortune to have Professors Daniel R. Beaver of the University of Cincinnati, Thomas E. Vadney of the University of Manitoba, Ellis W. Hawley of the University of Iowa, and Jordan A. Schwarz of Northern Illinois University read the manuscript and give me their perceptive comments. Of course, I assume full responsibility for whatever shortcomings that survived their inspection. Many librarians and archivists aided my research, and I wish that I could acknowledge them all by name; but the list would be too long. I would be remiss, though, if I did not single out the library staff of Mesa Community College for its diligence in fulfilling my countless requests for interlibrary loan items.

There are other debts as well. I am grateful for the permission granted by Hugh S. Johnston to use quotations from his father's and grandfather's materials; by Eric Wolman to cite the Reminiscences of Leo Wolman in the Columbia Oral History Collection; by Doubleday and Company, Inc. to quote from Hugh S. Johnson, *The Blue Eagle from Egg to Earth*, copyright 1935; by The Trustees of Columbia University in the City of New York to cite and quote from copyrighted reminiscences in the Columbia Oral History Collection; by Grace F. Tugwell to quote from the papers of Rexford Tugwell; by the Joint Collection, University of Missouri Western Historical Manuscript Collection—Columbia and State Historical Society of Missouri Manuscripts to cite and quote from the papers of Enoch H. Crowder and George N. Peek; by Princeton University Library to cite and quote from the papers of Bernard M. Baruch; and by the editor of *Montana: The Magazine of Western History* to draw upon material which first appeared in that magazine. I would also like to extend my appreciation to the staff of the Northern Illinois University Press, and in particular my editor, Wanda H. Giles, who skillfully guided my study from the manuscript stage to completed book.

Finally, and most importantly, I would like to thank Maria, my wife. A loving mother and a supportive partner, she gave much of herself to this book. For this reason I affectionately dedicate it to her.

Mesa, Arizona
September 1984

HUGH S. JOHNSON AND THE NEW DEAL

CHAPTER I

EARLY STUFF

A S CLODS of mud thumped against her Kansas-prairie sod house, accompanied by angry shouts, the alarmed mother of four-year-old Hugh Samuel Johnson opened the door. The target of a semicircle of outraged youngsters, backed up against the door, crying, and completely outnumbered, Hugh was nevertheless defiant, screaming to his tormentors that "everybody in the world is a rink-stink but Hughie Johnson and he's all right."[1] The reason for this altercation has not been recorded. But it shows Hugh Johnson, even in his tender years, as the fighter with a lusty flair for invective who would one day captivate the American people and also become one of the most controversial New Deal figures.

HUGH Johnson was the offspring of a vigorous frontier family. The Johnstons, as the name was then spelled, came to New York state from northern Ireland around 1812. A half century later, Hugh's grandfather, Samuel Johnston, who received serious wounds in his Civil War service as captain of a New York Irish regiment some fifty years later, moved his wife and children to Chillicothe, Illinois. There Sam Johnston, one of Samuel's four sons and Hugh's father, grew up, read law, and married his childhood sweetheart, Elizabeth Mead. Her ancestors had arrived in Connecticut from England in the seventeenth century and, in a familiar pattern of American westward migration, moved in successive generations from New England to western New York and then to the states of the Old Northwest.

Anxious to get away from prying relatives, the young couple moved to Pontiac, Illinois, where Sam, having passed the bar exam, established his practice. Pontiac, however, could not provide a lucrative practice, and the Johnstons' sojourn there was important solely because Pontiac was the place where Sam altered his name. Annoyed at having his mail and his practice confused with those of a fellow Pontiac lawyer bearing the same name, he dropped the "t" from his surname and inserted a meaningless "L." between Samuel and Johnson. In 1881, Sam and Elizabeth Johnson, hearing of greater opportunities, moved to Fort Scott, on the Marmaton River in southeastern Kansas; there, on August 5, 1882, Hugh, the first of their boys, was born.

As in Pontiac, Sam Johnson's law practice in Fort Scott had built-in problems. Too far from the main western roads, he could not turn a profit. Discouraged, he decided to try his hand at farming. Leading two horses, one carrying his wife and baby Hugh and the other a pack containing all the family's possessions, he trekked to Greenburg, Kansas, and staked out a homestead claim. As he soon grew restless with farming and began to buy and sell cattle and carloads of vegetables, the family followed this business first to Emporia and Greenwich, Kansas, and finally to Wichita, at that time a railroad boomtown. Sam Johnson prospered there by speculating in real estate. But the good times were short-lived. In 1887, a mounting drought triggered a great economic crash that brought severe distress to the whole state of Kansas. Many people who had recently settled in Wichita moved away; and Sam Johnson, overextended by one reckless plunge too many, was eventually forced to liquidate his holdings, including the fine house on Seneca Street he had proudly constructed for his family. As Hugh later recalled: "There is perhaps no word in the English language adequate to describe how completely and absolutely busted he was."[2]

Hugh intensely felt and remembered the terrible depression of the early 1890s. Past the family house streamed the prairie schooners of families moving west in hope of reviving their blasted fortunes. The abandoned and unfinished houses of the town, the visible wreckage of boom and bust, became magnificent play castles for Hugh and other children, their lead and copper pipe and iron-grilled doors and fences a miscellany of junk to be salvaged and peddled for a few pennies per pound. The family garden provided sufficient vegetables; but the Johnsons were clothed only by hand-me-downs sent from Chillicothe by the thrifty Meads. Despite the hardship, Sam Johnson never lost his spirit; and thereafter the memory of his father's indomitable resourcefulness in the face of economic disaster—getting a proper law degree from a boom-born, depression-killed university and working as a postal clerk and as a mail carrier—was a source of strength for Hugh. He was, Hugh later wrote, "the greatest man I ever knew."[3]

While Hugh Johnson would always remember the hardship of the Wichita days, he also recalled and cherished them for the beginnings of his acquaintance with music and literature. Elizabeth Johnson somehow acquired a wheezy old melodeon. The agonized and resentful hours he spent at its yellow keyboard provided the basis for his later appreciation of opera. Hugh remembered the town library more pleasantly, as a haven. Sam and Elizabeth Johnson were voracious readers—although Sam's reading tended toward the rollicking novels of Charles Lever—and they early directed Hugh to the treasures on the library's shelves. Without full understanding but with great appreciation of the impressive language, ten-year-old Hugh Johnson had worked his way through all of Shakespeare and most of Sir Walter Scott and Charles Dickens. Frank Merriwell, Nick Carter, and all of the Beadle series followed, but Mark Twain's *Huckleberry Finn* was Hugh's greatest delight. He read it five times in succession when he first discovered it, and endless re-readings followed.[4]

For the Johnson family, the hard times at Wichita came to an end in 1893, when President Grover Cleveland opened the Cherokee Outlet to settlement. Better known as the Cherokee Strip, this 58- by 100-mile area was squeezed between Huck Finn's Oklahoma "territory" on the south and Kansas on the north. As a reward for past services to the Democratic party, Sam Johnson received the postmastership of the unborn town of Alva. A week before the scheduled opening at noon on September 16, 1893, Sam Johnson, with post-office equipment, household goods, and wife and two small children loaded into a boxcar, arrived in Alva to prepare for the expected rush. Eleven-year-old Hugh was left behind in Wichita to come along in a surrey under the watchful eyes of two elderly deacons. Eight miles out of Wichita, however, the two deacons fell victim to a jug of demon rum; and Hugh was forced to make his way alone to Kiowa, Kansas, one of the primary jumping-off points for the mass of humanity lining up to make the rush.

At Kiowa, Hugh became a wide-eyed witness to the most spectacular land rush in American history. By the morning of September 16 between 80,000 and 100,000 people lined the border of the Cherokee Strip. At noon the cavalry released the mob of homestead hunters. Riding on a jam-packed train from Kiowa to Alva, Hugh saw along the way ponies, sulkies, buckboards, and buggies, all transporting the thousands of people to their hoped-for claims. As the train pulled into Alva around one o'clock that afternoon, he saw hundreds of his fellow passengers fearfully detrain and race for claims not yet staked out by horsemen who had reached the town minutes earlier. Inevitably, he saw some of the violence that followed as the latecomers drove their markers into the same quarter sections of land earlier arrivals might already be registering in the claims office. And, in a matter of hours, he saw Alva go from a town of five inhabitants to one of 7,000.[5]

Sam Johnson quickly emerged as one of Alva's leading citizens. He bought a claim on the high prairie west of the town, constructed a comfortable sod house, and began ranging cattle. In civic affairs he became a paragon of brisk action that his sons would long revere. He took the lead in getting a rudimentary school system established; brought the first church building complete with belfry and baptismal font, from Kansas to Alva; and, using his influence as an increasingly prominent figure in territorial politics, launched a campaign to have the Oklahoma territorial legislature authorize a normal school for Alva. Northwestern Normal School began classes in the Congregational Church in Alva in September 1897, and, thanks to Sam Johnson's initiative in engaging a contractor before the legislature had authorized construction, moved into the first building on its forty-acre campus two years later.[6]

Boyhood at Alva was exciting for Hugh. A Wild West oasis "in an encroaching desert of civilization," the Cherokee Strip attracted a rough lot of men.[7] Gunslinging frontiersmen walked the streets of Alva. On more than one occasion Hugh witnessed a gruesome shoot-out between trigger-happy deputy marshals and bands of outlaws. In addition, Cheyenne and Arapaho Indian reservations were nearby, and an inquisitive boy could easily find an aging brave willing to recount his exploits at the Little Big Horn. As he grew older, Hugh earned money for himself by gathering buffalo bones, which were shipped back East to fertilizer factories; and he carried an increasingly larger share of the work load at the family farm. Yet the demands of plowing, harvesting, and watching the herds were never so great that he did not have time to sit for hours and dream as he watched trains pass through Alva, roughhouse with friends, or take his best girl for an afternoon horseback or bicycle ride.[8]

In school Hugh impressed his teachers as a bright, alert youth, but he was more interested in mischief making and sassing his teachers than his studies. Only by relying on his own quick fists did one of Alva's elementary teachers temporarily subdue Hugh's rowdyism and pound a fair primary education into his head. In September 1897, Hugh enrolled in the first class at Northwestern Normal to prepare for a teaching career, though no record of his work there was kept.[9] Johnson, however, later remembered that the president of the college, James E. Ament, took a special interest in his education and "built where it was weak and guided where it was not so weak." Ament, in turn, remembered Johnson as a brilliant student, full of mischief but never malicious.[10]

An important noncurricular aspect of Hugh's two years at Northwestern Normal were the twice-weekly drills with the local militia company. His participation in these drills meant that Hugh was one of the first in Alva to hear news of Teddy Roosevelt's call for Rough Riders after war was declared against Spain in April 1898. As soon as they heard the news, Hugh and several squadmates, their heads filled with romantic notions of war, secretly resolved to go to Guthrie, Oklahoma, and enlist. But Hugh reckoned without his father, who had no intention of permitting a fifteen-year old—no matter that he looked older—to head off to war. Privy to most of the happenings in Alva, he quickly learned of their plan and easily collared his adventuresome son at the depot before Hugh could board the train to Guthrie. Hugh created such a disturbance, though, that his father, to restore peace in the family, had to promise to help Hugh secure an appointment to West Point. No one knows what led to Hugh's desire to go to West Point, but an investigation of the motives of other young men of similar background who sought West Point appointments in the late nineteenth century strongly suggests that a desire to escape the drudgery of farming and the dismal prospect of a lifelong career as a rural teacher was more important than any personal commitment to a military career.[11]

In the fall of 1898 Hugh took the examination used by Oklahoma's Populist congressman, James Y. "Eat a Mule" Callahan, to select his appointees to West Point. Hugh's performance was competent but only enough so to earn him an appointment as alternate. Here Sam Johnson's position as chairman of the central committee of the Oklahoma Democratic party served Hugh in good stead. First, he arranged a contingency: Callahan would permit Hugh to appear for the entrance examination at West Point in August 1899, if the principal failed to report at the usual time in June of that year. Then, after hearing Hugh remark that the principal looked old for the age he had stated on his appointment form, Sam checked the principal's application against his hometown information and learned that he was way over the maximum age limit for West Point. Learning of Sam Johnson's discovery, the principal failed to make an appearance at West Point in June, and Hugh left Alva for Highland Falls, New York, to prepare for the entrance exam. Two months of savage cramming with an experienced tutor lifted him over this hurdle, in spite of an examination-day attack of appendicitis. On August 30, 1899, Hugh Samuel Johnson, barely seventeen years old, was admitted to West Point.

In his adulthood Johnson wistfully looked back to his frontier upbringing. He treasured his exposure to the Wild West and never tried to submerge this part of his heritage. He was always eager to spin cowboy and Indian yarns, and one of his unfilled ambitions was the writing of a history of the West. Most of Johnson's yarns were oft-told tales distorted by the retelling. Yet they served in a roundabout way to advance his career. By making him an entertaining fellow, they helped open the doors to influence and power in both corporate America and government.

THE UNITED States Military Academy also had a lasting impact on Hugh Johnson, though it seemed at the outset very unlikely that he would even finish the first year. Nicknamed Sep because he entered the academy as a September plebe rather than as a June class member, Johnson, in his words, "was a very bad cadet."[12] Overly impressed with his own ability, he began his Fourth Class year thinking that West Point would be an academic breeze. As a result, his grades for the first six weeks put him close to the bottom of his class, in peril of being lopped off in plebe January and sent home. Like his father, though, Johnson was not one to give up when the going got tough. By January, after an enormous flurry of study, he climbed to the middle of his class. There he remained, completing the year standing 59th in a class of 134. He stood 46th in mathematics, 65th in English, 64th in French, and 80th in drill.[13] In deportment Johnson got off to an equally bad start. Independent in nature and essentially careless in small matters, he was impatient with the trivial aspects of authority and discipline at West Point. His demerits, or "skins," assigned for such casual and seemingly inconsequential offenses as missing a button, singing during call to quarters, or whispering in a classroom, mounted with amazing speed. At one point in the year, he had to go two months with almost no "skins" to avoid being judged unsatisfactory in deportment and dismissed.

Johnson's pugnacity as a plebe singled him out for special treatment from upper-class hazers. Hazing was extralegal; but upperclassmen, professors, and alumni viewed it as an essential means of ridding plebes of conceit and orienting them to the school's rigid system of obedience. Throughout the year plebes were forced to do exhausting physical exercises that sometimes resulted in permanent injury or even death, eat or drink large quantities of unpalatable foods, and in various ways humiliate themselves.[14] For some plebes hazing was a traumatic experience. Johnson took it in stride, however, feeling that the more he could take, the higher would be his status in the eyes of his peers. A year later, when his turn came to haze plebes, he gave back what he got, and then some.[15]

In his Third Class year Johnson was utterly indifferent toward his studies. Working no harder than necessary, he became a master at the art of "bugling"—avoiding daily recitation. At the end of the year his standing of 36th in mathematics, 46th in French, 52d in Spanish, 63d in military engineering, and 98th in drawing placed him 53d in a class of 104. He used the energy that should have been directed toward his studies in "a sort of sophomoric bravado and resistance to constituted authority."[16] Calling themselves the Salt Creek Club, he and a few other rebellious spirits played a constant cat-and-mouse game with the "tacs" (the assistants to the commandant of cadets), trying to see how many regulations they could break without getting caught. Their most common insurgencies were smoking after taps and playing craps in the bathroom. Not surprisingly, Johnson received 161 skins that year, a total many of his classmates did not approach in four years, and spent many hours walking punishment tours in the barracks area.

The Salt Creek Club also took pleasure in razzing the "nice boy" cadets of their class, particularly Douglas MacArthur and Ulysses S. Grant III, who slavishly sought the number one spot in the class standings. To Johnson, the seriousness of these grinds was worthy of contempt, and, at his instigation, the Salt Creek Club made them the target of numerous pranks. One characteristic prank occurred when the cadet corps went to Washington in March 1901, to participate in President William McKinley's second inauguration. Johnson and MacArthur shared a room on the top floor of the old Ebbet House. While MacArthur was out of the room on the evening before the inaugural parade, Johnson and his cohorts staged the battle scene from *Macbeth*, during which Johnson pinioned MacArthur's shako to the door with a cadet sword. MacArthur was furious when he returned and found his hat ruined, but fortunately for the Salt Creek Club, he chose to suffer the prank in silence rather than put them on report.[17]

At the end of his Third Class year, a cadet was permitted to leave West Point for two and a half months. Johnson used his furlough to indulge in the pleasures of New York City and to return to Oklahoma for the first time in two years. This trip home was a watershed in his development as a soldier. In his absence his best girl had found another beau; and his father had moved the family and his successful stock-raising business from Alva to Okmulgee, in the heart of the old Indian Territory. Okmulgee was thereafter the official family home for the Johnsons; but Hugh returned to West Point in August 1901 for his second-class year with full recognition that he had broken with his past and that the army was now his home.

Johnson continued his lackluster academic performance during his final two years at West Point. He ended his Second Class year 68th in a class of 97, standing 52d in philosophy, 64th in chemistry, 88th in drill, and 95th in drawing. In his last year, after which he would graduate 53d in a class of 94, he stood 32d in civil and military engineering, 18th in law, 24th in history, 34th in ordnance and gunnery, and 85th in practical military engineering. Johnson also continued to amass skins. His 133 skins in his final year placed him at the bottom of his class in soldierly deportment and discipline. But Johnson, fully aware of the West Point tradition that class standing bore little relation to military success, was not particularly concerned by his mediocre record.

Except for providing him with a solid knowledge of small-unit military tactics and the many types of ordnance, the best that can be said of Johnson's academic training at West Point is that it helped him develop a semblance of mental discipline and did not dampen his interest in literature. Moreover, West Point's strict disciplinary system failed to curb his pugnacity. Yet West Point left lasting marks on Johnson. West Point prided itself in developing in cadets unqualified acceptance of the intangibles a soldier must possess—devotion to duty, honor, and loyalty to superiors, personal no less than official. To Johnson, duty, honor, and loyalty were more than mere catchwords. They became a set of values that would inform his career and help him to judge others, both within and outside the military. Equally important, he found a camaraderie at West Point that would endure a lifetime. The shared hardships of the plebe year and the feeling of being a member of a select group combined to instill a solidarity among cadets that went beyond the idea of comradeship to almost mystic ties of brotherhood. Johnson was so taken by this camaraderie that he considered his fellow cadets as "bearing some

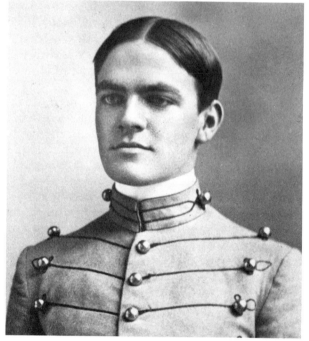

CADET HUGH S. JOHNSON. Courtesy of United States Military Academy Archives.

strong clannish or even family relationship" to him.[18] In later years, this camaraderie manifested itself in his appointment of West Pointers to important positions in the National Recovery Administration (NRA). In his eyes they represented a similarity of view to be depended upon, a trust that would not be violated.

At graduation ceremonies on June 11, 1903, Johnson received his West Point diploma from Secretary of War Elihu Root. Effective that day, he was commissioned a second lieutenant in the United States Army and assigned to the First Cavalry Regiment.

IN 1903 the United States Army was little more than a loose confederation of regiments scattered among a plethora of what the military called hitching-post forts in the United States and the Philippines. Loyalties and identities lay with the regiment. With place of work and residence combined and with frequent changes of post that prevented the establishment of permanent ties with local communities, the typical army officer moved about in a closed society that seldom came in touch with the problems and tensions that accompanied the nation's transformation into a modern industrialized state. Except for sporadic fighting in the Philippines, the nation was at peace; and from the perspective of

1903, Hugh Johnson "could look forward to an assured and reasonably comfortable but small-time" career with a minimum of challenging assignments.[19]

Johnson joined the Third Squadron of the First Cavalry just as it was settling in at Fort Clark, Texas, after returning to the United States from two years of guerrilla fighting and military government duty in the Philippines. Located on Las Moras Creek, Fort Clark had been established in 1852 to protect the San Antonio–El Paso road from Mexican and Comanche attacks. But in 1903 Fort Clark was a backwater, and Johnson's duties were confined to roll calls, drills, parades, reviews, target practice, practice marches, and the administration of the post and its men. As a second lieutenant, Johnson helped supervise the training and garrison work of his troop and took his turn as officer of the guard, whose duty was to stay at the guard house for a twenty-four-hour stretch, watching the captured deserters and sobering the drunks. Like many young officers, he was attentive to his experienced sergeants and was able to learn from them. He also went through the requisite manuals to be certified in everything from tactics and small arms to military hygiene and horsemanship. In off-duty hours he played polo, went horseback riding on the post's beautiful bridle paths and the endless plains nearby, and listened for hours to the old soldiers of the regiment recount their gory exploits in the Indian Wars and the Philippine Insurrection. To the impressionable Johnson there was a romantic, almost tragic, aura surrounding these hardened veteran soldiers, for he recognized that they were already a dying breed.[20]

While the romance in his life perhaps lay with history and with friends, in January 1904, Johnson married Helen Leslie Kilbourne, the daughter of a career army officer and the sister of one of his roommates at West Point. They had first met during one of her frequent visits to West Point to see her brother and became engaged during Johnson's First Class year. Slender, brown-haired, gentle, and refined, Helen Kilbourne was in many ways the antithesis of the irrepressible Johnson. They shared an interest in literature, however; and in the early years of their marriage they would spend many companionable evenings together reading poetry aloud.[21] Their only child, a son, Kilbourne, was born at Fort Clark in April 1907.

The Third Squadron changed stations with the First Squadron of the First Cavalry at Fort Sam Houston, Texas, in October 1904 but returned a year later to Fort Clark. In May 1906, all three regimental squadrons were rushed to San Francisco to help care for refugees from the devastating April earthquake and fire. Johnson's troop was assigned to the Presidio, where several thousand refugees huddled in army tents. Cavalrymen, many of them the greenest of farmhand recruits, were called upon for everything from feeding and clothing these refugees to census taking and attending births. In addition, refugee camps in the city were soon inundated with drifters from the western states who presented themselves as homeless and hungry victims of the disaster. In spite of all this, the Presidio was a model of organization. With the census records their men had compiled, the officers in Johnson's troop generated a card index from which they could locate bona fide residents from the destroyed neighborhoods of the city who would then confront drifters and disprove false claims for assistance. They then started an employment bureau to put men back to work and, as Johnson later related, "proceeded to clean out our camp at the very time when other camps were filling up."[22]

Johnson's work at the Presidio brought him appointment as second assistant to the quartermaster of Permanent Camps and Refugees. Because of accidents and illnesses that befell fellow officers, he soon became acting quartermaster, a position he continued to hold, at the request of the San Francisco Relief Commission, for two months after his regiment withdrew from relief work at the end of June 1906.[23] In this position he was responsible for feeding and clothing approximately 17,000 refugees, a number that dwindled through the summer, and for laying out and constructing sixteen camps to accommodate them.[24] As millions of dollars of private donations flowed into the city's coffers, Johnson and the other officers serving with him began to envision an ambitious relief program in which the funds would be used to finance large-scale housing projects in the city, rather than to construct temporary shacks in the relief camps. Their enthusiasm not only brought about arrangements for price concessions in labor, building materials, and architectural services but also led to such forward-looking ideas as a plan for a rapid-transit system into the industrial section of the city. However, their plans and much of the relief money were sidetracked by the graft-ridden city administration. One by one, Johnson and the other army officers, disgusted with civilian mismanagement of relief funds, returned to duty with their regiments.[25] Years later, when President Franklin D. Roosevelt asked him to administer early Works Progress Administration (WPA) funds in New York City, Johnson's memory of this political venality led him to sprinkle his staff with career army officers as an antidote.[26]

Johnson rejoined the First Cavalry at Fort Clark in September 1906 and, with his regiment, was dispatched to the Philippines for a two-year tour of duty that began in December 1907.[27] By this time the islands had largely been brought under American control, and Johnson's stay proved uneventful. Except for a brief stint at Baguio, in the high mountains of Luzon, Johnson spent his tour at Camp Stotsenberg, in Pampanga province. "In that tropical station," he later wrote, "you started drill before dawn, worked all morning, went to the club before lunch, slept until four, played polo until dark, dined, and sat around the club all evening—the day's work involving three showers and changes of uniforms and considerably more than that number of Scotch and Tan San highballs."[28] When not adhering to this regimen, Johnson devoted many hours to hunting with the Negritos in the nearby mountains, working as a "guard-house lawyer," and waging a fruitless battle to convince superior officers that a more realistic prophylaxis than abstinence was necessary to combat the rampant venereal disease encountered (and no doubt passed on) by American soldiers in the local barrios.

Johnson returned to the United States in February 1910 and was stationed for the next four years in California, first at the Presidio of San Francisco and later at the Presidio of Monterey. In the spring of 1911, Johnson, now a first lieutenant, spent several months at Yuma and Nogales, Arizona, where his squadron was sent after a revolution erupted in Mexico. During the summers Johnson was detailed to national park duty at Yosemite and Sequoia. Normally, two San Francisco Presidio troops of cavalry were sent to the parks each May, to remain until November, with the officer in charge of each troop serving as acting park superintendent. The cavalrymen's duties included expelling trespassers, extinguishing fires, constructing trails, protecting game, registering and advising visitors, collecting tolls, reading stream gauges, and planting fish. Eventually, at the insistence of the War Department, which thought that national park duty was too expensive for the army and detrimental to military discipline and training as well, the cavalry was replaced in Yosemite and Sequoia parks by a force of civilian rangers.[29] Johnson strongly endorsed the War Department's arguments against using cavalrymen on park duty in the report he submitted on his activities as acting superintendent of Sequoia in the summer of 1913.[30]

In many ways Johnson found himself during his years with the First Cavalry. He joined the regiment in 1903 callow and aimless. But the demands of regimental duty convinced him that as long as he was a soldier, he might as well do his job well. His latent promise emerged, and he earned an enviable efficiency record. One of his superiors referred to him as "one of the very ablest officers of his grade in the service." Another called him "the most conspicuous and able officer of his grade with whom I ever came in contact." Yet a third reported that "he is the most dependable and best qualified officer of his grade with whom I ever came in contact."[31] Henry L. Stimson, secretary of war for President William Howard Taft, was also impressed with Johnson. When he and his party visited Yosemite Park one summer, Johnson was in charge of a pack train of sixty-four mules. He so capably oversaw the handling of the baggage that even years later Stimson remembered him "as a very efficient young officer."[32]

During these years, two elements of the Johnson personality—and the way of life it necessarily led to—emerged. One was the habit of excessive drinking. The Old West glorified the hard drinker, and the cavalry added overtures of the hunt club to this potent tradition. In the hot

Southwest and in the Philippines, drills were normally scheduled in the cool of the morning before breakfast; but the "hooker" beforehand—or two—was the accepted ritual, breakfast or no. After drill, liquor and good fellowship abounded in the officers' mess. No great stigma was attached to drinking on duty or drinking heavily just before duty, so long as both the duty and the liquor were capably handled. The only prohibition was against reporting too drunk to assume one's duties, and even this restriction was frequently circumvented: the existence of the condition was simply not officially noted. Johnson was caught up in this liquor culture, as were many of his cavalry contemporaries; and the habit of excessive drinking continued after his cavalry days. By the 1930s he was an alcoholic, and doctors' warnings to stop drinking had no effect.

The other element of Johnson's emerging personality was a duality of demeanor. Standing five feet, nine inches tall and weighing a well-proportioned 170 pounds, his craggy facial features showing the ruggedness of frontier youth, Johnson was ready to mix it with fellow officers, enlisted men, or civilians and early chalked up a couple of fistfights in each category. In performing his duties, Johnson issued orders in a rasping bark, larded with the profanity of the barracks and the choicest specimens of stable-sergeant sweepings. He earned a reputation as a martinet. The careless transgressor of even the most minor army regulation more often than not felt the full sting of Johnson's considerable wrath. One sweltering summer day in 1918, Herbert H. Lehman, serving as a major in the Ordnance Department, learned about this aspect of Johnson when, because his uniform choker was unfastened, he received a scathing chewing out from Johnson in the halls of the Mills Building in Washington.[33] Johnson could be equally tough in his dealings with superiors. "When Johnson gets gruff," General John J. Pershing once attested, "he really seems ready to devour you, bones and all. Even I, as his superior, felt this way."[34] It is no wonder that Johnson's men called him Tuffy.

There was another side to Johnson, however; he was more than the hard-drinking, pugnacious, gruff cavalryman. His son Kilbourne described him as a sentimentalist who wept uncontrollably at arias from *Madame Butterfly*. He could be generous to a fault with money when somebody told him a sob story, and even the most violent chewing out of a wayward enlisted man often ended with a mild admonition to go and sin no more.[35] To his messmates Johnson was not hardbitten but simply a most likeable young officer, a warm and loyal friend with a disarming smile and a quick mind for wisecracks. He told good stories, was always up-to-date on the latest gossip, and did not hesitate to express his affection for those he cared about.

At one time or another, Johnson's friends in the First Cavalry included such notable future generals as George Van Horn Moseley, Jonathan M.

Wainwright, and James G. Harbord. His closest friend, though, was Malin Craig. A forceful, intelligent officer who in 1918 distinguished himself as a staff officer in France, Craig was Johnson's captain during most of the years of his lieutenancy. The Johnsons early became regular dinner companions with Craig and his wife Genevieve, and the Craigs' son taught Kilbourne (or Pat, as his parents called him) kite flying, top spinning, marble shooting, and other important boyhood accomplishments. Johnson's feelings for Craig approached the hero worship he felt for his father. In his opinion Craig epitomized the ideal officer. A natural leader, respected by superiors and subordinates alike, Craig combined a lively sense of humor and a flair for picturesque language with a tireless devotion to duty. Johnson consciously modeled himself after Craig, although he would never develop the tact and tolerance for individual differences that characterized Craig's command style. After leaving the army, Johnson closely followed Craig's career and did not hesitate to write the secretary of war or even the president to urge his promotion.[36]

WHILE serving with the First Cavalry, Hugh Johnson also pursued a literary career, rising to prominence and prosperity as a prolific writer of short stories about military life which were published in some of America's most popular magazines.[37] Johnson never stated a specific reason for his interest in writing short stories. Perhaps the literary interests awakened years before by his parents planted in his mind the idea that he too might some day become a successful writer. Perhaps he hoped that the financial returns of writing might assuage the woes of a newly married officer struggling to pay off debts. Perhaps he simply stumbled onto writing out of boredom with the routine at Fort Clark. Whatever the reason, Johnson, in his own words, turned to short story writing "in a mood that would have shot a rocket at the moon."[38] Unlike that of many writers, Johnson's early confidence was not unfounded. By the time he went to the Philippines at the end of 1907, he already had published two stories. The first, "How Caldwell 'Made Good,'" appeared in *Appleton's Magazine* in December 1906. The second, "Lascar," appeared in *Scribner's Magazine* the following August.

Both of these stories deal with military life on the Mexican border and reflect the application of a vivid imagination to the writer's own impressions of military life and the numerous tales he had heard at Fort Clark. "Caldwell" recounts the romantic struggle of a pampered second lieutenant to prove himself during a yellow fever epidemic. "Lascar" is the sentimental story of a troop horse who is saved from the bull ring by the old soldier who had been his groom for years. Although they are marked by one-dimensional, stereotyped characters and patently predictable turntable endings, these stories are nevertheless highly readable if for no other reason than Johnson's ability to turn a phrase. One cannot help but be delighted by a reference in "Caldwell" to an adobe hut as a "tarantula trap about the size of a hencoop."[39] And in "Lascar" one can find in considerably bowdlerized form a great deal of the stable-sergeant language that was so much a part of Johnson's vocabulary. Says one of the cavalry veterans to a recruit: "Why, you pimply-faced . . . herring-backed, horse-bluffed recruit, you, you botfly, I've worn more skin off-a-me on my saddle 'n ud make a regiment of boneless mounted marines like you!"[40]

After the publication of these two stories, Johnson's writing branched out in new directions. On the one hand, he began to write articles of a serious nature. Prompted by the Japanese war scare of 1907, he published two 1908 articles lamenting the failure of the United States to formulate a national military policy that was consonant with world realities. In the first of these articles, "The Lamb Rampant," which appeared in *Everybody's Magazine* in March 1908, Johnson questioned America's ability to defend itself and predicted how Japan would one day conquer the Philippines and, in conjunction with Germany, attack the coasts of the United States.[41] Later that year he developed the theme of unpreparedness in "The Mission of the Service Magazines." Appearing in the *Cavalry Journal*, this article called for the army's professional journals to dedicate themselves to the articulation of an effective military policy.[42]

Rather surprisingly, Johnson also turned to writing juvenile novels, and in 1908 Appleton and Company published *Williams of West Point*. It extols the traditions of the cadet corps and is "chockful of chivalry, courage and last-minute touchdowns."[43] Using an alleged incident circulated in his cadet days, Johnson created a hero out of Bob Williams, who had promised his dear old mother never to engage in fisticuffs because he had once seriously injured a playmate in a fight. He is ostracized by the entire corps because he refuses to respect the traditional cadet challenge to physical combat and will not explain the reason for his refusal. But Williams has become a member of the football team and comes into the dying moments of the Navy game to score three touchdowns, and the story ends happily in a sea of cadet cheers and motherly tears. A sequel, entitled *Williams on Service*, was published in 1910.

After he returned from the Philippines, Johnson devoted his writing energies to short stories, which flowed torrentially from his pen. Between October 1910 and December 1916, twenty-eight of his stories appeared in popular magazines such as *Century, Collier's, Everybody's, Hampton's, Scribner's,* and *Sunset.* The most popular magazine of the Pacific Coast region, *Sunset* was particularly receptive to Johnson's potboilers, publishing thirteen; *Century* and *Scribner's* each published five. These stories brought Johnson substantial financial rewards, and, compared to his fellow officers—and himself in his own past years of scrimping—he was "rolling in wealth."[44]

This success inevitably led Johnson to thoughts of resigning his army commission to embark on a career as a full-fledged professional writer. He shared his speculation with one of the "wisest of the old-time *Scribner's* editors," who reminded the overconfident Johnson that "the postman's bell had to ring before the dinner bell and that the postman might bring a rejection slip" and persuaded him to cast all such chimeras out of his head. He wisely suggested that Johnson use literature as an avocation, and, as the budding author later affirmed, "he was right on all accounts."[45] Although the returns for the stories were substantial, they were sporadic and could hardly supplant the steady—but smaller—checks from Uncle Sam that a young family man needed.

All but three of Johnson's stories dealt with military life. Set either along the Mexican border or in the Philippines, they followed the pattern that first brought Johnson success in 1906. A few of his subjects were the importance of a jester to troop morale, the hardships endured by army wives, the love between a soldier and his horse, the trials of a disgraced soldier struggling to redeem himself, the endless burdens of Anglo-Saxon officers in bringing the benefits of civilized government to America's "little brown brothers" in the Philippines, the conflict between bookish officers and those better able to empathize with their men, and the sometimes bizarre methods by which young officers win their mates and prove their manhood. Curiously, military action is subdued in these stories; and, in contrast to Johnson's gruff exterior, their thrust was invariably innocent and sentimental. Evincing no awareness of the growing trend toward realism in American fiction, Johnson felt at home with the romanticism of nineteenth-century America. In his stories, righteousness always triumphs over evil, and traditional virtues, such as loyalty, marital fidelity, and the sanctity of motherhood, are idealized.

In his later years Johnson denigrated his short stories, branding them "terrible trash," better forgotten.[46] Yet for a decade these stories had proved a healthy diversion for his leisure hours and had also provided welcome funds to supplement his army pay.

HUGH Johnson's service with the First Cavalry brought varied military experiences. But the years were passing; and as Johnson entered his thirties, anything resembling an extraordinary career seemed a remote possibility. The year 1914, however, saw a major turn in his prospects. For some time a shortage of trained legal officers had plagued the Judge Advocate General's Department. In an effort to upgrade his department the judge advocate general, Brigadier General Enoch H. Crowder, initiated a program to detail promising young officers to law school, with the expectation that they would be appointed to the army's legal arm as vacancies occurred.[47] He picked Johnson, on the basis of his outstanding efficiency record and the "emphatic" recommendations from his superiors that he was "a man with exceptional qualifications in this line," to be one of the first five officers to participate in the program.[48] Johnson approached it with mixed emotions. In eleven years with the First Cavalry he had developed a deep pride in the regiment and its traditions and a feeling of comradeship with its officers and men rivaling what he felt for West Pointers. Leaving the regiment and friends like Craig was akin to leaving a family. Crowder, though, assured Johnson that if he did well at law school, he would be recommended for appointment to a vacant majority in the Judge Advocate Corps. This meant about a twenty-year jump in promotion for Johnson and naturally "put a very different aspect on the whole matter."[49]

On October 5, 1914, Johnson entered the law school of the University of California, a month after the beginning of classes. During the remaining months of the term he worked hard for the first time in his academic life. Because of the outbreak of war in Europe, he was under orders to finish the three-year course of study in nineteen months or leave without a diploma. As a result, he had to double up on his courses and work eighteen hours a day. Spurred by Crowder's promise of the majority, he diligently applied himself to his studies in a manner his West Point instructors would have thought impossible. At the end of the term the dean refused him permission to take final exams because of his late start. Johnson, however, displaying the initiative and disdain for red tape that would later become one of his trademarks, slipped in and took one of the exams and scored the highest grade. The dean then let him take the other exams, and Johnson completed the term, earning either the highest or second highest grade in each of his courses. Johnson continued this brilliant performance through his remaining courses and graduated on May 17, 1916, "taking 1's in every subject carried and receiving honors."[50] He also found time to teach a course in the university's Department of Military Science and Tactics and to take enough regular academic courses that the university, by computing them with his West Point courses, could award him a bachelors of arts degree in addition to a law degree.[51]

Following his graduation from law school, Johnson immediately joined Brigadier General John J. Pershing's grueling expedition in pursuit of Pancho Villa in the rugged mountains of Chihuahua, Mexico. Sharing a tent with Lieutenant George S. Patton, he served as acting judge advocate for the expedition, an assignment that mainly involved reviewing courts-martial. From the outset, Pershing, who like Johnson had a law degree, was impressed with Johnson's work, writing to Crowder that "his briefs on various matters submitted to me are well drawn and show a very accurate knowledge of law."[52] Pershing also developed a personal fondness for Johnson and later told Kilbourne Johnston (Pat restored the "t" to his surname) that his father was one of the finest young officers he had ever known. In Pershing's words: "He was good cavalry."[53]

Johnson's work as acting judge advocate was not an "onerous duty" and did not tax his time. To keep him busy, Pershing gave him "a peach of an assignment" and directed him to determine why Mexico had never known any real peace except under a military oligarchy. Drawing upon the expertise of Mexican lawyers, judges, businessmen, legislators, and farmers, Johnson made an extensive study of the whole body of Mexican law. He concluded that the trouble lay with Mexico's adoption of an Anglo-Saxon common law constitution that was at variance with its Roman civil law traditions and what he considered the backwardness of the Mexican people. Johnson later wrote that his study was an important step in his growth. In order to understand and explain governmental conditions in Mexico, he found it necessary for the first time in his life, his legal training notwithstanding, to analyze American political institutions. This analysis, in his words, "soaked me through with the theory and practice of Federal, State and Municipal political structure in the United States" and permanently implanted in his thinking the crucial role of popular participation in the success of this structure.[54]

On July 1, 1916, Johnson was promoted to captain. A month earlier, Congress, in the National Defense Act of 1916, authorized the addition of nineteen new judge advocates to the Judge Advocate Corps, expanding its number from thirteen to thirty-two officers.[55] Awed by his record at law school and his "ability to express a proposition in legal language in strong, clear and concise style," Crowder advised Secretary of War Newton D. Baker that Johnson was the "best selection to fill one of these vacancies."[56] Johnson's candidacy was enthusiastically endorsed by Pershing and Senator Robert L. Owen, Democrat of Oklahoma.[57] But several other officers with considerably more political influence, including one in whom President Woodrow Wilson was personally interested, were likewise contending for one of the coveted appointments. Consequently, Crowder's buttonholing in favor of Johnson's candidacy went for naught. When the new judge advocate appointments were made in September 1916, Johnson was passed over. His emotions always lay near the surface and, in an early example of the sullenness that would later exasperate his NRA associates, he bitterly complained to his friends about the insidious nature of army politics and told Pershing that he would resign his commission if it would not seem that he was a quitter.[58]

In the meantime, Crowder, anxious to have Johnson assist in the mushrooming work load of his office, persuaded Pershing to release Johnson from the Pancho Villa expedition and in late September 1916, ordered him to Washington on temporary duty.[59]

CHAPTER 2

A STRONG RIGHT ARM

Hugh Johnson's first assignment in Washington was as assistant to the law officer of the Bureau of Insular Affairs. In this post he briefed insular cases docketed for argument before the Supreme Court. The work, however, did not last the winter of 1916–1917. Late in the afternoon of February 4, 1917, Enoch Crowder was unexpectedly summoned to the secretary of war's office where Baker, who had just consulted with President Wilson, instructed him to frame a bill by the next morning authorizing the adoption of conscription in case of war. The day before, Wilson had broken off diplomatic relations with Germany, an act foreshadowing American entry into the war in Europe, and the American army was grossly undermanned for a meaningful role in the war. After meeting with Baker, Crowder returned to his office and just before 5 P.M. met with Colonel Walter A. Bethel, Lt. Colonel Samuel T. Ansell, Lt. E. K. Massee, and Johnson. He explained Baker's instruction and asked them to return that evening to help frame the bill. All but Ansell returned, and Crowder gave each a section of the bill to write and told them to be finished before midnight.[1] Johnson's section dealt with the raising of the army.[2]

Through the night, the group worked on the exact phrasing of the bill and checked its provisions against the National Defense Act of 1916 and earlier laws governing the recruitment of the Regular Army and the National Guard. At three minutes before ten o'clock in the morning of February 5 Crowder submitted the bill to Baker. He thereupon pigeonholed it, for the administration had yet to settle on a policy for bringing a larger army into being.

The raising of armies had always been a troublesome matter for the United States. Historically, the nation had relied on volunteerism. Only during the Civil War had the United States resorted to conscription, and then only after the number of men enlisting had dwindled to a dangerously low level. For many people, volunteerism was a sacred expression of America's commitment to individual liberty; and they feared that conscription would inevitably impose Old World militarism and its hated coercion and regimentation upon the United States. But if volunteerism represented the American ideal, as some proclaimed, it was an unsatisfactory method for creating an army. In wartime the enlistment rates had generally fluctuated in response to public attitudes toward the war, and consequently the size of the army had usually been based not on strategic requirements but on considerations of public feeling and the number of men who could be induced to enlist.

The defects in the voluntary method had long been recognized, and by 1914 many military men were strongly urging the adoption of universal military training, or UMT, as a means of strengthening the nation's army in an increasingly threatening world. Others saw additional virtues in UMT, pointing out that "it would Americanize the immigrant, nurture the values of efficiency and 'service,' and overcome class antagonism." In December 1916 and January 1917, the War College Division of the War Department General Staff drew up detailed plans for UMT and presented them to the Senate Military Affairs Committee in February 1917. However, the administration refused to endorse UMT. Both Wilson and Baker were personally in sympathy with the voluntary tradition and were convinced that public opinion would not support the adoption of compulsory military service. Apparently, they considered the bill they had Crowder frame a standby measure, to be submitted to Congress only if enough volunteers did not come forward to bring the army up to desired strength.

Following the sinking of American ships by German submarines, the Wilson administration resolved on March 20, 1917, to ask Congress for a declaration of war. Shortly afterward, the administration reversed its position on conscription and decided to enact a selective draft, which would be the primary means for providing men for the army, as soon as possible. Two factors were paramount in this decision, the first of them political. Since the crisis with Germany had developed in February 1917, former President Theodore Roosevelt had been pleading with the War Department for permission to raise a division of volunteers and lead it in France. In Wilson's eyes Roosevelt's scheme was politically dangerous and "militarily daft"; by emphasizing a selective draft and largely closing off voluntary enlistments, he could effectively stymie it. The second factor that influenced the conscription policy was the experience of Great Britain, which had waited until 1916 to adopt conscription. As a result, it had suffered severe economic problems "as skilled and unskilled, needed and unneeded, replaceable and irreplaceable workers" randomly rushed to the colors. Moreover, thousands of Britain's most talented and best-educated young men had volunteered for war service, and the great number of deaths among them had serious implications for postwar British society. Hoping to avoid these problems, Wilson increasingly concluded that a selective draft was the best means of minimizing the disturbances that the manpower requirements of war inflicted on the nation's industrial and social structures. In other words, it would provide men for the army and "keep the right men in the right jobs at home."[3]

During the last week of March and the first week of April, a special War Department board ironed out the provisions of the conscription bill for presentation to Congress. As a basis for the work, it used a refined version of the bill framed by Crowder and a bill calling for UMT framed by the War College Division.[4] As soon as war was declared on April 6, 1917, Congress took up the draft bill. Approved on May 18 with only minor modifications, the bill designated the age limits for conscription as twenty-one to thirty and authorized the president to use the selective draft in raising the new National Army, which would constitute the great bulk of the men mobilized for the war effort. The Regular Army and the National Guard were to be filled out with volunteers, but conscription could be invoked if shortages occurred.

Johnson did not participate in the shaping of the Selective Service Act after that hectic evening in Crowder's office. Yet his involvement with the draft soon absorbed his energies and gave him his first taste of behind-the-scenes action and contact with men wielding nationwide power.

ON APRIL 2, 1917, the same day that Wilson asked Congress to declare war on Germany, Baker directed Crowder to prepare a preliminary plan for executing conscription. Crowder, in turn, delegated this task to Hugh Johnson, with instructions to design the draft so that it would be civilian in character and thus avoid the mistakes of the Civil War draft. An army-run draft, it had reinforced sentiment for volunteerism. Provost marshals, going door-to-door to enroll eligibles, had clothed it with a military character; and the suggestion of force bred resentment and, in some instances, violent opposition. Johnson, as were the other judge advocates in Crowder's office, was fully versed in the Civil War draft experience. The judge advocate general had made the 1866 report of Brevet Brigadier General James Oakes, acting assistant Provost Marshal for Illinois during the Civil War, required reading for all incoming judge advocates.[5] It detailed the defects in the Civil War draft and offered numerous constructive recommendations. In addition, at Crowder's direction, Johnson had made a comparative analysis of the Enrollment Act of 1863, the War College Division's UMT plan, and a plan for UMT prepared by the Senate Military Affairs Committee.[6]

With the aid of Captain Cassius M. Dowell, Johnson completed the plan for the draft in a week. In drawing it up he "scrupulously avoided" the methods that had made the Civil War draft so controversial and generally followed the recommendations in Oakes's report.[7] This was most evident in the all-important administrative and enforcement provisions. Unlike the Civil War draft, which was administered by a superimposed federal structure, Johnson cast the whole "execution of the draft back on local communities . . . made the governors of the states responsible and utilized to the fullest extent the existing institutions of state, county and municipal government." At the head of the administrative structure, Johnson set a small federal directing agency, the Office of the Provost Marshal General, whose primary functions were policy-making and supervision. Its responsibilities included promulgating regulations, computing and assigning quotas, and transporting draftees to training camps. The day-to-day administration of the draft, especially the distasteful responsibility for selecting and inducting draftees, would be left to state and local boards and officials. As far as the enforcement machinery was concerned, Johnson "eschewed" all use of military force. The Civil War draft, by relying on the provost marshal general to enforce it, had "bristled with bayonets." Johnson, in contrast, adhered to Oakes's recommendation that the task be left to local officials and the Justice Department.[8]

Johnson experienced considerable difficulty in persuading his colleagues in the Judge Advocate General's Department of the soundness of his plan. Major J. Reuben Clark, for one, advised Crowder that it was unconstitutional to use state institutions and officials to administer a federal draft. Only by resorting to the strongest language did Johnson convince Crowder that failure to overrule Clark would signify a weakening commitment to civilian control over conscription.[9] Johnson also had to counter criticism that his plan had "nothing behind it except the force of public opinion."[10] He readily agreed with this observation. But where others claimed that reliance on public opinion was a fatal weakness, Johnson saw it as the plan's principal strength. The study of Mexican law he had made for Pershing in 1916 had satisfied him that no venture in a democracy could succeed without popular support. If the public was unwilling to support conscription, no amount of coercive force could make it function effectively.[11] In the end, Johnson's arguments prevailed, and Crowder forwarded the plan to Baker with a minimum of changes. To Johnson's chagrin, however, the judge advocate general placed his own initials on the memorandum detailing the plan, prompting Johnson to complain bitterly to Dowell and Major James S. Easby-Smith that he was being denied just credit for his work.[12]

Johnson's plan, which meshed perfectly with Baker's commitment to localism, received the secretary's enthusiastic approval on April 10. Two weeks later the state governors were informed of Johnson's plan; and, with some congressional amendment, it was the plan eventually used.[13]

As soon as Johnson's plan received Baker's approval, Crowder began preparations for the first draft. He directed Johnson and Dowell to work out the details for registering the millions of potential draftees and Lt. Colonel Edward A. Kreger and Major Charles B. Warren to draw up regulations for their selection. While Dowell devised the registration forms, Johnson concentrated on the plan and regulations for registration. He rejected the registration scheme that the War College Division had outlined as part of its plan for UMT. Basing its planning on the premise that registration must be "strictly under Federal control," the War College Division had recommended that it be effected through the Post Office Department.[14] Johnson, in contrast, believed that the Post Office Department was not adapted to registration of large numbers of men. It lacked the clerical force, and the use of post offices as registration booths would disrupt the transmission of mail. Furthermore, the War College Division scheme, which required twenty days to complete, was obviously too protracted. Instead, Johnson endeavored to develop a conscription plan that was more genuinely local in character. However, he was uncertain as to which agency should be used for registration. He briefly considered local taxing or police agencies, but they presented too many drawbacks. Finally, former Representative Burnett M. Chiperfield of Illinois suggested the voting precinct. The thousands of these precincts throughout the nation already had the necessary personnel, and each was small enough that all eligible men within the precinct could be registered in only one day, without the taint of military control, and as "a great patriotic demonstration and outpouring."[15]

Johnson submitted his registration plan to Crowder at the end of the third week of April, but with little enthusiasm.[16] Since beginning work on the plan, he had come to see registration in a new light. Crowder and the other architects of the draft perceived registration simply as the first step in raising men for the army. Johnson, however, now saw it as an indispensable tool for mobilizing the entire nation for war. Rather than register only the age groups immediately subject to the draft, Johnson urged the registration of all men between the ages of nineteen and forty-five. This action, he contended, would provide the statistics so necessary for "mobilizing our industrial resources . . . guarding against insidious activity, and . . . casting up the strength of our available sources of men."[17] But this time Johnson's arguments and force were not sufficient to carry his proposal. The nation was not yet reconciled to the far-reaching demands the war might make, and Crowder vetoed the proposal on grounds of political expediency.

Johnson's registration plan was practical except for a gross miscalculation of the time needed to implement it. He assumed that Congress would approve the Selective Service Act on or about April 24 and proposed that registration be completed within two weeks following this approval. But after preliminary discussions with Cornelius Ford, the public printer, Johnson learned that the printing and distribution of the thirty million forms required for registration would take at least a month. This meant registration could not be completed in less than six weeks. Johnson, thinking it would reaffirm Germany's notion that

America was militarily impotent, considered this four-week delay intolerable. With Dowell and Ford's encouragement, he resolved to have the forms printed without waiting for congressional approval or Crowder's authorization, even though this step was clearly illegal.[18]

Johnson intended to store the bales of printed forms in the Government Printing Office. But neither Johnson nor Ford had correctly calculated the immense bulk of the forms, and before long the hallways of Ford's department were covered with mountains of bales. On the advice of the Washington postmaster, Johnson went ahead with addressing packages of forms and storing them in surplus mail sacks in the Washington post office, only to have this arrangement also break down when the supply of mail sacks ran out before the printing was half completed. Johnson decided his only recourse was to mail the forms to the thousands of precincts and pray that local officials would accept them and not make public their distribution.[19] For days Johnson was on edge for fear that the opponents of conscription would publicize his conspiracy and use this information to delay the passage of the conscription bill. Fortunately, the local officials cooperated; and, thanks to Johnson's audacious cutting of red tape, all the forms were in the hands of local officials by the time Congress approved the Selective Service Act, awaiting only the announcement of the registration day.[20]

During the first week of May, Johnson prepared the presidential proclamation announcing registration. Surprised, in view of Wilson's usual insistence on writing such statements himself, he used two days to familiarize himself with the president's literary style and writings. He finished the proclamation on May 12, and was again surprised when Wilson accepted the document in its entirety.[21] Issued on May 18 and declaring June 5, 1917, as the registration day, the proclamation explained the reasons for the draft, presenting it as "selection from a nation which has volunteered in mass"; it styled registration day as a "great day of patriotic devotion and obligation." Each American was "to see to it that the name of every male citizen of the designated ages is written on these lists of honor."[22]

In the meantime, Baker had determined that Crowder should administer the draft, and, at Crowder's direction, Johnson and Dowell, along with two assistants, moved into the old Land Office Building in Washington to set up shop for the Office of the Provost Marshal General. One of the assistants was Alvin Brown, a civilian clerk in the Judge Advocate General's Department who had received a law degree from George Washington University's law school and would later be a close associate of Johnson in business and in the NRA and the WPA. When Crowder was formally named provost marshal general on May 22, Johnson became executive officer in charge of administration—in effect, ratifying his de facto position as the number-two man in the draft.

Under Crowder's watchful eye, Johnson presided over the final preparations for the first draft. The whole body of regulations for the draft was formalized, the lottery for determining the order of selection arranged, and plans for mobilizing and transporting the draftees to training camps outlined. There never seemed enough time to do everything that had to be done; Johnson wrote later that for weeks he "worked on four to six hour's sleep on an office sofa." On June 5, despite some minor resistance in the Far West and in East Coast cities, over nine and a half million men registered in an orderly manner, and within forty-eight hours 90 percent of the totals were reported to Washington. In July the first great lottery was held to determine the order of selection. By September the initial "driblet" of the 687,000 men selected in the first draft began reporting to training camps.

Johnson's work on the first draft greatly impressed Crowder. Writing to Pershing in August 1917, he stated:

During my forty years of observation of the regular army, no officer has ever challenged and held my attention as has Johnson. He has ability, he has untiring zeal, and what is more he has genius. He has done a most remarkable piece of work for me in the course of which I have come to regard him as a man capable of carrying out any kind of professional burden; . . . I sometimes think that Johnson can carry the whole War College, including its president, on his back.[23]

For Johnson, however, his work on the first draft was only the beginning of his contribution to manpower mobilization. Crowder had other tasks in mind for him and was already making plans to use his writing and organizational skills to the fullest.

SOON after he was appointed commander of the American Expeditionary Forces (AEF) in early May 1917, Pershing told Hugh Johnson that he intended to ask for Johnson as his judge advocate. Johnson, throbbing with the excitement of the "Great Crusade" and the adventure it offered, was delighted by the prospect. He also realized that service in the war zone could be crucial for career advancement in the postwar army. Several days passed in which Johnson heard nothing more about the assignment. Then, in a chance encounter with Pershing, he learned that Crowder had asked the AEF commander to table the request for his services so that Johnson could finish working on the preparations for the first draft. Johnson "swarmed back to Crowder greatly aggrieved" and raised a storm with his superior. Only Crowder's assurance "that he and General Pershing had an arrangement for a new request" later that summer smoothed Johnson's disappointment and anger.[24]

On May 15, 1917, Johnson was finally appointed to the Judge Advocate Corps with the rank of major in the Regular Army. Several weeks later he was also named a lieutenant colonel of cavalry in the National Army. Johnson, however, was less concerned with these promotions than with the expectation that Pershing would soon renew the request for his services. But as July gave way to August and Pershing's call did not come, he began to fear that Pershing had forgotten him and badgered Crowder to ask the AEF commander to renew the request. Crowder sympathized with Johnson. He too longed for duty in France and realized that Johnson's opportunities to advance his career were limited in the provost marshal general's office. Yielding to Johnson's pleas, he sent a confidential letter to Pershing on August 16, lavishly praising Johnson and urging Pershing to renew the request for Johnson and use him as chief of staff of a combat division or as an assistant chief of staff at General Headquarters. "I would feel like I had given you a strong right arm if I succeeded in placing Johnson on your staff," he told Pershing.[25]

As it developed, Crowder's intervention was unnecessary, for Pershing's request arrived while his letter was in transit. Crowder, however, was not prepared for the immediacy of Pershing's request. As he considered Johnson essential to the operations of the Office of the Provost Marshal General, he refused to release him until the first week of October 1917, the projected completion date for the first draft. On October 2, 1917, Pershing asked the War Department to send him more staff officers. He accompanied this request with a list of officers, including Johnson, from which they were to be chosen.[26] But again Johnson's hope of joining Pershing was dashed. He was already engrossed in drawing up new draft regulations, and Crowder again deferred his transfer.

ON SEPTEMBER 4, 1917, Crowder and Hugh Johnson traveled to Camp Upton, New York, to view the first draftees from New York City. By this time the two men had determined that a new selection process was required. Under the existing process, each local board had "to call men for examination and keep on calling them until the culling out of the physically unfit and those with claims to exemption had yielded the requisite number."[27] To compile the selection list for the first draft, the local boards had to examine 2,501,706 men and, with the district appeal boards, adjudicate 1,560,570 exemption claims.[28] This long, grueling process worked against a rapid buildup of the army by generating a large amount of preliminary work on men who would probably be deferred.

Johnson had discerned this flaw in the draft as early as June 1917, and, at his urging, Crowder had proposed that enough men be examined and classified to provide a reservoir of men readily available for future draft calls.[29] At that time, though, the Wilson administration had yet to reconcile itself or the American people to the implication in Crowder's proposal that the war would cut deeply into the nation's fabric and rejected it out of hand. The Allies had indicated no pressing need for large numbers of American men; War Department planners, in fact, were just

beginning to question the War College Division's March 31, 1917, prediction that "the war must last practically two years longer before
we can have other than naval and economic participation."[30] By September, however, Russia was tottering on the brink of collapse, while
recent fighting on the Western Front had worn Britain and France down
to a dangerous level. It was clear that larger numbers of American men
would be required in 1918 than most planners had originally imagined,
and in a shorter period of time. With the difficulty in the selection process now exposed, the logic of Crowder's proposal could not be denied.
When he resubmitted it on September 12 as a cornerstone of a complete overhaul of the selection process, Baker readily approved it.[31]

At Crowder's instruction, Johnson began work on new regulations for
selecting men. As his first step, he queried the local boards for suggestions and criticism and, to enhance their sense of participation, called
some of their members to Washington to discuss problems with the
draft. Armed with the information provided by the local boards, Johnson
and two assistants, James Easby-Smith and Captain Harry C. Kramer,
"retired to a secret hideout in the Woodward Building" to formulate the
regulations.[32] They worked tirelessly, surfacing several days later to announce that they had devised a completely new selection process.[33]

The core of the new process was a self-administered survey of all of
the nine and a half million registrants. Each would be required to complete a questionnaire designed to inventory his circumstances. On the
basis of this information, his local board would place him in one of five
broad classifications. Class I would include those available for immediate induction, while Class V would include those totally unavailable
for service. The intervening classes would include those, graded in the
order in which they could be spared from service, who were entitled
to exemption. Exemption claims would be ruled on immediately, and
thus under the new process only those in Class I would have to be examined. No one would be called from the lower classes until Class I
was exhausted.[34]

Johnson designed this process primarily to create a reservoir of "fully
qualified availables," ready to be tapped in expectation of greatly increased draft calls in 1918. But equally important, all registrants now
would be classified by occupation. This would be invaluable in a war
where the demand for technicians might be more pressing than that for
infantrymen. In Johnson's mind the classification system was so explicit and thorough that it would be possible on short notice to honor a
call for "one hundred one-eyed pigioneers [sic] with wooden legs."[35]

The new selection process went into effect on December 15, 1917,
along with a War Department decree terminating voluntary enlistments in the Regular Army and the National Guard in the age group
subject to the draft. In early 1918 sentiment began growing to eliminate volunteerism in all age groups and in all branches of the service.

Johnson took the lead in advancing this position in Crowder's office. On more than one occasion he pressed Crowder to "seek all power" by "taking over the whole matter of recruitment, for all branches of the Army, Navy and Marine Corps and on the extension of the Selective Service System to the exclusion of volunteering." If Crowder would do this, Johnson said, "Instead of leaving a record of one who has done an incidental task . . . that came to his hand, you will leave the name of one who shaped the activities of a whole people."[36]

Crowder found Johnson's heady enthusiasm infectious, but he chose not to push the matter until he was certain that he had overwhelming public support. By the summer of 1918 the matter could no longer be postponed. Now that the nation was gearing up for a total effort, it could no longer afford the luxury of accepting volunteers who might better serve in factories than in trenches. Manpower had to be mobilized on a rational basis, rather than in response to patriotic sentiment, if the threat of economic dislocation from increased draft calls was to be minimized. At Crowder's request, Congress, on August 31, 1918, amended the Selective Service Act to require all branches of the service to obtain their manpower through the draft. The voluntary method, the mainstay of previous American mobilizations, had become a war casualty.

The new selection process that Johnson and his assistants designed was able to satisfy the large draft calls of 1918. In the first eleven months after the draft's inception in May 1917, fewer than one million men were inducted. Yet in the next three months 1,075,000 men were inducted, 375,000 in May 1918 alone; and by the war's end in November 1918, the draft had furnished nearly 67 percent of the four million men mobilized. If the war had dragged on into 1919, these large calls would have exhausted the reservoir of "fully qualified availables," necessitating the call-up of deferred classes and the risk of economic dislocation. As it was, the necessity for this action was postponed until 1919 only by the registration of all men who had turned twenty-one years of age since the first registration in June 1917 and the August 31, 1918, extension of draft-age limits from eighteen to forty-five.[37]

Another factor in the attempt to minimize labor shortages was a concerted drive to remove so-called idlers—men in Class I with high order numbers who loafed while awaiting their draft calls or persons exempted on the grounds of dependency who were engaged in nonessential work—from the streets. Idlers galled the families of servicemen and obviously "served no economic war purpose whatsoever." In early 1918, the Labor Department began work on plans to deal with the problems of idlers and labor shortages. Johnson, however, believed that Crowder's office should not forfeit the initiative in draft matters for fear that it would seem that it was "resting [on its] oars and going to sleep."[38] He had been giving thought to these problems for some time; and on

March 8, 1918, he informed Crowder of the general outline of a comprehensive plan he had devised to resolve them. Impressed with his ideas, the provost marshal general instructed Johnson to formalize the plan so that Crowder might present it to Baker and Wilson.[39]

In the resulting memorandum, "Selective Draft and Adjustment of Industrial Man Power," Johnson denounced those "who stood in saloons and pool rooms watching their contemporaries marching away to war" and postulated that "every man must serve, either under the battle flag or in the army of those usefully employed behind them."[40] He planned to handle idlers and labor shortages in two ways. First, he recommended that "the deferred classification or the deferment due to the order number . . . be withdrawn from any man upon a showing that he is not usefully engaged." Second, he returned to his proposal of April 1917 for legislation requiring the registration of all men between the ages of nineteen and forty-five. He now recommended that all men between the ages of eighteen and fifty be registered and that for those outside the designated military ages "their age alone will be their exemption, except that, those idle or not usefully engaged must either enter useful employment or become subject to draft."[41]

After reading the memorandum, Crowder wrote Johnson that "you have never done a better piece of work than this memorandum presents."[42] Equally impressed, the War Council, a group of high-ranking officers who advised the secretary of war on military matters, endorsed Johnson's memorandum on March 20, 1918. The Wilson administration, however, was averse to Johnson's recommendations because of the opposition of labor leaders who refused to admit the existence of a labor shortage and who expressed concern that Johnson's recommendations were intended to lay the groundwork for industrial conscription. This was not Johnson's intent. Through numerous discussions with individual labor leaders he had come to the realization that industrial conscription was political dynamite and that any effort to implement it on a wide scale would only damage the war effort. "Selective Draft and Adjustment of Industrial Man Power," in effect, was an effort to head off the industrial conscription that labor leaders feared.

After two months of temporizing, Wilson finally agreed to a modified version of Johnson's plan, and on May 17, 1918, Crowder issued a "work or fight" order. It warned deferred men who were either idle or engaged in nonessential work that they risked reclassification and induction if they did not find work in essential industries. The "work or fight" order did not get many men for the army. But as Johnson later boasted, it did put 137,255 "bartender[s], private chauffeurs, men hair dressers and the like that are pansies" into essential work and had, at least arguably, a beneficial psychological effect.[43]

IN JUNE 1918, a newspaper article reported that Enoch Crowder and

Hugh Johnson were "like father and son and that no better matched team ever worked in the same harness."[44] This characterization was overdrawn, but the close friendship between the two men was evident to all in wartime Washington. A gruff, frail-looking bachelor, Crowder early took a liking to Johnson. Like Johnson, Crowder had begun his military career in the cavalry and switched to the Judge Advocate Corps. Shortly after meeting Johnson, Crowder came to regard him as his protégé and even to talk about the prospect of the two entering into a private law practice at the war's end. Realizing that Johnson was a handy man to have around, Crowder increased his responsibilities and the challenge of his assignments. Crowder also recognized that Johnson worked best if sprinkled with generous doses of praise, and after the blowup over the credit for the first draft, he regularly commended Johnson. From time to time he brought Johnson's work to the attention of the secretary of war. More conspicuously, he reserved special praise for Johnson in the commendation section of his first annual report on the operations of the Office of the Provost Marshal General, writing that such "commendation as the administration of this office merits . . . will be found due, in a great measure, to Lieut. Col. Johnson, executive officer."[45]

In addition, in October 1917, Crowder recommended that Johnson be promoted to brigadier general in the National Army. Even with the flush of wartime promotions, Crowder's recommendation was unusual because of Johnson's relatively young age—thirty-five—and because the nation was only six months into the war. Crowder intended this promotion to compensate Johnson for his refusal to send the younger man to France as judge advocate for Pershing's AEF. He told Chief of Staff Tasker H. Bliss that if Johnson had gone to France, "he would have found himself in the position of Colonel Bethel who succeeded to the detachment now finds himself, namely nominated to the position of Brigadier General in the National Army."[46] Concerned that it might anchor him "to a Washington desk for 'the duration,'" Johnson declined the promotion in favor of Colonel Kreger, a much older officer whose promotion Crowder had been pushing since the spring of 1917.[47] However, in January 1918, Johnson did accept promotion to colonel in the National Army when he was appointed deputy provost marshal general.

If Crowder appreciated having a man of Johnson's talents to call upon, Johnson reveled at being at the side of one of the most powerful men in wartime Washington. He had influence and power rarely matched by officers of similar age and rank, and he was well-known in the nation's capital, in full view of men who could help his career. He was acting on a larger stage than he had ever occupied before, a vastly exciting and stimulating experience for one who only a few years before had been commanding cavalry troops at obscure frontier posts. At

LIEUTENANT COLONEL JOHNSON, GENERAL ENOCH CROWDER, AND ROSCOE S. CONKLING.
Courtesy of David A. Lockmiller.

times, though, the excitement became a little too much for Johnson.
He was justly proud of his accomplishments with the draft and never
shrank from asserting his contributions. However, his private conversations sometimes seemed to lead people to the impression that
Johnson assumed primary credit for the success of the draft. Crowder,
who was quick-tempered and prone to take offense, never accepted
this bombastic side of Johnson's personality. On more than one occasion, therefore, and most notably in the spring and summer of 1918
and in the fall of 1921, relations between the two men were temporarily strained.[48]

In public, however, Johnson was circumspect, always careful to make
it clear that he owed everything to Crowder. The provost marshal general had amassed a considerable number of enemies in his forty years of
military service. Both during and after the war these enemies circulated reports to the effect that Johnson should be "generally credited
with initiating and carrying through the burdensome work of the draft"
and that he was the "real author of the selective service draft."[49] Johnson
realized that these reports were inimical toward Crowder, and not
praise of him; and both friendship and his commitment to the West

Point creed of loyalty to superiors led Johnson to refute them. Each time such a report would appear, he would caustically condemn it and recount that all of his work "was done in the usual administrative manner, under the direction of General Crowder, as a member of his staff, in consultation with him and on his responsibility."[50] Even at the height of his career, several years after Crowder's death, he felt compelled to respond to these reports. It was his repayment for the interest Crowder had shown in him after 1914. He appreciated that without Crowder's interest he probably would have been "rejoicing in the exalted title of 'C.O. San Juan De Bac-Bac' or some other outlandish station—writing impassioned articles on drill regulations and lapsing into the final stages of a rotund human turnip."[51]

DURING the fall of 1917, Hugh Johnson's presence in Crowder's office became a matter of mounting concern to many of his colleagues. The problem lay with his temperament. When differences on policy arose, Johnson often resorted to intemperate tirades to reinforce his arguments. When he felt that he was being denied credit for his contributions, his reaction, whether a sullen withdrawal or a verbal tempest, had often been highly visible and had impeded his work until he felt fully vented. One of many such reactions came as the result of a feud with Major John H. Wigmore, a noted Northwestern University law professor whose work as a statistician in the provost marshal general's office so impressed Crowder that he came to consider Wigmore in all matters pertaining to the draft a "father confessor."[52] Johnson, using the old credit-for-work-done and other rationalizations, went so far as to advocate, to Crowder and others, Wigmore's dismissal.[53]

Crowder generally tolerated Johnson's outbursts, for he recognized that frequent and fierce as they were, they could usually be explained by Johnson's arduous working conditions. The man simply had to blow off steam. Yet the outbursts indicated more, an emotional instability that was troublesome enough to cause many of his colleagues, although not Crowder, to conclude that he had outlasted his usefulness. For nearly a year he had been Crowder's strong right arm, both in organizing the system for registering and selecting men and in administering it. But with the draft now firmly established, the Office of the Provost Marshal General required internal harmony in order to fulfill its responsibility. Johnson's outbursts threatened this harmony. One of his colleagues later surmised, not unreasonably, that if Johnson had remained, his temperament would have seriously hindered the day-to-day work required to fill the large draft calls of 1918.[54]

Johnson was aware that his temperament was a matter of concern to his colleagues, but he was blind to the intensifying disenchantment with him. His friendship with Crowder was unimpaired, and in January 1918, he again focused his attention on France, in expectation that

Pershing would soon renew the request for Johnson's services.[55] Although Crowder had three times opposed this transfer, Johnson was now buoyant. The new regulations would apparently supply the men for the 1918 draft calls, and he now had Crowder's firm promise to release him no later than mid-April. Pershing, however, cabled in February that Johnson's acceptance of the promotion to colonel in the National Army made Johnson ineligible for duty with the AEF staff in France.[56] For some time Pershing had been dissatisfied with the promotion system, believing that deserving officers in France were being passed over "by officers of the permanent staff departments whose chiefs happen to be in Washington urging greater promotion for their particular departments."[57] Johnson's promotion to colonel was merited on the basis of his performance. Yet it was based on performance in Washington and came at the urging of Crowder, and these facts were precisely at the heart of Pershing's major criticism of the system. Johnson's misfortune was that his promotion came just as Pershing was preparing to stress this criticism and the need for a new promotion system.

Although understandably disappointed by Pershing's stance, Johnson was not deterred. He immediately asked Pershing, through Crowder, whether he would renew the request if Johnson would relinquish his promotion to colonel.[58] Pershing waited a month to reply, during which time Johnson, fearful that he would never join Pershing's staff, grew desperate. To Crowder's dismay, he thought of transferring to the Air Service or the Tank Corps as an alternative means of getting to the war zone.[59] On March 24, when Pershing's reply finally arrived, Johnson's worst fears were confirmed: "Johnson's promotion along with many others in the various staff departments seems quite out of proportion, and the Line and Staff officers here feel that such promotions made at home are unfair to men who are serving in France."[60] The commander of the AEF did not indicate whether he would accept Johnson at reduced rank. Pershing's reply was devastating to Johnson. However, he had little time to brood. The next day he was relieved from duty with the Office of the Provost Marshal General and transferred to the General Staff.

BY THE time Hugh Johnson left Crowder's office, the draft was well established. A mechanism for raising the army had been devised and put in place and, as an operation of magnitude, it was an outstanding success. The army was raised efficiently and economically, with a reasonable balancing of military and industrial manpower requirements and with no serious political disruption. Of the many men who worked to make the draft a success, only Crowder stands out more than Johnson. Crowder's ideas and supervision gave form to the draft. But Johnson, more than anyone else, translated these into policy.[61] He penned the original plan for executing the draft, the registration plan, the revised selection regulations, and the rationale for the work-or-fight order. Each marked a major step in the development of the draft. In addition, as executive officer in charge of administration and later as deputy provost marshal general, Johnson oversaw much of the daily business of Crowder's office. For these contributions he received the Distinguished Service Medal.[62]

CHAPTER 3

DIRECTOR OF PURCHASE AND SUPPLY

TRANSFER to the General Staff thrust Hugh Johnson into the center of the ferment in industrial mobilization. In the decades preceding the war, business had outdistanced other segments of American society in organizing itself to achieve stability. Emphasizing the cooperative ethic, systematic coordination, and business-government cooperation, businessmen had formed hundreds of associations to reduce the waste and disorder of laissez-faire capitalism through a system of industrial self-government. In this way they hoped to protect themselves against labor unions, political reformers, and rival business groups and enhance their ability "to predict, plan, and control economic behavior." Moreover, many argued that industrial self-government offered a tool through which business could serve the common good. The maintenance of America's liberal heritage in the new industrial age seemed to require a regulatory and welfare apparatus. Yet in the opinion of the proponents of industrial self-government those proposed by many reformers threatened to impose a stifling European-style bureaucratic statism on the economy. Their answer to this dilemma was that the government should consign social duties to enlightened business and trade associations and develop, nurture, and legitimize machinery operating outside of government so that these organizations could act together for public purposes.

In theory and in practice, industrial self-government made significant headway in the immediate prewar period, but it still faced many obstacles. The pull of decentralization and regionalism continued strong, and in many industries "the older entrepreneurial spirit" reigned supreme. Even in the steel and farm implements industries, where oligopoly had emerged as a major characteristic, competition challenged market stability. In addition, the antitrust laws placed limits on cooperative activity; for example, corporations that exchanged information on production and prices within an industrywide organization were liable to prosecution.

The wartime mobilization presented a good opportunity for the advancement of industrial self-government. The mobilization effort was the biggest public endeavor since the Civil War, and the federal government lacked the personnel, the information, the experience, and the administrative structure to mobilize the economy in an efficient manner. By stepping into this vacuum, businessmen could prove their morality and patriotism and demonstrate on a grand scale that industrial self-government could maximize economic efficiency. Ideally, the demonstration would spark a reevaluation of the "government's antitrust disposition and policelike attitudes toward business" and possibly even the emergence of a business-government partnership combining the virtues of free enterprise and national planning. But if the war presented an opportunity for advancing industrial self-government, it also presented great dangers. The placement of large military orders would so alter supply and demand as to destabilize the price system. This, in turn, could lead to the creation of a government superbureau in the hands of those hostile to business or ignorant of its broad needs and conceivably even to the destruction of "the industrial economy's basic structure and character."

Anxious to promote their ideological aims and to preserve the edifice of private economic power, members of the business community moved to fashion an institutional order in which the producers of materials rather than the expenders would have the major voice in the wartime mobilization. Beginning their efforts in 1916, with the Industrial Preparedness Committee of the Naval Consulting Board, they progressed through a series of makeshift government mobilization agencies, culminating in the formation of the War Industries Board (WIB) in July 1917. Initially an advisory agency composed of representatives of the government's procurement departments and businessmen in government service on a dollar-a-year basis, the WIB was to assist the military in the placement of contracts and industry in the conversion to war production.[1]

The WIB was predicated on the assumption that voluntary cooperation between public agencies and private organizations would serve the interests of the nation and its components. But from the outset its effectiveness was weakened by the unwillingness of many businessmen to defer to the larger public venture. An even greater impediment was the refusal of the army to purchase exclusively through the WIB mechanism. It was dominated by old-school officers of the nineteenth century who had yet to realize "that it was no longer possible to compartmentalize civilian and military functions" as had been the case before 1917.[2] They believed that the dollar-a-year men of the WIB were motivated more by "paytriotism" than by sense of duty and sacrifice and that they were usurping legitimate military prerogatives. In their view, the army alone understood the battlefield necessity and the technical aspects of military production; therefore, it should determine its own requirements and procure supplies as it saw fit.[3] Any departure from this practice would violate the military dictum that he who controls strategy must also control supply.

Even if the army had been more amenable to cooperation with the WIB, its supply organization was ill structured to work with the WIB. The army was supplied through a series of semiautonomous bureaus, each responsible for procurement of specific functional items such as ordnance supplies, quartermaster supplies, and the like. Each bureau operated as a separate procurement agency with separate systems for purchase, finance, storage, and distribution. Theoretically, the bureaus were under the supervision of the General Staff. However, its work had been hampered by disputes with the bureau chiefs and their congressional allies, and in April 1917, the General Staff had yet to solidify its position in the army. As a result, there was no authoritative body charged with assessing needs, establishing priorities among the bureaus, assigning the accumulation of like purchases, or regulating interbureau competition for scarce supplies. Moreover, no one was able to speak before the WIB for the army as a unit; the board had to hear from all the bureaus before it could decide policy.[4]

Throughout 1917 the bureaus ruthlessly competed with each other and with other government departments for raw materials and finished goods. The army did not consult the WIB on the magnitude of its requirements, nor did the supply bureaus systematically utilize the WIB to locate sources of supply. They overloaded the Northeast with war contracts far beyond the capacity of the region, leaving firms in other parts of the country to beg for war contracts as nonessential business began to dry up from shortages of raw materials and fuel. Equally disruptive, each bureau shipped the supplies it procured to the embarkation ports without reference to the shipments of other departments, quickly congesting the nation's railroad network and overtaxing its berthing capacity.

By the end of 1917 the competition between government procurement agencies and transportation bottlenecks threatened to bring mobilization to a grinding halt. Businessmen demanded that all government procurement responsibilities be stripped from the military services and placed in a business-dominated ministry of munitions. The army was adamantly opposed to such a ministry; and in December 1917, Baker, under intense political pressure, moved to head off the businessmen by putting the army's house in order. The creation of two General Staff divisions to supervise the supply bureaus and the naming of a prominent businessman, Edward R. Stettinius, Sr., a partner in the J. P. Morgan banking firm, to assist the chiefs of these divisions were central to his reforms. Equally important, Baker determined that he must have an energetic and effective administrator in the post of chief of staff. On January 26, 1918, he ordered Major General Peyton C. March, a first-rate artilleryman who was highly regarded as an efficient administrator, to return from France and become acting chief of staff.[5]

Baker's patchwork reforms successfully forestalled a ministry of munitions, but changes in the relationship between the military services and the WIB were nevertheless forthcoming. The crisis in mobilization was so severe that the army supply bureaus could no longer be permitted to enter the market without regard for the impact of their procurement programs upon other government agencies and the national economy. On March 4, 1918, Wilson named the famous Wall Street speculator Bernard M. Baruch chairman of the WIB and granted him general coordinating authority over industrial mobilization, thereby terminating the army's independence in the market. The army, however, was able to preserve internal control of its supply, and to a great degree the effectiveness of the upgraded WIB would depend upon the establishment of harmony between the army and the WIB and the process of bureaucratization.[6]

March began his duties as chief of staff on March 4, 1918, after Johnson, at Crowder's instigation, attempted to sidetrack his appointment. Although Crowder was a powerful figure in the War Department, by the end of 1917 he longed for a more active role in the war. Combat command in France was out of the question because of his age and frail physical condition. Appointment as chief of staff, however, would bring him into the wider realm of army activities and serve as the capstone of his distinguished career. Bolstered by Crowder, Johnson exhorted Baker in late January 1918, to name Crowder to the post and detail March as Crowder's assistant chief of staff.[7] Arguing for a proven administrator, organizer, and executive, Johnson reasoned that "the appointment of General Crowder would be recognized by the American people as the greatest single thing that could be done in perfecting the War Department organization."[8] He also enlisted Senator Robert Owen to press the same viewpoint on Baker and persuaded Easby-Smith to discuss the matter with Joseph A. Tumulty, Wilson's secretary. Fortunately for the future of the General Staff, Baker was not moved by Johnson's scheming. Crowder was a "foe of the General Staff," and his appointment as chief of staff could have meant the gutting of that post.[9]

Ironically, it was March who arranged Johnson's transfer to the General Staff. In reviewing the operations of the War Department, March "observed the work of Colonel Johnson in the Provost Marshal General's office as being very high grade and considered him material for assignment to duty with the General Staff." Clearly, Johnson would be valuable in "building up the War Department into a more vigorous war machine."[10]

HUGH Johnson's General Staff assignment was to assist Brigadier General Palmer E. Pierce, director of the Purchase and Supplies Division, one of the two new staff divisions created by Baker at the end of 1917. Victimized by infighting and lacking a functional organization, it was languishing when Johnson joined the division. Pierce, already the army representative on the WIB and a member of the War Council, showed scant interest in the division. He made repeated overtures to Stettinius, in the hope that a man of that stature would assume responsibility for its organization and operations; he was repeatedly rebuffed.[11]

It was not long, however, before the droopy condition of the Purchase and Supplies Division began to change. Baker's reform of the War Department precipitated a three-cornered struggle among the General Staff, Assistant Secretary of War Benedict Crowell, and the bureau chiefs for control of army supply. Determined to concentrate control in his own hands, Crowell, who was serving as acting secretary of war while Baker was overseas, appointed a special committee on April 2, 1918, to investigate the supply situation and, he hoped, to give added weight to his position.[12] The committee, dubbed the Committee of Three, consisted of efficiency expert Charles Day of the War Council, T. Nelson Perkins of the Council of National Defense, and Johnson.

Although his experience with army supply was minimal, Johnson had begun to question the bureau system as early as the summer of 1917, when several bureau chiefs glibly claimed that they could furnish supplies as quickly as the draft furnished men.[13] Events soon proved them wrong. Unprepared for the demands of mobilization, the bureaus were overwhelmed in their efforts to provide supplies; the result was shortages of training-camp equipment that caused, in turn, postponed draft calls during the winter of 1917–1918. Johnson's initial doubts were reinforced by the Senate Military Affairs Committee's investigation of the War Department, beginning in December 1917. He assiduously followed the committee's hearings and was impressed by its scathing indictment of the bureau system. By the time he joined the General Staff, he was convinced that the bureau system was bankrupt and that centralized direction was the only answer to the chaos in army supply.[14]

Concomitant with centralized direction of the bureaus was improved army relations with the WIB. Johnson had given little thought to this aspect of mobilization before March 1918. Nevertheless, he understood the need for unitary army representation before the WIB and was prepared to push the matter with all the forcefulness he could muster.[15]

The report of the Committee of Three, completed on April 16, 1918, marked an important stage in the history of army supply in two respects. First, to the disappointment of Crowell, Johnson and his associates rejected the notion that the assistant secretary of war should control supply. Instead, they argued that control should be located in the General Staff, thereby laying the ground work for the General Staff's "bold entering," on an immense scale, onto the heretofore debated ground of Staff supervision of the bureaus.[16] Second, the report signified the army's commitment to the termination of its self-imposed isolation from the larger efforts of the business community to systematize mobilization. In no uncertain terms the committee made it clear that the bureaus were to cooperate with the WIB and that the Purchase and Supplies Division should be the sole intermediary between them and the WIB.[17]

While the Committee of Three was completing its work, March reshuffled the General Staff. The relentless chief of staff, who had no use for Pierce, was anxious to take advantage of the stature and administrative ability of Major General George W. Goethals, famed as the builder of the Panama Canal, then serving in the Storage and Traffic Division. Ordering Pierce out of the War Department, March fused Storage and Traffic with Purchase and Supplies, creating on April 16 the "somewhat unwieldy" Purchase, Storage, and Traffic Division, with Goethals as its head. March and Goethals had great respect for each other, and both were committed to General Staff control of supply.

Under March's new arrangement, the Purchase and Supplies Division became the Purchase and Supply Branch, one of four in Goethals's division. Johnson was named head of this branch over his heated objection that he knew nothing about industrial mobilization and wanted to go to France. March, however, deftly "softened the blow" by promising to dispatch him as soon as the organizational phase was concluded; Johnson was also promoted to a brigadier generalship in the National Army.[18] At thirty-five, Johnson was the youngest U.S. Army general since the Civil War and the first member of his West Point class to receive his star. The promotion persuaded many of Johnson's friends that he was a favorite of March and had special influence with him.[19]

The Committee of Three had recommended that the director of Purchase and Supplies should be the army representative on the WIB. But Goethals had preferred that the army operate through a civilian, preferably Stettinius. At Goethals's insistence, the committee revised its report and recommended that Stettinius, the second assistant secretary of war, represent the army.[20] Goethals did not prevail, however, for the dollar-a-year men of the WIB insisted that the army representative must have a comprehensive knowledge of "Army rules, Army regulations, Army law, and Army practice," criteria that Stettinius did not satisfy.[21] The matter remained unsettled for several weeks while Pierce stayed on as the army representative. March finally brought it to a head in early May by dispatching Pierce to France, intending to name Goethals as Pierce's replacement. But Wilson let it be known that the new army representative must be able to work harmoniously with Baruch.[22] An abrupt, old-school soldier who liked to dominate, Goethals was temperamentally unable to work with the civilians of the emergency war agencies except in a superior position. Moreover, Goethals and Baruch had clashed twice previously and had developed a strong dislike for each other.

With Goethals eliminated from consideration, George N. Peek, commissioner of finished products for the WIB, suggested that Johnson would be an acceptable representative. The two men had met only once, but Peek knew of Johnson "and his work intimately through General Crowder."[23] He wrote a friend: "He was a lieutenant only a year ago; is a young man and one of the most forceful, active fellows I have met. Unless I am greatly mistaken in the man he will bring about vast improvements in the War Department."[24] Following Peek's suggestion, Wilson, on May 14, 1918, named Johnson as the army's new representative on the WIB.

THROUGHOUT the spring and summer of 1918, Hugh Johnson worked to supervise bureau procurement within the framework outlined by the Committee of Three. He established sections in his branch to oversee and standardize every aspect of procurement, from the computation of requirements to the payment for supplies and recruited personnel to staff them.[25] However, Staff supervision of the supply bureaus was only a stepping-stone to a more far-reaching overhaul of the army supply organization by consolidating procurement of all standard items in a single agency. Goethals was the driving force behind consolidation of procurement. While building the Panama Canal, he had centralized authority and responsibility for procurement, and he was convinced that a similar approach offered the only satisfactory method of eliminating the mess in army supply and assuring that the troops in France were supplied.[26]

During late April and early May, Johnson devised the interbureau requisition system under which procurement of any item required by two or more bureaus was assigned to a single bureau, usually the one already procuring a large portion of that item.[27] However, this system was only a stopgap, for Goethals and Johnson had already decided to create a truly "consolidated service of supply" as soon as Congress provided statutory authority. Under their plan, procurement of all standard items and storage and issue of all army supplies would be consolidated in a single agency.

Goethals recruited Gerard Swope to assist in the project. A former vice-president of Western Electric, Swope had come to Washington in the spring of 1918 at the bidding of Stettinius. When Swope moved from Stettinius's office to the Purchase, Storage and Traffic Division, Johnson asked to use him in the statistical work of his office. But Swope's disarming manner and his undisguised zeal for an important post persuaded Goethals that he would be a superb troubleshooter in the larger project to consolidate army supply.[28]

In May 1918, Congress passed the Overman Act, which gave the president carte blanche to adjust the executive branch; and in early July, Johnson and Swope, with the assistance of Colonel William H. Rose of the Engineer Corps and Colonel Frederick B. Wells, director of storage in Goethals's division, "began to prepare a scheme of organization" for a "consolidated service of supply." The central concept of their plan, known as the July 18th memorandum, was that the director of Purchase, Storage and Traffic would have executive, rather than supervisory, authority. He would "be in *command* of the supply organization" with responsibility for computing and satisfying the army's supply requirements. The bureaus would be relegated to "strictly *operative* agencies," with each responsible only for the design and procurement of items peculiar to its specific function—i.e., aircraft in the Bureau of Aircraft Production and artillery in the Ordnance Department. Procurement of all standard items and the domestic storage and issue of all items would be consolidated in a single subdivision of the Purchase, Storage and Traffic Division.[29]

Goethals passed Johnson and Swope's plan to March on July 19 with the prediction that it could be implemented by October 1918, if approved immediately. March, however, moved slowly, and for the next month Goethals and Johnson waited impatiently for the chief of staff's approval.[30] Although March was desirous of expanding the authority of the General Staff, he had serious reservations about the July 18th memorandum. The granting of executive authority to the director of Purchase, Storage, and Traffic and the formation of a "consolidated service of supply" in the General Staff were radical departures from accepted theory, which said that the General Staff should not entangle itself in administration. Moreover, the July 18th memorandum was opposed by a majority of the bureau chiefs, who saw its recommendations as an attack on their personal fiefdoms and as an unwarranted affront to their own considerable efforts since the nation entered the war.

March finally granted his approval to the July 18th memorandum on August 26, 1918. His reservations about the General Staff's administration of army supply were overridden by the particular circumstances involved. War supplies had to be procured and shipped on schedule, and the Johnson-Swope plan seemed the best way to do it. It was drastic surgery, but centralized control over the bureaus was necessary to avoid disaster; and the General Staff was the only agency within the War Department able to do the job.[31]

AT THE same time that he was helping Goethals restructure the War Department supply organization, Hugh Johnson was also working to improve relations between the army and the WIB. In March 1918, he shared the prevailing army distrust of the WIB, presupposing that it was an "obnoxious civilian interference" in military matters and that the dollar-a-year men were "superfluous cooks."[32] But unlike most of his

fellow officers, Johnson had only minor misgivings. He had grown accustomed to working closely with civilians in Crowder's office and had
come to respect their efforts. He had also realized that many traditional
attitudes and practices were outdated. Because the draft was based on a
program of far-reaching cooperation between the civilian and military
sectors, Johnson learned that mobilization for total war was inextri-
cably intertwined with all of the nation's institutions. Once aware of
this reality in industrial mobilization, Johnson began to trust the WIB,
and he became "a zealous convert to its principles."[33] In July 1918 he
lectured a group of supply officers that the WIB, instead of threatening
army prerogatives, would actually serve them by insuring that facilities
be in place to meet military requirements and that supply be syn-
chronized with demand.[34]

Johnson's growing friendship with some of the dollar-a-year men
smoothed his acceptance of them as full-fledged partners in mobilization. Baruch, who was very adept at sizing up a man, soon appreciated
the substance beneath Johnson's bluster and grew to admire his capacity for work, his retentive mind, and his ability to cut through a complex maze and present his case with brevity. Equally important, Baruch
was attracted by Johnson's engaging personality and colorful language,
which were in marked contrast to the blandness of Pierce and the
acerbity of Goethals. He enjoyed the company of talented rambunctious
individuals who could be useful to him. Johnson had these qualities
and so was drawn into Baruch's entourage.[35]

Peek, a farm implements manufacturer from Illinois, was likewise
impressed with Johnson's ability and his willingness to cooperate with
the WIB. Relations between Johnson and Peek were, as Peek later commented, "close, necessarily so in order to get any results, because he
had control of this great amount of business that the Army had to have,
and I was looking after civilian necessities as well, and, of course, they
had to be considered together."[36] Before long the two were good buddies, and Peek was telling associates that Johnson had the potential for
an outstanding partner in business.

Johnson was flattered by the attention of Baruch and Peek. He always
wanted to belong to the "center of the gang," to be "one of the boys,"[37]
as he had been in Crowder's office and as he had hoped to be in the General Staff. But Goethals and March already had their courtiers, and he
was an outsider. As a result, Johnson gravitated toward Baruch and Peek
and increasingly espoused their views within the councils of the War
Department.

In Johnson's opinion, his "first job" in improving army-WIB cooperation was to furnish the civilian mobilization agency with a "statement
of gross requirements." Such a statement was essential to the WIB if it
was to coordinate government procurement and "provide for the long-
range program of raw materials and facilities."[38] In April 1918, however,

Johnson found that the army had failed to provide the WIB with even a semblance of a statement of gross requirements, despite repeated requests. Moreover, each supply bureau was making purchases on its own individual schedule.[39] The initial army program, based on thirty divisions in France by the end of 1918, had been adopted in October 1917; but bureaucratic bungling kept it from being officially transmitted to the bureaus by the Operations Division of the General Staff until February 26, 1918. Consequently, through the winter of 1917–1918 the bureau chiefs computed requirements on whatever information they could secure individually, thus breeding different constructions of the army program.

In April 1918, the thirty-division program was expanded to meet the threat presented by the German spring offensives. The Operations Division, however, delayed the issuance of a new program because the fluid manpower-shipping situation made it difficult for army planners to settle on a new program with any certainty. The delay in issuing a new program exasperated Johnson. Without it, the only guide for computing requirements was the outdated thirty-division program. He decided to prod March to issue a new program, arguing in a forceful memorandum for the "immediate determination of the military program not only for the balance of 1918, but for 1919." He emphasized that, unless this was done, there would not be time for the WIB "to create additional facilities to provide the necessary supplies."[40]

The memorandum was still in the formative stage, and when March came upon it he "hit the ceiling." Unlike Crowder, who had encouraged Johnson to submit unsolicited memoranda on policy matters, March regarded such actions by subordinates as impertinent. He severely castigated Johnson for his attempt at "running the army" and perfunctorily brushed aside the substance of the memorandum. Even more than Goethals, March was a "soldier of the old school who did little . . . to hide his low opinion of the WIB." His policy, as Baruch later noted, "was to get as many men as possible to France, and to let others worry about supplying them."[41] March's response to his memorandum shocked Johnson, he said, "like a bolt from the blue," leaving him greatly "discouraged"; and for several weeks he "perturbed" his associates with his pouting.[42]

On April 30, 1918, the revised army program was officially announced. But it did not provide the projected program Johnson felt was so vitally necessary. Based on the continuation of troop shipments to France until forty-two divisions were there by July 1919 and fifty-four divisions by the end of that year, it did not reflect the accelerated troop shipments. It was simply a makeshift that enabled the bureaus to make preliminary plans for 1919 procurement. During the late spring and early summer of 1918, monthly troop shipments were more than doubled over the projections in the approved army program. Instead of the 120,000 men originally scheduled to be sent to France in May 1918, actual shipments totaled 244,407 men. In June, 277,894 men were sent, and in July a peak in monthly shipments of 306,302 men. However, as Johnson later observed, the supply bureaus were not officially informed of the change in the troop shipments projected in the thirty- and fifty-four division programs.[43] When confronted with Johnson's criticism, March labeled it "ludicrously false in its broad sense." He replied that the "shipment of troops and the supply agencies were both under the same man, General Goethals . . . [the criticism] is like saying that General Goethals' right hand did not know what his left hand was doing."[44]

Certainly everybody knew that there had been an increase in troop shipments; and, in the fluid manpower-shipping situation of the spring of 1918, it was difficult to formulate a program. Yet these facts do not excuse March's failure to specify the army program.[45] When Johnson was vigorously queried at a May 17 WIB meeting about future army requirements, he could only reply that he "would not bet on any one of the statements of requirements to any great precision, but I know some big facts that make me feel just as sure as I am sitting here that the requirements are going to be boosted from this time forward."[46] While correct in its broad outline, Johnson's answer did not make the WIB's job easier.

A new army program reflecting the accelerated troop shipments began to take shape in late June 1918. Pershing wanted a program based on 100 divisions in France. March and Goethals decided, however, that 100 divisions exceeded available shipping and berthing capacity and that the new program should be based on eighty divisions. The eighty-division program, officially adopted by the War Department on July 25, 1918, sent shock waves through the WIB. It would unmercifully strain essential industry and "skeletonize" nonessential industry. Many dollar-a-year men, prompted by complaints from industries—particularly the automobile industry, whose supply of raw materials was being curtailed in favor of war production—questioned whether such an enlarged army program was feasible. The industrial sector also believed such sacrifices were unnecessary: the army was having trouble shipping the supplies to France that it was already procuring.

To answer the critics, Johnson assigned Swope to make a "study of production and available tonnage for overseas transportation." The study, completed on July 27, demonstrated that the charge that army orders were outrunning available shipping was, in Johnson's word, "unfounded." Liberal in his estimates of tonnage to be shipped and conservative on his available-shipping estimates, Swope optimistically predicted that "sufficient shipping will be available to maintain the army."[47] Armed with Swope's study, Johnson, at an August 1 WIB meeting, flatly denied that the eighty-division program was logistically unfeasible and thus quieted the critics.[48]

In the meantime, Johnson ordered the bureaus to prepare and submit requirements schedules based on the eighty-division program. Difficulties surfaced immediately when the Ordnance Department complained that it lacked statistical data on its reserve stocks. Johnson replied by warning the chief of ordnance that "the apparent inability of the Ordnance Department to make the desired estimates on a satisfactory basis . . . jeapordizes the entire program of the army . . . [and is] not acceptable."[49] The tough talk was apparently successful, for the Ordnance Department was the first bureau to submit requirements schedules. During the last months of the war, requirements schedules for approximately 2,700 items were transmitted to the WIB. The war ended, however, before a gross statement of requirements based on the eighty-division program could be completed.[50]

Providing the WIB with a statement of gross requirements was only one facet of Johnson's efforts to improve army-WIB relations. He also worked to shape the army supply organization to interact with the myriad of divisions, committees, boards, and sections of the WIB. The problem lay with the "hydraheaded" nature of army contact with the WIB. Each bureau pressed its own claims for clearance and priority, forcing the WIB to rule on conflicting army requests. To end this confusion, Johnson commanded the bureaus to submit all clearance and priority requests through his office and prohibited them from initiating contract negotiations until clearance was received. Furthermore, he established clearance and priority systems within the army so that conflicting interbureau requests were resolved internally, thereby answering the WIB's demand for "concerted presentation of such matters."[51]

Most of his attention in this regard, however, was devoted to coordinating army supply with the commodity organization of the WIB. Developed after Wilson's upgrading of the WIB, it consisted of a series of sections for items in which shortages either existed or were threatened. Each section was designed to serve as a clearinghouse for information for a specific industry—wood, rubber, hardware, chemicals, and the like. It maintained close ties with the war service committee of the industry's trade association and was staffed by industrialists from that industry and representatives of the government's procurement departments. The duties of the commodity organization included allocation of facilities and materials for war production, clearance for immediate military requirements, administration of curtailment and conservation programs, and advisement of the Price-Fixing Committee and the Priorities Board.[52]

Johnson noted that the army, with its functional supply organization, was not prepared to procure "in terms of commodities." In the case of automotive products, for example, several army supply bureaus bought, and without regard for the needs of other bureaus or the nation's requirements. Coordination between the chiefs of these bureaus was difficult because automotive products were only one of the many items that they were buying. If the army's demand for automotive products was to be measured against the supply, these bureaus would have to be brought together. The army had to shape itself so that it could respond to the situation with commodities.[53]

In late April, a number of commodity committees, made up of representatives from the various supply bureaus, were organized in Johnson's office; he directed that each one select a member to represent the army as a unit on all matters before the corresponding commodity section of the WIB.[54] He also advised the bureaus to approach industry only through the commodity committee-section arrangement so that they could "obtain suggestions" where best to place orders. In this way they would ensure speedy delivery and assist the WIB in its efforts to obtain "a scientific and common sense distribution of production."[55]

The commodity arrangement did not perform as Johnson intended. Many bureau officers serving on the army commodity committees were not committed to full cooperation with the WIB. Often they passed up the WIB's commodity-section meetings, and Johnson exerted considerable effort cajoling them about attending commodity-section meetings and lecturing them on the WIB.[56] His admonishments were of little avail, however, for most army commodity representatives resented Baruch's delegation of paramount authority in each section to the section chief, who was always a civilian. Many section chiefs, anxious to limit the army's field of discretion, acted without consulting the army representatives or even convening section meetings. Their arbitrary stance magnified the ingrained military distrust of businessmen, leading the army representatives to avoid rather than seek contact with the WIB. The situation became so serious by August 1918 that Johnson complained to Peek that "examination of the records of minutes indicates that the general statement that the Sections do not meet and conduct business as such, is justified in respect for a majority of cases."[57]

Johnson's response was two-pronged. He implored Peek to instruct the commodity chiefs to accord army representatives every opportunity to participate in the deliberations of their respective sections. Moreover, he successfully requested that the entire section be clearly endowed with the source of authority. At the same time, Johnson warned the army's commodity representatives to assert themselves before the WIB's sections and restated their responsibilities in *Supply Bulletin* #22, issued on August 28, 1918. He urged the army commodity representatives to consider themselves "as much a part of the . . . [WIB] as the officers of the War Industries Board themselves" and reminded them, in a heady vision of military-industrial cooperation, that we should consider it quite as much our function and duty as that of the War Industries Board to carry into effect the President's orders relating to the conversion of industry, the creation of new facilities, and the relief of congested districts. We should regard and constantly use the board and all its sections as our powerful help and auxiliary in carrying forward the Army program and never as in opposition or hindrance of that program.[58]

After the issuance of *Supply Bulletin #22*, the nature of army contact with the WIB's commodity organization improved dramatically. A new spirit of cooperation on the part of the army representatives was evident, and the commodity arrangement began to function as an efficient channel between the army and the WIB.[59] More than any other development, the organization and maturation of the commodity arrangement, under Johnson's watchful eye, symbolized the war-induced intertwining of the military and industrial sectors.

Johnson's efforts to improve army-WIB relations peaked with the issuance of *Supply Bulletin #22*. He had worked to furnish the WIB with a statement of gross requirements and shaped the army supply organization so that it would mesh with the organization of the WIB. He also had instilled a new vitality in army-WIB relations that was evident in the increased spirit of cooperation in the commodity sections. After months of wrangling, the army and the WIB had finally reached a modus operandi.[60]

THE summer of 1918 was a period of extreme tension for Hugh Johnson. Even for an individual of his energy and enthusiasm, the demands upon him as director of purchase and supply were grueling. The Purchase and Supply Branch was still in the embryonic stage, and organizational details demanded his attention. Conferences, reports, and administrative decisions seemed endless. Johnson also had to weld his office staff, a conglomeration of civilians and regular and newly-commissioned officers only recently brought together, into a smoothly functioning unit. Johnson attempted to effect cohesion with warnings of the dangers of "leisurely accomplishment."[61] But the staff, as in the case of the army commodity representatives, responded sluggishly, causing Johnson to fret and fume and drive himself harder.[62]

Johnson's worsening relations with March intensified the tension. Relations between the two men had deteriorated since March assailed Johnson for his April 1918 proposal on the immediate planning for the 1919 army program. Johnson's aggressive style offended March, who grew to regard the younger man as "more of a legal man than . . . a soldier."[63] This opinion was very likely induced by Johnson's past association with Crowder, March's bitter enemy since their service together as observers in the Russo-Japanese War. The chief of staff openly displayed his antipathy for Johnson and was quick to chastize him whenever he appeared to overstep his authority. Johnson, humiliated by the "dressing down" he had received from March, thereafter resented him. March's arrogant disregard for the WIB and disputes over the power of the General Staff with Baruch, Crowder, and Pershing reinforced this resentment. By the end of the war, Johnson's resentment toward March had swelled to the point of obsession. He looked on March with a jaundiced eye, seeing him as a modern-day "Richelieu" with megalomaniacal tendencies; he became convinced that March had intervened to prevent him from receiving the Distinguished Service Medal for his work in the General Staff.[64]

Another tension Johnson had to endure was his increasing fear that he would not get to France. A sliver of hope developed in early July when he heard that Baker planned to send Goethals to France to command Pershing's Service of Supply. Johnson immediately beseeched Goethals to take him along, arguing that "I represent you and your ideas and therefore I ought to go along with you and your ideas."[65] Stettinius, however, protested that "the whole shooting match in Washington would go to the dogs" if Johnson went overseas. Before Goethals made a decision, the plan for him to go to France was scratched by Pershing, who named General Harbord, an old cavalry buddy of Johnson, to head the Service of Supply in France.[66]

As soon as he completed work on the July 18th memorandum, Johnson again turned his eyes on France. Even though Pershing had not replied to his February 1918, offer to go to France at reduced rank, Johnson still thought his best opportunity to get to the war zone lay with Pershing. Therefore, on July 23, he renewed his offer to go to France at reduced rank and informed Pershing that he expected to be available by the middle of October, the projected completion date for the changeover to the new supply organization.[67] By now Johnson's rank was of no concern to Pershing, and at the end of August he asked March to send Johnson as soon as his work with the reorganization of army supply was completed. Pershing's first thought was to substitute Johnson for Brigadier General Johnson Hagood, chief of staff for the AEF Service of Supply. Later, he considered appointing Johnson as chief financial officer for the AEF.[68]

Goethals, meanwhile, decided that the Purchase and Storage Service, the "consolidated service of supply" outlined in the July 18th memorandum, should be formed out of the purchase and storage divisions of the Quartermaster Department. Johnson would hold the key post of director of purchase and storage, while Brigadier General Robert E. Wood, acting quartermaster general, would serve as director of purchase and Colonel Wells, as director of storage. But Wood and his principal deputy in the Quartermaster Department, Robert Thorne, informed Goethals that they preferred not to serve under Johnson, arguing that he was a lawyer with little knowledge of the day-to-day mechanics of procurement and storage and that he would botch the operation.

To the extent that Johnson was not an experienced supply officer, there may have been some basis for their objection. At the heart of it, however, was Wood's unwillingness to work under an officer of lesser seniority and Thorne's feeling that he could not work closely with Johnson's temperament.[69] Goethals thought that Thorne's concern was exaggerated. Yet, feeling that he could not risk breaking up the higher echelon of the Quartermaster Department just as its key divisions were to be formed into the Purchase and Storage Service, he reluctantly decided to divorce Johnson from the new agency and appoint him assistant director of Purchase, Storage, and Traffic, a largely titular post.[70]

Johnson's new post left him with little work, so in September 1918, Goethals and Baruch sent him on an ordnance-production inspection tour of industrial centers. By the time Johnson returned, later in the month, Goethals decided that this valuable lieutenant in the program to reorganize army supply and regularize army relations with the WIB now deserved the opportunity to go to France. A vacancy had developed in the command of an infantry brigade of the 8th Division; and on October 7, 1918, March, who now "wanted to see the last" of him, relieved Johnson from the General Staff and ordered him to Camp Fremont, California, to take command of it.[71] Orders were that the division would decamp and proceed to France.

Johnson was elated by the assignment, but his happiness clouded when he was stricken with influenza on the trip west. Upon arrival at Camp Fremont, he found the division caught in the rampaging Spanish flu epidemic. Johnson's 15th Infantry Brigade was scheduled to entrain first. But the brigade was so ravaged by flu that the division headquarters and the artillery brigade were sent instead. Johnson was to follow with his own and the other infantry brigade. The delay proved fatal to Johnson's hope of getting to France. When he finally got these troops to New York City and aboard ship, news of the "false armistice" of November 7, 1918, arrived, and they were disembarked.

His failure to get to France was a crushing disappointment to Johnson. The hope of serving with the AEF had nourished him for eighteen months; and now, after coming so close, he had missed the fighting. "Disappointed and disillusioned," he resolved to throw "twenty years of training and service [over his] shoulder" by resigning from the army. As he told his friends, "I spent my first 15 years listening to what my comrades had done at San Juan Hill. I don't want to spend the next 15 listening to what they did at Chateau-Thierry."[72]

Johnson's decision to leave the army, notwithstanding his comments about his failure to get to France, involved practical considerations at least equally. He realized that choice postwar army assignments would go to those with combat records. He would revert to his permanent rank of major in a Judge Advocate Corps already overcrowded with majors. Johnson was also concerned about his financial future. Staying in the army until 1946, when he would reach the mandatory retirement age, would yield him a commission worth only $100,000 in salary, allowances, and retirement benefits, in his judgment an insufficient amount to provide his wife, Helen, with a comfortable life after her sacrifices in the first years of their marriage and ensure his son a good education. Johnson believed he now needed a career that proferred greater professional and financial rewards than those of the postwar army. He presumed this career lay in business. His work with the WIB had provided "an unprecedented glimpse of the very vitals of the American industrial machine," priceless contacts with business leaders, and the confidence that he had assets to capitalize on in the business world. He had a law degree, and the organizational skill he had shown during the war had prompted several business leaders to express interest in him.[73]

After a brief stay at Camp Mills, New York, Johnson and his men were sent to Camp Lee, Virginia. There he was given charge of the demobilization of 60,000 men who, like himself, had failed to get to France. He found the routine and red tape deadening and cabled Harbord to ask whether there was a place for him in France during AEF demobilization. Harbord had no post "adequate for his particular qualifications."[74] Crowder, though, rescued Johnson from the red tape by summoning him to Washington in mid-December 1918, to help wind up the affairs of the draft. In January 1919, Johnson went over to the WIB, where he spent six weeks editing the reports of the WIB's commodity chiefs and writing a brief summary of the WIB for Baruch to use in preparing his report to the president. Baruch thought Johnson's work on this assignment was a "masterpiece"; however, he chose to use only parts of the material in his preliminary report in December 1919, and in his final report in March 1921, because of the length of the commodity reports and the outspokenness of Johnson's references to government procurement departments.[75] Now that the war was over, Baruch believed it was best to temper criticism of the army rather than carry on battles that could discredit both the army and the WIB.

Johnson's work with the WIB records was important to his growth. As the army representative on the WIB, he had been primarily concerned with improving army-WIB relations. Now he had the opportunity to examine more fully the operations of the WIB in the larger realm of the national economy, and he was particularly impressed with the extent of the cooperation between government and business during the war and the role of trade associations in helping to regulate business. America's tremendous industrial plant had been mobilized for a great national purpose, while at the same time business had made generous profits and eliminated some of the chaos of the marketplace. The key to this success, in Johnson's opinion, was the manner in which the WIB facilitated cooperation within the business community, and to his way of thinking there was no reason why this cooperation could not be carried over to peacetime:

No one will contend that there can ever be any peacetime necessity or reason for such close-held control over industry as was practiced during the war. . . . Still, the great lessons remain: efficiency is attainable only by cooperation; . . . industry is susceptible of such regulatory control as would prevent the abuses aimed at by the Sherman Act and yet attain the efficiency of cooperation without impairing the advantages of individual initiative.

Building on this base, Johnson postulated that "what is needed is a statute" legalizing trade association activities encouraging industrial self-government. He further postulated that "a mechanism" should be created to implement the statute so that the government would possess the capacity to act not as a "policeman . . . but a cooperator, an adjuster, a friend." It should take the form of a planning board made up of representatives from basic industries and pass upon prices, wages, investment plans, and trade practices.[76] Johnson's path to the National Recovery Administration began, essentially, with this report.

On February 20, 1919, Johnson submitted his resignation from the army. It was accepted four days later, leaving him, at the age of thirty-six, "to start all over again without the slightest idea of what . . . [he] would attempt to earn a living."[77]

CHAPTER 4

THE MOLINE PLOW COMPANY

HUGH Johnson's transition from khaki to mufti was extremely trying. Uncertain about what type of business career to pursue, he
initially accepted a temporary appointment as general counsel for the
Industrial Board of the Commerce Department. Chaired by George Peek,
it had been created in February 1919, ostensibly to protect business from
postwar deflation through government manipulation of prices. In actuality, it represented an effort by organized business to force the Wilson
administration to relax the antitrust laws. Before long the board was
mired in controversy, and in May 1919, it disbanded in the face of the
strong opposition within the administration to a price-reduction agreement it had negotiated with the steel industry.[1]

Johnson did not wait for the demise of the Industrial Board. In March
1919, he accepted Charles J. and Stewart Symington's offer to head their
Federal Liquidating Association. The Symington brothers, who had
met Johnson through the WIB, had formed Federal Liquidating to represent war contractors seeking favorable settlements with the government.[2] Johnson's $25,000 annual salary was to be supplemented by a
percentage of the profits.

The Federal Liquidating Association attracted sizable retainers, but it
soon aroused the enmity of official Washington when advertising from
some of the nation's industrial centers implied that Johnson and other
former army officers would ensure that the Symingtons' clients would
receive special consideration from the War Department. In retaliation,
the War Department proposed an amendment to the 1920 army appropriations bill prohibiting former army procurement officers from representing claimants against the government.[3] At the request of the
Symingtons, Johnson approached Representative Julius Kahn, Republican of California and chairman of the House Military Affairs Committee, and asked him to kill the amendment. Kahn, whom Johnson knew
as a result of their frequent consultations on matters relating to the
draft, refused the request. But Johnson was able to convince him to alter it so that it applied only to officers who were specifically respon-

sible for procurement. In this form, the bill would not adversely affect his work with Federal Liquidating. Yet Johnson, angry at what he believed to be an attack by March and his allies on his own integrity, left Federal Liquidating for other employment.[4]

With offers from Armour, International Harvester, Standard Oil, and Secretary of Interior Franklin K. Lane, Johnson was not lacking opportunities. But, looking for a place where he could take initiative and be his own paymaster, he set his sights on a law partnership with Crowder. The two had generally discussed a partnership for months, and in late July 1919, they made plans for one that would take advantage of Crowder's numerous Cuban business and governmental contacts. However, since Crowder would not resign from the army immediately (he was in Havana helping the Cuban government draft a new election code, and he wanted to be free to return to Havana if problems developed), Johnson decided to accept an offer from Peek to join the management team of the Moline Plow Company.[5]

Anxious to be top man in a large business, Peek, who had been president in charge of sales for Deere and Company before the war, had accepted the presidency of the Moline Plow Company shortly after the disbandment of the Industrial Board. Recently purchased by John N. Willys and headquartered at Moline, Illinois, it manufactured plows, drills, tractors, wagons, manure spreaders, and a host of other farm implements. It also controlled the Stephens Motor Car Company. Peek's acceptance of the presidency of Moline Plow surprised many of his friends, for the company was known in the farm implement industry as "a terrible lemon." It was virtually bankrupt and "on conservative accounting" had not made money for years.[6] But Peek, who was widely recognized as a man with shrewd insight and general business wisdom, was confident that he could turn the company's fortunes around, especially if the market for farm implements continued to grow at its prewar pace. Any doubts he may have harbored were overcome by Willys's assurance that he could have all the financial support necessary to make the company into a moneymaker.[7]

Persuaded by their work together in Washington that Johnson was "one of the big developments of the war," Peek asked Johnson to become assistant general manager and general counsel of Moline Plow at a salary of $28,000 a year. He was particularly impressed with Johnson's keen mind and "unusual faculty for clearly expressing himself" and saw in him potential for "the finest partner in business one can imagine."[8] "General Johnson," he wrote a friend, "is one of the best men I know."[9]

On first glance, the Johnson-Peek partnership was a match made in heaven. The two men were good buddies and in many respects complemented each other.[10] Peek brought vast experience in the farm implement industry to the partnership, while Johnson brought skills in writing and organization. Beneath this fair facade, however, the partnership was a dangerous mix of volatile personalities. Both had supreme confidence in their own abilities, and neither could tolerate opposition to his own views. Neither liked to lose an argument, and both relied on force rather than tact to win the day. A strain in the relationship was certainly predictable.[11]

WHEN he joined Moline Plow, in September 1919, Johnson was first assigned to review the company's books for the last ten years and devise an operations manual for the business. The work, Johnson said, "was no easy thing" for one new to business. But it thoroughly educated Johnson in the company's finances and operations and prepared him for responsibility. In the meantime, Peek, believing that the company must undertake a massive expansion program to survive, expanded production of all of the company's lines. Very quickly Moline Plow's business, financed largely by borrowed money, reached heights "it had never known before."[12]

The prosperity was short-lived. During World War I, American agricultural production had expanded greatly to meet European demands. But as the war-torn European nations began to get back on their feet in 1919, they curtailed agricultural imports; the result, in the United States, was mounting domestic surpluses. The termination of federal price supports in agriculture made matters worse. Beginning in July 1920, prices of agricultural products dropped precipitously, ushering in an agricultural depression that would last for two decades. Farm foreclosures skyrocketed, farm values fell, and the purchasing power of farmers in terms of prewar levels declined.[13]

The agricultural depression contracted the market for Moline Plow implements. At the same time, the money from Willys evaporated. As a result, Peek and Johnson found themselves at the head of a company saddled "with a new, heavy high-priced inventory, an enormous debt, and a portfolio of farm paper that had always theretofore been regarded as 'sound as wheat in the mill,' but which now turned into worthless chaff by millions."[14]

The sad state of Moline Plow unnerved Johnson. He was in debt because of unfortunate purchases of Moline Plow stock. He also feared that a company failure would irreparably tarnish his reputation. These were hardly satisfying circumstances for one who, two years before, had confidently expected a business career to bring unbounded professional and financial rewards. By the spring of 1921 Johnson was yearning for the more settled days he had known in the army. Pershing had just been named chief of a general headquarters in Washington, and news reports indicated that one of his major assignments would be planning for industrial mobilization. The thought of again working on industrial mobilization, a task for which he felt ideally suited, resounded in Johnson's head "like a tocsin." In April he queried Pershing about the prospect of being detailed to this work if he returned to the army. Pershing, "realizing not only . . . [his] ability as a soldier but as an organizer as well," was interested in securing Johnson's assistance. But he could not guarantee the detail Johnson desired, and in July 1921, Johnson temporarily shelved his thought of returning to the military.[15]

A month earlier, Moline Plow's creditors formed two overseers' committees which in turn formed a committee, chaired by Frank O. Wetmore, president of the First National Bank of Chicago, to reorganize and refinance the debt-ridden company. In 1922 Willys relinquished all interest in Moline Plow. Control of the company passed to the jittery creditors, and Wetmore became chairman of the board.

During the last months of 1922, "two or three of the larger" creditor banks and Peek split over the future of Moline Plow. Sales of implements continued to lag because of the depressed condition of the agricultural sector, and the banks contended that their interests would be protected only if the unprofitable implement lines were liquidated. Peek countered that it was bad business to liquidate. Having "grown up in the farm implement industry at a time when it was popular for the major implement companies to do a full-line business," he argued that the company would lose its dealers and jobbers if it did not provide a full line. He further argued that, given sufficient time and the freedom to operate normally, he could reduce the company's massive debt to manageable size and ultimately erase it.[16] Peek did not sway the banks, and in January 1923, they initiated steps "to get control of the company . . . or at least some of its important units" and effect the liquidation themselves.[17]

Needing funds to finance production of the spring line of implements, the Moline Plow board of directors voted on February 20, 1923, to defer interest payments on the company's bonds. One of the creditor banks immediately threatened to have the company placed in receivership.[18] Peek and Johnson were able to prevent this action. But the affair convinced them that they must seek new ownership if they were to manage the company successfully. Herndon Smith of Chicago and a New York banker associated with him expressed interest in buying the company, and in March 1923, Johnson prepared an optimistic prospectus. If ownership was willing to endorse full-line production and give the company time to get back on its feet, he prophesied that Moline Plow might anticipate annual profits of $1,000,000. Johnson's prospectus failed to persuade Smith to buy the company. Therefore, cash running out and additional loans refused, Peek and Johnson reluctantly accepted the inevitability of liquidating some lines. To preserve the largest amount of assets possible, Johnson devised a plan, dubbed the May 28 plan, calling for production to be cut back to the tillage, drill, and wagon lines.[19]

Peek and Johnson also began to experiment with a new marketing method. Known as the Moline Plan, it restricted the company's domestic business "to an area within one thousand miles of the main factory" in Moline and permitted sales "only in carloads or half carloads and only for spot cash." In this way distribution costs might be sufficiently slashed to permit Moline Plow to sell implements "at ten per cent less than the best cash and quantity deal of any competitor."[20]

The struggle to keep Moline Plow afloat exacted its toll on the friendship between Johnson and Peek. Whether because of extreme nervous tension or the natural erosion of the hard times, the two strong-willed men began to bicker over details of company policy. Johnson said, in a letter of February 25, 1924, that to his dismay, he found that "no opinion or advice" that he might offer "weighed a groat's worth" with Peek and that Peek was taking his disagreements as a personal affront.

The growing tension between the two men brought out Johnson's tendency to drink to excess under pressure. By the 1920s, scotch mixed with water was his daily working fuel, and no day was complete without an Occidental or a Harvey Wallbanger at bedtime. At this point, Johnson's drinking did not ordinarily impair his work. But as his relations with Peek deteriorated, he drank more than usual and was slowed down by hangovers often enough to lead Peek to suspect his judgments, thinking they were warped by alcohol.

In July 1923, saddened by his growing estrangement from Peek, Johnson again toyed with the notion of leaving Moline Plow. Secretary of Agriculture Henry C. Wallace offered him a job with the Department of Agriculture. But Eugene Meyer, Jr., who had served as director of the War Finance Corporation and knew Johnson through their mutual friendship with Baruch, advised him that he was not wealthy enough to afford the luxury of a government job and that he should attend to the business in Moline.[21] Johnson also considered joining with Robert W. Lea to form a consultancy specializing in industrial analyses, reorganizations, and general liquidations. Lea had served with Johnson in the Purchase, Storage and Traffic Division and had joined the Peek management team at Moline Plow in 1919 as president and general manager of the Stephens Motor Car Company. Johnson felt that he and Lea worked well together and told Peek that "he has many characteristics that I lack and . . . we would supplement each other in weak spots."[22] Before he and Lea could make a decision on the consulting firm, however, Wetmore convinced Johnson that his differences with Peek would work themselves out and that he should stay with Moline Plow and handle the liquidation.[23]

On September 6, 1923, the board of directors cancelled the management contract with Peek and his associates.[24] To meet current bills, it also authorized liquidation of all company lines except hay tool, tillage, drill, and wagon. On Wetmore's recommendation, the liquidation was assigned to Johnson. But the liquidators perfunctorily vetoed Johnson's May 28 plan as a basis for the reorganization of the company and heatedly demanded that all lines except tillage, the one profitable sales line, be liquidated. As a result, a final decision on the reorganization of Moline Plow was postponed to await business developments.

The failure of the May 28 plan to satisfy the liquidators aggravated the bickering between Peek and Johnson. They could not agree on a new strategy to save the company. Peek hoped to return to full-line production in the future.[25] As a first step, he instructed Johnson to negotiate a contract with the company's jobbers committing it to the manufacture of the harvester line. Johnson questioned the wisdom of this action, arguing that consideration of harvester-line production should be delayed until there was an "amicable atmosphere" on the board. Peek rejected Johnson's counsel and put strong personal pressure on him to negotiate the contract and vote for it at a board meeting. Against his better judgment, Johnson yielded to Peek. But, as he had predicted, the liquidators vetoed the contract. Their differences over the harvester contract left Johnson fearful that sooner or later he would be forced to choose between friendship with Peek and what he considered best for the company.[26]

AT THE same time they were fighting to save Moline Plow, Peek and Hugh Johnson were fighting on another front to solve the problems of agriculture. The wartime mobilization had taught the two men to think in terms beyond the immediate interests of individual businesses. After countless discussions they concluded in the summer of 1920 that "there can't be any business for us until the farmer is on his feet. There is nothing we can do here—let's find out what is the matter with agriculture."[27] In August 1920, the two Moline executives prepared an anonymous memorandum analyzing the nation's agricultural plight, emphasizing problems of transportation, finance, and labor.[28] The memorandum was edited by officials of the American Farm Bureau Federation and distributed to a select group of individuals, including James M. Cox and Warren G. Harding for their use in the 1920 presidential election campaign.[29]

During the spring and summer of 1921, Peek and Johnson followed up their initiative by devising a full-blown plan to aid agriculture. The plan was presented first in October 1921, to officials of the Farm Bureau, and then to the national convention of the Farm Bureau the following December. The Farm Bureau was not willing to endorse the plan, although one businessman suggested that it needed a name that would capture the attention and imagination of farmers and political leaders.[30] Accordingly, Peek and Johnson labeled their plan, and the unsigned pamphlet they were preparing to publicize it, equality for agriculture. Proof copies of the pamphlet were ready for distribution in the last days of December 1921, and 3,000 copies were printed in early 1922.

Most of the ideas in *Equality for Agriculture* were Peek's, while Johnson was responsible for the language.[31] They believed that the farmer's trouble lay in the operations of the protective tariff. By being able to control its output and withhold surpluses from the market, industry was able to guard against the price-depressing effects of overproduction and receive "the full tariff differential over world price" for a product. Agriculture, meanwhile, was unable to control its output or withhold surpluses from the market. Thus the domestic price for a product in which the United States produced a surplus, despite the tariff, was forced down to the world level. The result was an inequality for agriculture: Farmers received world prices for their products but had to pay protected prices for the industrial goods they purchased. To obtain equality for agriculture, Peek and Johnson declared, the tariff had to be made effective so that farmers received a fair-exchange price for their products. The fair-exchange price, or parity, as it came to be known, was defined as "one which bears the same ratio to [the] current general price index as a ten-year pre-war average crop price bore to [the] average general price index for the same period." The ratio price would be computed each year and protected by a fluctuating tariff. The price-depressing surpluses would be disposed of by a government-sponsored corporation that would buy up the surpluses at the ratio prices and dump them over the American tariff wall at world prices. The losses incurred by the corporation would be recouped by charging farmers an "equalization fee" on each bushel or pound of a product sold.[32]

The ideas in *Equality for Agriculture* were not original. For years farmers had realized the ineffectiveness of tariff protection for agricultural products, and the concept of parity went back at least to the 1890s. Nor were the ideas without fault. The plan totally ignored such long-range problems as reduction of costs, technical reorganization, and soil conservation. It would undoubtedly bring about increased agricultural production and steadily mounting surpluses. Peek and Johnson were also shortsighted in thinking that overseas sales would be a permanent solution to the problem of surpluses. Foreign nations would inevitably retaliate by adopting anti-dumping laws; and even if they let in increased amounts of American commodities, there was little reason to believe that they could indefinitely absorb or pay for all that Americans would have to sell. Despite its defects, *Equality for Agriculture* was, nevertheless, important in the evolution of American agricultural policy. For the first time, parity prices were identified as "a practical legislative goal." Moreover, by assigning responsibility for insuring parity to the federal government the Peek-Johnson plan broke "the restrictive bonds on farm thinking that held that government aid should be confined to education, credit, co-operative marketing, or regulation of business."[33]

An ideal opportunity for publicizing *Equality for Agriculture* developed when Secretary of Agriculture Wallace named Peek a delegate to the National Agricultural Conference. It was to convene in Washington on January 23, 1922, to discuss the agricultural depression. In preparation for the conference Peek and Johnson sent briefs of their plan to selected individuals and, upon their arrival in Washington on January 20, buttonholed officials to get permission to present it to the conference. Much to their disappointment, Wallace, who had not yet read the brief they sent him, refused to consent to the plan's presentation. He told the two Moline executives that he did not want the conference to get sidetracked on the political aspects of the tariff and was concerned that the ratio-price idea "was so broad" that nothing else might come out of the conference if it were injected into the discussion.[34] Peek and Johnson then went to see the permanent chairman of the conference, Representative Sydney Anderson, Republican of Minnesota. Anderson likewise refused to consent to the plan's presentation. He told them that the official position of the Republican party on the tariff was higher agricultural rates and, as Johnson later recalled, "that if we tried to raise this point [the plan] . . . he would steamroller us."[35] Thwarted in their efforts to present the equality for agriculture plan to the conference, Peek and Johnson had to settle for the conference's approval of a meaningless resolution calling for the establishment of "a fair exchange value for all farm products with that of all other commodities." Nothing was said about any mechanism for achieving this goal.[36]

Peek and Johnson were not deterred by their failure to get a hearing for equality for agriculture. On January 28, the day after the conference, they met with Wallace and asked him to call a meeting of "competent critics" to consider the plan's practicality. Though Wallace was intrigued by their presentation, he wanted the expert opinion of Henry C. Taylor, an economist in the Department of Agriculture, and George N. Warren, a department consultant, before agreeing to a meeting. Peek and Johnson also visited important senators but declined invitations to discuss the plan before congressional committees, feeling that they had first to sell the administration and then hope for action.[37] Wallace's economists completed their study of equality for agriculture in the first week of February. Although not in complete agreement with it, they advised Wallace that "some plan of this kind must be added to the tariff idea in order to make the tariff effective in holding up the prices of products."[38] Encouraged by their report, Wallace called for a semisecret meeting of business leaders to convene on February 13, 1922, to discuss the plan.

By this time equality for agriculture had gained a powerful opponent. Believing that he would be receptive to the plan, Johnson on January 16, 1922, had sent proof sheets of *Equality for Agriculture* to Secretary of Commerce Herbert C. Hoover. He wrote Hoover that "the best minds among our confidential friends" consider the plan economically sound and warned that rejection by the Republican party of the "essential principles deduced in the brief will seriously embarrass it in the coming election, if not permanently."[39] Hoover was not impressed. Although he had a member of his department study and criticize the plan, Hoover was already committed to a different approach to the farmer's plight. He believed that the farmer would best be served if the government helped him to organize cooperatives for the marketing of his crops. The government's role would be that of a facilitator and coordinator of cooperatives, and except in the most dire circumstances the government would keep its hands off the financing and marketing of commodities. Concluding that the Peek-Johnson plan would only lead to further surpluses and that it called for too much government intervention, Hoover spelled out his objections to the plan before the Interstate Commerce Commission on February 3 and thereafter was a leader in rallying opposition to it.[40]

The meeting to discuss the equality for agriculture plan convened in Wallace's office in the morning of February 13. Of the businessmen present, New York banker Otto Kahn was the most sympathetic; but even he expressed doubts about the practicality of the plan's administrative features. Julius Barnes, president of the United States Chamber of Commerce and a close friend of Hoover, led the opposition. Using information supplied by Hoover, he "damned the plan from cover to cover."[41] He charged that it would increase the surpluses, damage marketing channels, subsidize foreign customers, and necessitate the creation of a vast bureaucracy. It remained for Director of the Budget Charles G. Dawes to summarize the general attitude of the majority of those present. If the plan works, he said, it will "help these fellows sell plows; however, "where you undertake to institute a new theory that is revolutionary and paternalistic you want to go pretty slow."[42]

Peek and Johnson were dejected by their failure to get a more favorable verdict for equality for agriculture. Blaming Hoover for the failure, they went home on February 14. The meeting was not a total loss, however, for the two men gained an important proponent. Henry Taylor came out of the meeting cautiously in favor of their plan and convinced that Peek and Johnson had "thought out this whole question of the relation of tariff to agriculture more completely than any one else I know of." In the future Taylor would be a significant influence in getting Wallace to support the plan.[43]

After their return to Moline, Peek and Johnson transferred their campaign to gain acceptance for equality for agriculture from the administration in Washington to the public. In March 1922, they prepared a revised edition of *Equality for Agriculture*. Unlike the first edition, it was signed and omitted a discussion of the mechanics of obtaining equality for agriculture because the two men believed that discussion of the export corporation in the first edition had diverted attention from the general problem of the tariff and agriculture. A month later they printed a four-page letter summarizing their plan on Moline Plow stationery and distributed it as *To All Who May Be Interested in Equality for Agriculture*.[44] During the next year and a half they mailed hundreds of copies of *Equality for Agriculture* to farm leaders and visited numerous political figures, farm leaders, editors of agricultural journals, and business acquaintances to stimulate interest in the plan.

Peek and Johnson's lobbying made little headway in 1922. The Farm Bureau and the Grange were inclined toward cooperative marketing as a solution to the nation's agricultural depression, while vocal elements in the Farmers Union were demanding government price-fixing. In 1923, however, the campaign gained momentum. More and more farmers and farm organizations, particularly in the western Middle West, came to see equality for agriculture as the simplest, fairest, and most direct formula for quick relief. By the end of 1923 they were grouping round the plan and gravitating toward political action. Senator Thomas Walsh, Democrat of Montana, wrote a Senate colleague in December 1923, that "the farmers of my state, who border on desperation, quite generally, if not unanimously, are giving their endorsement to the so-called Johnson-Peek plan for an agricultural corporation."[45]

Equally important, Wallace became a fervent convert. In the months after the National Agricultural Conference he had the Department of Agriculture study various aspects of equality for agriculture. By the summer of 1923 he concluded that of the principal proposals being put forth to solve the agricultural depression—including cooperative marketing and price-fixing—the Peek-Johnson plan was the most acceptable and effective method of raising prices. In October 1923, Wallace sent Taylor on a tour of the West to investigate sentiment for equality for agriculture. He advised the secretary that there was strong grass-roots support for the plan. In the following month, Wallace, encouraged by Taylor's findings, broke with the administration, which was backing cooperative marketing, and publicly endorsed equality for agriculture.[46]

In the meantime, Wallace asked Charles J. Brand, a consulting specialist in the Department of Agriculture, to draft a bill implementing equality for agriculture. Before beginning work, Brand traveled to Moline to consult with Peek and Johnson, who, at Brand's behest, prepared a memorandum in October 1923 outlining the points to be emphasized in the bill. That same month Johnson visited Washington to explain equality for agriculture to President Calvin Coolidge and prepared a memorandum providing arguments for Wallace to use in presenting the case for a government-sponsored export corporation.[47] In December 1923, Brand's bill was reworked by the drafting sections of the Senate and House; and on January 16, 1924, it was introduced in Congress by

Senator Charles L. McNary, Republican of Oregon, and Representative Gilbert N. Haugen, Republican of Iowa.

The resulting battle over the McNary-Haugen bill dominated the debate over federal aid to agriculture from 1924 to 1928. Supporting the bill were most farm groups and the manufacturers of farm implements. The farmers were naturally attracted by the prospect of higher prices, while the farm implement producers, men like Peek and Johnson, believed that their business would benefit from the increased sales of farm machines that would grow out of the accelerated agricultural production implicit in the bill. Opposing the bill were groups such as the processors of foodstuffs, who saw the bill as a threat to their middleman profits, and most industrialists. They feared that it would raise the price of labor by increasing the cost of living. Exercising its considerable political clout, the Farm Bloc pushed the bill through Congress in 1927 and 1928. But each time Coolidge followed the recommendation of Hoover and pro-industry advisors like Secretary of the Treasury Andrew Mellon and vetoed it. Actually, Coolidge needed little persuading. The bill ran against the grain of his laissez-faire upbringing, and he reveled in branding it as expensive, wasteful, and counterproductive.

Johnson was largely inactive in the fight for the McNary-Haugen bill once it reached Congress. He dropped out in the spring of 1924 as the result of a quarrel with Peek that was so acrimonious that it virtually destroyed their friendship. However, his involvement in bringing the bill to life did not go for naught. It gave him great satisfaction again to be at the center of a national movement and to help make things happen. During the war he had been in regular contact with the power brokers in the nation's capital. The fight for equality for agriculture, at least to the degree that he was associating with Wallace, Hoover, and even Coolidge, enabled him to relive those glorious days. In addition, his involvement in the battle for agricultural relief expanded his circle of influential acquaintances among farm leaders, government officials, and Congressional figures and gained him recognition as an expert on agricultural economics.

THE break between Hugh Johnson and George Peek is a pathetic story. In January 1924, Wetmore determined that the split between Peek and the liquidators must be resolved by general liquidation or by sale of the company "as a going concern." He instructed Johnson to prepare a study showing the expected return from each of these actions and then to search for a buyer. At the same time, he intimated that the banks were inclined to give Johnson the liquidation job if the company could not be sold. Johnson immediately informed Peek that he would do his best to sell the company to a buyer willing to commit himself to the May 28 plan and to retain that firm as the manager. He also told Peek that if it came to liquidation, he wanted the job.[48] After all, he had already stated an interest in going into this line of work, and the fee would greatly improve his own anemic financial outlook.

For a month Johnson commuted between New York City and Chicago to talk to prospective buyers and to bankers. However, none of the prospects would agree to the banks' asking price of $6,700,000 or commit himself to the May 28 plan. In fact, several indicated that they were interested in Moline Plow only as a speculative investment. They saw no hope of operating the company on a full-line basis and simply planned to profit from its liquidation.

While Johnson was trying desperately to locate an acceptable buyer, another Moline director, Alfred J. Brosseau, president of the International Motor Company, asked him to determine the profitability of a tillage-line company. Johnson had originally opposed a tillage-line company, feeling, as did Peek, that the full-line companies would easily drive a single-line company out of business.[49] But after a ten-day study in early February 1924, he concluded that a tillage-line company, if it adhered strictly to the Moline Plan, could show a profit and survive any attempts by the full-line companies to smother it.[50]

His inability to locate an acceptable buyer and the Brosseau study, along with discussions with many friends and associates, convinced Johnson that liquidation to the tillage line was the only alternative to general liquidation.[51] Peek, however, would not admit that he was licked. "More than anything else in the world," he wanted to make a success of Moline Plow. In his mind liquidation of all but the tillage line was "tantamount" to general liquidation and would "discredit" him throughout the farm implement industry.[52] Believing that an acceptable buyer could be found, he vowed to continue the fight.[53]

For Johnson the dreaded choice between friendship with Peek and what he considered best for the company had arrived. During the last week of February he sought advice from friends and pleaded in vain with Peek to quit "beating a dead horse." Finally, after profuse soul-searching, Johnson sided with the liquidators at a board meeting on February 27, 1924.[54]

Peek responded with a scathing attack against Johnson. His nerves were frayed by the struggle with the liquidators and the long campaign to sell equality for agriculture. He saw Johnson at the center of a conspiracy to have a "hog-killing party" with Moline Plow and have his "guts hung on the fence." He scored his partner and former friend as a mere lawyer and actuary who had never sold a dollar's worth of implements or discussed business conditions with the company's jobbers and dealers. He bitterly accused Johnson of sabotaging the sale of the company and blasted the Brosseau study as trickery and deception. Johnson, Peek charged, had lost his perspective in a haze of booze and "double-crossed" him simply for what he could make out of the liquidation.[55]

In reply, Johnson vehemently held to the correctness of his position and chided Peek for turning an "honest difference of opinion" into an act of betrayal. He took pride in his adherence to the West Point creed of loyalty and honor and vigorously denied that his endorsement of liquidation was influenced by improper motives or booze. Never one to hide his emotions, Johnson told Peek that "I love you better than any friend I ever had" and "expect to go on fighting for you and protecting you."[56]

Peek was not mollified by Johnson's explanations and expressions of love and resisted his overtures to patch up their friendship. Although time would heal some of the bitterness, Peek never forgave Johnson.[57]

In the weeks following his break with Peek, Johnson was uncertain about what action he should take. Finding the tension between Peek and himself "unbearable," he again approached Pershing about reinstatement to the army. This time that possibility was permanently scotched when Pershing replied that reinstatement required special legislation and "is uniformly opposed by the War Department." He added that "I . . . regret to make such an unfavorable reply, as in your case the Army and the country would greatly benefit by your reappointment."[58] Stymied in his attempt to return to the army, Johnson went to Chicago and with Robert Lea formed Johnson, Lea and Company, an industrial consulting firm.

The struggle for control of Moline Plow culminated in June 1924. Using the Brosseau study, the liquidators persuaded the directors and bank trustees to support liquidation to the tillage line. On June 2, Peek resigned from Moline Plow, and the banks asked Johnson to assume "sole personal responsibility" for the liquidation and the reorganization of the company.[59] Johnson was reluctant to accept the job. The heartbreaking rupture with Peek had soured him on Moline Plow, and continued association with the company would be a festering reminder of the most unhappy episode in his life. He also was concerned that he might give credence to Peek's charge that he was self-seeking if he accepted. However, friends and business acquaintances who were familiar with the circumstances surrounding their break assured him that he had acted properly and that he should not be deterred by Peek's accusations.[60] Buoyed by their reassurance, Johnson accepted the assignment.

For Hugh Johnson the final years with Moline Plow brought vindication in regard to his dispute with Peek and showed that he could run a business. Whatever satisfaction he may have received, however, could not ease the hurt of the break with Peek or make him forget the desperate 1922–1924 struggle to keep the floundering company afloat.

After taking over the liquidation, he immediately closed "every shop and branch" of Moline Plow that had not operated at a profit and reduced the number of types and styles of implements "to a starvation minimum." He also redoubled sales campaigns in Argentina and South Africa "in order to straighten out and make equitable" the company's highly seasonal production curve. While these policies were being in-stituted, he settled the lawsuit Peek had initiated over the cancelled management contract and negotiated the sale of facilities rendered ex-pendable by the liquidation. In addition, Johnson went to Europe in a fruitless attempt to sell the harvester business in France and negotiate a business relationship with the Soviet Union.[61]

John D. Clark, chief engineer for Moline Plow, was at Johnson's side during the liquidation, providing him "with the inside dope" on the plants to be sold. At first, Johnson gave Clark the impression "that he was going to break you in two" and that "he just wanted you to snap at attention when you saw him." He soon found, however, that Johnson was "a peach to work for" and was amazed by his energy and power of concentration. Johnson, he recalled, would often sleep only two or three hours a night in the summer and fall of 1924 and then get up "fresh as a daisy and put in a hard day of concentration." At the time, Clark concluded, Johnson had to be "one of the five brainiest men in the country." Clark's judgment was seconded by an unnamed assistant for Johnson and Clark. The assistant spent several weeks on intensive research for Johnson, and finally late one afternoon he and Johnson got together to review his findings. Through the entire night, Johnson lis-tened; and when the assistant asked if he wanted a summary, Johnson declined and then gave a thorough analysis of the report, "and he hadn't taken a note."[62]

The liquidation decimated the once-sprawling Moline Plow organi-zation. Yet it enabled Johnson "to make substantial payments on the long-over-due debts." The reorganized company was named the Moline Implement Company. Johnson became chairman of the board, and Lea, president. Other officers included H. B. Dinneen, a member of the old Peek management team, and Alvin Brown, a former Federal Liquidating Association employee who had joined the Peek team in January 1920, rising within a year to comptroller and stock manager for Moline Plow.[63]

Many of the banks now had second thoughts about the profitability of a tillage-line company and urged that this last remnant of Moline Plow also be liquidated. Johnson, however, steadfastly maintained that a tillage-line company was profitable and that he "could make it go." Ignoring "dire predictions of disaster," he raised $1,500,000 from a syn-dicate of investors headed by Donald R. McLennan, a Chicago insur-ance man and real estate investor and a friend from WIB days. Johnson then "offered the creditors either their share of the whittled-down com-pany in stock or cash at fifty dollars a share." Most of the banks opted for cash, and in the fall of 1925 control of Moline Implement passed to McLennan's syndicate. To hold on to management people, Johnson underwrote 3,750 bonus shares of stock in his name and "gave every key man a share in our potential profits."[64] He retained ownership of 1,000 of these shares. Counting the liquidation fee and other investment, he emerged from the refinancing of Moline Implement worth nearly $400,000.[65]

As Johnson had forecasted, the little company was a money-maker. From the very first month after the unprofitable implement lines were liquidated, Moline Implement made money. It "kept on making money and piling up cash," so that before long its "balance sheet began to look more like that of a bank than of an industrial company."[66]

By 1926, Moline Implement was running so smoothly that Johnson felt comfortable enough to turn his attention elsewhere. On the recommendation of Cyrus Dietz, a prominent Moline lawyer, he accepted an appointment as a special assistant to the Illinois attorney general to help defend the state in the Great Lakes diversion case. Johnson began work on the case, which involved Chicago's use of Great Lakes water to flush its sewage into the Mississippi River, by studying lake transportation, sewage disposal, and the hydrology and hydrography of the Great Lakes and the Mississippi River system. On November 9, 1926, he presented Illinois's plea to former Supreme Court Justice Charles Evans Hughes, who was acting as special master for the court. At the outset Johnson was uneasy, fearing that Hughes might remember a 1917 encounter in which he had inadvertently kept Hughes waiting in the selective service office, where he had come in behalf of his son;[67] but to his relief, the incident was not a problem.

During the spring of 1927, Johnson prepared the digest and argument for Illinois's plea. It was one of the most difficult jobs he ever had, for he had to reduce five million words to ten thousand.[68] Dietz, who was also serving as a special assistant and was now a close friend, later remarked that Johnson worked so hard on the digest that he would "strain the muscles of his brain the way an acrobat strains his arm muscles."[69] Completion of the digest and argument in June 1927 brought an end to Johnson's appointment, although the case dragged on until 1930, when the Supreme Court sustained Hughes's finding against Chicago.

While Johnson was wrapping up his work on the Great Lakes diversion case, McLennan decided to sell Moline Implement. Although the company had made money, it was clear that, without a long-term program of plant expansion, its earnings were limited. Moreover, feelers from prospective buyers indicated that its sale would enable the syndicate to more than double its original investment. In the summer of 1927, Johnson, at McLennan's instruction, negotiated the sale of Moline Implement to the J. I. Case Threshing Machine Company. The Case representatives agreed to the asking price of $4,000,000. But to Johnson's amazement, the Case board of directors refused to approve the purchase. Blocked in his effort to sell the company, Johnson recommended that it be liquidated.[70] However, the Minneapolis Steel and Machinery Company was also interested in Moline Implement and after buying the firm in May 1929, merged it with the Minneapolis Threshing Machine Company to form the Minneapolis-Moline Power Implement Company.

Johnson himself was somewhat depleted by the liquidation and merger; for, if he had gained at least temporary financial security in the ten years since he left the army, he had also lost Peek's goodwill and friendship. And if he had been an up-and-comer in 1919, he was no longer that after ten years with Moline Plow. On the credit side, however, Johnson could not say he had wasted his time. He had achieved some financial security. Additionally, he now had substantial practical experience. He had come to Moline a novice in business. He left knowing what it meant to meet a payroll; he knew how to deal with bankers and how to analyze the complexities of business organization and the dynamics of production and marketing.[71] Later, as an advocate of industrial self-government in the 1930s, he would be well served by these lessons, which enabled him to present arguments to the nation's political and industrial leaders as an experienced industrialist.

CHAPTER 5

SERVING THE CHIEF

I N T H E years immediately following his association with Moline Plow, Hugh Johnson's career centered around his work for Bernard M. Baruch. Tall and courtly, with "finely chiseled features," Baruch was a figure of great influence in the interwar period in his twin roles as background political strategist and publicist on national issues. Many factors account for Baruch's influence, but none was more important than the friends and advisors who opened doors for him in Washington and provided him with information on political and economic issues. Although his retinue included many who would become men of stature in their own right, few were more prominent than Johnson. For two decades he served the Chief, as Baruch was affectionately called by his protégés, and was proud to be known as a Baruch man.

Johnson was initially drawn to Baruch's side by the realization that Baruch's friendship and support could be of inestimable value as he tried to make a new career for himself after the war. Baruch could use his contacts to help him get a job or cement a business deal; Baruch could provide wise investment counsel and even funds for a good deal; and Baruch could help Johnson play an ongoing role in national affairs. Baruch was also widely known for his generosity toward his helpers and toward friends who were down on their luck. A man like Johnson, who had reached middle age without establishing himself in a permanent career, could do a lot worse than to attach himself to Baruch.

In addition to the prospect of aiding his career, Johnson was drawn to Baruch by his companionship and the chance to hobnob with important businessmen and politicians. Baruch, who liked to blend business and social relationships, showered pet names and endearments upon those in his circle; the humor, intimacy, and camaraderie used by the group also gave one a sense of belonging. Moreover, membership in Baruch's circle brought invitations to parties and dinners; the chance to travel in private railroad cars and stay in the finest hotels, often at the Chief's expense; and visits to Hobcaw, Baruch's South Carolina plantation for gambling, hunting, and conversation with wealthy and talented people. Being part of Baruch's circle was as close as Johnson could come to reliving his days of comradeship at West Point and in the First Cavalry mess.

Baruch could also gain from a relationship with Johnson. Here was a man with many talents and tremendous energy, just the type to be useful in Baruch's numerous activities. He could write; he could analyze; and he did not mince words. Johnson was also good company. His masculine sense of humor, his well-told yarns about the West, and his aggressive manner all made him a joy to have around. Johnson had flaws, as Baruch would come to realize. But he was never boring, and in Baruch's opinion, to be boring was the worst crime.

The Johnson-Baruch relationship would never go the way of the Johnson-Peek relationship. Johnson had always regarded Peek as his equal and felt free to speak his mind, to raise his voice, and even to cross him. Baruch did not expect Johnson to be a mere mouthpiece, for he realized that was not Johnson's nature. Johnson liked to interject his ideas and to argue too much to be a yes man. But Baruch expected Johnson to remember that he was Baruch's employee, his representative, and was quick to chastize when Johnson forgot his place. Johnson appreciated the character of their relationship and dutifully played the loyal subordinate by regularly making flattering statements to the press about Baruch's "unmatched" business ability, generosity, and patriotism. These statements were not mere sycophantry. The Chief was everything Johnson wanted to be—a man of wealth and power—and said all the right things about duty, honor, and country. For these reasons, at least in Johnson's view, Baruch was a man deserving of respect and loyalty. He could do no wrong.

Baruch did not hold Johnson in similar esteem. He enjoyed Johnson's stories and wisecracks and heaped praise on him. However, he was too aware of Johnson's faults—his emotionalism, his impetuousness, and his tendency to drink to excess—to give him too much responsibility and was always careful to supervise him closely in important tasks.[1]

Hugh Johnson and Baruch first worked together in the interwar period in the planning for economic mobilization for future wars. The WIB alumni believed that the World War I mobilization showed that the military was incapable of handling the manifold problems of mobilizing a modern industrialized nation for war. Baruch, in particular, believed that it was too riddled with personal jealousies and selfish interests to procure its own supplies effectively and also that it simply did not appreciate the destabilizing impact of military orders on the civilian economy. What was needed if the nation was to avoid the chaos of 1917 and 1918 in the future, he emphasized, was another WIB to serve in an advisory capacity in peacetime and in a coordinating capacity in wartime. The military, however, showed little interest in Baruch's call

HUGH JOHNSON, BERNARD BARUCH, AND EDWARD MCGRADY. Historical Pictures Service, Chicago.

for an industrial strategy board. It feared that an advisory WIB would undercut the authority of the president's cabinet and suspected, correctly, that Baruch was a maudlin man who wanted to relive the exciting days of 1918 by again serving as the head of the industrial mobilization agency.[2]

Baruch was not one to give up without a fight. He had vast resources to call upon, not the least of which was his band of brothers from the WIB. Johnson was of special value to him in several respects. Because of his work on the final report, Johnson knew as much about the WIB as anyone. Second, Johnson could organize ideas and write. Baruch worked by hunches and intuition and required assistance in ordering his thoughts and putting his views into digestible form for public consumption. In these respects, Johnson complemented Baruch.[3] Finally, Johnson was an army man. He understood the army mind, spoke the army language, and was a friend of many of the officers now in the highest army positions. Baruch would have to convince these men first if his ideas were to prevail; and Johnson, with his close ties to the men in khaki, could be an entree to them and an effective proselytizer. The crucial target was Pershing, chief of staff from 1921 to

1924 and a figure of awesome influence in army circles after his retirement. In the early 1920s Baruch had yet to establish close relations with Pershing. He was confident, however, that Pershing had "absolute faith" in Johnson and was determined to use the friendship between the two one-time cavalrymen to establish his own intimate relationship with Pershing and "to get [him] absolutely straight" on the problems of economic mobilization.[4]

Johnson needed little urging to work with Baruch on this project. He considered himself an expert on industrial mobilization and was certain that Baruch's message was correct. From his perspective, the army seemed to have forgotten the lessons of the war, and the "experienced actors" of the World War I economic drama had a responsibility to make the case for a WIB "so that the lessons . . . would not have to be learned over again."[5] Johnson also looked forward to being part of a national issue, through which he could experience again the days of his glory. Being an executive in a major corporation had its rewards, but for one who had briefly had power and influence in Washington it was not enough. By working with Baruch on industrial mobilization, Johnson could once more feel that he was a man of importance.

During the 1920s Johnson worked hard to sell Baruch's ideas. At the Chief's behest he had frequent discussions with Pershing on industrial mobilization and followed these up with strongly argued letters and memoranda.[6] In addition, he wrote many of Baruch's speeches on industrial mobilization.[7] Most important, in his own lectures and articles he hammered away at the "necessity for industrial strategy, or a War Industries Board, or whatever you may call it."[8] In these presentations Johnson spelled out his conception of the ideal program for industrial mobilization. It included a selective service law, a "work or fight" order, a WIB "comprised of the very cream of American industrial leadership," presidential powers to fix wages and prices, and an excess profits tax.[9] There was nothing original about the Johnson program. It was a refinement of that in effect at the time of the Armistice and did not depart one iota from what Baruch was preaching. On the question of industrial mobilization, Johnson was not paving new ground. His job was to teach the lessons of the past as interpreted by Baruch.

Johnson and Baruch made little headway in their efforts to bring about a new WIB in the 1920s. The National Defense Act of 1920 empowered the Office of the Assistant Secretary of War to plan for the entire economy. But to Johnson's dismay this office was hesitant to assume what it considered civilian responsibilities. Instead of focusing on the larger questions involved with the national economy and the need for a super agency to oversee mobilization, it concentrated on the narrow question of military procurement. The army service schools, meanwhile, including the newly created Army Industrial College, merely served as forums before which Johnson and Baruch could spout their views. By themselves, these bodies were ineffectual for serious discussion of and planning for industrial mobilization.

In 1929 the War Department, prodded by Major General George Van Horn Moseley, deputy chief of staff, finally began to include economic mobilization in its planning. Its first tentative plans failed to satisfy Johnson. Reviewing their general outline for Baruch, he warned that they lacked an appreciation of the interrelation "of functions in the process of mobilizing resources" and were too "tangled up on the question of military and naval design."[10] In 1930 the War Department produced its first official economic blueprint for war—the Industrial Mobilization Plan of 1930. But it was little more than a general proposal for using the methods of World War I to regulate a wartime economy. In no way could it be interpreted "as an army embrace of Baruch."[11] The army, as in 1917–1918, continued to fear a business abridgement of its prerogatives.

During the following decade, the Industrial Mobilization Plan of 1930 underwent several revisions which had the effect of simplifying the proposed mobilization apparatus and patterning it even more explicitly after the World War I model.[12] In this regard, another Johnson, Louis Johnson, was more valuable to Baruch than Hugh. Appointed assistant secretary of war in 1937, Louis Johnson, with the encouragement of Baruch, pushed hard for rearmament and the creation of an advisory board on industrial mobilization.[13]

The culmination of the prewar planning for industrial mobilization was the Industrial Mobilization Plan of 1939. It called for the creation of the supervisory agency that Hugh Johnson and Baruch had been advocating for two decades. In fact, Johnson pronounced it as "about as good as it could be."[14] President Roosevelt, however, rejected the plan, complaining that it drained too much power from his office and turned too much power over to businessmen, many of whom had opposed the New Deal. As Johnson caustically noted, "the present pack of semi-Communist wolves"—New Dealers—do not "intend to let Morgan and DuPont men run a war."[15]

Baruch and Johnson's opposition to schemes for a universal draft paralleled their concern for an overall strategy for economic mobilization. In the early 1920s the American Legion, whose rank and file resented the alleged wartime profiteering of business and the unequal burden carried by the fighting forces, spearheaded a campaign for a universal draft of industry, labor, and capital. The universal draft was presented as a measure for promoting peace by removing the promises of riches as an inducement to war and by equalizing wartime burdens. Beginning in 1922, a Legion-sponsored bill for a universal draft was repeatedly introduced in Congress, although Congress did not seriously deal with the economics of war until the 1930s. Both Baruch and Johnson considered the universal draft anathema. As Johnson wrote Baruch after examining the scheme, it is "a fantastical project, inhibited by our Constitution, subversive of the essence of our social and political institutions, abortive in theory and impossible in practice."[16]

As an alternative, Johnson encouraged Baruch to support a scheme for "taking the profit out of war," a misleading concept, for clearly profit would not be excluded, only profiteering.[17] But in Johnson's mind, this could be accomplished through a program of government price-and-wage controls and an excess profits tax. Many in Congress, however, fueled by the investigation of the munitions industry by a special Senate committee chaired by Republican Gerald Nye of South Dakota, appended the shibboleth "taking the profit out of war" to a bill designed to curtail all profits in an emergency by limiting profits to 3 percent and personal annual incomes to $10,000. Baruch, Johnson, the War Department, and even the Nye Committee opposed this bill; and periodically Johnson testified before legislative committees to voice his opposition.[18] His principal argument was essentially the same as that voiced by his master and other opponents of the bill: to change the economic system during a war would threaten production and invite disaster. Proponents of the bill found it difficult to discredit this argument. After the Roosevelt administration let it be known that it too believed curtailing the profit motive would be counterproductive, the proposed legislation was doomed.[19]

The work with Baruch on industrial mobilization was often frustrating for Johnson. A firm believer in what he had to say, he could never understand why others failed to see what history so obviously taught, at least to him. The work, however, played an important role in Johnson's career. He had worked tirelessly for Baruch's cause, had given form and flair to Baruch's often fuzzy notions, and had demonstrated unwavering loyalty. Here was a man, in Baruch's opinion, who could be valuable in other areas as well.

HUGH Johnson's work with Baruch on industrial mobilization blended into a business relationship between the two men. This relationship began with the moderately profitable Okmulgee Oil Syndicate. Formed at Johnson's instigation in 1922 to acquire and develop oil and gas leases in Oklahoma and partly financed by Baruch, it consisted of Johnson, Peek, and Johnson's brothers, Mead S. Johnson and Alexander Johnston.[20] As Johnson proved himself in the work on industrial mobilization, Baruch expanded their business relationship. In 1926 he gave Johnson "a few special jobs—examining companies in which he had been asked to invest." In his initial assignments Johnson investigated three "highly propagandized companies of very large capitalization." In each case, as he later wrote, he "had the good luck to call the turn of their sorry future with at least the accuracy of the Prophet Isaiah."[21]

Johnson's evident knack for industrial analysis affirmed Baruch's high estimate of his abilities, and in April 1927, the Chief asked him to come to New York City and serve as an investigator of business and economic conditions. Johnson jumped at the chance. McLennan had decided to sell Moline Implement, so there was little left for him in Illinois. Moreover, Johnson was intrigued by the open-ended nature of the work Baruch had in mind and could hardly resist Baruch's generous terms. Their informal working relationship called for Johnson to receive an annual salary of $25,000 and for Baruch to underwrite Johnson up to 10 percent on any joint enterprises Johnson might recommend.[22]

During the next five years the Chief kept Johnson busy investigating the investment potential of firms so that he might judge "whether he should go long or short." Johnson was never more valuable to Baruch than in this job. His investigations were quick, thorough, acute, and accurate. Johnson was able to go through a company's affairs in two or three days and emerge with seemingly more knowledge about it than its chairman of the board possessed.[23]

The investigations were exhausting work for Johnson, for they required extensive travel. A typical trip might take him to Buffalo, Detroit, Toledo, Indianapolis, Auburn, Kenosha, and Milwaukee, with no more than one night spent in a single city.[24] "All of this was in addition to the daily grind of reports on balance sheets and income statements of companies listed on the Stock Exchange to try to arrive at some idea of the worth of their securities."[25] Nevertheless, it was time well spent for Johnson. The investigations enabled him to expand his contacts in the industrial and financial communities and his knowledge about the operations of American industry.

While devoting most of his effort to the investigations for Baruch, Johnson never lost sight of profitable investments for himself. He and Baruch jointly invested in several companies, including a chromium company, a rock asphalt company, and an automobile carpet company.[26] By 1929 these investments, along with his salary from Baruch, brought Johnson annual earnings of $100,000.[27] Dabbling in the stock market on the side added to his earnings, and one day, by playing a few market tips, Johnson was able to make $17,000.[28]

In the 1930s Baruch claimed that he saw the financial crisis of 1929 coming and sold his stocks in time to get out of the market before it hit. This claim to financial sagacity did much to advance his subsequent reputation for wisdom in economic matters. Johnson, in turn, claimed that he was instrumental in shaping Baruch's decision to get out of the market so that he could preserve "the bulk of what he had."[29] In fact, the story is not that simple. As early as September 1927, Johnson sounded warning signals about the economy, writing to Baruch that

business is distinctly 'off' in nearly all lines so that we have the cheapest money rates known, declining activity in business [and] a stock market already as high as a cat[']s back and getting higher. This seems a great anomaly. I don[']t see how the three things can be reconciled.[30]

Johnson's warnings, however, did not have that much impact upon Baruch. Fundamentally, Baruch was an optimist. He underestimated the gravity of the situation in the fall of 1929 and sold his stocks only belatedly. As a result, he bore a significant loss, although by no means was he taken to the cleaners. At the top in 1929 he was worth $22 to $25 million. At the end of 1931 he was still worth $16 million.[31]

Johnson was not so fortunate. Most of his money was tied up in companies that he was trying "to develop and couldn't get out of."[32] Lea Fabrics caused the greatest concern. Originally incorporated in 1928 under the name Oryx Fabrics by Johnson, Lea, and others of the old Moline crowd, the company, using money borrowed from Baruch and McLennan, among others, acquired the small automobile carpet plant of Duratex Corporation in Newark, New Jersey. The new company had slow going at first because of excess overhead on its rather small production. Johnson responded, in August 1929, by reorganizing the company's management and expanding its production capacity.[33] Lea Fabrics proceeded to produce an excellent line of luxurious automobile carpet as well as "a line of cheap carpet." Car sales slumped with the onset of the depression, however, and by the spring of 1930 the company's future was bleak. Johnson assumed responsibility for attracting customers and made numerous trips to automobile producers to persuade them to adopt Lea carpet. But, as he wrote in the summer of 1930,

conditions for such an effort are simply terrible. Outside of Ford and Chevrolet the industry is *flat* with enormous inventories and commitments. It is really a pity to have finally evolved a sound industrial unit just at the time when to do anything with it seems next to impossible.[34]

In the last months of 1930, Lea Fabrics experienced an upswing because of some "flash-in-the-pan business." But the success of the company depended "solely on volume," and at the end of 1930 a price war obviated any hope of garnering a significant share of the market. The established companies, already heavily burdened with inventories, reduced their prices to figures below production costs and "caused almost complete stagnation" for Lea Fabrics.[35] In January 1931, Johnson, who had taken over management of the company the year before, put it "on a paying basis" by negotiating orders from Chrysler and Willys-Overland.[36] Repeated efforts to get other car companies to buy significant amounts of carpet were disappointing, however, for Johnson could not match the low prices quoted by competitors on carpet for lower-priced cars.[37]

For the next four years Lea Fabrics limped along. In 1935 Johnson finally rescued it by securing a loan from the Reconstruction Finance
Corporation. In one of the few instances when he opposed Johnson in a
business matter, Baruch had argued against Johnson's recourse to the
loan. In his opinion, the loan could subject Johnson to charges of im-
properly using political influence for private gain. It was wiser, he advised, to reduce management overhead and secure a bank loan.[38] Johnson
rejected the Chief's advice, noting that there was nothing improper
about the loan from the Reconstruction Finance Corporation and that
it was in the best interest of the stockholders. The loan provided needed
capital to expand production capacity, and within a year Lea Fabrics was
in a "solvent liquid condition of moderately profitable operation."[39]

Although the battle to save Lea Fabrics "had been one continuous
headache" for Johnson, he was proud that it changed, "under my direction, from a gigantic flop to an actually earning and going concern."[40]
The effort, however, was not financially remunerative for Johnson. He
had refused the board of directors' 1930 offer of a salary of $30,000 in
order to hold down management expenses; instead, he took a small re-
tainer fee. This decision, along with the sorry state of Lea Fabrics and
his other investments, seriously depleted his financial resources. His
assets dropped precipitously, and in the early 1930s his salary from
Baruch was his only reliable income.

HUGH Johnson's work for Baruch inevitably drew him into politics.
Baruch considered himself a sage on matters of political economy and a
power broker in the Democratic party. Although he never retired from
speculation, public affairs commanded most of his interest and attention after 1920; and, as in other areas, Johnson was a handy man to have
around.

Baruch first used Johnson in this way in the 1928 campaign, when he
offered Johnson's services to the Democratic party. Johnson took a desk
at Democratic headquarters in New York City and began working on
the agricultural activities of the campaign. The job again brought him
into close association with Peek. Nominally a Republican, Peek had
turned away from the GOP after it nominated Herbert Hoover, a staunch
foe of the McNary-Haugen bill, as its standard bearer in 1928, and the
Democrats endorsed the bill in their platform. In August 1928, Johnson
met Peek at Democratic headquarters and discussed the possibility
of organizing an independent farm-state campaign for Al Smith, the
Democratic presidential nominee.[41]

Both men realized that two things made this a tough fight. First, farmers traditionally voted Republican. More difficult, they would have to be
convinced that economic issues were more important than Smith's Ca-
tholicism and his big-city background. Yet Peek and Johnson were confident that a well-financed campaign could make deep inroads into this

bastion of Republican strength. Encouraged by their optimism, Smith's campaign managers authorized them $500,000 to canvass and organize eleven farm states, from Ohio to Montana.[42]

In a spirit of cooperation that amazed all who knew them, Peek, working from Chicago, and Johnson, working from New York City, prepared newspaper advertisements, wrote speeches and position papers, arranged for speakers in the Farm Belt, and formed independent organizations for Smith in many states. At first, Johnson was optimistic, believing that Hoover's past record clearly tied him in "with the grain exchanges, packers, [and] millers" rather than with farmers. By hitting this point "with almost violent emphasis," they could make Hoover "squirm" and place him "on the defensive good and proper."[43] But they had trouble getting coverage from major midwestern newspapers, most of which were Republican. Even more exasperating, the promised money from Democratic headquarters was slow in coming. On more than one occasion Johnson had to badger John J. Raskob, chairman of the Democratic National Committee, to speed up the flow of necessary funds to keep their campaign alive. "I do not know," Peek wrote Johnson in the last weeks of the campaign, "what we would have done had it not been for your activity in getting action on this."[44]

Notwithstanding their strenuous efforts, Peek and Johnson had no impact on the outcome of the election. With prosperity apparently rampant, except in agriculture, and with cultural and religious issues paramount, Hoover easily defeated Smith. The eleven states where Johnson and Peek concentrated their campaign went for Hoover. Yet the two had not worked totally in vain. The Democratic vote in many of these states increased significantly over that in 1920, more so than did the Republican vote. This indicates that the Peek-Johnson farm campaign at least helped sow anti-Republican seed that would bear fruit for the Democrats in the 1930s.[45]

When the stock market crashed, Johnson, like most Americans, never imagined that it was the prelude to the Great Depression, much less that the depression would last so long and have such a searing effect on the nation. But from the outset he provided Baruch with insightful and candid descriptions of business conditions. Thus in July 1930, after returning to New York from a trip through the Midwest, he reported that while businessmen and journalists in that region were basically optimistic about the future, he was less sanguine. There was not "one fundamental sign of improvement," he emphasized, while "wage and salary cuts—some under cover, some boldly—are general," Hoover's plea to maintain wages notwithstanding. "The last half of 1930," he predicted, "will be worse than the first in nearly all lines."[46]

By the summer of 1931 Johnson was even more pessimistic, reporting that "I . . . am afraid things will be worse instead of better." This bleak conclusion was based on a tour of midwestern industrial centers in which he had discussed economic conditions with manufacturers and bankers. The extent of unemployment and lack of work relief had stunned him. Manufacturers like Ford were shutting down or laying off workers, while the administration in Washington was "making no preparations beyond a few futile conversations between Hoover and the Red Cross." People who had helped feed the unemployed last year "are going to have to be fed themselves this winter." Conditions were so bad, he concluded, that the "government is going to have to provide between five and six billion dollars this winter for the relief of unemployed in nearly every industry."[47] On the basis of reports like this, Johnson obliged the Chief, a hidebound fiscal conservative, to declare that the jobless were Washington's reponsibility and to consider expansion of federal public works.[48]

As the depression worsened, Baruch and Johnson directed much of their attention to the federal budget. The nub of Hoover's recovery program was the restoration of business confidence through the bolstering of the nation's credit system. Central to this program was a concerted effort to balance the federal budget. Budget surpluses had been the norm in the 1920s. But the depression brought unbalanced budgets, reflecting a decline in tax revenues and substantial increases in expenditures for public works, agricultural relief, and veterans benefits. To balance the budget, Hoover, in December 1931, called for draconian cuts in agricultural and public works spending, while Secretary of the Treasury Ogden L. Mills, Jr., called for new taxes. Even with these measures, Mills estimated the deficit for fiscal 1933 at $920 million, an extremely large figure in relation to a federal budget which ranged from $3 billion to $4 billion in the early 1930s.[49]

Hoover's budget proposals disturbed Baruch on two accounts. First, Hoover's proposed budget cuts were part of a political maneuver by the White House to blame the Democrats in Congress for an unbalanced federal budget that hurt business confidence. Therefore, Baruch privately suggested that if the Democrats were not to be caught in Hoover's trap, they had to "out-tax and out-economize Hoover."[50] More important, however, Baruch was philosophically committed to a balanced budget; too much public spending would inflate the dollar. To those who argued that increased public spending and an unbalanced budget could be tolerated in hard times Baruch turned a deaf ear. He could countenance minimal gestures toward those most hurt by the depression and thus supported limited aid to agriculture, self-liquidating public works, and the Reconstruction Finance Corporation. But all depression-fighting programs, he emphasized, must be aimed at restoring business confidence. In his opinion, this could be accomplished only within the maintenance of federal fiscal integrity.[51] Since Hoover's retrenchment would not balance the budget, Baruch recommended further spending cuts and a general sales tax to increase revenues.[52] In effect, he wanted taxation of the lower classes, not increased taxes for those on the level of job makers.[53]

To amplify the need for a general sales tax, Baruch had Johnson examine the Hoover administration's estimates of revenues and expenditures for fiscal 1933. With the assistance of Alvin Brown, who, at Johnson's request, came to New York City to aid in the analysis, Johnson concluded that the administration's estimates were "wrong by many hundreds of millions." In early February 1932, he presented his findings to Mills, and in March he assured Mills that Baruch would use all of his influence in the Congress to help Hoover balance the budget. Mills, meanwhile, revised the administration's estimates of revenues "below even . . . [Johnson's] worst figures" and estimated the deficit for fiscal 1933 at $1.241 billion.[54] Johnson quickly proclaimed that the administration's revisions were largely the result of his efforts. Irritated by Johnson's grandstanding, Mills retorted that "the revision was based . . . on our own assumptions and calculations."[55] Privately, Mills "swore that if anyone came to him with more figures, he would have him put out the door."[56]

Contrary to Johnson's pledge to Mills, Baruch was unable to line up the House Democrats behind a revenue bill containing the sales tax. Revolting against their leadership, they killed the levy, and Congressional interest now increasingly focused on the question of public works. On Baruch's instruction, Johnson drew up a plan for self-liquidating public works, which Baruch, in turn, gave to Senator Joseph Robinson, Democrat of Arkansas, to introduce into the Senate. Although debate over the Robinson bill and a similar bill proposed by Hoover was hot and heavy, a version of the two eventually passed the Congress as the Emergency Relief and Construction Act of 1932.[57]

Johnson, meanwhile, was crystallizing his own thoughts about the causes of the depression and developing a cure. He perceived the depression as an outgrowth of the imbalance between supply and demand in the national economy. Agriculture had been prostrated by production surpluses, while industrial production, spurred by technological advances and false hopes about the prospect of an ever-expanding export market, had outstripped consumption. The result was spiraling unemployment. To make matters worse, the public, seduced by the rosy statements of Republican spokesmen, had gone on a speculative spending spree in the stock market in the late 1920s that brought a "headlong incurment of debt." When the market crashed, both the industrial sector and the consuming public reduced their buying, plunging the nation into an endless spiral of lower sales, lower prices, lower wages, and layoffs. As a result, the nation was mired in the incongruous condition of starvation in the land of plenty. Johnson believed that the long-term answer to the nation's economic ills was the reestablishment of balance in the economy. Agriculture had to be restored to health and placed in balance with industry through McNary-Haugenism, while industrial production and consumption needed to be balanced through a program of industrial self-government modeled after the WIB experience.

Realizing that the enactment and implementation of these programs would take time, Johnson in June 1932, spelled out, in "a jazzed-up form" proclaimed by "Muscleinny, Dictator pro tem," a plan to get the wheels of the economic machine turning in the short run. The proclamation, which was privately distributed to a small circle of associates, began facetiously by calling for the establishment of an economic dictatorship and the deportation of Congress. In a more serious vein, however, Johnson itemized specific actions to instill confidence in the business community and stimulate recovery. They included a 25 percent cut in the federal budget, a variety of taxes to meet specific federal relief expenditures and maintain a balanced budget, tariff revision, and, to lessen the crushing burden of debt, a reduction of the gold content of the dollar.[58]

Johnson's critics later claimed that "Muscleinny's" call for an economic dictatorship indicated a serious desire to bring fascism to the United States. Exchanging "fool ideas" with friends was characteristic of Johnson, however, and hardly indicated serious intent. As "Muscleinny" noted, not one action was suggested "that did not reside in Congress and the President." What was needed, in his opinion, was not a dictator, only the election of a Democratic president who would take forceful action to restore confidence among the nation's business leaders.

In the months before the 1932 Democratic convention Johnson's conception of which potential nominee met his criterion mirrored Baruch's. The Chief wanted the party to nominate an economic conservative. Al Smith was acceptable. So were Albert C. Ritchie, govenor of Maryland and an old WIB associate; Owen D. Young, an executive with General Electric; and Newton D. Baker, now in private law practice. None of these men, however, had enough broad-based support to command the nomination without a fight. Recalling the embarrassment he had suffered in 1924 by backing a hopeful who failed to get the nomination, Baruch refused to endorse any candidate before the convention.

If Baruch was not clear on whom he favored for the nomination, he was clear on whom he opposed: Franklin D. Roosevelt. The popular and successful governor of New York, Roosevelt was the Democratic front-runner. But Baruch had little time for him. He had known Roosevelt since World War I, when Roosevelt had served as assistant secretary of the navy, and questioned his competency for the White House. Equally important, he questioned Roosevelt's commitment to fiscal integrity and, of some special concern, suspected that he would have little influence in the White House if Roosevelt became president. Roosevelt, he complained to friends, was too willing to listen to the ill-digested schemes of academicians and theoreticians and ignore the advice of men who knew the ways of practical business.

Johnson shared the Chief's sentiments. When Peek inquired in May 1932, about his opinion of Roosevelt, Johnson replied that "it doesn't do any good to talk to this bird. He answers according to Hoyle and then gets on the radio and says something somebody fixes up for him. He's all wet all right in more ways than one."[59]

At the convention in Chicago, Baruch, with Johnson at his side, maneuvered behind the scenes to block Roosevelt in favor of Baker. Once it was apparent that Roosevelt would be the nominee, however, he moved quickly to make his peace with the Roosevelt camp, knowing that influence resided with those who went along, not those who sulked.[60]

On the morning of July 2, 1932, the day after Roosevelt's nomination, Baruch, with Johnson in tow, went to the suite of Louis Howe, Roosevelt's intimate political advisor, in the Congress Hotel. Ostensibly, Baruch's mission was to offer their services to the Roosevelt campaign. In actuality, however, Baruch wanted to examine Roosevelt's acceptance speech and judge whether he would be a "safe" candidate. After briefly introducing Baruch and Johnson to the Roosevelt men lounging in the suite, Howe whisked them into another room and "banged the door shut." Then Jesse Straus, head of New York City's Macy's Department Store, approached Raymond Moley, Roosevelt's principal speech writer, and asked: "Can we let Baruch see the acceptance speech? We want to be nice to him because he can contribute a good deal to the campaign." Moley was furious, seeing "visions of party compromise and expediency" in the request. But he consented, and Straus disappeared into the room where Howe was talking with Baruch and Johnson. Johnson spent twenty minutes reading the speech and briefing Baruch on its "harmlessness from their point of view." Shortly afterward, Baruch ended the encounter by concluding an agreement with Howe for the Roosevelt "Brain Trust" to confer with Johnson and himself in the near future on the strategy for the upcoming campaign against Hoover. The Brain Trust, primarily a group of Columbia University professors who served Roosevelt as speech writers and thinkers, included Moley, Rexford Tugwell, and Adolf Berle, Jr.[61]

In preparation for their meeting with the unenthusiastic Brain Trust, Baruch and Johnson drafted a lengthy memorandum on their economic principles.[62] The Brain Trusters, meanwhile, dreaded the meeting, knowing that their ideas on what had to be done about the depression conflicted seriously with Baruch's. Although the Brain Trusters had differences among one another, they agreed on a fundamental advocacy of social and economic intervention by the federal government for the

"forgotten man." Baruch, in contrast, cared for business and would sacrifice the helpless in order to salvage it. Aid for the forgotten man, he
believed, should be shelved in favor of a balanced budget to encourage
private investment.[63]

Considering their mutual distrust, the meeting between the college
professors and Baruch and Johnson, held at Baruch's house in New York
City during the second week of July, went rather well. The Brain Trusters' fear about Baruch's conservatism was calmed after they examined
the Baruch-Johnson memorandum and Baruch indicated willingness to
retreat on his opposition to federal intervention in return for a balanced
budget. In reporting to Roosevelt on the meeting, Moley pronounced
the memorandum "excellent" and suggested that it could serve as the
basis for the governor's opening campaign speech at Columbus, Ohio,
which was intended to be a biting indictment of the Hoover administration. Moley added that "the subjects . . . [it] treats might in large part
be amplified into speeches" dealing with the tariff, the budget, and foreign debts.[64]

In the morning of July 18, 1932, Baruch, Johnson, and the Brain
Trusters went to Albany, New York, to discuss campaign strategy and
issues with Roosevelt and his political advisors. Their meetings lasted
through that day and the next. Baruch and Roosevelt quickly realized
that they were in general accord on most matters. Hardly a radical,
Roosevelt readily acknowledged the importance of a balanced budget
and economy in government. He also agreed in principle with Baruch's
notion that private business was the key to recovery and would assume
the responsibility for leading the country out of depression once it
knew the government meant it no harm and followed honest fiscal policies. Pleased by Roosevelt's essentially conservative remarks, Baruch,
as a peace-making gesture, offered a $50,000 contribution to Roose-
velt's campaign, conditioned upon the inclusion of Johnson in the Brain
Trust.[65] Johnson, he told Roosevelt, was an economist, an experienced
administrator, an expositor of the business community's thoughts, and
a ready writer; he would be a positive addition to the campaign team.
What he intended, however, was that Johnson would be his watchdog in
Roosevelt's inner circle; he would also ensure the inclusion of Baruch's
views in the campaign.

Roosevelt was fully aware of Baruch's purpose. But he and Howe
agreed to the condition. Johnson in the campaign team was a small exchange for Baruch's vaunted purse. Moreover, Roosevelt believed that
Baruch owned sixty senators and congressmen, whose support he would
need if he was to get his legislative program through Congress. Losing
that support by excluding Hugh Johnson would be rash, especially
since Roosevelt and Baruch had no essential disagreement on the direction government should take. Finally, by accepting Baruch's factotum
into his inner circle, Roosevelt could reassure Baruch that his con-

servative views would be heard and that a Roosevelt presidency was nothing to fear.

HUGH Johnson was a valuable addition to the Roosevelt compaign team. His indefatigableness, encyclopedic knowledge, versatility, and practical experience in business and politics made him an excellent speech writer and idea man, and his smoking-car stories added levity to a dreary meeting. But his abusive and domineering nature caused stormy sessions for the Brain Trust. Charles Michelson, one of Roosevelt's speech writers, later wrote that Johnson's "roaring voice dominated their meetings. His voice was that of a commander of troops ordering a charge."[66] And Tugwell recalled that Johnson was "always condescending to those of us who were 'theorists,' and always voluble." Fortunately, the college professors and the gruff old soldier developed enough mutual acceptance to make "life tolerable among the tensions."[67]

Johnson's relations with the individuals in the Brain Trust varied. Initially, the professors were suspicious of Johnson, afraid that, through him, Baruch's "sinister influence" would destroy the progressive thrust of the campaign. They also doubted his fidelity, since he had been part of the "Stop Roosevelt" movement before the convention.[68] Before long, however, relations between Johnson, Moley, and Berle mellowed. In part, this was an outgrowth of the changing attitude of Moley and Berle toward Baruch. Following the July meeting of the Brain Trust and Baruch and Johnson, their concern about Baruch's conservatism had lessened; and as the campaign progressed, their concern about his loyalty to Roosevelt did the same. He was no longer the ogre (Berle, in fact, would even accept employment with Baruch before the year's end). It was only natural, therefore, that as the attitude of the two men toward Baruch changed, so would their attitude toward Johnson, his man. But more significantly, the two Brain Trusters soon recognized Johnson's abilities. They were also fascinated by the "gutsy drama in everything" he did. The breakthrough came, really, when Moley and Berle realized that their ideas and Johnson's were not far apart. Like Johnson, Moley and Berle accepted the need for achieving balance in the economy, and their specific ideas on how this should be achieved were similar to his concept of industrial self-government.[69]

The Johnson-Tugwell relationship, however, would always be strained. Tugwell grew to like Johnson and respect his abilities. But in contrast to Moley and Berle, he remained deeply suspicious of Baruch's conservatism; since Johnson was Baruch's man, this attitude carried over to him. Johnson, in turn, never got past seeing Tugwell as a dangerous radical. Tugwell advocated a form of national planning (coordinating of the various industries by the government or organized non—business groups through a planning mechanism), which Johnson regarded as the forerunner of a Soviet-style collectivization of the American economy.

Johnson was also irritated by Tugwell's claims to expertise in agricultural economics. Because his father was in the cannery business and he himself knew some fruit growers, and because he taught "a kind of course in agricultural economics," Tugwell believed he was an expert on agriculture and its problems. In actuality, his links with farm people were limited, and what knowledge and experience he brought to agricultural matters were more academic than practical. To Johnson, accordingly, Tugwell was nothing more than a "theoretician" whose views were hardly worthy of notice when compared with the views of men like himself who had business experience and had been in the front line fighting for farm parity for a decade.[70]

Not even a day passed between the Roosevelt-Baruch rapprochement and the beginning of Johnson's work as Baruch's ambassador to the Brain Trust. Following dinner on the evening of July 19, Roosevelt, Johnson, and several other Roosevelt associates met in the governor's study at the mansion in Albany to discuss the speech Roosevelt was to give at Columbus. Johnson produced a memorandum on the economics of the Hoover administration he and Baruch had prepared and read it with great flourishes. Comparing Hoover to the captain of a sinking ship, Johnson said in a roaring voice that if he had only "followed the honorable tradition of the sea and elected" to go down with his craft, "we might entertain respect and regret. But no! He seeks vindication and reward of another term!" Thoroughly entertained by Johnson's presentation, Roosevelt remarked to Moley, "It's great stuff. Water it down 70 per cent and make it into a speech."[71]

The evening's work in Albany initiated an exhausting four months for Johnson. Except for twelve days in August when he went to England to come back with Baruch—over on one ship and back on the next, with one night in London—he worked unceasingly in the Brain Trust headquarters, an office in the Roosevelt Hotel in New York.[72] His "literary output," as Moley recalled, "exploded like an elaborate fireworks display into a series of enchanting patterns." Yet his speeches, like Tugwell's and Berle's, underwent review and revision by Moley and even Roosevelt. The other Brain Trusters accepted the revisions. But Johnson believed that his drafts were perfect as written. When Moley "tried to edit his stuff he would scream and swear at every blue pencil scratch," as if Moley was "hacking his child apart before his eyes." Johnson's inability to be a good team worker compounded the problems created by his outbursts. Moley preferred that the Brains Trusters collaborate with each other in every stage of drafting a speech. In contrast, Johnson preferred to receive an assignment, vanish, and return "after an all-night and solitary session with a whole assignment in his own handwriting." Johnson's industriousness could hardly be faulted. But it gave many worrisome moments to Moley.[73]

Johnson's contribution to the campaign was limited. Following his nomination, Roosevelt was buffeted by ways to end the depression. Tugwell advocated national planning and social management. Felix Frankfurter of the Harvard Law School and Louis Brandeis, an associate justice of the United States Supreme Court, urged a policy of trust-busting and government regulation. And Baruch and Johnson urged retrenchment and budget balancing. Determined to keep a free hand, Roosevelt refused to commit himself, giving each group just enough to keep it quiet. Thus his speeches contained elements of all three approaches. While Johnson contributed to many of these speeches, his contributions, with two noteworthy exceptions, generally consisted of fulminations against the Hoover administration, wisecracks about Hoover's blundering, and catchy phraseology.

One of the exceptions was Roosevelt's tariff speech, delivered at Sioux City, Iowa, on September 29, 1932. Many Democrats, led by Senator Cordell Hull of Tennessee, believed that the Republicans' high tariff policies of the 1920s had been the major factor in causing the depression. In their opinion, the tariff, which made it difficult for foreign nations to sell goods in the United States and build up credits with which to buy American goods, had encouraged retaliatory tariffs that drastically reduced U.S. exports, thereby prostrating industry and impoverishing agriculture. Adhering to this line of reason, Hull urged Roosevelt to pledge an immediate 10 percent reduction in the Hawley-Smoot Tariff of 1930. This reduction, he argued, would encourage other nations to reduce their tariffs and promote recovery by the restoration of a world market for American surpluses.

In early September 1932, Charles W. Taussig, president of the American Molasses Company and a strong exponent of "free trade," presented Moley with a draft of a speech espousing the Hull view. Moley, however, was disinclined to use the Hull-Taussig draft as a basis for Roosevelt's tariff speech, for the Brain Trust had serious doubts about Hull's "free-trade" analysis of the nation's economic plight. Economists themselves could not agree on what caused the depression, let alone a formula for recovery, and the Brain Trust was wary of committing recovery to a single theory.[74]

In the meantime, Johnson, at Baruch's instigation, drafted a speech calling for a different approach to the complex problems of tariff. Like Hull, the two men considered the Republican tariff policy absurd. But they were unwilling to support a campaign commitment to unilateral tariff reduction. The world's high tariff system was a formidable economic reality, and there could be no assurance that unilateral reductions in American tariffs would produce favorable economic benefits or a reduction in foreign tariffs. Instead of Hull's unilateral 10 percent cut, Johnson urged negotiated tariff reduction on a step-by-step basis, conducted in "good old Yankee trading fashion." "What is here proposed," Johnson emphasized in his draft, "is that we sit down with each great commercial nation separately and independently and negotiate with it alone . . . for the purpose of reopening the markets of these countries to our agricultural and industrial surpluses."[75]

During the third week of September, Roosevelt, who was on a tour of the West, consulted numerous Democratic leaders on Taussig's and Johnson's tariff speeches. Roosevelt wavered between the two speeches until Moley and Senators Key Pittman, Democrat of Nevada, and Thomas Walsh persuaded him to use the Johnson speech as the basis for his Sioux City address, which was billed as his major tariff pronouncement. The Hawley-Smoot Tariff, Roosevelt told a large audience, had been suicidal; it had to be remedied by tariff reduction. But the reduction, he promised, would be secured by Yankee horse trading designed to open markets for American surpluses, not unilateral reduction.[76]

Johnson's other noteworthy contribution to Roosevelt's campaign was the governor's speech calling for retrenchment and budget balancing, delivered at Pittsburgh, Pennsylvania, on October 19, 1932. Baruch had been urging federal retrenchment as a stimulus to business confidence for months. Johnson reiterated Baruch's recommendations after he joined the Brain Trust, arguing that a balanced budget was essential to restore business confidence.[77] Once the campaign was under way, Johnson pressed Roosevelt to make a speech in support of a balanced budget. On September 14 he drafted a strong economy speech and had Roosevelt political advisor James Farley deliver the draft during Roosevelt's western state campaign swing. The speech, Johnson wrote Moley, "is a terrific indictment [of Hoover's failure to balance the budget] and I believe will do much to solidify the Governor in the East and do him no harm in the West."[78]

Johnson was anxious for Roosevelt to deliver the speech in San Francisco on September 23. But Roosevelt was "frankly reluctant" to launch an attack on the Hoover budget. Secretary Mills was scheduled to make a campaign swing across the country, and Roosevelt knew from personal experience that Mills "was in possession of all the facts on federal finance; he was a master of his subject, a dangerous fighter, and a resourceful campaigner." Roosevelt feared that a strong budget speech would give Mills more of a hearing than he might otherwise command. He also considered that he might be hurt by an effective rebuttal from the secretary. It was better political strategy, Roosevelt advised, "to emphasize the positions he had already occupied and which he was certain he could hold."[79]

When Roosevelt failed to use the speech in California, Howe, whom Johnson and Baruch convinced of the necessity for the speech, argued Johnson's case with Roosevelt by telephone and telegraph at every stop on Roosevelt's way back from the West Coast. He did not cease his badgering until Roosevelt reached Chicago and ordered him, face-to-face, to "hush up." Johnson also pressed Roosevelt to deliver the speech, wiring Moley that Roosevelt should deliver the budget speech in Chicago, before Hoover could pledge heavy cuts in government spending at a scheduled speech in Des Moines. At the time, the Roosevelt people believed that the Republicans were experiencing an upsurge, and Johnson despaired that they might steal the issue of a balanced budget from the Democrats. "Budget speech unanswerable," he wired Moley, "if they beat us to it with a new economy program at Des Moines. Our budget speech later will lose half its strength as a forced and trumped-up reply and a me-too remedy. If we shoot first at Chicago our opponent's new economy pledge will look like confession and repentance."[80]

Back in New York, Roosevelt faced relentless pressure from Johnson, Howe, and Baruch. Howe insisted that Roosevelt had to counter Hoover's charges that Democratic "radicalism" would destroy the American economy and American individualism. Johnson added that the economy was faltering even more because Roosevelt had given no assurance that he would follow a conservative course.[81] Their arguments appeared compelling, and Roosevelt capitulated. Moley asked Roosevelt to go over the speech very carefully, since it was one of the few speeches that committed him to a specific policy. Roosevelt, in turn, handed it to Basil O'Connor, his law partner, but neither made any revisions. On the morning of the speech, Moley revised it slightly with the assistance of former Democratic Congressman Swager Sherley of Kentucky, and Roosevelt made a few stylistic changes. For the most part the speech stood as Johnson had written it.[82]

The Pittsburgh speech criticized the Hoover administration for living beyond its means and warned that its prolifigate spending had put the nation on the road to bankruptcy. The federal budget, Roosevelt charged, had gone up 50 percent between 1927 and 1931 "in the most reckless and extravagant past that I have been able to discover in the statistical record of any peacetime Government anywhere any time." This spending produced a deficit for the two fiscal years preceding June 30, 1932, of $3.75 billion. The cause for these deficits and the economic distress they produced, Roosevelt explained, was Hoover's "novel, radical and unorthodox economic theories of 1928." When the stock market collapsed, the administration unavoidably increased costs by centering "control of everything in Washington as rapidly as possible." As a remedy, Roosevelt pledged to "approach the problem of carrying out the plain precept of the Party, which is to reduce the cost of current Federal Government operations by 25 per cent."[83]

Conservative Democrats praised the speech; and Frankfurter, speaking for many Democrats, labeled it an extraordinary and devastating presentation of the Hoover fiscal policies. But viewed within the context of the New Deal the speech seems absurd, for the Roosevelt presidency did not lead to reduced federal expenditures or balanced budgets.

At the time, though, Roosevelt was sincere in his call for a balanced budget. It represented his basic belief not only during the campaign but well into the New Deal.

As the campaign neared its conclusion, there was little question that Roosevelt would win the election. The only doubt was by what margin. Johnson recognized the likelihood of Roosevelt's victory, writing Peek at the end of October that "the hog's eye is soot and the battle is over."[84] In the last days of the campaign, Johnson began to drink heavily, and on November 2 he went on a drinking binge that put him "out of action" for six days.[85]He was still recovering from this bender on election day, November 8, when the returns began to show Roosevelt's overwhelming victory.

Johnson returned to his work with Baruch as soon as the campaign was over. The months he had worked on it had been exhilirating. It had been great fun "dashing off biting assaults upon Hoover" and sparring with the professors and lawyers over what would stimulate recovery. It had also been exciting to be at the side of the next president and to be part of a winning team. After tasting the sense of importance that came from knowing that his views carried weight with Roosevelt, working with Baruch would never be the same. The Roosevelt people, meanwhile, had been greatly impressed with Johnson. They were alternately amused and infatuated by his aggressiveness and expressiveness and recognized that his explosive energy and acute intellect made him a good man to have on the team. In addition, Roosevelt considered him an entertaining fellow and enjoyed his company. Had Johnson not been so closely associated with Baruch and part of the "Stop Roosevelt" movement, there might have been a spot for him in the Roosevelt administration from the outset. Instead, he was in limbo for the first three months.[86]

IN THE weeks following the election Hugh Johnson's major assignment from Baruch was to work with the National Transportation Committee. In the fall of 1932 an association of banks, insurance companies, and universities with large financial investments in depressed railroad securities had convened the committee to study and make recommendations for the restoration of the economic vitality of the railroads. It consisted of former President Coolidge; Alex Legge, a WIB alumnus and an executive with International Harvester; Al Smith; Clark Howell, publisher of the *Atlanta Constitution*; and Baruch. Coolidge was chairman, and Baruch, vice-chairman. Baruch was sick during part of the committee's deliberations, and often he had Johnson sit in for him. The Chief also had Johnson "get together" the evidence accumulated by the committee and prepare the final report, a job which required three months of work during the winter of 1932–1933.[87] The final report, which proposed the elimination of excess and obsolete lines and the regional consolidation of railroads, looked toward the ultimate creation of a national railroad system. Like many such projects, however, it was ignored because of the opposition from major railroads and the trucking industry.

His work with the National Transportation Committee starkly revealed the belligerent side of Hugh Johnson's personality and laid the foundation for one of his most prominent feuds. In committee meetings Al Smith, who was associated with John J. Raskob and the DuPonts, major stockholders in General Motors, had as his second Robert Moses, who argued against Johnson's contention that trucks and buses had an unfair advantage over railroads and condemned his proposal for additional highway taxes to equalize the competition. Both Moses and Johnson were proud of their verbal abilities and pugnacious to a fault. One day they argued their cases so strenuously that they nearly came to blows, and thereafter they were bitter enemies.[88]

As it developed, the National Transportation Committee report was Johnson's last major assignment for Baruch, for he was about to embark on a new career that would take him out from under Baruch's shadow and thrust him to the forefront of national policymaking. The years with the Chief had been critical to Johnson's rise to prominence. They had prepared him for big things, expanding his business and political contacts and knowledge of American industry and quickening his interest and involvement in national issues. Moreover, these years were unmarked by bitterness or personal rancor; they led to a lifelong relationship of goodwill between him and the Chief. Even after Johnson moved up, he happily performed occasional services, like speech writing and business writing, for Baruch and repeatedly praised his sagacity. Baruch, in turn, repaid his loyalty with financial assistance and fatherly advice on many public and personal matters.

CHAPTER 6

INTO THE SADDLE WITH NRA

H UGH Johnson expected to have a major role in New Deal policy-making, especially in the area of agricultural relief. He had been a hardworking member of the Brain Trust, and he was widely recognized as an expert on the farm problem. The first months of the New Deal left him sorely disappointed, however; he had entered the fray too late to have a significant impact.

During the late 1920s and early 1930s Johnson continued to argue that McNary-Haugenism was the salvation of the farmer. By the early 1930s, however, McNary-Haugenism had an enticing rival: the domestic allotment plan. Developed by several economists—John Black of the University of Minnesota and Harvard University, William J. Spillman of the Department of Agriculture, and Beardsley Ruml of the Rockefeller Foundation—the domestic allotment plan was advanced most forcefully by Milburn L. Wilson of Montana State College. It proposed to restrict acreage, levy a tax on the processors of agricultural commodities, and pay benefits to farmers who agreed to limit production. Support for the plan was slow in coming. But by 1932 it had won the backing of numerous concerned groups, particularly among producers of corn, hogs, and cotton.

From the outset, Johnson vehemently opposed the domestic allotment plan. In his mind, the whole notion of the plan was wrong because it rewarded nonproduction and foreshadowed a planned economy in the hands of bureaucrats. Moreover, Johnson was concerned about the impact of the tax on processors. He had long had business and personal ties with them, and he feared that they could not afford additional reductions in investment and purchasing power.[1] Finally, he doubted the practicality of the plan. It called for the secretary of agriculture to estimate the percentage of crops to be consumed at home each year and levy a tax on the crops produced to finance the benefit payments. Johnson considered both tasks impossible. There were too many shifting factors for the secretary to consider in estimating domestic consumption of crops, and there was no way to know whether the tax he levied would be sufficient.[2] Johnson also questioned Wilson's insistence that participation in the program be on a voluntary basis and that farmers themselves play a major role in its administration. As he told Wilson at a meeting in Tugwell's New York City apartment in July 1932:

Hell, this thing of having a bunch of farmers together, in farmers' meetings and cooperatives, doesn't sound too effective. If you don't want to do something, have a meeting. If you want to get something done, put somebody in charge, tell him to go out and do it, and he'll get it done.[3]

Shortly before the 1932 convention, Roosevelt, who had originally endorsed McNary-Haugenism, accepted the domestic allotment plan. Converted to it by Tugwell, he inserted a general proposal for the domestic allotment into his acceptance speech, leaving the actual wording of the bill to responsible farm groups. Johnson, however, did not believe that Roosevelt's conversion to the domestic allotment was irrevocable and was optimistic that Peek and other conservative farm leaders could bring their influence to bear and wean him away from limits on production. Within an hour after reading Roosevelt's acceptance speech in Howe's suite, he wired Peek that "we will get what we want. Hold all fire."[4] Peek found it difficult to accept Johnson's advice, replying that "my training was holding the plow not holding fire but will try." Instead of "holding fire," he wanted to press Roosevelt to call upon the Democratic majority in Congress to pass farm relief legislation immediately, even though Hoover would undoubtedly veto it. Johnson thought Peek's idea had little merit and, through Baruch, admonished him. "Hold your horses," Baruch wired Peek. "Our man is not yet the boss. He honestly intends to act. The job now is to let us know exactly whom he should consult and whom he should ask to prepare a specific plan."[5]

Johnson was unable to exert any significant influence on the formulation of Roosevelt's farm policy during the campaign against Hoover. He wrote a draft of a farm speech, but it was not used. Instead, Roosevelt consulted a wide range of farm leaders before making his major farm pronouncement. The speech, delivered at Topeka, Kansas, on September 14, 1932, was phrased so generally that supporters of domestic allotment and various other major proposals could read into it his endorsement.[6] Johnson accepted this politically expedient course. Before there could be any effective farm relief, the Republicans had to be out of the White House; and he judged that he could win the battle against the domestic allotment when it came time to draft farm relief legislation.

Roosevelt moved quickly after the election to formulate specific farm-relief plans. During November and December 1932, representatives of many farm groups and specialists in agricultural economics worked to frame an emergency bill to be presented to Congress at its lame duck session. Johnson, who was vacationing at Baruch's estate in South Carolina and then working on the National Transportation Committee report, was not a participant. Anxious to have his views aired, on November 29 he wrote Moley a long letter pungently expressing his opposition to the domestic allotment. In its place, Johnson, who now realized that McNary-Haugenism had no support among Roosevelt's closest advisors on farm policy, recommended that the farm problem be solved by eliminating the multiplicity of distribution organizations. "It seems possible," he told Moley, "to make such contracts between farm cooperatives or a corporation to be owned by them and existing organizations for the distribution of farm products as will make the farmer a partner . . . in the journey of his product all the way from the farm through the processor, clear to the ultimate consumer." Although he had yet to check thoroughly the "figures and circumstances" of this scheme, Johnson predicted that it would bring higher prices to farmers, lower prices to consumers, and avoid the administrative nightmare inherent in the "half-digested plans sponsored by very earnest gentlemen who have no experience whatever in the field in which they are projecting their theories."[7]

Johnson's efforts to use Moley to influence Roosevelt's agricultural policy went for naught. The members of Roosevelt's circle most directly charged with farm relief—Tugwell, Wilson, Henry Morgenthau, Jr., publisher of the *American Agriculturalist* and a Hyde Park neighbor of Roosevelt, and Henry A. Wallace, an Iowa newspaper editor and son of Henry C. Wallace—were strong advocates of the domestic allotment. Moley could only present Johnson's views to them.[8]

At a meeting in Washington on December 12–14, 1932, Roosevelt's spokesmen worked with congressional leaders and leaders of some fifty farm organizations to draft agricultural relief legislation embodying the domestic allotment. In January 1933, the House of Representatives approved the legislation, but opponents of the plan blocked it in the Senate. As an alternative they proposed a scheme for federal rental of acreage in states producing a surplus. Johnson, Baruch, Baruch's friends in the Senate, and even Hoover enthusiastically endorsed it. Roosevelt, however, rejected acreage rental, even though "it need not have varied much from the domestic allotment and might have worked about as well." The lame duck session of Congress ended on the eve of Roosevelt's inauguration on March 4, 1933, with farm relief legislation postponed until the new Congress could meet.[9]

Four days after the inauguration, Tugwell and the newly appointed secretary of agriculture, Henry A. Wallace, persuaded Roosevelt to move immediately to get farm relief legislation. The next morning Wallace telephoned farm leaders and asked them to convene in Washington on March 10 in order to draft emergency legislation. Desirous of a broad base of support, he suggested blanket authorization for the secretary of agriculture to use several plans to deal with the farm surplus as the solution to differences between the supporters and opponents of the domestic allotment. He also invited Johnson and other opponents of the domestic allotment to participate in the discussions. Welcoming the opportunity to present his views, Johnson, on a train from New York City to Washington with Moley on March 9, again denounced the domestic allotment and urged the development of a government supervised "dumping" program and marketing agreements to control the flow of products into the nation's markets.[10]

The next few days were filled with feverish activity as administration officials and farm leaders worked to draft legislation. Wallace, Tugwell, and Wilson, supported by spokesmen for the Farm Bureau and the Grange, insisted that the domestic allotment be included in the legislation, while Johnson and Peek, with frequently telephoned support from Baruch, focused on marketing agreements and rental arrangements. Johnson argued that the legislation should be limited to acreage rental and marketing agreements. He maintained that all agricultural difficulties could be remedied by applying these two devices, with principal reliance on marketing agreements. Johnson also spoke out against the proposals to limit the application of the processing tax to a list of "basic" commodities and to grant the secretary of agriculture discretionary power to levy taxes and allocate the revenue from them. He regarded this grant as unconstitutional and suggested that instead there should be a specific appropriation to cover acreage rentals only. It would be financed by a lighter tax imposed on a wide range of agricultural and competing commodities.[11]

Johnson and Peek lost the battle to block provision for the domestic allotment in the drafting stage of farm relief legislation. Yet it was not a total defeat, for the legislation included provision for marketing agreements and, at the insistence of Representative Marvin Jones, Democrat of Texas and chairman of the House Agriculture Committee, an acreage rental program. The latter program, to Johnson's disgust, "suffered shipwreck" shortly afterward on the claim of Federal Farm Board economist Mordecai Ezekiel that it was "not good economics."[12]

Roosevelt sent the farm relief legislation, known as the Agricultural Adjustment Act, to Congress on March 16, 1933. Even then Johnson refused to give up the fight. He continued to question the taxing and spending provisions of the legislation; and in letters to Roosevelt, Howe, and Wallace, he warned that the legislation was "clearly unconstitutional as an invalid appropriation and an invalid delegation of the taxing power."[13] Roosevelt glibly replied that "there is a lot in what you say."[14] But Johnson was ignored; too many people had lined up behind the domestic allotment.

Realizing that he had failed to have a significant influence on the legislation, Johnson dejectedly wrote Moley that the draft was so far set when he got it that he could not obtain modifications to make it workable. "It nearly breaks my heart," he moaned. "I began this farm fight twelve years ago and I think I know as much about it as anybody in the country."[15]

Johnson now placed his hopes for the effectiveness of the farm program on the prospect that its administrator would emphasize marketing agreements over the domestic allotment. He expected Baruch to be that administrator and thought the Chief would take him along as a lieutenant. But Baruch did not want the job, and, his claims to the contrary notwithstanding, it is not even clear that he was seriously considered for it. When it became obvious that Baruch would not head the farm program, Johnson concluded that it would now be completely in the hands of the "theoreticians" and that he had lost a great opportunity to play a major role in farm relief. Discouraged, he privately lashed out at Tugwell, blaming everything on his behind-the-scenes machinations. Tugwell, he told Peek, was "a damned Communist, and . . . the whole idea of benefit payments was communistic."[16] It was little consolation to Johnson that Roosevelt named Peek to the job to finalize Senate passage of the legislation.

The first months of the New Deal deeply frustrated Johnson. Despite his work as a Brain Truster and his expertise, he had not been a prime mover in the formulation of farm relief legislation. Instead, Roosevelt had been more receptive to the schemes of theoreticians, like Tugwell, Wilson, and Ezekiel. Johnson felt this president, for whom he had worked so valiantly, had let him down. He deserved something more, something better.[17]

THE FIRST part of April 1933, saw Hugh Johnson chafing on the sidelines while the New Deal took shape. Baruch, worried over his despondency, took Johnson to Hobcaw for a hunting trip, and while it did little for Johnson's spirit, he soon afterward began work on a new project that put his talents to good use and propelled him to the center of the planning for industrial recovery.

On April 25, one day after his returning to Washington from Hobcaw, Johnson ran into Moley in the lobby of the Carlton Hotel. The two had a leisurely lunch in the hotel's dining room and then went upstairs to talk with Baruch, who kept an apartment at the Carlton. Moley described the many industrial recovery plans submitted to the administration and the need to bring them together into a single proposal for presentation to Congress. On the basis of Johnson's World War I experience as an industrial mobilizer and the many industrial studies he had made for Baruch, Moley asked Johnson to draft the bill. Johnson was elated. His failure to influence the formulation of agricultural policy was past; he would again be at the center of the action. Moley told

Johnson to waste no time and gave him a vacant office in the State, War and Navy Building. That afternoon, Johnson went to the office with Moley, who dumped all the plans on the desk and instructed Robert Straus, the son of Jesse Straus, to assist him. It being a hot day, Johnson took off his coat and tie, rolled up his sleeves, and "plunged into a job that was to make him, next to Roosevelt, the most talked about member of the administration during the year ahead."[18]

By the time Johnson began his industrial recovery work, Roosevelt had been deluged with ideas to rehabilitate industry. Several senators and Cabinet members urged Roosevelt to initiate large-scale public works. Organized labor favored legislation limiting working hours in the belief that the limits would spread jobs, stabilize labor standards, and increase workers' purchasing power. Labor also endorsed Secretary of Labor Frances Perkins's proposal for minimum wage regulation. Others suggested plans for "restarting industry" either through government loans to industry for reemployment purposes or government guarantees against losses for firms increasing their work forces. Finally, significant groups within the business community favored industrial self-government, with trade-association control of markets. During the 1920s trade associations had attempted to stabilize many industries on the basis of voluntary cooperation. But in the absence of any legal sanction these agreements often broke down. Revision of the antitrust laws so as to institutionalize and legitimatize agreements limiting competition, they argued, would combat the overproduction and lowered prices that, in their opinion, had destabilized industries and caused the depression.[19]

Roosevelt was uncertain about which plan to support and was moved to action only after the Senate on April 6 passed a bill sponsored by Senator Hugo Black, Democrat of Alabama, providing for a thirty-hour week. Judging that it was too inflexible and would make matters worse by bringing about an actual drop in purchasing power since it contained no wage provision, Roosevelt opposed the Black bill. Yet it was too popular for him to oppose publicly; therefore, his opposition had to consist of "substitution of a better proposal for stimulating employment and recovery." During the following weeks Roosevelt searched for an effective substitute, although at the time Moley brought Johnson into the work he had yet to decide what form the substitute should take.

Unlike Roosevelt, Johnson had little doubt about what needed to be done. His experience as a WIB administrator and numerous discussions with Baruch and Alexander Sachs, an economist with Lehman Corporation, had given him well-developed ideas on the subject of industrial recovery. Working quickly, he reviewed the plans Moley presented to him and within twenty-four hours produced the first draft of a bill. It contained only one paragraph and was written on less than two sheets of foolscap.[20]

The central feature of the Johnson draft was provision for the legalization of business agreements (codes) on competitive and labor practices. Johnson believed that the nation's traditional commitment to
laissez-faire was outdated. Laissez-faire had been acceptable in the
nineteenth century when those displaced by the economic dislocations inherent in laissez-faire capitalism had the opportunity to move
to the vast expanses of the frontier and start over again. That was what
his father had done in migrating across the Kansas prairie to settle
finally in Oklahoma. But in the twentieth century, with scientific
and technological improvement outdistancing economic progress and
with the frontier only a memory, laissez-faire had led to excess production capacity and chronically unstable markets. This, in turn, led to
the more extreme methods of competition, such as sweatshops, child
labor, and the ruthless price slashing and low wages that marked the
spiraling downturn of 1929 through 1932. "Nothing like this could
have happened," he later wrote, if the nation's industries had not been
prevented by the antitrust laws from checking "uncontrolled competition" through "counsel and united action."[21]

In providing for the legalization of codes on competitive practices,
Johnson was adopting a program that supporters of industrial self-
government had been urging since 1918. He himself had endorsed it in
1919 in the preliminary report on the WIB's operations. In his draft of
the recovery bill, however, Johnson went beyond the program of many
of the supporters. They envisioned industrial self-government as a partnership between government and business, with business as the senior
partner, administration largely lying in the hands of trade associations,
and government merely providing permission and some measure of supervision for their activities. Johnson, meanwhile, envisioned more
governmental power, including authority for the president to license
industry. The president, in his view, had practically unlimited power to
do in the industrial sector whatever he believed was best.

Johnson included federal licensing to inject an element of compulsion into industrial self-government. One might have wished that businessmen would cooperate out of enlightened self-interest, but the WIB
experience had shown that many businessmen had trouble looking beyond their own immediate profits. Despite appeals to patriotism, they
had hoarded materials, charged exorbitant prices, given preference to
civilian customers, and even refused to convert to war production. The
WIB had dealt with these "slackers" by threatening to commandeer
their production or to deny them fuel and raw materials—in other
words, by presenting the prospect of closure. These threats usually won
grudging cooperation, and Johnson knew that compulsion was also necessary to any industrial recovery program. Under his scheme, federal
licensing would serve as a stick that would codify industry and enforce

the codes. Firms refusing to cooperate would lose their licenses to do business.[22]

The provision granting the president sweeping power in the industrial sector stemmed from Johnson's conceptions of the depression and of presidential powers. To Johnson, the depression was as grave an emergency as the Great War, and in his thinking presidential powers in wartime were unlimited. That was how he had written and administered the selective service law in 1917, and that was how an industrial recovery law should be written and administered. As he later lectured Frances Perkins:

This is just like a war. We're in a war. We're in a war against depression and poverty and we've got to fight this war. We've got to come out of this war. You've got to do here what you do in a war. You've got to give authority and you've got to apply regulations and enforce them on everybody, no matter who they are or what they do. . . .
    The individual who has the power to apply and enforce these regulations is the President. There is nothing that the President can't do if he wishes to! The President's powers are unlimited. The President can do anything.[23]

Moley rejected Johnson's first draft since it would have given the president dictatorial powers that Roosevelt did not want.[24] Johnson continued to work on the bill, refining it almost daily. The labor provisions were particularly troublesome, as Johnson had given little initial thought to this aspect of the recovery program. Except for some incidental wartime contact with American Federation of Labor President Samuel Gompers, Johnson had just enough experience with labor to feel incompetent to deal with the bill's labor provisions. At Moley's recommendation, he sought and received help from Donald R. Richberg, a Chicago lawyer who had close ties with the railroad brotherhoods and seemed to have the confidence of the labor movement.

By now Johnson was also including provision for a relatively modest public works program in his bill. He realized that business codes on competitive and labor practices would raise prices; if purchasing power did not rise correspondingly, the nation would remain mired in depression. Public works spending, he believed, could bring about the necessary increase in purchasing power. After considerable thought, Johnson determined that the spending that activated the capital goods industries, which had the bulk of the nation's unemployed, should be emphasized. Until these businesses were back on their feet, purchasing power would be insufficient to sustain reemployment in light manufactures, commerce, and the service industries. Johnson also saw that public works spending would complement federal licensing as a means of dealing with firms that failed to demonstrate a social responsibility. As in WIB practice, contracts for materials and jobs could be used to compel cooperation with the recovery program. Finally, public works could be used to stimulate an industry in which a code was insufficient. If a code did not stimulate the electrical industry, he told Perkins, "we'll give out a public works program that will require a lot of electrical wiring to stimulate Westinghouse Electric, which isn't in a position to make larger electrical operating units unless it has some orders."[25] Such orders would also stimulate those industries that supplied Westinghouse with raw materials. The appropriations for public works, he calculated, should extend from three to four billion dollars annually and, so as not to be inflationary, should be financed by new taxation.[26]

Another group, Johnson soon learned, was also drafting a bill. Headed by Senator Robert Wagner, Democrat of New York, and John Dickinson, assistant secretary of commerce, it produced a bill in early May calling for a program of public works, government loans, and industrial self-government through trade associations; it also guaranteed labor's right to collective bargaining.[27] Although Moley later wrote that when he asked Johnson to draft a recovery bill, he was unaware that anyone else in the Roosevelt circle was working on a bill, historian Robert F. Himmelberg has noted that he knew of the existence of the other group as early as April 18. Moley's reason for bringing Johnson into the operation was most likely a personal power play, to gain control of the drafting process for himself, or, a shrewd political gambit, to guarantee the support of Baruch and his conservative friends on Capitol Hill.[28]

At any rate, Johnson was predictably dismayed to hear of the competition. He regarded the draft as his private preserve. Johnson knew that Dickinson was working on plans for industrial recovery, but Moley had led him to believe that no one else was drafting a bill. Greatly angered by Moley's apparent deception, Johnson pressed him to bring the two groups—the Johnson-Richberg group and the Wagner-Dickinson group—together to integrate the two bills. At about the same time, Perkins, herself working with the Wagner group, learned of the Johnson-Richberg group and urged Roosevelt to bring both groups together to draft a bill. Following discussions in the White House on May 10, Roosevelt ordered Johnson, Richberg, Dickinson, Wagner, Perkins, Tugwell, and Lewis Douglas, director of the budget, to "shut themselves up in a room" until they could come up with a common proposal.[29]

Work on the bill, which in its final form was largely hammered out by Johnson, Wagner, Richberg, and Douglas, was completed on May 14. In general, it followed the draft of the Wagner-Dickinson group, but Johnson's voice dominated in the bill's specifics. As Perkins recalled: "Things would appear in one draft that hadn't been in the previous draft, when we were meeting in committee. I would question as to how they got in and would get, 'Well, Johnson thought it ought to be that way. Johnson put that in,' and so on.''[30] On one occasion Johnson, without consulting the other conferees, inserted a provision for vast naval construction in the public works section. On another occasion, he fought Dickinson to gain approval for his provision for federal licensing of business. Dickinson, who opposed federal licensing as too tough a measure to squeeze by the business community, went after Johnson's weaknesses; Tugwell records that he was ''biting and arrogant'' toward Johnson. But Johnson doggedly resisted his baiting and, with the crucial support of Tugwell, prevailed.[31]

Johnson's most important contributions to the bill followed disputes with Wagner, whose draft gave the Congress the power to lay down guidelines for the implementation of the recovery program. At Johnson's insistence, though, the conferees agreed that the president should be vested with vast legislative powers relating to allocation of resources, production, organization, wages and working conditions, and labor-management relations. In effect, Johnson removed administrative control of the economy from the traditional purview of Congress and transferred it to the executive branch. Johnson also won out over Wagner in a dispute over the scope of the recovery program. Wagner's draft called for the formulation of codes only by the major industries, like steel and automobiles. Johnson, however, persuaded the conferees that the bill should provide for the codification of all industries engaged in interstate commerce. This action eventually led to efforts to extend industrial self-government—and red tape—to the dog-food industry, poultry markets, and even burlesque theaters.[32]

Only in one instance of consequence did Johnson fail to get a provision he advocated. Wanting an additional sanction in the bill for non-compliance with codes, he recommended that it provide for a high tax (10 to 20 percent) on the gross receipts of a non-complying business, a drain that would mean ruin for most firms.[33] Johnson's penalty tax appalled the conferees, and Douglas somehow scotched it.[34]

Except for Tugwell, the other conferees had not known Johnson before the spring of 1933, and after they finished drafting the bill few knew what to make of him. During their meetings Johnson's thinking about industrial problems had been ''excellent,'' and he had been a stubborn, effective advocate at the conference table. But he had also been impatient for action, bored increasingly with the wrangling over legal points. He would squirm in his chair like a restless child, run his hand through his hair, pull his legs up onto his chair, and then stretch himself forward in a crouch. Once he grew so bored that he completely ignored the discussion, prompting Wagner to complain to Roosevelt that he ''wouldn't talk up.'' Later, when discussion focused too long for his tastes on a constitutional point, Johnson suddenly jumped from his seat and roared that he could no longer tolerate such ''poppycock discussions.'' He told the startled group:

Well, what difference does it make anyhow, because before they can get these cases to the Supreme Court we will have won the victory. The unemployment will be over and over so fast that nobody will care. We'll go on doing it somehow under some other name, because this is the answer.

When Dickinson remarked that he should not be so flippant about such a serious matter, Johnson retorted:

You don't seem to realize that people in this country are starving. You don't seem to realize that industry has gone to pot. You don't seem to realize that there isn't any industry in this country unless we stimulate it, unless we start it. You don't seem to realize that these things are important and that this law stuff doesn't matter. You're just talking about things that are of no account.[35]

Their meetings left the conferees uncertain about which Johnson was the real man: the clear-thinking, effective advocate or the man of emotional outbursts.

On May 15 the conferees presented their bill to Roosevelt. Two days later he sent it to Congress with the recommendation that it be approved quickly. The bill easily passed the House (323 to 76) on May 26. The Senate was another matter. Rural progressives and antitrusters, claiming that the bill would cause trusts to blossom and that well-heeled industrial spokesmen would organize to dominate the code-making process at the expense of the consumer and labor, attempted to attach many amendments to the bill, some of them designed to make it more politically attractive and others intended to gut key provisions. The most important was proposed by Senator William E. Borah, Republican of Idaho. It prohibited any code from permitting "combinations in restraint of trade, price fixing, or other monopolistic practices." Though the Senate approved Borah's amendment, Johnson successfully lobbied the House-Senate conference committee to mute its effectiveness by removing the specific prohibitions against "price fixing or other monopolistic practices." Johnson considered the bill useless if these words were in it, and Johnson's zeal prevailed over Borah's interests.[36]

The Senate finally approved the industrial recovery bill on June 13 by a vote of 46 to 37; three days later, Roosevelt signed it into law. Known as the National Industrial Recovery Act (NIRA), it contained three titles. Title II authorized the expenditure of $3.3 billion on a variety of public works projects, while Title III provided for a new system of capital stock and excess profits taxes to help finance it. The most significant and controversial portion was Title I. Limited in application to a period of two years, it laid down the rules for code making and exempted the codes from the antitrust laws. Little was said about the specific provisions to be contained in the codes except for the labor standards mandated in Section 7. These included provision for maximum hours, minimum wages, desirable working conditions, and the right of workers to organize and bargain collectively.

Some businessmen saw the passage of NIRA as opportunity and looked forward to the implementation of price and production controls, or to obtaining greater profits through emulation of their monopolistic colleagues, or to saving themselves from technological advances, or to halting the inroads of mass distributors. Millions of exploited and suffering workers, meanwhile, looked forward to improving labor standards through such measures as higher wages, shorter hours, and the organization of unions. The recovery measure, however, had serious flaws. Title I was vague as to what should be included in the codes, and underlying the act's provisions were two approaches to recovery. One anticipated that the checking of destructive price cutting and other competitive practices through industrial self-government could restore business confidence and encourage expanded operations. The other held that the raising of wages and the spreading of work would increase purchasing power and induce employers to take on more workers. The danger was that the former might outpace the latter, in which case the increased purchasing power would be negated by higher prices.[37]

Johnson recognized that there were flaws in NIRA. But he told reporters on May 18 that the best bill might be "spoiled" by poor administration, while good administration could make a bad bill work. NIRA would work, he concluded, as along as it was administered by a man with common sense.[38]

GIVEN this essential ambiguity, much would depend on the administrator who would define NIRA. In Roosevelt's mind there was only one man for the job: Hugh S. Johnson. He made this decision shortly after sending the recovery bill to Congress and apparently without consulting advisors or seriously considering anyone else. Roosevelt picked Johnson, first of all, because he agreed with Johnson on industrial self-government. His presidency, during the 1920s, of the American Construction Council, an industry trade association, left him committed in principle to the virtues of industrial self-government, and he was particularly attracted to Johnson's version. Like Johnson, he believed in the necessity of governmental compulsion in industrial self-government; cutthroat competition had to be controlled. Moreover, he favored Johnson's emphasis on granting the president virtually a free hand in the industrial sector. An experimenter, he liked a program with a minimum of explicit legislative guidance. A strong-willed man, he liked having full rein.

In addition, Roosevelt appreciated Johnson's ability to press his ideas. On May 15, when the drafting committee for NIRA had presented its bill to Roosevelt, Johnson acted as spokesman for the group. As Perkins recalled, "Johnson made a very good appearance that day. I remember how well he argued, how well he spoke, how clear he was. It was his best foot forward. . . . He showed himself in his most competent and most effective side."[39] Roosevelt found Johnson's vigor and enthusiasm irresistible and was impressed with his knowledge of the industrial sector and his experience with the WIB, the sole large-scale precedent for industrial self-government. Here, in his view, was the man with the know-how and drive to make this novel program a success.

Political considerations also played a role in Johnson's selection. Despite the considerable financial aid Baruch had given the Roosevelt campaign in 1932 (estimates range as high as $200,000; variations are due to the inclusion or exclusion in the figure of contributions he facilitated), the Chief had not yet received an appropriate return.[40] He had not been appointed secretary of state, as he secretly desired; nor had he had much influence in shaping legislation. In fact, during the spring of 1933 Baruch was not even on speaking terms with Roosevelt because of a dispute over gold policy. By appointing Baruch men to key positions in the administration (Peek to administer the agricultural recovery program and Johnson, the industrial recovery program), Roosevelt hoped to mollify Baruch and ensure that his Senate friends supported administration programs.[41]

Johnson learned of Roosevelt's decision to appoint him administrator of the industrial recovery program while "going over a chart of the proposed organization for both titles with the President." Suddenly, Roosevelt said, "Hugh, you've got to do this job." Johnson's first response was a self-deprecating remark suggesting Roosevelt should pick another man. But that moment past, he grabbed the offer. For most of his career, he had been someone else's lieutenant. Now he would be heading his own operation, the largest peacetime attempt at organizing industry in American history. Besides his pride, he felt security, believing that his work with the wartime mobilization, his experience as an industrialist, and the studies he had made for Baruch had uniquely prepared him for this job.[42]

As he later told the story, Johnson fully realized that the assignment was fraught with pitfalls. The recovery bill was vague in its mandate, and his was a job never tried before. The public would be supportive at first; but as decisions were made, those not favored would undoubtedly unleash a flood of criticism. "It will be red fire at first and dead cats [criticism] afterward," he told friends. "This is just like mounting the guillotine on the infinitesimal gamble that the ax won't work."[43] But at this point, the prospect of criticism did not frighten Johnson. "I can take it," he cockily told inquiring newsmen.

On May 18, word of Johnson's selection to head the industrial recovery program leaked to the public, immediately drawing praise from conservative columnist Arthur Krock, who hailed the president for selecting a practical man like Johnson, rather than an educator or theoretician, to head the program.[44] Despite their differences during the 1932 campaign, a "rather surprised" Tugwell recorded his pleasure in the selection:

Had got used to thinking of him as Baruch's man rather than independent personality, not doubting of course, the strength of [his] character and real brilliance, which are obvious. I think his tendency to be gruff in personal relations will be handicap and his occasional drunken sprees will not help any; but on whole quite happy about it. . . . Hugh is sincere, honest, believes in many social changes which seem to me right, and will do good job. It would doubtless be better if he had been further from Baruch's special influence and if he believed more in social planning, but the one gives him wider knowledge which will be useful in his dealings with business and [the] other is something which comes out as it is done.[45]

Others were alarmed by Johnson's selection. Jerome Frank, once a Chicago lawyer who had worked with Johnson during the liquidation of Moline Plow and now a Department of Agriculture employee, went to Wagner and warned that Johnson "will not think things through. He's impulsive and you don't want to trust legislation of this kind to him." Frank repeated the warning to Wagner "three times on consecutive Sundays." But by the time he finally convinced Wagner of the possible dire consequences of the selection, Roosevelt was irrevocably committed to Johnson. "I was in despair about it," Frank later told an interviewer.[46] Senator Huey P. Long, Democrat of Louisiana, was also concerned about Johnson's selection, but for another reason. During the Senate debate over NIRA, the "Kingfish" thundered that Johnson was nothing more than an employee of Baruch who would permit the most conservative elements in the Democratic party to do as they pleased with American industry.[47]

The most poignant warning about Johnson came from an unexpected source: Baruch. Learning that Roosevelt planned to appoint Johnson to head the industrial recovery program, Baruch rushed to Perkins and advised her to intercede with the president to block the appointment. He had been pleased to have Johnson working on the recovery bill and even thought that Johnson could play a role in its implementation. But he questioned his ability to head the program. In his opinion, Johnson's excesses and weaknesses were too pronounced, and Baruch feared that sooner or later they would counterbalance any good that he could achieve as administrator of the recovery program. "Hugh isn't fit to be the head of that," he warned.

He's been my number-three man for years. I think he's a good number-three man, maybe a number-two man, but he's not a number-one man. He's dangerous and unstable. He gets nervous and sometimes goes away without notice. I'm fond of him, but do tell the President to be careful. Hugh needs a firm hand.[48]

Perkins was dumbfounded. Like most others, she thought Baruch would welcome the appointment. When she carried Baruch's warning to Roosevelt, he grilled her about her own impressions of Johnson. "I've only known him for these few weeks," she replied. "But he's a driver and able." Perkins's assessment calmed Roosevelt. The two briefly discussed other potential selections, including Charles Dykstra, former city manager of Cincinnati, Ohio, and Philip LaFollette, former governor of Wisconsin; and Roosevelt abruptly ended the discussion with the comment that he could handle Johnson. Roosevelt appeared more intrigued that Baruch did not deliver the warning personally than by its content.[49]

During the next several weeks Perkins had ample opportunity to observe Johnson. The more she saw of him, the more she appreciated the substance behind Baruch's warning. Nelson Slater, a cotton textile manufacturer and close friend of Johnson, corroborated the rumors that she had heard about Johnson's drinking, although he did point out that Johnson was not presently drinking heavily. In addition, Johnson made remarks about the recovery program that disturbed her. Johnson had just read Raffaello Viglione's *The Corporate State*, an adulatory account of Benito Mussolini's Fascist Italy. One day he gave Perkins a copy of the book with the enthusiastic comment that "this idea of code committees is good. Read this book and you'll see they've got the idea of the committees here." Perkins knew that Johnson was no fascist and that his statement was merely thoughtless. But she also recognized that such frivolous comments could fuel charges that he harbored fascist leanings.

Perkins was even more disturbed by Johnson's notion of code making. In one discussion Johnson announced that he intended to draft a code for an industry simply by meeting with the representatives of its trade association. This was the way things had been done during the war, and Johnson believed that a similar approach would speed up and ease the code-making process. Perkins recognized that the backroom dealings of the wartime government-business partnership could be justified on grounds of national security. But she saw no compelling reason for them in 1933. Concerned that a repeat of the wartime approach could spur opposition to the recovery program from those left out of the negotiations, she informed him that everything must be done in public hearings at which anyone, particularly representatives of labor and the public, could make objections or suggest modifications. Johnson thought the idea was "perfectly crazy." "I can't see it," he exclaimed. "I think this is crazy. . . . Why, we'll spend all our time on public hearings." Perkins reminded him that public hearings were essential to public support, but Johnson was unconvinced and accepted public hearings only when Roosevelt insisted.

Her observations of Johnson led Perkins to conclude that he should not be entrusted with the administration of the public works provision of NIRA. Public works administration required attention to detail, and she doubted his inclination to read through the thousands of contracts. He was not a man to check accountants' figures, she believed; instead, his strength was "splurging enthusiasm." If he had the freedom to splurge money, his impatience for action would soon open the administration to politically damaging charges of boondoggling. Perkins shared her concerns with Roosevelt, suggesting that he consult someone else if he questioned her judgment. Marvin McIntyre, one of Roosevelt's assistants, confirmed Perkins's evaluation. "She's absolutely right, boss," he told the president. "Hugh is an easy mark for any grafter in the U.S.A. He doesn't know the difference. I don't know what he would do. He would throw those public works around to please anybody and to get him off his back. I think it would be terrible."

It was not hard to convince Roosevelt to restrict Johnson to the administration of Title I; for different reasons, he was already leaning in that direction. Believing that large-scale public works spending was fiscally unsound, he had refrained from proposing such a program during the 1932 campaign and had agreed to its inclusion in the NIRA only because of pressure from members of his cabinet and important senators. In his mind, public works was not an essential ingredient of the recovery effort, and he was determined to keep its spending to a minimum. By separating Johnson from Title II and placing its administration in the hands of a more cautious and less hard-driving man, he could effectively limit public works expenditures. A bonus of this plan was that it prevented either NIRA man from having too much power. If Johnson administered both titles, he would overshadow the rest of the recovery program and possibly even the White House. Roosevelt decided to separate administration of the two titles shortly before Congress approved NIRA. But recognizing Johnson's hypersensitivity, he delayed telling him of his decision until he could do so in some "glorious manner."[50]

A few days later, Roosevelt took further action to ease staff worries about Johnson. Title I vested complete authority for organizing industry under codes in the president, who would have to delegate much of this authority to Johnson. Since Roosevelt himself could not supervise Johnson, he created a cabinet-level board, the Special Industrial Recovery Board, for this purpose. Originally suggested by Secretary of Commerce Daniel C. Roper as a means of coordinating NIRA with the rest of the recovery program, it was chaired by Roper and included Perkins, Wallace, Secretary of the Interior Harold L. Ickes, and other key administrators.[51] While publicly stating that the purpose of the Special

Industrial Recovery Board was interbureau coordination, most of the board privately understood that they were to keep a rein on Johnson and cushion Roosevelt from any ill-advised action he might take.[52]

As it developed, the Special Industrial Recovery Board, its members burdened with other responsibilities, was unable to supervise Johnson effectively. When they did question him seriously, he circumvented the group or blustered his way to freedom. For better or worse, Title I was going to be Johnson's show.

LONG before Congress finally approved NIRA, Hugh Johnson was busily putting together the staff for his agency—the National Recovery Administration. As a first step, he had Baruch arrange for meetings with industrialists and labor leaders so that he could explain the recovery program to them, enlist their support, and ask their cooperation and assistance in recruiting the "best material in industry" to implement it.[53] With abandon, Johnson asked old friends in San Francisco, Detroit, New York City, and Moline to fly to Washington immediately and take jobs at his side. Johnson tendered many of these job offers without consulting Roosevelt or his political advisors, who, of course, wanted state Democratic endorsements for all appointees.[54] Irritated by Johnson's naive presumption, Roosevelt let him off with a joking reprimand and instructions to make no major appointments without consulting the White House. By June 15, most of the key positions were filled, and without further problems.

Felix Frankfurter turned down Johnson's offer of the general counsel position, recommending that Johnson choose Donald Richberg.[55] Thus, Johnson picked as his number-two man someone much like himself—a big man in his middle years, cunning, and highly sensitive and emotional. Johnson had been impressed by Richberg during the drafting of NIRA. He had ability. He also had the confidence of organized labor though he was no radical; he and Johnson shared opinions as well as personal traits. In Johnson's view, it was wise to take into the organization people who, simply because they were outside, might be potential opponents. Richberg, although in apparent agreement with Johnson's ideas, might follow a different course if he stayed outside and maintained his close ties with labor. Richberg "ought to be with us," Johnson told Perkins; "otherwise he would be against us."[56]

For his "girl Friday" Johnson chose Miss Frances Robinson. He had been impressed during his years with Baruch with the Chief's Miss Mary A. Boyle. Ostensibly Baruch's secretary, Miss Boyle was actually his chief of staff; she ordered his affairs and assumed responsibility for their smooth operation. Johnson wanted a "Miss Boyle" at his side at the NRA. Getting one was a problem. Robert Straus hired Johnson's first secretary, who lasted only three days before Johnson fired her for incompetence and nosiness. Another woman came and went in a matter

THE BRAINS OF THE NATIONAL RECOVERY ADMINISTRATION. Frances Robinson and Edward McGrady stand to Johnson's left in the first row. In the second row, H. N. Slater stands third from the left; and Robert Straus, John Hancock, Dudley Cates, and Robert Lea are, left to right, fifth through eighth. The Bettmann Archive, Inc.

of days. Straus next tried two men, but both were like the women—"no good, lousy." The by-now exasperated Straus went to ask exactly what Johnson wanted in a secretary and got an offhanded, irritable bark: "[someone] that knows the business, that will do it right, that will keep me reminded, will keep track of things, [and] not come asking me questions and fluttering around."

This large and vague order reminded someone of Miss Frances Robinson, known to her friends as Robbie. She had worked as a volunteer stenographer at Democratic headquarters in New York City in 1932. She had prior secretarial experience with the Radio Corporation of America. There was no problem, then, with loyalty or competence. And her personal assets were encouraging. Although a devout Catholic, at twenty-six she was no schoolgirl. She was pert, auburn-haired, and experienced at flattery and strong language. A superb secretary, she was unshockable by Johnson. She had, like Miss Mary A. Boyle, drive and ambition and moved quickly to make herself important by taking hold of Johnson's affairs. Within days, she seemed to be everywhere—attending meetings with Johnson, guarding the door to his office, giving orders to fellow NRA workers. She was becoming a power in NRA.

Johnson, who did not want to be bothered with details, appreciated her efforts and was soon telling friends that "every man should have a 'Robbie.'"[57]

Most of Johnson's other key subordinates were old friends from the military and business. They were men, he told reporters, who were as "loyal as brothers." They would not disgrace him or "have their pants taken off" in the rough-and-tumble of code making. John Hancock, a New York banker who had handled navy procurement during World War I, became assistant administrator for general policy. Hancock left at the end of the summer of 1933, but he "whipped and kept in shape" NRA's first organization; his successor was Alvin Brown. Dudley Cates, of the old Moline crowd, became assistant administrator for industrial policy but left in August 1933 after a policy dispute with Johnson. Bob Lea took his place. Alexander Sachs headed the research division, and Robert Straus became an administrative assistant. Johnson's deputy administrators included Kenneth M. Simpson, William L. Allen, Carl D. Howard, Nelson Slater, and Major General Clarence C. Williams, army chief of ordnance when Johnson was director of purchase and supply. The only major exception to this pattern of familiar appointments was Edward F. McGrady, assistant administrator for labor policy. Short, soft-spoken, and looking more Italian than Irish, McGrady was a veteran lobbyist for the American Federation of Labor. He was recommended to Johnson by William Green, president of the labor federation. According to Pat Johnston, his father and McGrady, each rough and tough in his own way, "cliqued as unique" and became "bosom friends." McGrady "literally loved" Johnson, while Johnson liked nothing more than to relax and exchange tall tales with him.[58]

Johnson delegated the recruitment of the NRA rank and file to Hancock and the administrative heads. Roosevelt's patronage people were anxious to staff the agency with political appointees; but Johnson steadfastly fought off their efforts to turn the NRA into a political dumping ground, insisting that those charged with dealing with a specific industry be experienced in that industry. Nevertheless, he was forced to accept many sheerly political appointees. Initially rather small, the NRA staff numbered only 400 in August 1933. But it grew rapidly afterward; and at its peak, in February 1935, it had a staff of 4,500 workers and a sprawling array of divisions, councils, committees, and boards.

At the time when he was organizing NRA, Johnson made a crucial policy decision that seriously weakened his position in code making and enforcement. Johnson had insisted on the tough sanctions in the form of federal licensing power that had been written into NIRA. But on May 20, three days after the bill was sent to Congress, Alexander Sachs undermined Johnson's confidence in the use of legal compulsion as a big stick. The economist had reviewed the bill and concluded that the United States Supreme Court would very probably declare the act unconstitutional on the grounds that it ignored the distinction between intra- and interstate commerce and that it represented too great a delegation of power by the Congress to the executive branch.[59] From a purely intellectual point of view, Sachs's argument did not impress Johnson, who considered the distinction between intra- and interstate commerce "obsolete" (in the long run, he was upheld in this opinion). He also believed, even if Sachs's argument had merit, that the need for action overrode the need to boggle at constitutional questions that might not be settled for years.[60]

Despite his disdain for the constitutional question, Johnson could not brush aside Sachs's warning. An influential group of businessmen already planned to seek an early court ruling if NRA did not turn out to their liking. This prospect convinced Johnson to bypass the constitutional issues by avoiding any "semblance of czarism." NRA would not be an agency of direction; he would make it a forum for bargaining. Johnson would not invoke the licensing powers he had written into the law.

IN THE afternoon of June 16, Roosevelt convened his cabinet to brief it on the industrial recovery program. Near the end of the meeting Johnson was called into the room to hear Roosevelt announce that he was about to sign NIRA and officially appoint Johnson as administrator. Almost as an aside, the president added that Harold Ickes would administer Title II. Roosevelt, apparently oblivious, rode out the storm of Johnson's emotions (Perkins recalled his face turning deep red, then purple) and adjourned the meeting in good cheer. Johnson remained seated in his chair muttering "I don't know why" as the others left the room.

In part, Johnson's consternation was the result of the unexpectedness of Roosevelt's decision. In the month since Roosevelt had informed him that he was to administer NIRA, he had expected to be in charge of both titles. Now, in important company and without warning, Title II had been snatched away. Roosevelt's behavior struck Johnson as a humiliating display of lack of confidence. Even more important, Johnson believed Roosevelt's action doomed the recovery program. Unlike Roosevelt, who saw the linking of industrial self-government and public works in NIRA as merely coincidental, Johnson considered their linkage mandatory. Through perfectly timed public works spending, he would ensure that the public could afford the higher prices that codification would bring. Without control over Title II, he had lost this necessary "engine of expansion." Equally damaging, the separation of Titles I and II removed his last stick for compelling cooperation with the recovery program. Since he had already ruled out invoking the licensing powers in NIRA, the only major weapons left to him were moral suasion and public pressure; and these, the war experience had showed, were of limited value in government's dealings with business.

Perkins, realizing that Roosevelt's separation of Titles I and II had left Johnson "just about wild," informed the president that "Hugh is about crazy." He, in turn, asked her to "get him over it" and not let "him talk to the press." She escorted Johnson out of the White House through a seldom-used exit and, with Robert Straus, took him on a calming automobile ride to the airport, where Johnson was to board an airplane for Chicago to deliver a speech that night before a convention of coal executives. During most of the ride Johnson was beside himself. He swore repeatedly as he struggled with his emotions, and "then he would go into a great deep melancholy, saying 'The President has disgraced me. I can't do anything. If he doesn't believe in me, why doesn't he get somebody else?'" Several times he told Perkins, "I've got to get out. I can't stay." Perkins soothingly replied that Roosevelt "does believe in you. He thinks you're a genius. He thinks you've got lots of qualities. You've got the drive and leadership for the great new enterprise that has never been done before. Public works is nothing." She raised the possibility that he might work with Ickes to coordinate Titles I and II, and she reminded him "that there was an immense social service to be performed anyway." Her charm and arguments persuaded the distraught Johnson to stay, although he knew he had no business associating himself with a program whose future success he now severely doubted.[61]

CHAPTER 7

CODIFYING INDUSTRY

Hugh Johnson's first task as NRA administrator was the codification of American industry. According to the ideology of industrial self-government, each industry had group interests that transcended those of individual members. Among these was the elimination of predatory practices that were destructive to the industry and to the nation as a whole. Recognizing their group interests, industry representatives would draft a code of fair competition prohibiting the undesirable practices. This action would increase stability, employment, and investor protection in the industry and encourage general economic progress and social peace. Since business leaders were thought to know the most about economic processes and were expected to be broad-minded in considering the welfare of their workers and the well-being of society, they would be given a virtual free hand in codifying an industry and administering its code. Labor and consumer participation was anticipated, though; these views were to be heard. Government was assigned a supervisory role, which, for the most part, would be limited to advising and supporting business efforts to codify and punishing violations.

Johnson, who was charged with translating this promise of industrial harmony and enlightenment into reality, found it a difficult assignment. For one thing, Johnson had to chart a tortuous path through a bewildering maze of competing business pressures. Despite the political success of the proponents of industrial self-government, businessmen were not of one mind on its desirability or goals. The less prosperous industries generally favored codification in the belief that it would restore profitability. The more prosperous ones, however, were less interested in codification than in putting brakes on it, so that it would not lead to unwanted government interference. Some businessmen were willing to make sacrifices for the common good; others were interested only in their own profits. Some shrank from any program that allowed the majority within an industry to dictate business and labor norms of behavior. Inter-industry conflicts between new and declining industries and intra-industry conflicts between large and small firms, manufacturers and distributors, regions or sections, further complicated matters. These divisions portended lengthy code negotiations with industries and industry subgroups trying to shape the codes to their advantage. The outcome would inevitably reflect their relative bargaining strength.[1]

A second difficulty facing Johnson was the need to ensure that the interests of labor and the general public were not neglected as businessmen rushed to raise prices and profits. The ideology of industrial self-government granted businessmen the dominant voice, and the circumstances of code making enhanced their position. In his public pronouncements, Roosevelt had stated that he wanted the wages and hours provisions emphasized during codification. This meant that business was to make concessions at the beginning and set the stage for it to ask for concessions in return. In this respect, it had the upper hand. Businessmen knew what they wanted and, through their trade association activities in the 1920s, had experience in drafting industry-wide agreements dealing with prices and production. Moreover, they controlled most of the information about industrial operations on which code-making and enforcement would be based. Perhaps most important, many NRA officials were sympathetic to business aspirations and had little knowledge about regulating or planning "with 'the public interest' and some conception of the whole economy in mind." Labor and consumers were at a clear disadvantage. In most industries, trade unions, if they existed at all, were a minor element; consumers, too, were largely unorganized.[2]

Johnson was in a weak position to deal with the competing business pressures, and he was no better empowered to protect labor and the public interest. He knew the fragmented character of the industrial sector and the hunger of businessmen for profits; for these reasons, he had included coercion in his version of industrial self-government. Through federal licensing and the ability to grant or withhold public works contracts, he would bring everyone to the code-making table, resolve conflicts, and keep businessmen from turning code making into an orgy of profit taking. However, his own decision to shelve federal licensing and Roosevelt's decision to deny him control of public works spending greatly reduced his ability to coerce. He could threaten business with the imposition of a code. But this was a last resort, for it ran the risk of alienating businessmen and "would have required the full force of the Federal power, judicial, military, and executive to do it."[3] Johnson concluded that he had to rely on the voluntary cooperation of business.

Notwithstanding his concern about profit taking, Johnson was convinced that code making include the opportunity for business to increase its profits. He was aware that most businessmen had endured a long drought in profits, and he understood their desire to improve their balance sheets. Even more fundamentally, he believed that business, as the source of jobs, was the key to recovery. The recovery program would fail without the rehiring of large numbers of workers. Corporate executives could not rehire without confidence, and Johnson realized there was little of that in 1933. Confidence depended on the expectation of profits, and Johnson was prepared to hold out the prospect of reasonable profits if business would consent to higher wages and shorter work weeks. Working with business, not fighting it, would launch the spiral of recovery.

Johnson's determination to complete code making in sixty days was also both a problem and a necessity. The collective bargaining provision of NIRA, in particular, contained the potential for considerable discord, and he feared that protracted negotiations over it would lead to a long period of unrest and labor disputes and a delay in the codification and recovery of industry. In the process, vital support for the recovery program, both among the business community and the public, would be lost. So that the full benefits of higher wages and shorter hours could be reaped, quick industrial codification was necessary. If some mistakes were committed, they could be corrected later.

Johnson's reliance on the voluntary cooperation of business, his belief in business as the key to recovery, and his drive for the quick codification of industry were his theoretical foundations for the recovery effort. In the kind of difference so often observed in applications of theory, though, the chief result of Johnson's plans was only to mollify business leaders.

EVEN before Congress approved NIRA, Hugh Johnson decided to concentrate on codifying the nation's ten largest industries. Textiles, coal, petroleum, iron and steel, automobiles, lumber, garments, wholesale trade, retail trade, and construction comprised the bulk of employment. After surveying each industry, Johnson concluded that he should focus on cotton textiles, steel, petroleum, automobiles, lumber, and coal. These were either strong NIRA supporters or sufficiently organized for speedy codification. The others were "too complex for immediate action."[4]

The cotton textile code was the first Johnson considered. Responding to his call for industries to organize code-drafting committees, cotton textile industry representatives began work on a code at the Mayflower Hotel in Washington on May 24, 1933. Excess output, price-cutters, and low profits had pushed the industry to a catastrophic state, and its leaders looked to industry-wide agreements to bring order to production. With little debate they lined up behind the Cotton Textile Institute's 40-40 plan. Under this trade association plan, production would be limited by having mill hands work no more than forty hours a week and by operating machines no more than eighty hours—two forty-hour shifts—a week. The wage question, however, proved troublesome. The code-drafting committee favored a minimum wage in the South of $8 or $9 a week and in the North, $9 or $10. At the time wages in the industry were as low as $5 a week for fifty to fifty-five hours of work. In heated meetings on May 24 and 25 Johnson told the committee that an $8 minimum wage was "ridiculously low" and would do nothing to raise the standard of living of workers. He suggested the minimum wage should be as high as $15 a week; $12 a week might be acceptable, although even that was low. Johnson added that the forty-hour week might not spread the work around enough and that the committee should think in terms of a thirty- or thirty-two-hour week.

Johnson next met with the committee on June 1. Backed up by an impressive array of statistics, the members took the offensive to tell Johnson that the 40-40 plan would stabilize production and employment at 1929 levels and that a minimum wage of $10 and $11 a week was as high as the industry could afford. For the next week, NRA officials and industry representatives haggled over the proposed code, completing it by June 16. Its provisions included minimum wages of $10 per week in the South and $11 in the North; a forty-hour week for workers; Section 7a of NIRA, which guaranteed workers the right to organize and bargain collectively; the 40-40 plan; and control of new firms entering into the industry and expansion of existing plants.[5]

Although the minimum wages were not as high as he desired, the draft code generally pleased Johnson. Wages were, nevertheless, to be raised substantially, and industry representatives had evidenced a cooperative attitude in working with government to meet the goals of NIRA. Initially, he had also been concerned about the 40-40 plan and had expressed the hope that the committee would eliminate destructive competition without limits on production. But he was most anxious to raise wages, and his staff had convinced him that he had to accept some limits on production if the industry was going to afford higher wages. In addition, not to accept limits on production defied the logic behind NIRA. The law provided for the relaxation of antitrust laws, and there was little reason to relax them if the codes did not include provisions such as 40-40.[6] By bowing to industry's designs, basically a cartel, however, Johnson took a self-defeating step. As Bernard Bellush has written, "At one of the most critical moments in the nation's history, when a great need was to increase the purchasing power of the consumer through immediate expansion in production, jobs, and income, the NRA established a restrictionist policy."[7]

The public hearing on the cotton textile code began on June 27 in the auditorium of the Commerce Department building, with Johnson himself presiding. The high point came on the second day. For years, reform groups had been working to eliminate child labor in the Southern mills; and during the early weeks of June 1933, they had flooded Washington with letters calling upon the industry to include a provision in the code abolishing it. George Sloan, head of the Cotton Textile Institute, had argued that child labor would be effectively eliminated by the minimum wage requirement; manufacturers would not be willing to pay this wage to children. Johnson, though, suggested that the reformers' demand should be met, pointing out that in an industry suffering from overcapacity, getting rid of child labor was a relatively painless gesture and was good public relations. Following this prodding, the code-drafting committee met during the night of June 27 and decided to recommend that the code prohibit the employment of minors under the age of sixteen. The recommendation was announced at the hearing on June 28, and it stunned the audience. As Johnson later wrote: "There was a moment's silence in that over-crowded audience, and then a tremendous burst of applause. The Textile Code had done in a few minutes what neither law nor constitutional amendment had been able to do in forty years."[8] In his view it was one of NRA's finest hours.

The abolition of child labor took much of the attention away from labor's criticism of the code. Labor spokesmen William Green, president of the American Federation of Labor; Senator Black; and Thomas McMahon of the United Textile Workers all attacked the forty-hour provision. They argued that it was too long a week and would not spread the available work around enough. But Johnson was not moved. McMahon had participated in a minor way in the code-drafting process and had offered no objections to the forty-hour week. Apparently, his turnabout was sparked by his own union's refusal to support the provision he had previously accepted.[9] Since those opposed to the forty-hour week were unable to present any statistical evidence controverting the industry's position that the forty-hour week would bring employment up to the 1929 level, Johnson gave them little heed.

Labor critics had more success in attacking the minimum-wage provision. They blasted the $10–$11 minimum wage as a "bare subsistence wage" that would provide workers with little more than "an animal existence." These charges made a deep impression upon Johnson, who had never been happy with the penurious minimum wage in the code. Furthermore, members of the Special Industrial Recovery Board had suggested that acceptance of the low minimum wage in the first code "may possibly have the result of creating discouragement with the operations of the Act and dampen the ardor of industry, since obviously such low wages cannot contribute much to [the] increase of purchasing power."[10] Concerned that the minimum wage in the code might undercut recovery and cause Roosevelt to reject the code, Johnson warned the code-drafting committee that it should reconsider the minimum wage or risk seeing its work go for naught. That little encouragement was enough. As Johnson had judged, the industry could afford more, and the committee quickly concluded that a higher minimum wage was a small price to pay to ensure acceptance of the 40-40 plan. On June 29 it announced that the minimum wage would be raised $2, from $10 and $11 to $12 and $13. This was more in line with Johnson's original thinking and "certainly as much" as he "had ever thought he could get."[11]

Johnson also had to deal with the complaint of Russell E. Watson of Johnson and Johnson, a major producer of cotton surgical supplies and bandages, that the machine-hour limitation penalized the efficient producer. Johnson and Johnson's plants were set up to run on a twenty-four-hour basis, Watson testified, and the machine-hour limitation served only to hurt it, and ultimately the consumer, by giving more work to inefficient plants. Johnson struck back at Watson's complaint with a barrage of questions designed to show that Watson had "presented a strong self-serving case but not a position that is . . . in accordance with the objective of the Recovery Act." Watson, in effect, had argued for the continuation of unrestricted competition, which, in the short run, offered no solution to the unemployment problem. Johnson intended to stabilize production and spread the existing work among a large number of individuals.[12]

Except for the child-labor provision and the increase in the minimum wage, the only important measure to be added to the code during the hearing was a provision transforming the code-drafting representatives of the Cotton Textile Institute into a cotton textile industry committee, the code authority that would officially administer the code. Johnson readily endorsed this provision, even though it effectively turned the policing of the industry over to the industry itself. In his opinion, the code-drafting committee had performed admirably, and the duties outlined for the code authority were in harmony with the notion of self-regulation that was at the heart of his concept of industrial organization.

On June 30, the final day of the hearing, Johnson announced that he was satisfied with the code and intended to present it to the president for final approval. "You men of the textile industry have done a very remarkable thing," he said.

Never in economic history have labor, industry, government and consumers' representatives sat together in the presence of the public to work out by mutual agreement a 'law merchant' for an entire industry. . . . The textile industry is to be congratulated on its courage and spirit in being first to assume this patriotic duty and on the generosity of its proposals.[13]

His enthusiastic sentiments were echoed by others. Writing to Johnson on July 6, 1933, Felix Frankfurter praised the code as a "notable achievement" and commented that "to go as far as you have gone in constitutionalizing that cut-throat, anarchic industry is a most auspicious beginning."[14]

All was not yet smooth for the code. On July 9 Roosevelt approved it but demanded the addition of thirteen amendments suggested by the Special Industrial Recovery Board because of its concern over the restrictive character of the 40-40 plan and its desire to give the government a greater voice in industrial self-government. The most important amendment limited presidential approval to a four-month period, after which the code would be subject to renewal or modification. Johnson and the code-drafting committee were aghast. They had been operating on the assumption that NRA was a venture in business-government partnership. Now the government was amending the code without negotiations.

Johnson, caught offguard by the amendments, saw the recovery board's action as one that undermined his position and made him look bad in the industry's eyes. He immediately apologized to the code-drafting committee and told the members he would support any understanding they worked out with his deputies. Within a few days the NRA people and the committee arrived at an agreement. They completely dropped the four-month trial period; they altered five other amendments and accepted seven without change. On July 15 the committee presented the amended code to Johnson, who accepted it without objection. As Louis Galambos, the most important student of the cotton textile code, writes: "In a sense Johnson had undercut the President's authority in order to preserve the partnership concept."[15]

On a July 16 Potomac cruise on the presidential yacht Johnson endeavored to sell the amended code to Roosevelt. For Johnson this day would be a test of his ability to serve as an effective broker between industry and the president; for the industry, it could mean that all its hopes of stabilizing itself on its own terms might be dashed if Roosevelt insisted on the four-month trial period. Roosevelt and Johnson took their time discussing the code; but in actuality neither Johnson nor the industry had much to fear. For political reasons, Roosevelt in 1933 talked in terms of public goals and made gestures toward many clients. However, his commitment to business was greater than his commitment to any other of his constituencies. In accepting the Special Industrial Recovery Board's amendments, he had made a half-hearted concession to those members who were concerned that Johnson had moved too far into business's corner. When Johnson made it clear that the four-month trial period was unacceptable to the industry and would undermine the industry's confidence in the administration, Roosevelt readily agreed to go along with the industry-amended code.

The public greeted Roosevelt's approval of the cotton textile code with great excitement, for it seemed to take the nation a giant step toward a social and economic millennium. Leaders of the cotton textile industry, under Johnson's watchful eye, had agreed to collective bargaining, the abolition of child labor, greatly reduced maximum hours, and significantly increased minimum wages. In reality, however, the code established ominous precedents. Determined to secure codes without any semblance of czarism, Johnson had conceded to the industry almost everything it wanted and then assisted it in beating back the recovery board's belated effort to strengthen the government's role in the NRA-inspired business-government partnership. He had simply shoved labor aside; for in 1933 organized labor had little strength in textiles and Johnson had no intention of permitting it to slow the pace of codification. As for consumers, he had all but ignored them.

COMPARED to the problems that developed in codifying some of the other industries, the job with cotton textiles was easy. Work on the lumber code began in late May 1933, and a preliminary draft was approved by industry representatives in June. Complications materialized when foresters and conservationists urged that acceptance of the industry's proposals for controlling prices and production be linked to a requirement for regulating cutting practices on private timberlands. Dickering between the industry and NRA officials continued through much of the summer; not until mid-August did they arrive at an accommodation on cutting practices.[16] Hugh Johnson involved himself only slightly with the lumber code. He knew little about the industry and was devoting much of his attention to the codes for the vital steel, petroleum, and automobile industries. Major problems stalled the codification of these industries, and in each case Johnson personally intervened and, with great impatience, pushed them through to conclusion.

Like cotton textiles, the steel industry looked to cooperative action to solve its problems. Since the early months of the depression, industry leaders had been active in the movement to relax antitrust laws. Johnson therefore expected the steel industry to submit a code almost as soon as the cotton textile industry, and he engaged in several preliminary discussions with industry representatives before the end of May 1933.[17] Talks bogged down, though, and it was six weeks before the industry trade association, the American Iron and Steel Institute, submitted a workable code. Production and capacity controls, pricing policies, and wages and hours provisions caused disagreements within the industry and with NRA officials. The labor provision was an even greater problem. The champion of the open-shop movement in the United States, the steel industry was determined to include an open-shop clause in its code despite the fact that such a statement ran counter to the spirit of Section 7a. Adopted by United States Steel in 1909, the open-shop principle was the basis of employment in the industry and had been upheld for more than two decades, bitter strikes notwithstanding, through a combination of managerial repression and welfare programs. By keeping the workers unorganized, management had been able to keep a firm grip on working conditions, paying little more than subsistence wages to its many unskilled workers.[18]

Although Johnson made it clear that he would strike from the code any clause that qualified the law, the Iron and Steel Institute submitted a draft code on July 6 containing an open-shop clause. NRA officials promptly rejected it. A second draft, also containing an open-shop clause, was submitted on July 12 and was also rejected. Finally, a third draft, somewhat more in line with NRA thinking, was submitted on July 15 and became the basis for the final code.

Getting to a workable draft had required unusual action by Johnson. Because of recent and substantial pre-code upturns in steel production, he was under intense pressure to get the steel code. Prices were rising rapidly, and calls abounded for a steel code to bring about a corresponding rise in wages and employment. Despite his rejection of the industry's first two draft codes, Johnson knew that he could not wait much longer for steel to submit a workable draft. Therefore, he resorted to a policy of hectoring and appeasing steel leaders. At Johnson's instigation, Roosevelt met on July 11 with Myron C. Taylor of U.S. Steel and threatened him with the imposition of a thirty-five-hour week and a $14 minimum weekly wage. At the same time, Johnson contacted industry leaders and assured them that he was willing to cooperate. Through economist Leo Wolman, a member of the Labor Advisory Board of NRA, he also let them know that he now had no objection to the inclusion of the open-shop clause in the draft code but that it would have to be cut out during the public hearing. Johnson's approach brought the industry into line, but it gave steel the chance to score a major victory at the public hearing.

The public hearing was held on July 31. After Johnson opened the hearing by praising the industry for its spirit of cooperation, Robert P. Lamont, president of the Iron and Steel Institute, presented the code. As soon as he finished reading the open-shop clause, Johnson immediately interrupted him and stated "that that matter is inappropriate in that particular section of this Code." Following a brief recess, Lamont agreed to the removal of the clause. The audience applauded heartily; however, the industry's willingness to strike the clause did not mean that it was retreating from the open shop. Before the recess Lamont had insisted that "the omission of this section does not imply any change in the attitude of the industry."

Johnson appeared to win in this affair; he had managed to get the steel industry to submit a code without the permanent inclusion of an open-shop clause. But it was a meaningless triumph; for, in effect, the affair gave industry leaders a "two-fold victory." On the one hand, they "served notice" on everyone that they intended to maintain their "historic labor position." On the other hand, they removed from the hearing labor's "chief point of attack on the code."[19]

The wage and hour provisions were the most troublesome issues left. Johnson favored a higher minimum wage and a lower maximum work week than the industry was prepared to offer. On August 15 he convened a meeting of industry leaders and NRA officials in the office of Frances Perkins to wrap up the code. But twelve hours of tough negotiations to get the industry to grant higher wages brought no resolution.

The steel industry's obstinate stance reminded Johnson of the World War I mobilization when the industry, particularly in 1917, had feuded with the navy and the WIB over their efforts to restrain steel prices in favor of patriotism and the national interest. An unyielding, unenlightened self-interest had seemed to dominate the industry's thinking. With considerable vehemence the industry had argued, in one aspect of the wartime price controversy, that it was entitled to charge what it could command from the public and the Allies. Only President Wilson's threat to nationalize mills brought the industry around to the government's position that the maintenance of the nation's economic health required a set price for all customers.[20] Now the industry argued, with similar vehemence, that it could not afford higher wages even though Roosevelt had identified them as a major priority of the recovery program. At one point an exasperated Johnson, hearing steel barons claim the imminent bankruptcy of the industry if it had to pay higher wages, shouted to Lamont and his associates that "you guys have been handing me that guff about long enough." He told reporters that the steel men were like "a den of lions."

In some despair, Johnson appointed a commission from the assembled group to study the wage and hour problems. He kept it in session until the night of August 17; still, there was no agreement. Further conferences were held with no breakthrough. Then, at one o'clock in the morning of August 19, Johnson emerged from a conference and, waving the code in his hand, announced that an agreement had been reached.[21]

The turning point apparently came after Johnson suggested to Roosevelt that Charles W. Schwab of Bethlehem Steel and Myron Taylor be summoned to the White House for some presidential persuasion. They met with the president on August 16. Schwab said that the government's proposed wages were too high and that he could not accept the code because of his obligations to his stockholders. Roosevelt replied by asking whether he had been looking out for his stockholders by paying a million-dollar bonus to Bethlehem Steel president Eugene Grace while his miners lived in coke ovens. Schwab and Taylor left the White House visibly shaken, and Roosevelt told a visitor afterward that "I scared them the way they never have been frightened before and I told Schwab he better not pay any more million dollar bonuses."[22]

The code that Roosevelt signed on August 21 was a compromise. The complex wage and hour provisions were expected to raise wages to an average in excess of forty-five cents an hour, and as soon as production in the mills reached 60 percent of capacity then the maximum workday would be eight hours. This in an industry which had argued only the week before that it could not afford more than a thirty-five-cent hourly wage and which for years had required its employees to work ten or twelve hours a day, often seven days a week. In return for these concessions, the industry gained most of what it really desired. All manner of fair trade practice had been written into law, and production and capacity controls were now permitted if they became necessary. The industry could also combine to set prices and to divide the market.[23] Johnson best summarized the struggle to codify steel when he told the Special Industrial Recovery Board that he did not regard the code as "altogether satisfactory" because of the considerable leeway it gave the industry in controlling prices and in "cutting out chiseling" (violating the code) in regard to wages, hours, and prices; but "the main thing is we got them under a code."[24]

The petroleum code provided another tough problem. Conditions in this industry were chaotic. Technological advances, the discovery of enormous pools, the breakdown of state proration regulations, and ruinous competition had brought about an oil glut that depressed prices and profits. In the spring of 1933 the Marland-Capper bill was introduced in Congress; its purpose was to stabilize the oil industry by giving the federal government sweeping powers to establish the amount of oil to be produced, imported, or withdrawn from storage and to fix both minimum and maximum prices.

The industry was divided on the question of federal regulation. Many independent oil producers generally favored the Marland-Capper bill in the belief that federal regulation was the only remedy to the chaos in the industry. But the major companies opposed it, preferring to rely on the continuation of state production controls, combined with a federal ban on the shipment of oil produced in violation of state regulations ("hot oil"). Through the states, they could probably keep much of the control in their own hands rather than give it to a federal government that might transform the industry into a public utility. Finally, many small refiners in the Southwest and southern California and the well owners in the flush fields of East Texas also opposed the bill. Organized into the Association Opposed to Monopoly, they argued that monopoly control, not overproduction, caused the industry's problems. Calling for strict enforcement of the antitrust laws, they spoke out against the bill on the grounds that federal regulation might be "exercised for the benefit of the big companies in the industry." Roosevelt, meanwhile, was reluctant to throw the administration's weight behind the bill for fear that it would precipitate a major fight in Congress that would delay the passage of NIRA. As a result of all this, Congress failed to approve the Marland-Capper bill, although it did amend the NIRA to give the president authority to ban interstate shipment of hot oil.[25]

Negotiations for the oil code began in Chicago in mid-June 1933 and were essentially a continuation of the debate over the Marland-Capper bill. The major oil companies, aware that a unified front would lessen the chances of the administration imposing undue federal controls, relaxed their opposition to federal regulation by agreeing to federal production controls. But federal price controls were the snag, and the industry failed to reach agreement on this issue. Preferring security over autonomy, Wirt Franklin of the Independent Petroleum Association and several other major industry heads argued for price-fixing as the only way to raise prices. Most major companies feared, however, that in the long run, price controls would diminish profits. They countered that the limiting of production would naturally force prices to an acceptable level, obviating any need for federal monitoring. In effect, the price-fixing issue became the battleground on which the independents and the major companies struggled for control of the industry.[26] The conference majority favored price fixing and were able to include a provision for it in the proposed code. The battle was not over, though, for the board of directors of the American Petroleum Institute, which reflected the thinking of the major companies and some larger independent oil associations, voted to approve the code with the provision that any member was free to oppose price fixing at the upcoming hearing. Following the lead of the API board, Gulf Oil, Dutch Shell, Standard Oil of Indiana, Standard Oil of New Jersey, and other major companies endorsed the code with reservations opposing the price-fixing provision.

The rifts in the industry were apparent at the public hearing, which was held during the third week of July. The independents and the major companies continued their fight over price fixing, while the Association Opposed to Monopoly criticized price fixing and production controls and renewed its call for enforcement of the antitrust laws. Johnson tried to resolve the differences by appointing special committees to work out compromises on price fixing, production, and other divisive issues. These efforts narrowed the differences; otherwise, nothing significant was accomplished.[27] Johnson warned the factions that he would have to write the codes himself unless they could quickly work out a compromise, but even his warning did not break the logjam. After three days, the hearing ended with the fate of the code uncertain.[28]

Since the industry seemed "hopelessly divided," Johnson decided to push it toward a settlement by drafting a tentative code himself. His goal was to reconcile the most important elements in the oil industry, since no workable code could be developed without their support. And if this basic industry were not included in the recovery program, the prestige of NRA would suffer.

For all practical purposes, Johnson's code ignored the recommendations of the Association Opposed to Monopoly. Determined to gain the support of the major companies and the independents, he called for federal control of production. When one small refiner argued that production quotas would be his downfall, Johnson frankly admitted that someone had to be "squeezed" if production was going to be reduced. In his opinion, any refinery that was harmed by production controls was obviously inefficient and would hardly be missed. Johnson's only concession to the small refiners was to include a provision giving any refiner who believed the NRA was treating him unfairly the right to appeal to a local board comprised of representatives of other refiners in the area. On the issue of price fixing, Johnson sided with the major companies and opposed price fixing in any form. His family had been involved in the oil business in Oklahoma for years, and he had well-developed ideas about the undesirability of price fixing. He later wrote that "if they would control production, price would take care of itself, and we would then need a maximum price to protect the public rather than a minimum price to protect the companies."[29]

Johnson convened a meeting of all interested parties on July 31 and presented his code. He sternly told them "that was it"; they had twenty-four hours to register protests, but "essentially, that was it."[30] This was the closest Johnson ever came to cracking down on an industry. As soon as he had completed his brief speech, he adjourned the meeting, only to see the oil men rushing him and the pile of mimeographed papers he had brought. Johnson reacted by gruffly commanding them to "sit down. Sit down or I'll stop it immediately." Buffaloed, the oil men retreated to their chairs; and "Johnson, leaving the distribution to flunkies, put on his hat and strode out."[31] The matter was not settled, though, for the Independent Petroleum Association refused to accept Johnson's code until it included a provision for price fixing.

At this point, Johnson encountered a new problem. In the spring of 1933 Secretary Ickes, a strong supporter of the Marland-Capper bill, had been at the center of the debate over federal oil policy. Following the passage of NIRA, however, he had sat on the sidelines while Johnson handled the administration's negotiating for a code. But when Johnson had trouble bringing the divergent interests together, Ickes reinjected himself into the oil picture and began work on his own version of a code. Unlike Johnson, he favored price fixing and quickly enlisted the backing of Wirt Franklin and several other important oil men.

Johnson had no intention of seeing his code supplanted. During the first weeks of August he modified it to meet the objections of those who wanted price fixing. Retreating from his earlier position, he proposed a watered-down version of price fixing. A ratio of 18.5 to 1 between gasoline and crude petroleum prices would be established and, equally important, the president would be given discretionary power to fix the minimum wholesale price for gasoline.

These revisions satisfied no one. Price-fixing opponents thought it was unwise to give the president the opportunity to tamper with prices. But price-fixing proponents were also disappointed; if gasoline prices fell, so would crude prices, thereby defeating one of the major goals of the code—to raise profits for well owners. The Association Opposed to Monopoly, meanwhile, totally rejected Johnson's revisions, arguing that the 18.5 to 1 ratio was unfair to small refiners.

On August 17 Johnson went to the White House to present his oil code to Roosevelt. Later that same day, Ickes and his aides made a similar trip and presented Roosevelt with their draft. Not wanting to fail so late in the code-making prosess, Johnson met with industry leaders and secured their backing for his version. They recognized that Johnson's code was the only way to bridge the gap dividing the industry and feared that Roosevelt would impose a code if they failed to reach an agreement. Ickes too recognized that Johnson's code was the only one acceptable to most of the dominant elements in the industry; he grudgingly accepted it with some minor alterations.

Johnson resubmitted his code to Roosevelt on the night of August 19. Roosevelt approved its provisions, with one major exception. Johnson's code called for the creation of a federal agency to determine the allowable production for each state. This meant that ultimate power over domestic production would rest with Washington rather than Austin, Oklahoma City, and the other oil centers. The powerful Texas Railroad Commission, however, not wanting control of Texas's greatest industry to slip from its hands, successfully lobbied Roosevelt to change Johnson's code so that the proposed federal agency would only "recommend" production quotas to the states.

The final code was "an hermaphroditic compromise" between the major companies, the Independent Petroleum Association, and the Texas Railroad Commission. They were the dominant elements in the industry, and Johnson and Roosevelt had no intention of alienating them. In response to the demand of the independent producers for greater federal regulation, the code included provisions for production quotas and price fixing. But in response to the wishes of the major companies and Texas officials the provisions were not so strong as to undermine their traditional power. The code contained none of the antitrust reforms that the small refiners and others in the Association Opposed to Monopoly demanded, and, not surprisingly, their representatives refused to sign it.[32]

Ten days after approving the oil code Roosevelt named Ickes to administer it, thereby removing the code from the jurisdiction of NRA. Johnson felt slighted by Roosevelt's decision, although he tried to put the best public face on it by saying that the industry was a "disorganized mob" and that he was more than happy to turn it over to someone else. There was some truth in this statement. Two months earlier Johnson had told Ickes, possibly in an effort to curry his goodwill and provide for a smooth relationship in regard to public works, that he

NRA Chief Happy as Oil Code Appears Certain. The Bettmann Archive, Inc.

could have the administration of the oil code "with my blessing."[33] Washington pundits saw Ickes's appointment as part of a struggle between Johnson and Ickes for power within the Roosevelt administration and a victory for Ickes. But it was something less. By naming Ickes as petroleum administrator, Roosevelt was simply trying to continue the cooperation that had existed between the industry and the Interior Department for some years.[34]

Unlike the other industries that Johnson was working to codify, the automobile industry evidenced little interest in codification. It did not suffer from overproduction or destructive price cutting, and auto manufacturers had already standardized their trade practices through the auspices of the National Automobile Chamber of Commerce. They did not want to go further for fear of opening a Pandora's box, especially in regard to their relationship with dealers and suppliers. They also feared that Section 7a would compel them to bargain with unions, which they considered anathema. In addition, there was a very real prospect that Henry Ford, the foremost individualist in the industry, would gain a competitive advantage if they agreed to a code and he did not. To a great degree, then, NRA needed the automobile industry more than the industry needed NRA.

Despite its lack of interest in NRA, the auto industry could not afford to stand aloof from codification. In his speeches, Johnson was equating support of NIRA with patriotism, and the public might interpret its failure to cooperate as treason. Even more important, it ran the risk of an unsatisfactory code imposed by Roosevelt if it failed to submit one. Therefore, on June 22, 1933, the auto chamber of commerce began work on a code, which went through eight drafts. Section 7a was the most crucial issue. Not wanting to change the prevailing character of labor relations in the industry, the auto manufacturers added a provision interpreting Section 7a to permit the open shop:

The employers in the automobile industry propose to continue the open shop policy heretofore followed and under which unusually satisfactory and harmonious relations with employees have been maintained. The selection, retention and advancement of employees will be on the basis of individual merit without regard to their affiliation or non-affiliation with any labor or other organization.

Before submitting the code to Johnson, however, they wanted unequivocal assurances from him on two crucial matters—what would happen to Ford if he refused to agree to the code and the acceptability of its labor provisions.[35]

Recognizing that Ford could be a stumbling block, Johnson had early resorted to personal diplomacy to gain his cooperation. As he later wrote, on June 24 he "took a fast army airplane, arrived in Dearborn before dark, spent the evening with Mr. Ford, left early the next morning and was in my office before it opened."[36] Everything about the meeting was cordial, and Johnson came away with the impression that Ford "would play ball" with the recovery program "to the limit and even beyond." As it developed, Johnson was mistaken. After permitting his representatives to sit in on the early stages of the code drafting, Ford had second thoughts and refused to have anything to do with NRA on the grounds that Section 7a and the possibility of industry-wide price and production controls could place him "under the orders" of others.

In response to a telephone message from auto leaders that they had doubts about codification, Johnson flew to Detroit on July 27 "to straighten out the kinks." At a news conference after he arrived, a reporter asked whether it was "undignified" for him to come to Detroit at the industry's bidding. "Dignity hell," he snapped. "I'm here to button this thing up." There are "many misconceptions about the law and dignity has no place." His job, he told the reporter, was "to put 5–6 million men back to work by Labor Day," and he was not squeamish about doing whatever was necessary.[37]

Johnson held three meetings with auto chamber of commerce leaders on July 27 and 28. The most significant took place on July 28 in the

General Motors Building. Talking "in direct fashion" and frequently profane, he told them that he was "damn serious" about getting the industry codified. Beneath this tough-guy exterior, however, he was fully prepared to give the auto men whatever assurances they sought. From experience he knew that they could be intractable. During the war they had dragged their feet in converting to military production. They had been unmoved even by Baruch's threat to shut them down if they did not cooperate with the war effort. In the end the industry relented and agreed to enter the military market. But it did so on its own terms, and only after casting into doubt the efficacy of industrial self-government as a tool for mobilizing industry.[38]

Johnson did not want to go through a similar fight with the industry in 1933. All the large industries had to cooperate with the recovery program if it was going to succeed, and he could not afford prolonged negotiations with Detroit over the details of the auto code. Addressing himself first to the auto men's concern about Ford, Johnson said that if Ford failed to go along with NRA, he would not be permitted by NRA to upset the industry's code. The auto men, however, were most apprehensive about Section 7a. Seeking to assure them that they had nothing to fear, Johnson proclaimed that it was not the "function" of his office to promote organized labor. Employers would still be permitted to bargain individually with their men, although they could no longer refuse to bargain collectively with the chosen representatives of the workers. But even the latter prospect need not frighten them, he added, for "the fact that you bargain with the men doesn't mean that you have to agree." When the interpretive language in the code regarding Section 7a was read to him, Johnson unhesitatingly replied, "I am glad you put it just that way." He had it read a second time. Again he gave his approval, commenting simply, "100%."[39]

Johnson's hasty approval of the auto industry's interpretation of Section 7a became a major source of controversy. Recognizing the consequences of his remarks, Johnson later lamely downplayed the incident as "a slip as I suppose might be expected of anybody in such stress." Certainly, Johnson was under stress when he sanctioned the industry's interpretation of Section 7a. But he could hardly claim that his approval was "a slip." The wording of the interpretation was carefully read to him twice, and his other comments and actions during the meeting clearly indicated that "he was on the whole sympathetic with the industry's point of view." He told the auto men that when he was at Moline Plow, it had been customary to fire workers who carried a union card. And when Walter Chrysler, a close friend, replied that only recently his company had "fired a fellow who was going around agitating" in favor of a union and would continue to do so, Johnson conspicuously raised no objection or asked no questions.[40]

Satisfied by Johnson's assurances, the auto men agreed unanimously to submit their code for approval. Johnson left Detroit that same day, taking it to Washington himself. Before leaving, he jubilantly told reporters that he had got what he "came here for" and was not overly disturbed about Ford's refusal to agree to the code; he would eventually come around. Realizing, however, that the code was going to arouse the ire of labor and compromise his position in dealing with other industries, Johnson attempted to minimize his whole role in securing its submission. Asked by reporters what the code specifically provided, he jauntily remarked, "Hell, I don't know—haven't read it."[41]

Organized labor and its supporters heavily criticized the code in the prehearing discussions. The Labor Advisory Board of NRA, whose job it was to advise NRA administrators on labor matters, charged that the open-shop clause was blatantly not in keeping with the "spirit" of NRA. Johnson had refused to accept a similar clause in the steel code, and the Labor Advisory Board argued that the auto industry should not be treated differently. But Johnson turned a deaf ear. He had given his word to the auto men that the clause was acceptable, and he could not discern any compelling reason to change his mind. He had persuaded the American Iron and Steel Institute to remove the open-shop clause from the steel code because the industry had too much to gain from codification to risk a last-ditch battle to retain it. In contrast, the auto industry, as Johnson appreciated, had no overriding interest in the success of codification and was fully determined to wage war against NRA, if necessary, to keep its open-shop clause. Moreover, organized labor was impotent in the industry, and Johnson believed that it was foolhardy to endanger the whole recovery program by battling the auto men for the benefit of labor, especially since he was convinced that the auto men had treated workers more fairly than any other large group of industrialists. The only significant code alteration that he would countenance was Donald Richberg's suggestion that the phrase "may continue the open shop" be dropped; the words "may continue" appeared to sanction past labor practices that might now be in violation of the law, while the words "open shop" were too ambiguous.[42]

On August 24 representatives of the auto chamber of commerce visited Johnson and assailed him for running out on his "promise" regarding Section 7a; after long discussions Johnson and the auto men finally arrived at a compromise. Reference to the open shop would be dropped from the code; however, the industry retained the merit provision. Johnson had won his point on the open shop. But after the commitment he had made in Detroit he was "in no position" to insist that the auto chamber of commerce make any additional concessions.[43]

Three days later Roosevelt signed the code. In all probability Johnson had informed him that he had given his approval to a stronger affirmation of the industry's open-shop position than was contained in the final code and that the industry was unwilling to make further concessions. Fully aware of the industry's strong bargaining position and anxious to have the code, Roosevelt was as willing as Johnson to accept it without additional qualifications.[44]

Johnson's acceptance of the merit provision in the automobile code was a major defeat for organized labor. In spite of Section 7a it insured that labor relations in the open-shop auto industry "remained unchanged" and encouraged other industries to demand similar treatment.[45] Aware that widespread adoption of the merit provision would totally undermine NRA's standing with labor, Johnson attempted in early September 1933 to recoup the situation. At a press conference he agreed with labor critics that the provision had become a source of trouble and stated that the wisest course would be to omit any interpretive language in future codes. Critics of Johnson were not assuaged. But at least he could find some solace in comments on his press conference he received from Felix Frankfurter: "Your refusal of . . . [the] insertion [of the merit provision] in other codes is courageous and wise statesmanship."[46]

THE CODE for the bituminous coal industry required more work for Hugh Johnson than any other code—twice as much time "as all the rest of the work combined," he told the Special Industrial Recovery Board.[47] Talks with the industry began before Congress passed NIRA, and codification was not completed until the end of October 1933. Throughout the process Johnson was compelled to act as a broker and mediator among the operator groups. It was, he later proclaimed, NRA's "hardest fight."[48]

Following June 1933 meetings in which Johnson explained the purposes of NIRA to coal industry representatives, the National Coal Association produced a "model" code to guide the various producing districts in framing their own codes. Johnson, however, had little use for the model code. It lacked substantive provisions for hours, wages, and prices. Most importantly, it set forth no meaningful provision for the actual organization of the industry under one code. In his opinion, codification of this industry had to be accomplished under one code if it was to be successful; codification under more than one code, as in the model code, would only exacerbate the regional differences that had plagued the industry for decades. In an address to the association convention on June 16, Johnson urged the delegates to put aside regional differences and organize under a broad, meaningful code.[49] But the delegates ignored the plea and approved the model code by a large voice vote.

The action of the National Coal Association was a major defeat for Johnson. Instead of drafting a unified, industry-wide code, it in effect informed the operators in different regions that they should all produce their own. Everywhere operators formed trade associations to submit codes that would favor their locality, protect regional interests, and keep their labor out of the United Mine Workers. In all, more than thirty codes would eventually be submitted. Most followed the model code in the prohibition of unfair trade practices; most contained provisions designed to circumscribe Section 7a; and all were based on the assumption that government regulation of the industry was unacceptable.

While the operators were drafting codes to favor regional interests, the United Mine Workers was working for a single code. It had been hard hit by the depression and the wage slashing of Southern operators; and John L. Lewis, the union leader, believed that a national code—with one nationwide wage scale—was the best way to end the hated wage differential between North and South. With that in mind, he persuaded union operators to work with representatives of the United Mine Workers on a national code. More important, he stepped up union organizing drives. NRA's negotiations with other industries had already revealed to him unorganized labor's inability to extract significant concessions in codes. Proclaiming that NRA heralded "a New Deal for miners," Lewis and his aides increased union membership from 100,000 to 300,000 in the spring and summer of 1933 and aggressively sought to use this new strength to negotiate contracts with the operators. The traditional open-shop operators in the South and the captive mines (those owned by steel companies) fought the United Mine Workers with every weapon available. Union leaders were discharged, racial antagonisms between black and white miners exploited, company unions created, and the repressive police power of local government exercised. Miners fought back with strikes.

Johnson had been concerned with other matters since the dealings with the National Coal Association in June and did not reenter the coal fracas until the beginning of August. On July 31, Joseph Guffy, the Democratic political leader in Pennsylvania, telephoned Roosevelt from Pittsburgh that the serious trouble in the Pennsylvania coalfields might be brought to a quick end if Johnson issued "an appeal urging the restoration of peace in Pennsylvania" and asked the striking miners to go back to work pending the working out of a code.[50] Governor Gifford Pinchot of Pennsylvania also contacted Roosevelt and pressed for immediate presidential action. Since Johnson was scheduled to make a recovery appeal in Harrisburg, Pennsylvania, on August 2, Roosevelt instructed him to see what he could do to get the miners back to work.

Although admittedly ignorant of the specific circumstances of the Pennsylvania situation, Johnson eagerly jumped into the cauldron of swirling forces at work in the coal industry. Coal was vital to the American economy; if the miners remained on the picket lines for any length of time, every industrial activity would be adversely affected, just as he was trying to get recovery underway.[51] Johnson was less concerned with the causes of the strikes, which he thought grew out of both sides misrepresenting the purpose of NIRA to the miners, than with settling them quickly. By appealing to patriotism, he believed that he could simultaneously settle the strikes and move the code negotiations forward. In Harrisburg on August 2, Johnson told a joint labor-business gathering that the national interest compelled strikers to return to the pits and industry to get on with codification.[52]

Johnson returned to Washington that night with Pinchot and Thomas Moses, president of the H. C. Frick Company, in tow. Moses had been the most vocal United Mine Workers opponent among the captive mine operators, and Johnson hoped that he could arrange a strike settlement and speed code drafting by bringing Moses and Lewis together. He quickly summoned a late-night conference of operators and announced that public hearings for the coal code would begin on August 9. He coupled the announcement with a plea for a strike truce until the code was finalized.[53]

Johnson first tried bluster as a means of getting the coal operators to deal with Lewis, lambasting Moses on one occasion with an outburst profusely interlaced with "goddamns" for his intransigent opposition to the union. He then turned to tact and stealth. In meetings on August 3 and 4 he relied on "interminably patient negotiations sprinkled with appeals to every angle of persuasion." Johnson was never better as NRA administrator than he was during these two days. He put Pinchot in one room in the Shoreham Hotel, Lewis in a second, the captive mine operators in a third, and the commercial operators in a fourth. "At the psychological moment," Roosevelt later glowingly told a press conference in off-the-record comments, "he would bring two out and get them together and then the other two and get them together and work them around." Johnson also made extensive use of his personal relationships with key industrial and financial leaders. He conferred at length by telephone with William A. Irwin, president of U. S. Steel. He also persuaded Walter Teagle of Standard Oil of New Jersey to call Andrew Mellon. A Pittsburgh banker and former secretary of the treasury, Mellon was the principal supporter of the Pittsburgh Coal Company; and, at Teagle's behest, he convinced the company to cooperate. In addition, Johnson recruited old friend Gerard Swope of General Electric to use his superb powers of persuasion on other financial powers "to bring the coal men into line." Johnson's endeavors produced a putative truce on August 4. Summing up his performance in the negotiations, Roosevelt dubbed it "amazing. . . . Hugh Johnson has done a swell job on this."[54]

The settlement called for the commercial mines to reopen with no discrimination against the strikers and, until a code was drafted, for the operators and miners to settle all future disputes through a mediation board appointed by the president. Moses agreed to a similar settlement for the captive mines. Lewis, meanwhile, consented to call off the strikes if the operators fulfilled their pledges. Flushed with exuberance by the settlement, Johnson flew to Poughkeepsie, New York, that night to report to Roosevelt. Possibly only his elation saw him through the flight, during which he had to sleep on the floor of the plane, with a cushion for a pillow. Johnson first announced the settlement when he landed at Poughkeepsie and then motored to Roosevelt's home at Hyde Park for his approval; it came at midnight.

The public hearing brought no agreement on a coal code. Johnson now resorted to direct presidential intervention, convincing Roosevelt to meet with four of the operators and pressure them to be more forthcoming. In their meeting, Roosevelt warned the operators that if they did not soon draft one code for the whole industry, he would draft one for them. Johnson was elated by the president's performance. Roosevelt, he reported to the Special Industrial Recovery Board, "waltzed all over them, up one side and down the other, and that softened them up a little."[55]

Just as success appeared to be within reach, Johnson commited two serious blunders. Following the hearing, he had asked each of the major operators associations to choose representatives for closed-door discussions. But rather than force them to meet together and compromise their differences, he tried to deal with them separately. Perhaps Johnson believed that a joint meeting would simply produce further argument and that he could more effectively use his power of persuasion as he had done on August 3 and 4, by meeting with the coal representatives separately. If so, he was wrong. They were now accustomed to him; his tough act no longer moved them. Rather than yield to Johnson's demands for a national code, they held back and hoped that time would work in their favor.[56]

Johnson's second blunder was even more calamitous. On August 21 he telephoned Louis Howe, Roosevelt's confidant, to report that he was optimistic that an understanding on collective bargaining could be reached when southern operators and United Mine Workers officials met the next day. Others were also optimistic. According to Louis Stark, labor reporter for the New York Times, "this conference was in the bag." There was a good possibility that these two implacable foes could settle; if they did, the northern operators would probably quickly fall into line. But as the conference was about to begin, Johnson unexpectedly announced that he would "clarify" Section 7a. He thought that this maneuver would enable him to repeat his success in getting the auto code. In that case his sanctioning of the industry's interpretation of Section 7a had swept away the final obstacle to codification by convincing the auto men that they had nothing to fear from unionization.

With the coal industry, the strategy proved disastrous. The coal men were more opposed to unionization than Johnson had imagined and were not prepared to make any concessions. Aware that he had given in to the auto industry when it had stood firm, they concluded that

Johnson's willingness to "clarify" Section 7a would bring more concessions if they did the same. Hoping Johnson would eventually consent to the open shop, they declared that they would not bargain. Miners and the pro-union operators were dismayed by Johnson's blunder, and on August 23 Stark wired Roosevelt that "the coal situation has become acute. Both operators and miners want to take the matter out of General Johnson's hands because of his inability to understand the problem."[57]

Johnson's blunders slowed the momentum to such an extent that only Roosevelt's convening of a special White House conference of the negotiating participants kept the codification process afloat. Discussions were resumed; however, they abruptly ended on September 7 when Johnson repeated the ploy he had used in wrapping up the petroleum code. During the last week of August, Johnson, at the industry's request, had prepared the code himself.[58] It followed the code drawn up by the United Mine Workers–union operator group and called for five regional divisions. The non-union operators promptly vetoed Johnson's code on the ground that it was too pro-labor. But Johnson was now convinced that there was no other way to end the maddeningly slow pace of codification than for him to impose the code.

Increasingly impatient and frustrated, Johnson called together industry representatives, presented them with his own code, and told them that they had two days to register objections. Most balked, denouncing his tactics as "paternalistic interference of the Administration in management." Johnson did not respond well to this frustration. Exhausted, lacking sleep, he received a telegram from Walter Jones of the Central Pennsylvania Operators Association while lunching at the Occidental Restaurant in downtown Washington. He read of that group's opposition to his code and exploded in a public tantrum, tearing up the telegram, throwing pieces of it on the floor, and shattering the ambience with references to that "goddamn SOB."[59]

In spite of the dictatorial way in which he had presented the code to the industry, Johnson now realized that he could not force it upon the coal men. When the hearing resumed on September 12, Richberg, at his direction, informed the 500 operators present that the code had been drafted "only as a focus for discussion." The various associations then appointed two committees of nine men each to discuss aspects of the code with Johnson that afternoon. Two days of discussion produced no result, at which point Roosevelt told the operators that he was prepared to impose the Johnson code if no agreement was reached within twenty-four hours. One hour past the deadline, the sleepy-eyed negotiators emerged from their meeting with a final draft for the entire industry. Roosevelt signed it on September 18. Three days later the Appalachian operators and the United Mine Workers reached a wage settlement, the Appalachian Agreement.[60]

The coal code brought dramatic gains for miners. It included Section

7a and the right of miners to a checkweighman and payment on a net-ton basis and prohibitions against child labor, compulsory scrip wages, and the compulsory company store. In addition, it provided for a maximum workweek, while the Appalachian Agreement provided for higher wages than recent levels. But in getting the operators to agree to these provisions, Johnson eventually had to give them, among other things, the opportunity to establish nineteen divisions and subdivisions. These made the coal code "only the shell" of the national code Johnson had originally sought.[61]

Nor was Johnson's job finished. The captive mines were willing to concede to miners the wages and working conditions prescribed in the Appalachian Agreement. But they refused to sign the code or deal with the union, prompting angry miners in Pennsylvania to strike. Again Johnson was on the phone to negotiate with the leaders of Bethlehem Steel and U.S. Steel. One day, briefly hospitalized for a minor ailment, he even turned his room at Walter Reed into a conference room for a meeting with representatives of the American Iron and Steel Institute. Finally, on September 29 the captive mines agreed to abide by the wages and hours "prescribed under or pursuant to the coal code." When on October 1 he arranged for a meeting between Moses and Philip Murray, one of Lewis's principal aides, Johnson concluded that the coal fracas was now ended.

He could not have been more mistaken. Moses still refused to bargain with the United Mine Workers and told Murray that the September 29 compact did not include union recognition. At Murray's request Johnson wired his understanding of the compact, stating that it included the checkoff for collection of mine workers' dues and the right of miners to select their own checkweighmen. Since the checkoff meant ultimate union recognition, Murray was satisfied and ordered the strikers back to work. Johnson, meanwhile, wired Roosevelt at 3:18 A.M. on October 2 that "This settles it."[62]

But the controversy would not go away. In a last-ditch effort to avoid union recognition, the captive mine operators now contended that the checkoff was not part of the working conditions prescribed in the Appalachian Agreement. Johnson was infuriated by the operators' delaying tactics and bitterly told reporters that "it is perfectly clear to me that the check off is part of the contract and binds the operators. I can see no room for argument on that point."[63] Johnson's pronouncement did not move the captive mine operators, and Roosevelt was again forced to intervene. With Johnson now in the background, the president settled the matter by the end of the month, largely in the union's favor. The coal industry, commercial and captive, was finally codified.[64]

CODIFICATION of the coal industry was the capstone to Hugh Johnson's campaign to codify industry. Virtually all major industries were now codified, and hundreds of small industries were also submitting codes. In Johnson's mind, and in the minds of many others, codification laid the foundation for a new industrial era in which the few could no longer exploit the many. Through industrial self-government, business had eliminated destructive competition and dramatically improved conditions for workers, thereby insuring economic growth and social harmony. Business had showed, in other words, that profits and the public interest were not incongruous.

The reality, however, bore little resemblance to this bright picture. Holding most of the trump cards in the code-making process, the more organized segments of the industrial sector had generally shaped the codes for their own purposes. Practices that had been defined as "conspiracy in restraint of trade" were now sanctioned by the government as legitimate and even as public services. Price and production restrictions were common, and enforcement of the codes was essentially vested in the industries themselves. In this manner, organized business had successfully used NRA to achieve its long-sought goal of market control and had committed the nation to a restrictionist economic policy designed to defend the position and wealth of business. Organized labor and consumers, meanwhile, had received little from codification. Except in the coal industry, where the United Mine Workers was already a significant force, their "hopes and expectations" had been largely "circumscribed or suppressed."[65]

CHAPTER 8

PUBLIC MAN AND PRIVATE COMPLICATIONS

HUGH Johnson was virtually unknown to the public at the beginning of 1933. After his appointment as NRA administrator, though, he "burst like a flaming meteorite on the country." His name appeared daily in the newspapers, and everything about him was now news. Across the nation people marveled at his versatility, physical energy, gusto, ruthless drive, and ability to coin a phrase. In Washington, Johnson became the most discussed and best known figure in the administration after Roosevelt, and in Boston thousands of people besieged the Statler hotel just to catch a glimpse of him.[1] The job of codifying industry, however, exacted its toll. The exhausting grind pushed him to excess and magnified his flaws. Before long his personal life embarrassed himself and the administration.

THE PRESIDENT'S Reemployment Agreement was the factor that catapulted Hugh Johnson to the forefront of national attention. A voluntary blanket code for all employers, it established a thirty-five hour week for industrial workers and a forty-four hour week for white-collar workers, with a $12 to $15 weekly minimum wage. It has usually been assumed that Johnson launched the President's Reemployment Agreement as a hasty response to conditions in July 1933. In actuality, however, he had given considerable thought to such a code during the initial planning for NRA, believing that it would be the quickest way to bring about a dramatic improvement in wages and hours. His idea was simple: Promulgate a uniform rule and then deal with the exceptions in code negotiations.[2]

Johnson first gave some indication of what he had in mind in a speech he wrote and Baruch delivered to the Brookings Institution on May 20, 1933. In it Johnson outlined the purpose and features of the blanket code, placing particular emphasis on its voluntary character. He further spelled out the purpose of the blanket code in the negotiations for the cotton textile code. In order to persuade the industry to adopt a higher minimum wage, he advised industry representatives that they would not lose any competitive advantage if they raised wages, for he intended to see that wages were raised as quickly as possible in all industries through a blanket code.[3]

Despite the importance he attached to a blanket code, Johnson did not move immediately to implement it. He reasoned that several major industries must submit codes before a blanket code would be accepted by enough industries to ensure its success. "If several major industries declined to sign a general agreement," one NRA official later wrote, "smaller industries would also refuse and the whole program would fail."[4]

In the first week of July 1933, Johnson decided he could wait no longer. Two factors shaped his decision. The first was the snail's pace of codifying industry. Many industries were reluctant to codify because they feared the impact of reduced workweeks or what they regarded as enforced unionization. Others held back in expectation that noncodified business might have a competitive advantage over those who came in quickly. Organizing industries which were not sufficiently integrated to submit codes was also a problem, as was bringing into the national program workers who were not involved in interstate commerce. The negotiations with the cotton textile industry indicated that even in a highly homogeneous industry it would take a minimum of six weeks "to put one of the great major codes completely through the NRA mill from original negotiations to final approval." At this pace, with more than 400 industries already announcing their intention to submit codes, codifying industry would take a decade.[5]

The other factor was the state of the economy. Beginning in March 1933, there had been an upswing in production and employment. Factory production shot up from an index of 56 in March to 101 in July 1933, industrial stocks swung from 63 to 109. By July, however, it was becoming apparent that the upswing in business activity was chiefly fueled by forward manufacturing and purchasing before the implementation of codes increased costs and that its tempo would slow as inventories accumulated. It was also apparent that it would be some time before the public works program pumped sizable sums of money into the economy. As a result, Johnson was confronted with the question of how to fuel the economy once the upswing ran its course.[6]

"With failure staring him in the face," Bernard Bellush writes, Johnson determined that something must be done "to whip up an atmosphere in which trade associations would be more willing to quicken the process of codification" and to give the economy "a new injection of confidence."[7] His answer was a blanket code, known formally as the President's Reemployment Agreement. All the nation's employers would be asked to agree to a code eliminating child labor, decreasing hours, and increasing wages. It would be in effect from August 1 to December 31, 1933, or until the employer's specific industry was codified. Though enforcement was an all-important matter, Johnson did not see the blanket code as a source of discipline over industry. Section 3 of Title I contained provisions for the punishment of those who violated the codes; but Johnson had already ruled out coercion in regard to individual codes, and he did the same with the President's Reemployment Agreement. Recalling that the WIB had urged compliance with its conservation programs by having businessmen place government insignia on their doorways, letterheads, and invoices, Johnson planned to have those that complied with the blanket code place an insignia in their windows and on their products. Consumers would be encouraged through a massive propaganda campaign to patronize only firms displaying the insignia. Compliance would be entrusted to local committees, which, like the wartime draft boards, would be made up of what Johnson called the very "best" people in town.[8]

Skeptics opined that public opinion would never enforce such a large-scale program and that ultimately coercion would be needed. In reply, Johnson harked back to the way public opinion had enforced the draft, ignoring the distinction that draft dodgers were arrested and sent to jail. "What will happen to objectors who won't go along with the code?" a reporter asked Johnson in late July. Johnson, lunching on pork chops and beer, shot back: "They'll get a sock right on the nose."[9] He was more grandiloquent in a speech in St. Louis on August 13. Rhetorically asking about what would happen to those "guilty of trifling with this great chance to lift this country out of economic hell," he answered:

As happened to Danny Deever, NRA will have to remove from him his badge of public faith and business honor and 'takin of his buttons off an' cut his stripes away' break the bright sword of his commercial honor in the eyes of his neighbors—and throw the fragments—in scorn—in the dust at his feet. It is a sentence of economic death. It will never happen. The threat of it transcends any puny penal provision in this law.[10]

During the first weeks of July 1933, Johnson focused on the massive publicity campaign necessary to rally public opinion behind the blanket code. He addressed himself first to the design of a distinctive and striking insignia for the President's Reemployment Agreement. A chat with Henry Wallace about the thunderbird made by the Navajo Indians of the Southwest persuaded him that it would be appropriate. He sketched a figure patterned after the Indian ideogram and then called in N. W. Ayer and Son, a Philadelphia advertising agency, to turn the sketch into an insignia.[11] Working all day and all night on July 14, it designed an insignia with a Blue Eagle holding a factory wheel cog, symbolizing industry, in its left claw and a sheaf of lightning bolts, symbolizing energy, in the right. Underneath the eagle was the legend "We Do Our Part." The insignia was exactly what Johnson was looking for. He said to Wallace several days later "that he *hoped* it would be full of thunder."[12]

While the finishing touches were being made on the insignia, Johnson searched for an organizer for the publicity campaign. Seeking advice, he contacted William G. McAdoo, former secretary of the treasury. McAdoo had headed the Liberty Loan drives during World War I, the closest precedent for what Johnson was attempting with the President's Reemployment Agreement. At McAdoo's suggestion, Johnson recruited Charles F. Horner, a Kansas City, Missouri, advertising man. Horner, who had organized and administered the Liberty Loan drives, quickly agreed to handle the organization of the Blue Eagle campaign. For the crucial publicity work, Johnson brought in Charles Michelson, a close friend from the 1932 presidential campaign.[13]

On a Sunday cruise on the presidential yacht *Sequoia*, Johnson presented the details of the plan and the Blue Eagle insignia to Roosevelt. Besides the president and Johnson, the July 16 meeting included Wallace, Rexford Tugwell, and George Peek. These three, arguing that it would provoke resentment from the agricultural sector, expressed doubts about the ballyhoo aspects of the campaign and objected to its implementation. But Roosevelt was most receptive to Johnson's plans and quickly granted his tentative approval.[14] He was particularly impressed with Johnson's vision of a speedy recovery. During the winter and spring of 1932–1933 Roosevelt had been attracted to the proposals of start-up planners whereby the economy would be jolted back to normal by the infusion of self-generating purchasing power and the psychology of expansion. Johnson presented the blanket code in the same light. He told Roosevelt that rapid codification of industry and widespread agreement with the reemployment agreement would bring recovery "with an irresistible sweep." If all employers simultaneously expanded their work forces, maintained wage rates, and kept prices stable, the resulting wage payments would buy the enlarged product. "A self-supporting recovery 'spiral' would get started." The president, Tugwell recorded in his diary, "fell for it."[15]

Another element was also at work. That same day Roosevelt gave his final approval to the cotton textile code, which opened the door to cartelization of the industry. He was committed to business's approach to fighting the depression; but he was uncomfortable in committing himself too much to one approach. He liked room to maneuver, and possibly he was so willing to approve Johnson's scheme because he saw in it the last chance to moderate cartelization in the other codes and keep the door open for another approach if NRA stalled. By establishing a uniform wages and hours standard through a blanket code, NRA could hopefully avoid the substantial concessions to the goal of cartelization that industry was demanding as the price of its cooperation in improving wages and hours.[16]

In contrast to Roosevelt, the Special Industrial Recovery Board was cool toward the President's Reemployment Agreement and questioned

Johnson for three consecutive days about the principles and details of the plan and its potential pitfalls. Tugwell expressed sympathy with Johnson's objectives but had "very serious misgivings as to whether the thing will work or not." He told the recovery board: "I am just scared to death. I am afraid of the commitment and of getting the President into this. If we strike what a number of us anticipate, which is a flattening out of markets and maybe a precipitous drop right in the midst of a ballyhoo campaign we will look like ten cents." John Dickinson of the Commerce Department, in pointedly caustic remarks, called the plan "white magic" and questioned whether "you can create consumers' purchasing power by magic." Fearing that it "would almost certainly destroy at the outset the great advantage which may be expected from organizing the industries of the country one by one," he was even more skeptical of Johnson's intention to universalize codification. He asked Johnson, "Suppose you start all this ballyhoo and then the agreements do not come in, or if they do, the people do not keep them, where will you be?" Get the big boys first, Dickinson advised Johnson; the corner grocers and barbers can wait. "If you can get enough of the big industries in with your agreement, there will be enough increase of purchasing power on the part of their employees to help things along without having to take the barbers and corner grocers into it." Attorney General Homer Cummings agreed with Dickinson's concern about the pitfall of including the whole nation in the campaign. It was not wartime, he added:

If you start out to get the whole nation to sign the pledge, you are going to run into enormous difficulty. . . . This is not war time. When the nation is in peril, people can be appealed to on the basis of patriotism, which is a very simple thing to appeal to. This is much more subtle and difficult. The idea of sending out seven million and having five hundred eighty thousand of them that never come back worries me.[17]

Johnson conceded "that there is a great deal of gamble about the success of the drive." But "I think it is a good gamble. I think I can put this thing over." Almost every person, he told the group,

has either suffered terribly or knows of friends and relatives who have, so there is waiting there to be appealed to what I regard as the most fertile psychology that you could imagine for such a thing; namely that the President of the United States has a plan by which all can do things together and get back to work. I don't think there was anything in the War that lent itself to a sounder psychological field than this.[18]

Budget Director Lewis Douglas gave Johnson "very hearty support." Tiring of the board's detailed questioning of Johnson, he concluded on July 19 that "General Johnson knows more about this than anybody else in the Administration. . . . If he thinks this thing ought to be done and should be done to prevent collapse, I am heartily in favor of having it done, and done when he thinks it ought to be done."[19] Most of the members of the board remained unconvinced, however, and only reluctantly agreed to endorse the Blue Eagle campaign.

The Special Industrial Recovery Board's concerns did not diminish Roosevelt's support for Johnson's plan. Its boldness appealed to him, and he was always inclined to favor the "player as against the kibitzer."[20] Moreover, on July 19 the bottom fell out of the pre-code economic upswing when prices on the New York Stock Exchange dropped precipitously. Roosevelt now desperately needed something to revive the economic momentum, and Johnson's plan was the only game in town. Johnson also brought personal pressure to bear on Roosevelt. Fearful that the recovery board's criticism of the plan might spur Roosevelt to withdraw his tentative approval, Johnson telephoned Louis Howe on the morning of July 19 and told him that the blanket code was crucial to NRA and that he would resign unless it "went thru."[21] Sensing the public's need for action and not wishing to lose Johnson's services at this inopportune moment, Roosevelt told Johnson to go ahead. On July 21, Johnson telegraphed presidents of the Chamber of Commerce in every city with more than 10,000 people and asked them to organize committees "to direct a campaign of education and organization which is to be part of a national movement to spread the return of prosperity through the expansion of consumer purchasing power."[22] The flight of the Blue Eagle was underway.

Johnson based the campaign for the President's Reemployment Agreement on a war mobilization psychology. In a replay of 1917 he asked Americans to unite voluntarily behind the Blue Eagle to win the battle against the depression.[23] Beginning on August 1, Horner unleashed a great outpouring of ballyhoo and patriotic appeal. Four-minute speakers took to the radio, the pulpit, and the rostrum and assaulted the nation's "conscience and eardrums" with propaganda. Motorcades, torchlight processions, and mass rallies, complete with brass bands and cheering crowds, were held in cities from Boston to San Diego. Songs were even written exhorting the public to join the war against the depression. The Blue Eagle appeared on posters, billboards, flags, movie screens, magazines, newspapers, automobile windshields, and countless products. On Broadway stars formed an eagle as part of the finale of the musical *Footlight Parade*. In a San Francisco baseball park 8,000 children stood in the formation of a gigantic NRA eagle. A Philadelphia socialite searching for a name for his entry in the professional football league showed his allegiance to the bird by dubbing his team the Eagles. And millions of consumers signed their own pledge. It read: "I will cooperate in reemployment by supporting and patronizing employers and workers who are members of NRA."

During the first week of August 1933, Johnson was too involved with the coal strike negotiations to devote much attention to the Blue Eagle campaign. As soon as the strike ended, however, he plunged into the campaign with the same energy that marked his efforts to codify the major industries. He began on August 6 with a telephoned address to a rally in Cleveland, Ohio. In the next five weeks he gave numerous speeches, called frequent press conferences, issued many news releases, and made himself readily available to any reporter who wanted a story. A contemporary noted that "a newspaper correspondent could always see General Johnson, whereas an industrialist called to Washington to assist in the recovery program might be kept in the outer office cooling his heels."[24] In effect, Johnson became the chief publicist for the Blue Eagle.

In this hectic period, Johnson had to break up his work in Washington and travel to many cities "to confer with local leaders and to make speeches—sometimes three a day." The Army Air Service aided greatly by lending him "a big fast Condor plane with a desk in it." He wrote his speeches on hops from city to city, and he "visited every important town in the country except New Orleans, and flew a distance considerably greater than the earth's circumference."[25] Cheers, banners, music, and fireworks met him at each airport. "There was no time for thought of what was happening or what it was all about." It was as if Johnson was in "a dream or a motion picture."[26]

Johnson had never given a major speech before the Blue Eagle campaign, and his delivery showed it. He talked rapidly, never once looking at his audience, eyes on the speech in his left hand, his right hand waving and shaking in short earnest gestures.[27] Yet his vivid language captured the public's attention and made him a popular speaker. Those who opposed NRA he branded "social Neanderthalers," "Old Dealers," and "corporals of disaster." Those who engaged in the time-honored practice of reducing prices to gain a larger share of the market he likened to Judas Iscariot and dubbed "chiselers."

But his optimistic predictions of the results the Blue Eagle campaign would produce mattered most to his receptive audiences. On July 25, announcing the details of the campaign in a nationwide radio address, he presented the Blue Eagle as the goose that would lay the golden egg. The blanket code, he predicted, would create six million jobs by Labor Day.[28] This estimate was a wild guess, and Johnson soon realized that he had erred in giving a specific figure. The results of the President's Reemployment Agreement could be measured against this number, and Johnson hastily retreated from it. Yet he never departed from the image of the Blue Eagle as a savior. On August 23 he stated that the Blue Eagle "is putting people back to work by the hundreds of thousands . . . and is raising payrolls by the millions." A week later, after conferring with NRA chairmen from various states, Johnson estimated that the recovery drive had put two million unemployed workers back into factories and shops. What did this mean to the economy? Johnson elucidated:

Well, 2,000,000 people represent, at the lowest estimate, $30,000,000 more in the payrolls each week . . . and this money goes right back into the hopper of trade and is spent over and over again; which means more work, more comfort, more happiness. And yet this great effort has just started.[29]

In a Labor Day speech in Chicago, Johnson announced "that people have gone back to work in vast swarms and that those who had work are getting better pay." If everyone does his part, he prophesied, "we shall be on our way out of this depression before snow flies." Choosing to overlook the reemployment figures he had previously stated, Johnson now admitted that he could not document the "facts" on reemployment. However, he did not back away from his rosy predictions and still expressed unbounded confidence that the Blue Eagle was the nation's salvation. In a speech delivered in New York City on September 12 he opined that "there is a distinct stirring of hope throughout this country. That hope is not without substance. Every economic index has moved substantially upward since those dark days in March. Signs of a broad advance are everywhere."[30]

On all accounts the Blue Eagle seemed a success. The national surge around the Blue Eagle broke the logjam in code making. Draft codes by the hundreds now flowed into Washington. Millions of employers had pledged themselves to NRA labor standards, and millions of consumers were pledged to support them. Hundreds of thousands of people were back at work. In fact, Johnson claimed that 2,785,000 "breadwinners were back on pay-rolls" and that their annual earnings increased purchasing power by $3 billion, which was "several times the aggregate result accomplished by all of the other Recovery Administrations put together."[31] Most important, as Roosevelt observed, "there is a unity in the country . . . not seen since April, 1917."[32] A government agency had been transformed into a mass army, and Hugh Johnson was its general.

The price for this success was high. In mobilizing Americans into his Blue Eagle army, Johnson had promised sales for the salesmen, profits for employers, higher wages for the employed, and work for the unemployed. His emotional appeals and optimistic statements about the ability of the Blue Eagle to hatch recovery had caused millions of Americans to regard NRA and its supercharged chief as the saviors of the nation. But "trumpets, placards, and parades," by themselves, do not make for recovery; and some were already wondering whether Johnson had promised more than he could deliver.

DURING the summer of 1933, Hugh Johnson was at least once called the "busiest man" in the United States.[33] Whether sitting at the desk in his "plain, uncomfortable office" in the Commerce Department or on the platform in the auditorium, Johnson, with his coat off, shirt open at the neck, sleeves rolled up, and perspiration streaming down his cheek, "labored like ten demons." He chain-smoked Old Gold cigarettes, often lighting up one while two others were still burning in a nearby ashtray. Between visitors, sometimes over a hundred a day, and telephone calls, he scanned official documents and hurriedly scribbled his signature on letters brought in by his secretary. At a moment's notice he would bolt out of the office to deal with a snag in code negotiations, conduct a hearing, see the president, attend a meeting of the Special Industrial Recovery Board, or rush to the airport and fly almost anywhere in the United States on one mission or another. Johnson seldom worked less than sixteen to twenty hours a day, and there were nights when he did not return to his suite at the Carlton but instead caught a little sleep on his office sofa, showing up at the nearby Childs Restaurant for breakfast at five or six in the morning. Then, without a change of clothes, he would return to his office ready for another day's work.[34] His hectic work schedule made it difficult for Johnson to be on time, even for the White House, which reported in October 1933 that Johnson was the first guest ever to arrive late at a state dinner.[35]

Johnson was so busy that he often could not keep track of everything he was doing. Soon after NRA was created, George Creel, an old friend who had been wartime head of the Committee on Public Information, offered his services on a volunteer basis. In early July, Johnson wired Creel and asked him to help administer the Blue Eagle campaign on the Pacific coast. There was no followup, but Creel soon read a news story reporting that he had been appointed. He accepted, but it was days before Johnson gave him any indication of his duties.[36]

William H. Davis, a New York City lawyer, had a similar experience. In response to a wire from Johnson, he came to Washington to see about a position with NRA. Arriving at Union Terminal early in the morning, he immediately went to the Commerce Department, where he was kept waiting all that day and the next in Johnson's outer office. Finally, he bumped into John Hancock, who told him to come back at eight o'clock in the morning on the third day, at which time Hancock promptly ushered him into Johnson's office. Without waiting for a formal introduction, Johnson looked up from his cluttered desk, mumbled some sounds, and told Davis to look over some legal matters. Hancock then quickly escorted Davis outside and swore him in as a deputy NRA administrator.[37]

At times, Johnson seemed to be running out of control. Roosevelt told his cabinet in late July 1933 how one day Johnson rushed into his office and handed him three codes to sign. As he was signing the last code, Johnson said he had only five minutes to catch a plane and dashed out of the White House, the codes stuffed in his pocket. "He hasn't been seen since," Roosevelt amusedly added.[38]

Johnson did thrive on hard work, but this unrelenting pace wore him down. Lack of sleep made his eyes bleary.[39] He frequently lost his temper and threatened bodily harm to staffers and businessmen who angered him. "Get the hell out of here before I throw you out," he barked at one startled staffer who lingered too long in his office. Public displays of his emotionalism became commonplace. In August 1933, bad weather forced Johnson's plane to land at Dayton, Ohio, on a flight back to Washington from St. Louis. A hotel clerk failed to recognize him and, judging him a probable hobo because he had no luggage, refused to accommodate him unless he paid for a room in advance. Rather than meet the clerk's request, Johnson exploded in a rage, stormed out of the hotel, and went to another hotel where he was recognized as the nation's number-one depression fighter.[40]

Outbursts like the one in Dayton made Roosevelt increasingly concerned about Johnson's health. On August 14 he summoned Johnson to the White House and "ordered" him to quit working so hard or be "fired." Johnson replied that there was too much to be done and hurried back to his office, telling reporters that "I'm getting along fine."[41] Johnson continued to work at a murderous pace through August; by September, reporters were commenting that he was so tired that he looked closer to seventy than his fifty-one years of age. When they asked whether he was going to take a vacation, he answered that he was too busy and that reports that he needed a rest came from enemies of NRA.[42] An opportunity for a rest came in late September when Johnson was hospitalized for minor surgery. Even then, rest took second place to negotiations on the coal code and the reading of reports.[43]

Those around Johnson worked just as hard. Many of his assistants were at their desks until the early hours of the morning. When they finally were able to go home, greet their families, and prepare for sleep, the phone would ring and Johnson would growl, "Come on over right away." Some found it too much of a grind and were let go because of jangled nerves. By the end of August, Johnson realized that he was driving his troops too hard and decided for the physical and mental health of his staff to close down the office and give everybody a three-day break over Labor Day. He did the same at Thanksgiving.

Not surprisingly, Johnson tried to run NRA the same way an officer commands troops. In the formative days he ordered Edward McGrady to record the name of every person he saw and what took place. McGrady had only started to complain when Johnson interrupted, sternly glared at him, and testily snapped that such meticulous record keeping was the army way and would be the practice for NRA.[44] In conferences Johnson left no doubt who was in charge. He would say little and press the participants to get things done. But if they bogged down, he would rise from his seat and abruptly close the discussion with the command, "We'll do this!"[45] Johnson expected those around him to be as loyal to him as regimental officers to their commanders; he expected a fellowship similar to that among the men of the First Cavalry. He often told them that "they were separate and different from other people and all bound up in . . . [the] great cause" of licking the depression.[46]

The steady round of hearings, press conferences, speeches, and parades was "heady medicine" for Johnson and "had the effect of getting him into a kind of a mood of elation." He liked people to greet him as he walked down the corridors at Commerce, and nothing "jacked" him up more than going to a hearing with NRA employees coming out of their offices, standing at their office doors, clapping their hands, and wishing him "Good luck. Good luck to you General Johnson. Bully for you. Get a code."[47]

Johnson's belligerent, domineering style, his military background, and the Mussolini-like manner in which he waved at crowds during parades led some people to see in him the material from which dictators were made. One young man in Johnson's entourage told writer Matthew Josephson that the depression and continuing labor disturbances were creating the need for a "Man on Horseback" and that Johnson was the man. Rumors were rife that Johnson had a military map of Washington in his desk, with every public building plainly marked. Why, it was asked, did the administrator of an economic program keep this map handy?[48] Johnson, however, was hardly a would-be dictator. His underlying sentimental nature and the major concessions he granted to business suggest how little of the dictator there was in him.

Johnson was initially very popular with the Washington press corps. He enjoyed considerable press attention, and his press conferences were only slightly less eagerly attended than Roosevelt's. They were, columnist Mark Sullivan wrote, the most "enjoyable entertainment" in Washington.[49] Johnson's full and penetrating voice seemed to echo off the walls of the room, and he often showed his dramatic flair, looking fiercely at the reporters, sticking out his already pronounced lower jaw, waving his arms, and talking about getting tough with chiselers and slackers. One reporter early likened Johnson to Captain Flagg in Maxwell Anderson and Laurence Stallings's play *What Price Glory?* Newsman Westbrook Pegler soon gave Johnson the sobriquet that seemed best to epitomize him—"Old Ironpants."[50] Johnson perhaps needed hardness for self-protection, for caution was unnatural to him. He regularly blurted out more information than necessary when he answered questions and fueled controversies with intemperate or injudicious statements. He also could be replied upon to say graphic and florid things that were meat for reporters hunting quotes. Typical was Johnson's answer to a question after he had announced the appointment of Lieut.

Colonel George A. Lynch, a West Point classmate, to a NRA post. Asked if he might appoint any other old army buddies, Johnson responded that reporters were "welcome to anything here of interest to the public. . . . but if you want to see my stud book, I'll be damned if I am going to show it to you."[51]

The Washington press corps was fascinated by Johnson's variety. Just when they thought they had him, he would reveal himself in a new light. In meetings with them he would alternate between blustery, self-confident moods and disarming humility. At one minute he would be a hard-boiled and threatening top sergeant; the next minute he would be cracking a joke, quoting an apt piece of Scripture, or, almost childlike, scribbling profanity on a scratch pad while talking or abruptly holding muttered conversations with himself. When a reporter asked if he harbored political ambitions, Johnson stunned him by insisting that all he wanted was "to be down between Brownsville and Matamoros where the owls fucked the chickens."[52]

Depending on the moment, Johnson appeared to the press as any one of a half a dozen people. Much of the time he was a cavalry officer leading the troops of the Blue Eagle army. At other times he would be the professional lawyer grappling with the constitutional questions raised by NRA, the "minor industrialist" who was familiar with the day-to-day problems of the business community, the theoretician expounding on a new industrial order, the government administrator trying to protect the public interest amid swirling and quarrelsome private interests, or the humanitarian "for whom human values stand above either sordid profits or performed hypotheses." He was, as one contemporary commentator noted, a marvelous "quick-change artist."[53]

Johnson thrived on the newspaper attention, for it gave him an added tool with which to publicize NRA. He deliberately made himself newsworthy (NRA = Johnson) to dramatize the Blue Eagle campaign.[54] Johnson also established good working relationships with a number of newsmen, including Paul Y. Anderson, a regular contributor to the *Nation*, Howard Davis of the *New York Herald Tribune*, and Emory Thomason of the *Chicago Daily News*.[55]

In August 1933 Johnson's honeymoon with the press began to sour. The cause was the strained negotiations for the newspaper code. From the outset, newspaper publishers were critical of NRA. The wages and hours requirements caused fears that smaller newspapers would be put out of business and larger ones would lose too much money. They were also traditionally anti-union and questioned Section 7a. Most of the arguments, however, centered on NIRA's provision allowing the president to license businesses. The publishers argued that this was a threat to freedom of the press and insisted that the code include a clause guaranteeing First Amendment rights. Believing the clause unnecessary and fearing that it would lead other industries to clutter up their codes,

Johnson opposed the clause before representatives of the American Newspaper Publishers Association. When the publishers went ahead and included the clause anyway, Johnson withheld his approval of their code.

During August the negotiations grew increasingly bitter. The publishers association and NRA were even at odds over the definition of the paramount issue. The publishers argued that freedom of the press was the issue and threatened to stay out of NRA if they did not get what they wanted. But to Johnson the real issue was Section 7a and NRA labor standards. In his mind, the freedom of the press issue was a smoke screen the industry used so that it could dodge codification and avoid collective bargaining, minimum wages, and maximum hours requirements.

The controversy dragged on during the fall of 1933, with many publishers denouncing the administration and Johnson from editorial pages and podiums. NIRA, one publisher proclaimed, could be likened to a Nazi "edict abolishing the right of free speech and freedom of the press in Germany." Johnson considered such statements politically motivated bunk. But he could not force his will upon the publishers. The final code, which Roosevelt approved in February 1934, included a freedom of the press clause. Johnson, though, would not let the matter rest. In the letter of approval he prepared for Roosevelt, he clearly indicated that his mind was unchanged. The whole debate, he implied, had been motivated by the desire of the publishers to get special favors for themselves and maintain sweatshop working conditions. The inclusion of the freedom of the press clause, he went on, "is pure surplusage"; it in no way meant that the publishers could avoid NRA labor requirements. This statement served no purpose but to further antagonize the publishers, and Johnson apologized for it in a speech before the American Society of Newspaper Editors; by then, the newspaper men were only partially mollified. After cheering him roundly at their convention, they promptly adopted a resolution declaring the freedom of the press clause essential.[56]

Certainly the publishers used the freedom of the press issue, both to try to carve out a special position for themselves in regard to NRA labor requirements and as a whipping stick to beat the Roosevelt administration. Johnson erred, however, in seeing the issue only as a smoke screen. Historically, publishers had been touchy about anything that seemed able to threaten the First Amendment, and in their eyes the specter of NIRA being used to oppress the opposition was within the realm of the possible. This fear was exaggerated; Johnson and the administration simply did not possess the power or the inclination to war on the press. But Johnson too readily ignored the publishers' concerns; as a result, negotiations for the code took longer than necessary and engendered needless acrimony. Even if he had been correct in regard to the freedom of the press issue, a wiser course would have been to agree to include the provision at the outset. In this way he would have stripped the First Amendment veneer from the publishers, thus forcing them to oppose him openly on NRA labor requirements and giving NRA a more favorable exposure.

Johnson's troubles with the press were exacerbated by his feud with James True, who published his own "industrial control reports." He had been critical of NRA, and on October 14, 1933, Johnson, piqued by the criticism, barred True from his press conferences. Informing True of his action, Johnson wrote: "Your last industrial control report is full of misinformation and sabotage of NRA. I encourage constructive criticism but your statements have been consistently without foundation in fact and in one case distinctly libelous."[57] True immediately claimed that Johnson was violating the First Amendment and attempted to attend Johnson's next conference. He was turned back by an NRA press officer. In barring True, Johnson was acting within his prerogative; admission to press conferences in Washington had long been considered to be under the control of the person holding the conference. Yet his action, his claims that he could take it notwithstanding, revealed a thin skin for criticism and a dangerous penchant for overreacting. Despite common knowledge that True was more a tipster seeking inside information than a full-fledged newsman, many reporters and columnists came to his defense.[58] For the next few weeks Johnson had to endure impassioned outcries that he was a petty tyrant engaging in censorship. All of this negative publicity could have been avoided if Johnson had ignored True or refuted his criticism. Even those sympathetic to Johnson's position were disturbed by his bad judgment, although they charitably attributed it to a case of frayed nerves.

IN THE fall of 1933, Hugh Johnson's personal life became a lively source of controversy. Fatigued by long hours of work and overexcited by public adulation, he had trouble relaxing, even for a few minutes. Always tense, he inevitably turned to drink for release. Johnson had not been drinking heavily since 1930, when Baruch had him go dry out. Even during the summer of 1933 he had largely confined himself to drinking beer.[59] But as the excitement and pressures of running NRA mounted, Johnson began to drink more. Initially, his drinking did not impair his faculties. Years of heavy drinking had enabled him to consume large amounts of alcohol with no loss of perspective. Frances Perkins recalled that he could do his job loaded with "booze." Although he would often be loose-tongued from drinking, people who knew him "felt perfectly all right doing business with him."[60] Periodically, however, Johnson would go over the edge. Those talking with him could not be sure that the glassy-eyed, groggy Johnson understood what they were saying, and it was hard to make sense of his comments. He began to say contradictory things. He would agree to a code provision and later refuse to sign the code because he had never agreed to it. In the meantime, the enforcement apparatus would have been set up, ready to go, leaving trade associations angry over all their wasted work. On occasion, and without designating who was in charge in the office, Johnson was known to disappear for days to sleep off a bender.

Tales of Johnson's excessive drinking became commonplace in Washington. Peek was the source of some of these tales, as was True.[61] Reporters who exploited celebrities' personal lives were anxious for real and imagined accounts of Johnson's drinking bouts, and they worked the drinking angle into their stories and columns whenever possible. One perceptive reporter even noted with a touch of irony that Johnson's mother prominently displayed her WCTU white ribbon on her black dress when she visited the White House for one of Eleanor Roosevelt's teas.[62]

Fortunately for NRA, there were steadying influences around Johnson. John Hancock helped for a time, and Nelson Slater and George Sloan, now a good friend, could be relied upon to sober him up. Johnson's son, Pat, was also a steadying influence. A lieutenant in the army, Pat had followed in his father's footsteps, graduating from West Point in 1928 and later studying law. Presently, he was assigned to NRA's legal staff. Pat usually could tell when his father had drunk too much and could tactfully take him away before he made a fool of himself.[63]

The most important steadying influence, however, was Frances Robinson. Always more than Johnson's secretary—no job description covered her ambition or her sense of responsibility and regard for him—she early began looking after Johnson. With an instinct for recognizing his childlike quality and needs, she made sure that his desk drawer was always full of Old Golds and that sardines and crackers were nearby if he wanted a snack.[64] She became Johnson's guardian-nurse. At code hearings she would bring him a glass of water to drink every half hour; at press conferences she would keep him from talking too long; and when he went to the hospital, she would shoo away photographers. Most important, Robbie recognized that Johnson had a serious drinking problem. Fiercely loyal to Johnson, she cleverly covered for him when he was on a binge. If someone needed to see Johnson for a decision on some matter, she would say that she was putting together the information for his deliberation and that it would be forthcoming. In some instances she even made the decision herself and then got Johnson's approval. Frances Perkins later commented that Robbie's decisions were "nearly always right" and that more than once she "saved the day."[65]

Having little personal life outside her job, Robbie made Johnson's cause her cause. She worked at his side for as much as twenty hours at a stretch, stood with him as he reviewed parades, accompanied him on many of his trips, and attended hearings and White House functions with him. She became as knowledgeable, if not more so, about NRA than Johnson and was an indispensable source of facts and statistics for him. Before long Johnson was referring reporters' questions to her, flippantly remarking, "I don't know. Ask the little skirt."[66] In effect, Robbie became Johnson's "one-woman brain trust." Johnson formally ratified this role by changing her job from secretary to administrative assistant and increasing her salary three times in 1933. Next to Donald Richberg and Alvin Brown, Robbie was the highest-paid employee of NRA, receiving a salary of $5,780.[67]

At first people in Washington thought Miss Robinson was just a tireless, exhibitionistic shadow. But within a month, Robbie was a recognized power. Despite her diminutive size—she was five feet tall and weighed 100 pounds—Robbie was ruthless at work and could be rough with subordinates. Once she learned that a stenographer assigned to one of Johnson's deputies was hinting about her availability for an affair with her boss. Refusing to tolerate hanky-panky at the office, Robbie met with the deputy administrator and decided with him to handle the flirt by quietly transferring her to another office. But Robbie decided first to put the stenographer in her place. After meeting with the deputy administrator, she growled that she would "tell that bitch where to head in," a promise she fulfilled on the spot.[68] From that point on, office workers knew that they had better keep their minds on work if they did not want a chewing out from the feared Robbie.

Robbie was good at self-advancement; and as her importance increased, so did her assertive style. Smartly dressed, and with a bejeweled blue eagle at her throat, she frequently played hostess to important NRA visitors and dropped winks to those who had her favor as she trotted from one office to another. "People began to realize that if you wanted to get something done, you got to know Miss Robinson, you got on the good side of Miss Robinson."[69] She was privy to all that was going on in NRA and guarded the door to Johnson's office; nobody could see the general without her assent. Newsmen began to play up to her because her word was law. In return, she would straighten their neckties and dust their lapels while telling them about the $1 breakfast she had to leave untouched that morning at the Shoreham Hotel in order to rush to the office.[70]

Several of Johnson's associates grew quite concerned about Frances Robinson's power and tried to keep her at arm's length. Richberg particularly resented her aggressiveness, and the two had a nasty run-in a few weeks after NRA was launched. One day Robbie entered Johnson's office while Richberg was talking to the general. Believing that their conversation was none of her business, Richberg glared menacingly at Robbie and told Johnson he would "come back and see you when I can see you alone." Robbie retorted that "if I'm not wanted I'll leave," prompting Richberg to reply: "You are not wanted." Stung by Richberg's

HUGH S. JOHNSON AND HIS SECRETARY, FRANCES ROBINSON. United Press International Photo Library, The Bettmann Archive, Inc.

abruptness, Robbie stormed out of the office; and thereafter, the two waged undeclared war.[71]

As the months passed, Richberg found it increasingly difficult to see Johnson alone. Once in 1934, wanting to speak to Johnson without Robbie hovering about, he took matters into his own hands. Slipping into Johnson's office while Robbie was talking to someone else, he locked the door behind him and started outlining a problem to the general. An infuriated Robbie began banging on the door, shouting that she must come in. Johnson then motioned to Richberg to let her in, whereupon Robbie stomped into the room and rebuked both men. "What do you mean by locking yourselves away from me in this way?" she exclaimed. Shaken, Richberg picked up his coat and retreated. Never, he later told Secretary of the Treasury Henry Morgenthau, had he had such an experience.[72]

Richberg saw no good in Robbie's presence at NRA. Others, however, considered her a positive influence. Raymond Moley recalled that she fought Johnson's drinking as much as anybody could, and Henry Wallace commented that she was necessary in order for Johnson "to survive properly."[73] Frances Perkins also appreciated Robbie's contributions. Like Richberg, she resented Robbie's presence whenever she talked to

Johnson. But "I really think this country owes Miss Robinson . . . a real debt," she later remarked. If Robbie had not been minding Johnson's business, he "would have been a total flop a great deal earlier. . . . There would have been a terrible scandal if she hadn't been able to do that."[74] Nothing would have been gained if Johnson's career in government had ended in a noisy, drinking spree.

Robbie's association with Johnson soon extended beyond her role as secretary-guardian-nurse. Helen Johnson was absent from Washington during the early summer of 1933, while Robbie was always at Johnson's side. Johnson enjoyed Robbie's company and felt completely at ease with her. He did not have to restrain his language around her and many times changed clothes in his office while she was in the room. They visited Dallas, Texas, in November 1933 and shocked local officials by reserving a whole hotel floor for themselves and lounging around together in their night clothes.[75] If the belief that Robbie had become Johnson's mistress had not already been current, this episode would have generated it.[76]

Johnson's close relationship with Frances Robinson severely strained his marriage, which had been deteriorating for years. Unabashedly self-centered, Johnson had always subordinated the marriage to his own interests. He "thought the world" of his wife, Helen, but he expected her to live through him. Otherwise, Johnson had no time for her; his interests had to come first.[77]

Overwhelmed by the exploitive nature of their relationship, Helen had failed to develop any techniques for managing Hugh or establishing a separate identity for herself. While Johnson concentrated on his career, she withdrew into mothering their son, Pat. But after Pat went to West Point in 1924, Helen was at a loss. She craved attention from Hugh, wanting him "to send her flowers" and "court her." She grew jealous of his associates; and when Johnson failed to show her any attention, she transferred her attention to her pet dogs. By the 1930s Helen "was utterly incomprehensible to him and he to her." Unable to see that he might be responsible for her condition, Johnson often complained to friends that she was "always hysterical" and getting in his way.[78]

It was not long before Helen Johnson heard of Robbie and came to Washington "to see what was going on." Frances Perkins recalled that she did not come with "blood in her eyes. . . . She just came because she heard about Miss Robinson. . . . She heard that Miss Robinson had possessed the General, was telling him what to do . . . and that everybody was snickering when Miss Robinson went somewhere with him."[79] Johnson had no idea how to deal with his wife. He was too busy to give her any attention and recruited Perkins and Mary Rumsey, daughter of railroad magnate Edward Harriman and head of the Consumers' Advisory Board of NRA, to entertain her. They hosted a party

RECOVERY ADMINISTRATOR AND WIFE APPLAUD PRESIDENT'S RADIO APPEAL. The Bettmann Archive, Inc.

for her; Rumsey escorted her around town; and, confused about what to do next, Helen left Washington and returned home.

She had no intention, however, of being "shoved into the corner." She soon came back to Washington and insisted that Johnson find a job for her in NRA. Out of desperation, he placed her on the Consumers' Advisory Board without pay. It was a bad situation. Helen had no experience for the job, and she embarrassed those around her by coming to work in "fussy, dressy clothes" that were more suitable for a "Southern ladies' tea party." People considered Helen little more than a helpless wife trying to preserve some semblance of her dignity and something of her marriage.[80]

For a time things went fairly well; Perkins and Rumsey arranged a tight schedule of luncheons, teas, and dinners to keep Helen busy. Then Helen began to grow "very jealous of Robbie," prompting Johnson to "blubber and carry on." One night he complained to Perkins that "he never could accomplish anything because she had to come into the limelight" and that she had "never been able to comprehend that he had a mission in life." She was "always jealous," he added. The situation was difficult, and only their son Pat's joining NRA helped it. He understood that his parents could not be forced together and that his mother was confused about "what her place in life was." Pat and his wife gave Helen some attention and made her happier.[81] By the end of 1933 Helen had reconciled herself to Johnson's relationship with Robbie enough that she attended White House functions in their company.[82]

Johnson was amusingly naive in explaining Miss Robinson's role to reporters. On the demand of Senator Lester J. Dickinson, Republican of Iowa, the NRA payroll was made public in December 1933, giving reporters their first knowledge of Robbie's high salary. She was listed as a secretary; yet her salary was $5,780, four times that of most government secretaries. Implying something improper in their relationship, reporters asked Johnson to justify Miss Robinson's salary. Johnson hotly retorted: "I think that was one below the belt." While the reporters were still giggling, Johnson added that she was paid so much because she was more than a secretary, a comment that delighted the reporters even more and produced a number of "more-than-a-stenographer" headlines.[83] This exchange was a poignant example of the "man-boy" that Hugh Johnson was: on the one hand, tactless; on the other hand, innocent.

HUGH Johnson's emergence as a national figure was confirmed at the end of 1933 when *Time* named him its "Man of the Year." The magazine praised him for his hard work, success in codifying industry, and the flair he brought to his job—all cases of deserved honor. Yet *Time* clearly indicated that Johnson's personal life was one of a number of embarrassments that were also part of him. In suggesting that Johnson was gallivanting with Frances Robinson, *Time* wickedly used two pictures. One was Robbie standing slightly behind a seated Johnson and whispering into his ear; its caption read: "Secretary-of-the-Year/She works for $5,780." The other Helen Johnson; its caption read: "Mrs. Johnson/She works for nothing."[84]

CHAPTER 9

WARS AND DEAD CATS

B Y T H E fall of 1933, Hugh Johnson himself called NRA the stormy petrel of the New Deal. Controversy engulfed the agency as Johnson warred with other government officials and businessmen in his relentless struggle to do the job. At the same time, public enthusiasm for NRA began to lapse. Johnson downplayed the controversy by blaming it on a capital press corps that had little else to do with its time but stir up trouble; he shrugged off the growing skepticism about NRA by referring to its critics as malcontents who were not worthy of a hearing.[1] But NRA was in trouble, and Johnson knew it. He responded by taking the offensive, and for a time his tactics shored up his position. Yet confidence in NRA and his leadership was waning, and the prospect for his success as NRA administrator was fading fast.

HUGH Johnson's tenures at the Provost Marshal General's office, the General Staff, and Moline Plow had been marked by bitter feuds with his associates, and this pattern early reappeared in NRA. Johnson's most conspicuous NRA feud was with Dudley Cates. A Chicago businessman who had been associated with Johnson in Moline Implement and Lea Fabrics, Cates was assistant administrator for industry. Trouble between Johnson and Cates erupted in July 1933, when Cates spoke out against the President's Reemployment Agreement. He argued "that it was unworkable upon the intricate pattern of industry and commerce, and that it would arouse false hopes on the part of honest working people which cannot be fulfilled." Johnson only persuaded him to go along by including in the blanket code "provisions contemplating special consideration for industries or individual units where the agreement did not fit the conditions." In practice, however, Johnson was leery of allowing any modification, believing that it rendered enforcement of the blanket code impossible. Cates regarded Johnson's approach as destructive to small business and blasted him for his "the hell with them" attitude. "For God's sake," he chided Johnson, "recover the perspective you have lost, else you will plunge the country into chaos."[2]

Johnson and Cates also clashed over NRA labor policy. Cates had little time for the American Federation of Labor. He believed that it was "a wornout cult" and was perverting the intent of NIRA by seeking "to *force* unionization throughout industry." Johnson, in his opinion, had become a pliant tool of the federation. He had ignored his repeated pleas for a "show-down" with the federation, thereby encouraging its "agitating," and, at its behest, had excluded him from discussions of labor policy. Johnson was choleric over Cates's blasts and replied that Cates failed to understand that, under the law, NRA was to deal with the workers' chosen representatives and "cannot take a stand based on a concept that unionism as such is a worn-out cult." Cates had been excluded from labor discussions, Johnson added, "because . . . you are opposed to a fundamental mandate of this law on this score." Tiring of his opposition to many of his plans, Johnson further told Cates that "your attitude . . . has given me more trouble and concern than any other feature of my almost impossible task. . . . My dear Dudley, if it had been anybody but such an old friend as you, I would not have stood this constant implacable opposition in my own organization for twenty-four hours." Cates tried to smooth over the breach with Johnson, but he refused to retreat from his "stricture on unionism."[3] On August 31, 1933, Cates resigned from NRA.[4]

Publicly, Johnson and Cates attributed Cates's resignation to differences over labor policy. Later, Johnson wrote that "the Dudley Cates episode was nine-tenths overwork," although he did not specify whose overwork was at fault.[5] But neither policy nor overwork caused the break. Johnson expected his assistants to be loyal. He was willing to listen to their arguments during the planning stage. But once he had made up his mind, he would brook no further opposition. Because he had been close to Johnson for years, Cates often continued to question him after a decision had been made. For more than a month their bickering stoked the "smouldering underground fires of controversy in NRA."[6] By the end of August, Johnson could no longer countenance Cates and insisted that he leave the organization.

Johnson engaged in a more prolonged and heated feud with the Special Industrial Recovery Board. It stemmed from a mixture of jealousy, personality clashes, and differing opinions over the functions of the board. As head of NRA and architect of the Blue Eagle campaign, Johnson, though outranked, had become more of a national figure than the cabinet members who sat on the recovery board. Several were jealous of the newspaper space he attracted and resented the special attention he received from other government agencies. They were galled, for example, when the War Department ordered that no civilian except Johnson could have use of an army plane.[7] By the middle of July 1933 they were "sharpening knives for him."[8]

Relations between Johnson and Secretary of Commerce Daniel Roper were particularly strained. A Roosevelt political ally of long standing, Roper was a quiet man who only rarely raised his voice. He considered Johnson's bluster at meetings of the Special Industrial Recovery Board out of place and early developed a strong dislike for him.[9] Almost from the start the two men were at odds. As secretary of commerce and chairman of the recovery board, Roper had expected to approve and supervise all of Johnson's plans and appointments. But Johnson had no intention of clearing his actions with someone else and bluntly told Roper that "he wanted him and his subordinates to keep hands off of the recovery program."[10] Roper was not deterred by Johnson's tough talk. When Johnson publicly complained that NRA did not have enough office space in the Commerce Department and threatened to move to the Land Office Building, where the wartime draft had been headquartered, Roper ordered him to stay where he was.[11] Since Roper's ruling seemed to Johnson the cause of any and all NRA inefficiency or confusion, Johnson retaliated by acting as if Roper's questions at recovery board meetings were foolish or by petulantly stating that Roper should already know the answers.[12] Although Johnson's insolence angered Roper, the secretary strove to avoid any outright break. He refused to get involved in a shouting match with Johnson and regularly issued statements of confidence in him.

Johnson's relations with Secretary of the Interior Harold Ickes were equally fractious. Ickes had regarded Johnson's appointment as NRA administrator as "a terrible mistake." Johnson, in his estimate, was too pro-business and "especially dictatorial and absolutely beyond control."[13] Feeling a proprietary interest in public works because of his previous work in supervising two cabinet-level committees dealing with public works legislation, Ickes had been appalled by Johnson's high-handedness in drawing up an organization for public works even before Congress had approved NIRA. During June 1933, he participated in the maneuvering that excluded Johnson from public works and then for himself won control of the Public Works Administration (PWA), the agency for implementing Title II of NIRA. Once established as PWA administrator, Ickes scrapped most of Johnson's organization and plans. Whereas Johnson had intended to emphasize speed and the expenditure of vast sums of money in public works, Ickes followed a cautious, miserly approach that only dripped money into the economy.[14]

Johnson was very piqued by Ickes' handling of public works.[15] It rendered useless the expansionary arm of NIRA that he believed was necessary to stimulate heavy industry and make NRA a success. "If we don't get heavy industry moving [through public works spending], we're sunk," he preached. But Ickes ignored his pleading and finecombed each public works proposal for every hint of potential graft while industry continued to limp along. Johnson also resented the manner in which Ickes had barged into the negotiations for the oil code. Ickes, in turn, was angered by Johnson's indifference at recovery board meetings. More than once he complained that Johnson was too "fluffy" in answering questions and not forthcoming with the recovery board. Unlike Roper, who avoided confrontations with Johnson, Ickes spoke up. Johnson and Ickes often dealt with each other more like "a couple of snapping turtles" than two government administrators with a common goal.[16]

The most important factor in Johnson's feud with the Special Industrial Recovery Board, however, was differences over the board's functions. Despite Roosevelt's instruction to clear his actions with it, Johnson had assumed that the recovery board was formed merely to give him advice and to legitimatize his policies, whereas the board took Roosevelt's charge seriously. As it had lengthy contact with him, many members became concerned. To them he seemed to be a bull charging "into the china shop, usually in behalf of business." In contrast, Ickes, Frances Perkins, and Henry Wallace, in particular, were accustomed to proceeding more cautiously and from a viewpoint that was "non-business . . . and pro-labor." They believed that Johnson was permitting the larger industries "to get a stranglehold on the economy" and suspected that these industries would use their power to raise prices, restrict production, and allocate capital and materials among themselves.[17] They were predictably determined to monitor Johnson closely and guard against hasty action.

Johnson bristled at this monitoring. Regarding NRA as his private preserve, he expected unquestionable support, not interference, from its board. When members began to quiz him, Johnson defensively took the stance that involvement with them bored him.[18] The worst irritation, which led him to contemplate resignation,[19] was to be questioned at board meetings by assistants of Perkins and Roper. In addition to that demeaning process, Johnson was flabbergasted by the amount of time the board members would devote to minor jurisdictional and administrative questions. He had no time to waste on these details while the battle for recovery was raging. In his opinion, it was better, if details could just be ignored, to let underlings tidy them up. The board never agreed, and Johnson fumed that the recovery program was failing while it debated which department was to have what little job and which was to have that man and at what salary. By September 1933, Johnson was telling friends that the recovery board was a waste of time; he begged off attending its meetings and sent Alvin Brown or Donald Richberg in his place.

The Special Industrial Recovery Board doggedly fought back. Concerned that Johnson was giving too much to business, it proposed in November 1933 that all NRA codes be brought to it for approval.[20] For Johnson, this was too much. He stormed to Roosevelt, bitterly complaining that the recovery board was a nuisance that only interfered in and delayed code making. As he later wrote: "They felt that they had to edit all the orders and regulations that NRA might publish and they actually proposed to pass on the validity and substance of all codes. . . . I resisted that. I had to resist."[21] Mincing no words, Johnson told Roosevelt that his choices were to terminate the recovery board or lose his NRA chief.

For several reasons Roosevelt yielded to Johnson. The recovery board wanted to review the codes against a general standard in matters of prices and the like. Roosevelt, in contrast, wanted room to maneuver— to give a little here in order to get something there. Moreover, he wanted code making to be completed quickly. In part, he believed that after code making was completed, business would start producing. And, in part, he believed that it was better to establish broad principles at first and then wrap up details later. Once an industry was codified, the experience and the code authority would be the bases for pressuring a given industry toward proper regard for consumer and labor interests. Finally, Roosevelt was still hopeful that business would not abuse the concessions granted to it under NRA. Was it not better for business to have the chance to demonstrate its reliability in regard to the public welfare before condemning it?[22]

The Special Industrial Recovery Board held its last meeting on December 12, 1933; a week later it was absorbed into the National Emergency Council, established on November 17 as the forum to clear away confusion and administrative competition in decision making. The National Emergency Council proved no more effective in monitoring Johnson than the recovery board. It was too large, and its agenda too broad, to examine NRA policy in detail. Furthermore, the exact relationship between the council and NRA was never specifically defined.[23] Johnson's triumph over the Special Industrial Recovery Board was complete.

BEFORE the end of 1933 Hugh Johnson was also feuding with other government agencies. The Department of Labor criticized NRA for turning statistical reporting over to the code authorities. The Federal Trade Commission (FTC) branded the codes a perversion of the whole concept of regulated competition. The PWA held Johnson responsible for the mounting number of identical bids on public works contracts. And, to his consternation, the Civil Works Administration (CWA), a public works program established by Roosevelt to see the nation through the winter of 1933–1934, ignored Johnson's views on setting wage scales.[24] His most rancorous and long-lasting feud with another government agency was with the Department of Agriculture, perhaps because it employed several onetime friends and associates. In the case of George Peek, head of the Agricultural Adjustment Administration (AAA), the conflict was, as in Moline, one of personality and power; in the case of Jerome Frank, AAA's general counsel, and Rexford Tugwell, assistant secretary of agriculture, it was one of principle and policy. Before running its course the Johnson-Agriculture feud, which provided the capital press with some of the most entertaining epigrams, aroused some of the most heated passions in Washington.

Peek regarded Secretary Wallace as a Johnny-come-lately to the agricultural field; he was deeply hurt when the secretary "usurped his role as *the* leader of the agrarian drive for economic equality." His ego was further bruised when Roosevelt gave Johnson the NRA, an independent agency, to direct while requiring him to be subordinate to Wallace. Accustomed to having his own way, Peek chafed at his stature in the Roosevelt administration.[25] And, given his deep-seated grudge against Johnson, he found Johnson a ready target on which to vent his frustration.

The line of demarcation between the agricultural and industrial recovery programs was another source of friction between the two men. The NIRA gave Johnson jurisdiction over labor matters "all the way down the line in every industry everywhere." AAA, meanwhile, did not want any roadblock in the path of its efforts to raise farm prices. Fearful that Johnson might make a ruling that would interfere with AAA's operations, Peek early sought an understanding with Johnson on the division of responsibility between NRA and AAA and assurances that NRA would cause no problems for the farm sector. After these discussions between Peek and Johnson, Roosevelt issued an executive order on June 26, 1933, assigning all industries primarily engaged in processing agricultural commodities to AAA, with the proviso that working hours, rates of pay, and other conditions of employment would be decided in collaboration with NRA. Four days later, in a news conference held in Wallace's office, Johnson and Peek spelled out the arrangement for reporters, emphasizing that approval of both agencies would be required for co-administered codes.[26]

Cooperative words in a press conference did not lead to cooperation in practice. Before long the negotiations between Johnson and Peek and their administrative staffs over the details of specific codes were as stormy "as those with the leaders of the industries in question."[27] Congressman Marvin Jones later commented that both Johnson and Peek believed they knew all there was to know about the industries in question and that both, in their customary determination, wanted each dispute settled his way. When Johnson could not prevail, he would often announce how NRA had intended to handle the disputed issue and then try to get industry leaders to enforce it.[28] The Johnson-Peek clashes soon found their way into the Washington press, of course. For a time, reporters were so preoccupied with their quarreling that Wallace, weary of the constant arguing and harsh words, only half jokingly asked the press corps to report as "news unexpected points of agreement" between them.[29]

The feud between Johnson and the Department of Agriculture became more pronounced when Johnson proposed the President's Reemployment Agreement. Primarily concerned with the needs of the farmer, Peek argued that the agricultural sector must take precedence in the recovery program. During meetings of the Special Industrial Recovery Board on July 18 and 19 and in correspondence bracketing the meetings, he questioned the impact of the blanket code on farmers and recommended that it exclude rural and farm labor until AAA had an opportunity to consider its effect on agriculture. Otherwise, he warned Johnson in a letter on July 17, "any fixation of minimum wages and maximum hours" in farm-related industries, "even though the labor involved is urban labor, is bound to have its effect upon the prices which we are seeking to obtain for the farmer for his production of basic and other agricultural commodities." Peek was even more hostile toward the blanket code in the recovery board meetings. He told the board that if processors had to pay the higher wages required by the code, they would make it up by paying lower prices to the farmer, thereby impeding agricultural recovery.[30]

Johnson exploded at Peek's implication that NRA was undermining the agricultural recovery program. Like small boys arguing in the schoolyard, they jawed at each other until Roper brought the meeting back to order from the chair. Despite the vehemence of Peek's presentation against the blanket code, he did not convince the recovery board to block Johnson's plans. Before adjourning on July 19, it approved the code, with the stipulation that Johnson and Peek work out any differences between them with Roosevelt. Impressed by Johnson's performance, Wallace told a reporter: "Johnson is a determined man and usually gets what he wants."[31]

The following weeks brought no agreement between Johnson and Peek. Johnson suggested that Peek draw up a list of agricultural and food industries that might be exempted from the blanket code until August 15, 1933. But Peek rejected the suggestion; in turn, he asked Johnson to continue to deal with agricultural and food industries on the basis of the executive order of June 26.[32] In letters, Peek badgered Johnson to go slowly and to give detailed study "to the relation of increased labor costs to increased prices to the farmer and to the market."[33] He also enlisted the leaders of most of the nation's large farm organizations to press Johnson to go slowly and chastized him for failing to "readily recognize the purpose of our act [AAA] and my present effort to equalize the differential between agriculture and other industries."[34] Johnson, however, would not relent, arguing that he could not "be moved" to grant exceptions to the blanket code "by unsupported statements of exaggerated fears."[35]

In August 1933, Peek attempted to outflank Johnson by having Roosevelt exempt from the President's Reemployment Agreement "any industry which has to do with agriculture or any of its products." Johnson, however, effectively stymied Peek. He convinced Roosevelt that Peek's proposal was simply "a move on the part of the food chains and others who thought they would have a better chance under Agriculture." He also reminded the president that exemption of any agriculture-related industry from the blanket code would practically exempt most major industries in the nation and bring an end to the code. Even if it were possible to minimize the exemptions, Johnson added, it would not be efficacious to approve Peek's request. NRA worked at top speed, while AAA worked more deliberately; and from a psychological perspective, the first should not be geared to the latter.[36]

During the late summer and fall of 1933, members of the Department of Agriculture attacked Johnson almost daily. Jerome Frank recalled: "All of us took a hand at it—Peek for his reason, Wallace and Tugwell and the economists for other reasons."[37] The feud carried over to Washington social circles, always somewhat incestuous with government. One August night at a party given by columnist Drew Pearson, Johnson had "a hell of a hot discussion," which lasted for hours and took the form of a "powwow against Hugh Johnson," with Frank, Tugwell, and others from Agriculture. Though Johnson had only Robbie to back him up, he more than held his own.[38]

On October 12, 1933, Johnson had "a fine visit" with Peek and Wallace, prompting Wallace to write to newsman Paul Anderson that "things in the official family are beginning to straighten out."[39] Wallace, however, was too optimistic. As the NRA codes began to take effect, industrial prices climbed, forcing farmers to pay more for the products they bought. Frank, Tugwell, Mordecai Ezekiel, and others in the Department of Agriculture responded by stepping up their attacks on Johnson and NRA. Johnson retaliated by branding the farm "intellectuals" as "professors who wear the heaviest of horn-rimmed glasses." The professors hurled back such epigrams as "Johnson is a sheep in wolf's clothing."[40]

During the last months of 1933, Johnson's feud with the Department of Agriculture centered on the marketing agreements Peek was arranging to control the quantity of commodities released for sale. In order to raise prices paid to farmers, Peek was willing to give the food processors almost any type of controls they wanted; Frank and Tugwell, however, were appalled by these agreements. In their opinion the processors owed something to the government in exchange for immunity from the antitrust laws. They also believed that there should be a check on excessive prices and unreasonable profits, ideally in the form of clauses providing for quality standards and full access by the government to company books and records. Whenever possible, Frank held up approval of Peek's marketing agreements with questions about their legality, while others from Agriculture protested them in the name of the consumer.[41]

Since the marketing agreements often overlapped with NRA codes,

Johnson was drawn into the struggle. In this instance he stood with Peek. Peek labeled Frank's proposals as "un-American nonsense," and Johnson joined in by calling them "just part of Mr. Frank's general sabotage of N.I.R.A."[42] In Johnson's view, Frank's proposals had frightened the food processors and left them with little incentive to accept the upgraded labor standards advocated by NRA. Johnson spelled out his concerns in detail at the end of December 1933 in a memorandum to Richberg. "The issue is this (although it may not be diplomatic to say so)," he wrote:

(2) A.A.A. thinks that government should run business. N.R.A. thinks that business should run itself under government supervision. This takes the particular form of A.A.A. insistence on these points to which we do not agree:
  (a) That government should practically appoint the Code Authority.
  (b) That unlimited search of books and accounts should be forced on industry without regard to the purposes of the Recovery Act. . . .

Now I think all this is subversive and bad and that we cannot maintain the economic team work necessary to success on any such prescription.[43]

Roosevelt agreed with Johnson. Holding to his belief that the government's primary commitment was to business, he rejected the Frank-Tugwell position. On January 8, 1934, he assigned all agricultural and food codes except those for "first processors" of raw products to NRA.[44] There the processors would receive a friendlier hearing.

Johnson followed up his victory with an effort to ameliorate his relations with the farm "intellectuals." Writing to Tugwell, he thanked the former Brain Truster for his assistance in the writing of NIRA and expressed his hope that they were not in disagreement on substantive matters. He was cooler toward Frank, whom he blamed for gossip to the press that Johnson's industrial orientation made him unable to administer the agriculture and food codes fairly. In the future, he scolded Frank, they should talk out their differences with each other, not with reporters or other outsiders.[45] This peacemaking effort took some heat out of the passions in Johnson's feud with Agriculture. But his critics in the department were not silenced. Tugwell and Frank were convinced that the NRA codes were a monopolistic device aimed at maintaining prices and continued to say that NRA was impeding agricultural recovery.

IN ADDITION to feuding with NRA associates and other government agencies, Hugh Johnson also feuded with numerous businessmen. The most important feud was with Henry Ford, whose refusal to sign the automobile code presented Johnson with a dilemma. Ford had been a pioneer in high wages, and he apparently intended to meet the wage and hour provisions of the code or even improve on them. Yet Johnson could not let Ford stay outside NRA, since his above-the-rules position would leave little incentive for others to sign codes or adhere to their provisions. Ford, therefore, became the major test of the disciplinary power of NRA.[46]

Johnson's principal weapon for disciplining Ford was the boycott. Taking shape during the last week of August 1933, it centered around the refusal of the federal government to award contracts to the Ford Motor Car Company and a propaganda campaign urging the public not to purchase Ford vehicles.

Ford initially made action on the first matter unnecessary by refusing to bid on federal contracts. But a serious hitch developed in September 1933, when an independent Ford dealer, the Northwest Motor Company of Bethesda, Maryland, submitted bids for government business. Northwest had agreed to the motor vehicle retailing code, and it had submitted the low bids on some trucks for the United States Coast and Geodetic Survey. Johnson was in a very embarrassing situation. If the federal government accepted Northwest's bids, his boycott of Ford was meaningless. Yet the government would be in very hot water if it bought Chevrolet trucks when a Ford dealer was the low bidder. Many members of the Roosevelt administration were inclined to buy the Ford trucks and let the matter rest there. Johnson, however, argued that the federal government should not purchase vehicles from Ford dealers, even if they had accepted the President's Reemployment Agreement or the dealers' code. "If we weaken on this," he wrote Roper, "it will greatly harm the Blue Eagle principle and campaign."[47]

Agreeing with Johnson, Roosevelt told an October 27, 1933, press conference that the federal government would buy products manufactured not only in accordance with NRA standards but also "by people who have gone along with the general agreement." The important consideration, he declared, "is the article rather than the person you buy it from."[48] Johnson reinforced Roosevelt's remarks by getting rid of his own Lincoln and replacing it with a Cadillac.[49]

Roosevelt's announcement had little effect. On October 28, Comptroller-General John R. McCarl opined that government contracts must go to the lowest bidder. Two weeks later he ruled that nothing in NIRA required a company actually to sign a code or a compliance certificate. A company had only to comply with the code. Since even Johnson had acknowledged that Ford was complying with the automobile code, McCarl's ruling opened the door for government agencies to award contracts to Ford dealers.[50] Before the year's end the Civilian Conservation Corps was buying trucks from Northwest Motors, and by March 1934, approximately $1 million in federal contracts had been let to Ford dealers.[51]

In 1934 Johnson again tried to force Ford into line. At his request,

General Johnson Presenting President Roosevelt, March 5, 1934. The Granger Collection, New York.

Roosevelt issued an executive order on March 14 declaring that the federal government would not contract for any materials produced by a firm that had not signed a compliance certificate. Notwithstanding his position the previous November, McCarl ruled in favor of the executive order.[52] Johnson now believed it was only a matter of time until Ford signed a compliance certificate. In late June it appeared that Johnson had finally won. He received an unsigned letter, allegedly from the Ford Motor Car Company to a dealer, stating that the company had been complying with NRA standards and would continue to do so in the future. Hoping that the letter was the breakthrough that he had sought for ten months, Johnson buoyantly announced that a Ford official had only to sign the letter, which he would consider a compliance certificate; he would then also call off the crackdown campaign against Ford. But his hopes were quickly dashed when Ford officials disavowed the letter, which finally appeared to have come from a Ford dealer who was anxious to bid on government contracts.[53]

Johnson's crackdown campaign against Ford continued through the summer and fall of 1934, but it had clearly lost its steam. Despite all the pressures Johnson brought to bear, Ford stubbornly refused to sign a compliance certificate. Simultaneously, many government agencies were grumbling about the rigid terms of the president's executive order. Gradually, the federal government relaxed its ban on business with Ford, first by permitting the purchase of repair parts and then the purchase of vehicles on the basis of compliance certificates provided by dealers. Both practices were deviations from the executive order; however, Johnson advised the NRA Compliance Division in October 1934, "not to make an issue of this" in the hope that negotiations with Ford would resolve the dispute. Nothing came from the negotiations; and once the ban had been relaxed, it could not be reinstated.[54]

Ford's refusal to go along with NRA was a major defeat for Johnson and one that undermined his whole effort to enforce the codes. Nettled by Ford's resistance, Johnson had resorted to the boycott to force him to knuckle under. But Hugh Johnson was no match for the nation's number-one industrialist. The boycott cost Ford the possibility of gaining his share of government contracts, particularly between March and October 1934 and may have cost him a small percentage of his normal car and truck sales in 1933. But the company, after losses in 1933, made a healthy profit in 1934; and by the end of the year it had regained its share of the market. The price of being out of step with Johnson, in other words, was not enough to make Henry Ford, "a wild horse of pioneer America," give up his accustomed independence. Ford's success may even have had a negative advertising value, as NRA soon declined in public esteem.[55]

In November 1933, Hugh Johnson announced that NRA had put 4,000,000 men back to work. This statement, like so many others he made in the fall of 1933 about the extent of recovery achieved by NRA, was a shot in the dark. His estimate of reemployment probably exceeded the total increase in employment up to that time from all causes; Johnson apparently based his estimate on the assumption that had it not been for NRA, there would have been no gains whatsoever.[56] Actually, the number of workers reemployed did not approach Johnson's estimate. NRA's research staff later calculated total reemployment under NRA at 2,750,000, a figure which Johnson maintained was too low and based on faulty statistical methods. The American Federation of Labor, meanwhile, said that even that figure was too high and estimated the total of reemployment under NRA by the end of 1933 at between 1,750,000 and 1,900,000 workers. In early 1934, total employment actually decreased, although later figures showed a slight improvement.

Other economic indices told a similar story. In March 1933, the business activity index of the *Annalist* stood at 58.5. It rose until June 1933, when it reached 89.5. Thereafter, it declined until November 1933, when it was down to 68.4. A gradual increase followed, but it was more a result of federal spending through AAA and CWA than NRA. At the same time, total wages had declined instead of rising, and with no compensatory fall in the cost of living.[57]

Johnson's defense of himself and NRA in the light of these statistics was lame. Speaking before an NRA gathering in Washington on February 27, 1934, he stated:

If yesterday approximately three million people were out of work and tomorrow they are put on steady substance wages, and if in the meantime the cost of living has gone up five per cent, are those people better or worse off than if nothing at all had been done for them? If I have no money to buy a beefsteak dinner, does it make much difference to me whether it costs $1 or $1.05? I say—and I think these three million reemployed will all agree—that I will take the $1 and buy liver and bacon with it. The claim of all this criticism (that purchasing power among wage earners has not increased), even before we consider its truth, is cruel, cynical buncombe.

Later in the same speech Johnson pointed out that the cost of living index had dropped from 77.9 in September 1933 to 77.5 in January 1934 and then added:

In the meantime the NRA increase in payrolls was $3,000,000,000. In other words, with the cost of living stationary, NRA reemployed three million people, who were without jobs before, and added $3,000,000,000 to the annual wherewithal of workers to live. It must be remembered, too, that all this happened during a downward cycle of production when, without NRA, we would probably have had a fresh deluge of unemployment. That, as I have said before, was why we hurried. Now there are the cold, hard facts of the NRA job, and of these underhanded, tricky and dishonest criticisms of NRA. I ask you—can you beat it? [58]

The "cold, hard facts," however, were very different from Johnson's recitation. There was no credible evidence that anywhere near three million workers were reemployed under NRA. Nor could one assume, as Johnson did, that the wages of the reemployed represented a net increase in purchasing power. Often the reemployed were hired at the expense of other workers who were having their wages cut or were being fired. Despite the obvious inaccuracy of his statistics, Johnson continued to recite them as if saying them loud enough would make them true. But the reality, as the American people were increasingly recognizing by the end of 1933, was that NRA, despite all the hoopla and effort, had not brought any significant recovery.

In this respect, NRA was like most early New Deal programs. AAA had placed more money in the hands of farmers, but they had frugally hoarded it at the very time that crop reduction programs were raising farm prices. PWA was proceeding too slowly to have any meaningful effect on recovery. The Federal Emergency Relief Administration (FERA) and CWA were modest relief programs that pumped only minimal funds into the economy. Because Johnson had made such glowing promises about what NRA would achieve, however, people expected more from it. When the results did not match expectations, it attracted most of the criticism.

Problems with compliance put Johnson more on the defensive. From the outset there was considerable chiseling on the codes. (Even Johnson's own firm, Lea Fabrics, was accused of violating code labor standards, a charge that was rejected by the New Jersey Bureau of Complaints and Compliance.) Johnson first looked the other way at code violations. His concern was to get industry codified, and he believed that it was "wise not to press too harshly the disciplinary measures on the one hand and investigation on the other" during code making for fear that it would scare companies off. By mid-September 1933, however, codification was largely achieved, and Johnson was now ready to move on to "disciplining these people."[59]

Enforcing the codes was harder than Johnson's plan had suggested. He had said to the recovery board in August 1933 that "if we get a few cases . . . and by holding a public hearing under circumstances of great publicity and with absolute fairness demonstrate that they have misused the emblem, I am going to take the Blue Eagle out of all those stores. I think we can control this chiseling very effectively in that way."[60] The compliance problem, however, was not that simple. There were too many loopholes in the codes, and there were too many businessmen who were willing to agree to a code and then continue business as usual. The public quickly realized that a Blue Eagle in a window was not an infallible sign of compliance.

Johnson's hope that removal of the Blue Eagle would chastize chiselers boomeranged. He took away the Blue Eagle from small businesses—a restaurant in Gary, Indiana, and a New Jersey dry-cleaning shop. In the case of the dry cleaner, a crowd stormed his shop with clothes to clean and press as soon as his name was published; competitors' cleaning shops lost money. As other small shops lost their Blue Eagles, the public saw to it that they did not suffer greatly.

Giant firms, meanwhile, violated codes at will. In the cotton textile industry, mill owners fired employees and rehired them as "learners," who could be paid less than the minimum wage. They also made greater use of the industry's brutal "stretch-out system," whereby one worker manned more than one machine, and they often refused to pay overtime. In August 1933, a representative of the American Federation of Labor reported that "no mills that I know of are living up to the code as signed by the President." Johnson hysterically denounced the mill owners and threatened a crackdown, but he would go no farther.[61] Johnson's critics were quick to note his double-standard approach: While the Little Fellow lost his Blue Eagle, big business was allowed to thumb its nose at NRA.

Johnson's defense of NRA's enforcement procedures conveyed a frank recognition of the difficulties inherent in enforcement—and evidence of his ability to deny reality. At the convention of the American Society of Newspaper Editors in April 1934, he was asked why NRA did not take action against large business interests in apparent code violation. Johnson gave three reasons. First, the large corporations "have the best legal pilots in the world—men who can and do steer them so close to the rocks that it is difficult to determine whether they are scraping the ledges or not." Second, forceful action could throw thousands out of work at a time when the administration was doing everything to increase employment. These were honest reasons and made sense to the editors. But the third left them dumbfounded, for it seemed to fly in the face of what everyone knew. Johnson stated that "we haven't any case against a large employer that we think could stand up against prosecution. This is literally the fact. . . . They are complying with the law as they see it."[62] Left unsaid was the real reason. If Johnson turned on business and forced it to live up to all the codes, he risked losing its support. And such action would also be an admission that the notion of industrial self-government, the essence of Johnson's thinking about political economy, was fallacious.

By the fall of 1933 the nation increasingly felt that NRA was not working. Economic indices were falling, chiseling was a national pastime, and Johnson was making himself look silly by his bloated claims of reemployment. The result was the storm of "dead cats" Johnson had predicted. Consumers complained that businessmen were raising prices faster than wages. Labor leaders complained that industry was circumventing Section 7a. Small businessmen complained that code authorities were ignoring or overriding the needs and conditions of their firms. And the industrial giants complained about the administrative maze stemming from the code provisions. Everywhere there was discontent over code enforcement. Newspaper mogul William Randolph Hearst summed up the attitude of many when he suggested that the initials NRA really stood for "No Recovery Allowed." An equally caustic critic suggested that the initials stood for "National Run Around."[63]

Johnson responded to his critics with exhortations. He called on businessmen to forgo profits made by excessive price increases and to treat their customers and employees justly. He also launched a "Buy Now" campaign. But no one listened. Businessmen continued to do as they pleased, and the Buy Now campaign was "a resounding fiasco." An Illinois farmer summed up the exasperation of many with a recovery program that was not bringing recovery when, in response to one of the general's radio addresses, he wrote Johnson: "Over the radio you shout, 'Buy, buy, buy now!' In reply we farmers of the Middle West would like to ask you one question—'What With?'"[64]

When critics survived exhortation, Johnson resorted to invective, branding the critics of NRA as "witch doctors . . . making incantations" about the recovery program and "seeing things under the bed."

He likened businessmen who refused to cooperate with NRA to Al Capone. For them, he had an embroidered warning:

Away slight men! You may have been Captains of Industry once, but you are Corporals of Disaster now. A safe place for you may be yapping at the flanks but it is not safe to stand obstructing the front of the great army. You might be trampled underfoot—not knowing and inadvertently—because of your small stature and of the uplifted glance of a people whose 'eyes have seen the glory' and whose purpose is intent on the inspired leadership of your neighbor and friend Franklin Roosevelt.[65]

Refusing to concede on any point, Johnson convinced himself that "only fools and crooks could find flaws in the NRA."[66] Even many of the NRA sponsors, however, were losing confidence in the government-sanctioned experiment in industrial self-government. They especially resented the determination of the NRA labor and consumers' advisory boards to impose "untried and impractical ideas upon experienced businessmen" and to raise disturbing questions about the provisions of codes. Henry Harriman of the United States Chamber of Commerce commented that business had supported NRA the previous spring; but "I know of no representative groups of businessmen today in which some do not question the whole program." The National Association of Manufacturers endorsed NRA at its December 1933 convention, but with noticeable lack of enthusiasm. NRA, with its Blue Eagle, Section 7a, and the like, had become more far-reaching than business had ever envisioned. Too many groups were clamoring for a voice in industrial self-government; and although Johnson had so far kept them at arm's length, he could always be replaced, and the next man might not be so solicitous of business.[67]

Epitomizing business discontent with NRA, Gerard Swope proposed on November 1, 1933, that NRA be scrapped and replaced by a National Chamber of Commerce and Industry. Centered around the United States Chamber of Commerce, it would administer the codes; the industrial recovery program would be delivered from government and given to business. Johnson's reaction to the Swope plan was mixed. Recognizing that it represented a growing business disenchantment with NRA, he told reporters that "what Swope's speech was, he and I have talked about for years. I am in thorough agreement with his statement and it was almost a joint operation. It is a kind of goal to shoot at." Though claiming in philosophical agreement with Swope, Johnson also stated that business was not yet sufficiently organized to run itself and made it clear that he intended to keep a directing hand on industry for the time being. Everything that is done in the name of industrial self-government, he explained to reporters, will continue to be "subject to government control."[68] Johnson's comments satisfied no one. Busi-

nessmen wanted out from under the "intolerant and dictatorial attitude" of the advisory boards immediately, while Johnson's endorsement
of the Swope Plan in principle persuaded many critics that he was leading the nation down the path to fascism.[69]

The mushrooming criticism of Johnson and NRA spawned rumors
that he was now ready to leave the agency, but Johnson turned these
reports aside. "I am conscious of the dead cats. I expect them," he told
reporters. Asked about the criticism, he responded that "I can take it.
I have no political ambitions and so I don't care what they say." He had
no intention of leaving NRA, he reiterated, "until the job is done."[70]

IN EARLY November 1933, Hugh Johnson went on a barnstorming tour
of the Middle West to pump up support for NRA. Hoping to convince
farmers that NRA was not making things more difficult for them by
raising prices for consumer goods at the same time that farm prices
were falling, Johnson proudly boasted to his audiences that "N.R.A. *has*
succeeded" in bringing a better life for Americans. Farmers should not
let themselves "be played for a sucker," he roared, by the "tom-tom
beaters" of despair who were urging a revolt against NRA. While con-
ceding that midwestern agricultural prices were lagging behind industrial commodity prices, Johnson was quick to add that "N.R.A. is
creating the market and the urban price for your products."[71] Back in
Washington on November 15, he reported to Roosevelt that the mid-
westerners were behind NRA. But Johnson was only deluding himself.
The audiences on his tour had applauded and cheered his highly print-
able aphorisms and verbal barrages against Old Guard industrialists
and carping critics. However, he had not erased their doubts about
NRA, and one perceptive newsman remarked on Johnson's return that
the country was "getting bored with continued exhibitions of a fighting
man 'cracking down' on everybody who gets a little out of line."[72]

CHAPTER 10

THE PRICE PROBLEM

As NRA administrator Hugh Johnson envisioned a harmony of consonant interests between producers and consumers. Through codes of "fair competition," business would achieve price stabilization (i.e., higher prices) to eliminate the negative effects of competitive price cutting and to insure that it could afford higher wages. Johnson appreciated, however, that price increases must not outrun wage increases. Otherwise, the increased payrolls would be absorbed in the payment of higher prices rather than in the purchase of more goods. The same volume of goods would be sold without any movement toward recovery. As a result, Johnson exhorted business to restrain price increases and to share a small part of its increased earnings from higher prices with labor. In summary, therefore, Johnson espoused a political understanding whereby producers received price floors, while consumers received price ceilings.

Unfortunately, Johnson's concept of community proved faulty, making price policy one of the major fields of controversy for NRA. Many businessmen were primarily concerned with getting their profit-starved firms out of the red. Taking advantage of their dominant position in code making, they wrote a variety of price-control devices into the codes with little regard for their impact on consumers and raised prices faster than wages. Price ceilings based on exhortations, in other words, were not sufficient to protect consumers. As it became apparent that organized business had dominated code making and that the codes were moving in the direction of higher prices and reduced purchasing power, numerous critics charged that NRA was retarding recovery and fostering monopoly. They demanded either the removal of the price-control devices from the codes or broader representation on code authorities and closer government supervision of business. Forced to choose between the business supporters of NRA and the critics of NRA price policy, Johnson sided with the former. He vigorously resisted the onslaught against the codes and only reluctantly made concessions to consumer interests.

HUGH Johnson's initial statements on price policy emphasized that price increases should lag behind wage increases. In press conferences and in discussions with business leaders, he stated that business should hold down prices until the program to reemploy workers was well underway. "We are going to ask something in the nature of an armistice on increased capacity and prices until we get this thing started," he told the press. While recognizing that "the tendency of higher wages is higher prices," he cautioned that

if we do a thing like this and do not also put some control on undue price increases so that prices will not move up one bit faster than is justified by higher wages, the consuming public is going to suffer, the higher wages won't do any good and the whole bright chance will just turn out to be a ghastly failure and another shattered hope.

Johnson added that he would "not stand" for "any wild-cat price lifting," although he was careful to tone down his tough talk with the observation that business could be relied upon to cooperate:

Our best people understand that this is not time to get rich quick. It is the time to pull our country out of a hole. We need every good man on the ropes and nobody is going to do a thing that makes him a peace profiteer by taking advantage of the patriotic unselfishness of his fellow man.[1]

In Johnson's opinion, however, there was an additional dimension to the price problem—sales below cost. He was convinced that sales below cost inevitably led to the sweating of labor and accelerated the downward spiral of the economy. Humanity and recovery, he argued, demanded the end of destructive price-cutting.[2] Consequently, Johnson early took the position that "in these codes it will be proper to have a provision that they are not going to sell products at less than the cost of production." In this way he hoped to raise prices enough so that employers could afford decent wages but not so much that they would soak up purchasing power and introduce new rigidities into the economy. He was careful to remind businessmen, therefore, that sales-below-cost provisions should not be considered license to fix extortionate prices. "If prices are found to be extortionate," he informed reporters at a news conference on July 3, 1933, "and complaint is made and the prices are found to be unjustified, the offending company could be withdrawn from the benefits of the industry's code and that company would then be subject to all the penalties of the Sherman Act."[3]

Despite these pronouncements, there was much to be determined about NRA price policy; and the early codes submitted to NRA contained provisions reflecting almost every shade of opinion on the subject of prices. Since neither NIRA nor Johnson's statements had been very explicit, Stephen M. DuBrul, chief of the Code Analysis Division, pressed Johnson to make a general ruling on price policy, or, failing that, not to approve any codes until an in-depth analysis of all the issues was made.[4] Johnson did not take DuBrul's recommendation, as each industry faced a different set of conditions, and it was "important to the concept of industrial self-government not to have general rules of what should and what should not be in the codes." He emphasized that NRA was experimenting, and "resolutions requiring the Administrator to include or not to include this or that thing" were "very embarrassing to the Administration." Not until October 25, 1933, did Johnson consent to the issuance of a policy memorandum with a standardized guide to price policy and a general idea of what NRA would accept. In the meantime, policy was largely made "by improvisations, by day-to-day responses to contested proposals, business disputes, and emerging problems."[5]

Under these circumstances Johnson's vision of a harmony of interests between producers and consumers meant little in code making. The pressure from business for price protection was terrific. For years trade associations had been seeking a mechanism to stabilize competition through the private control of prices; they had supported NRA primarily out of the hope that it would help them make price agreements. Johnson himself admitted the need to "pretty nearly . . . fix a minimum price" in some industries and told the industrial recovery board that "the purpose of the Act just goes out the window if you don't."[6] Alexander Sachs suggested that in the wild scramble of code negotiation, price-fixing became almost "a panacea for American business, like the brazen serpent in the Book of Numbers which restored to health all those who had been bitten in the wilderness."[7] Business demanded a wide variety of price-fixing powers; and although Johnson sheared off many schemes, few codes went through without some price-controlling device.

Johnson's willingness to give in to business demands for price protection stemmed, in part, from his bad bargaining position. Concerned about the constitutionality of NIRA and believing that industrial acceptance of NRA labor standards had somehow to be greased, he felt compelled to hold out to business the prospect of regulated prices. Recognizing Johnson's attitude, businessmen naturally made the most of their position in the early code negotiations and gained his acceptance of price-control devices in return for agreeing to the higher wages and shorter hours for workers.[8] Moreover, once Johnson had committed himself to the Blue Eagle campaign, he became so involved in the drive for the President's Reemployment Agreement that the drama of code making became more important to him than the details of the codes. Sometimes he inadequately reviewed reports on the possible effects of codes he was to approve. In the case of the copper industry, he was so impatient to codify the industry that he sanctioned whatever price-protection devices the industry wanted.[9]

But the main thing was that Johnson, at heart, agreed with many of the price goals of businessmen. In his opinion, the depression had been brought about by excessive price competition, and price stabilization was necessary to prevent "economic slaughter." Before long his admonition to employers to raise wages first and prices afterward was interspersed with requests simply to raise prices no faster than wages. And his exhortations to keep prices down alternated with prophecies that they were surely going up and even with statements that higher prices were among the NRA goals. As he stated in August 1933:

In the first place, don't forget that nobody expects employers to pay the increased costs of re-employment. This is not possible. The consumer—as always—pays the bill. It is no argument to say, 'Oh this will cost his great company $1,000,000 a year,' or 'this small employer $200 a month.' Of course it will do nothing of the sort. It is inevitable that the employer will raise his prices and will himself pay nothing at all. The only restraint that is asked of him is that he not raise his prices any more than his costs are raised. Except in a limited class of cases there is simply nothing to the claim that any employer pays the bill.[10]

The price-control devices that Johnson encouraged took several forms. The most controversial were devices designed to establish, directly or indirectly, minimum prices through outright prohibitions against sales below cost. Businessmen had repeatedly urged the outlawing of sales below cost, and Johnson had early indicated that he would look favorably on these prohibitions. Critics complained that "cost" was an arbitrary value in such cases, that it was almost impossible to compute and tended to be based on high rather than low costs, that it protected the inefficient producer, and that it increased prices. Johnson, however, retorted that everyone knew what his costs were (or could hire an accountant to find them out) and repeated his dogma that sales below cost constituted chiseling.[11] His statement did little to clarify what actually constituted cost, and only gradually did NRA include additional provisions in the codes for the development of uniform cost-accounting formulas.[12]

In a few instances Johnson sanctioned direct price-fixing. Most conspicuous was the code for the cleaning and dyeing industry. Plagued by low prices and urged by NRA to raise wages and shorten hours, the industry demanded permission to fix prices. The Advisory Committee of the Research and Planning Division of NRA opposed the plan by a vote of nine to one. By oversight, Johnson read only the report of the lone dissenter and mistakenly signed the code in the belief that it had the committee's approval.[13]

Substantial price increases accompanied industrial codification. In fact, many industries raised prices in anticipation of labor cost increases, so that by the time the codes raised wages, they were catching up with prices, not leading them.[14] Johnson was alert to the rising tide of prices. As early as July 20, 1933, he warned that "the rapid rise of retail prices ahead of consumer power may precipitate another crisis."[15] He was thinking of the impact of price increases on labor; if business raised prices too quickly and profits fattened, then labor would want its share too and might resort to disruptive strikes to get it. With little result, Johnson emphasized in his speeches that purchasing power, and only secondarily profits, was the key to recovery. He had given business the opportunity to profit through price increases, and business was going to make the most of it. As price increases outraced wage increases, people slowly began to realize that the codes were promoting cartels in the interest of scarcity profits instead of broad-based recovery.

OPPOSITION to price control developed quickly. Initially from within the Roosevelt administration, the opponents were those economic planners dissatisfied with the dominant role business was playing in code making and wanting greater government supervision. Represented by Rexford Tugwell, they believed that business was using the codes to adopt restrictive price policies and argued that the higher prices fostered by NRA were cancelling out the gains brought by AAA and the wage-and-hour provisions of NIRA. Persuaded that the higher prices hindered recovery, they preferred to see business decisions left to the free market rather than cartels. If there were to be price controls, they wanted planned price ceilings, not the planned price floors Hugh Johnson sought for producers.

Even before the first code was approved, Tugwell and others argued, in the meetings of the Special Industrial Recovery Board, in opposition to price controls and called Johnson's attention to the need to protect purchasing power. Johnson angrily perceived this as nagging. Tugwell noted in his diary: "I protested as violently as I could, so much so that Johnson and I nearly had a personal row." When Tugwell openly challenged him in the fall of 1933, Johnson persuaded Roosevelt to kill the recovery board.[16]

The demise of the Special Industrial Recovery Board did not silence the critics of NRA price policy. Even as Johnson warred with the board, opposition to his price policies was emerging from the liberal, consumer-oriented economists and sociologists who staffed his own NRA Consumers' Advisory Board and Research and Planning Division. Headed by Johnson's friend Mary Rumsey, the Consumers' Advisory Board was made up of individuals who represented varying economic outlooks. But whether they were semi-collectivist in their goals or still confident believers in laissez-faire, they were united in their opposition to the price and production controls Johnson was sanctioning in the codes. Johnson, however, shunted them aside. He had never intended that consumers would play a major role in NRA and had consented to the formation of the Consumers' Advisory Board only to avoid charges that the consumer was being sacrificed by price-fixing and price lifting in the interest of labor and capital. He certainly had no intention of permitting the board to function as a free agency and did not even require reports from it on specific codes until mid-September 1933, by which time the precedent-establishing codes had already been adopted. In Johnson's view the board's expressions of concern about price policy were "troublesome and useless nonsense."[17] He sometimes bluntly summarized his attitude toward the board: "Who the hell cares what your board thinks?"[18]

Johnson's first blowup with the Consumers' Advisory Board occurred in August 1933. From the outset he was at odds with William F. Ogburn, a University of Chicago economist who was serving as Rumsey's executive director. Ogburn was supposed to advise Johnson of the potential harm of codes to consumers, and his early reports were generally critical of the codes. He cautioned Johnson that they lacked adequate machinery for measuring and reporting price increases and suggested numerous changes in code making and administration to protect consumer interests. In addition, he privately complained to Johnson that Rumsey was too amateurish to head the board and called for her replacement with a champion of what Ogburn called "good judgment and discretion."

Johnson had little time for Ogburn. He believed that his code analyses were too complicated to "make heads or tails" of and that his suggestions for safeguarding consumer interests would only delay code making. Hoping to rid himself of Ogburn without a public fuss, Johnson tried to kick him upstairs. But Ogburn rejected that offer, although he promised that he would not publicly air their disagreements before again consulting Johnson. But then he had a change of heart. Breaking his promise, Ogburn resigned from the Consumers' Advisory Board with a blast against Johnson and NRA policies that favored producers.[19]

Ogburn intended his highly publicized departure from NRA to be an alert to Roosevelt and the Special Industrial Recovery Board about the weaknesses of Johnson's direction of the early NRA. But Johnson, furious over Ogburn's blast and his broken word, was able to deflect the criticism and continue business as usual. In reporting his differences with Ogburn to the industrial recovery board, he obscured the fundamental issue. Rather than emphasize the substance of his criticism of NRA price policy, he played up Ogburn's "violent attack" on Mary Rumsey and the circumstances of his resignation. Simultaneously, he took the bite out of much of Ogburn's criticism by creating an NRA section to handle price complaints. Lacking an adequate staff and a well-organized constituency, it proved ineffective in dealing with prices;

for the time being, however, it served Johnson's purpose by pacifying many of his critics and enabling him to ignore any critical governmental group.

Notwithstanding Johnson's indifference toward the Consumers' Advisory Board, it increasingly played an aggressive role in the battle over prices. During the fall of 1933 it issued memoranda and policy statements criticizing the concessions Johnson had made to industry and publicized their detrimental effect on the consumer. At board meetings, Rumsey often interrupted Johnson to make some comment in "defense of consumers of which he was certainly to disapprove." Exasperated, he one day told her to quit harping on the consumers and focus more on the real job of NRA—"to get industry back at making a profit," a comment that in a nutshell summarized the price controversy.[20]

Johnson fumed at the Consumers' Advisory Board, later writing that "I never heard of the Consumers' Advisory Board supporting anything in NRA." On several occasions, with the board obviously in mind, he called upon all members of NRA to "be personally loyal to me" and pleaded with them to "not embarrass the administration" with their statements and reports. In one instance, Alvin Brown, speaking for Johnson, even threatened to abolish the board unless it adopted a conciliatory attitude on code matters and recognized that its job was not simply "to make a record" by objecting to everything.[21]

By November 1933, the disenchantment with NRA price policy was too strong for Johnson to ignore. Reluctantly, he gave in to the Consumers' Advisory Board's demand for public hearings on the price question. Johnson originally scheduled them for December 12; but he postponed them for a month when merchants convinced him that bad publicity from the hearings might dampen their holiday business.[22]

Mary Rumsey, aware that Johnson's postponement of the price hearings disappointed consumers' groups, invited representatives from these groups to meet with her in Washington on December 17. Immediately after the meeting, she took fourteen of the consumer spokesmen to see Johnson. A shouting match between Johnson and Leon Henderson of the Russell Sage Foundation quickly ensued. Henderson protested the delay in the hearings and complained that Johnson was pushing consumers around. Johnson pounded his desk, damning Henderson for his "unjustified complaints." An uncowed Henderson shouted back, and Johnson, caught offguard, roared, "If you're so goddamned smart, why don't you come down here and be my assistant on consumer problems?" It was a dare Henderson quickly accepted.[23]

By bringing one of the most vocal consumer spokesmen into his organization Johnson wrongly thought he had co-opted consumer attacks on NRA. Henderson was a hard worker, a fighter, and a man of ability; and after his appointment as head of the Research and Planning Division in February 1934, he became a major figure in NRA. Previously headed by Alexander Sachs and Stephen DuBrul, the Research and Planning Division had been ineffective. For example, in November 1933, the Cotton Textile Code Authority had proposed that production be curtailed by 25 percent in order to prevent the price decline that usually accompanied seasonal changes in demand. The Research and Planning Division opposed the proposal. But Johnson, who was sympathetic to the proposal and looked on Research and Planning as only a statistical office, bypassed the division and approved the curtailment. Henderson tried to make the division more of a force in NRA and used his post to become one of the most effective critics of NRA's "business-oriented price and production policies."[24] He also became an outspoken proponent of strengthening government, labor, and consumer representation in the code-making process and on the code authorities.

The long-promised price hearing was finally held on January 9 and 10, 1934, in the Commerce Department building, with Arthur D. Whiteside of Dun and Bradstreet, Johnson's most conservative assistant administrator and a long-standing champion of price-fixing, presiding. A parade of witnesses charged that the codes had brought uniformity of bids on government contracts and unjustified price increases. The testimony of the witnesses was buttressed by the work of the Consumers' Advisory Board, which had prepared a series of reports documenting the price situation in specific industries. Certain business leaders were aware of these reports and, threatened by their content, had pressured Johnson and Whiteside not to admit them as evidence. Whiteside, under pressure from the Consumers' Advisory Board, finally relented and permitted the board at least to present statements of its findings. By this time, the credibility of NRA had been damaged, and word that Johnson was gagging the Consumers' Advisory Board was already in the papers.

Johnson had hoped that the price hearing would deflate criticism of NRA price policy, but instead it gave critics more ammunition to use against him; and they put it to good use. Moreover, the drumfire of criticism at the hearing compelled Johnson to modify NRA policy, particularly in regard to the codes' open-price provisions, which sanctioned arrangements requiring businessmen to file prices and exchange price statistics. Witnesses had charged that these arrangements had facilitated monopolistic price-fixing and that they "illustrated the true nature of self-government in industry." Realizing that the criticism could not be glossed over, Johnson, on January 25, 1934, issued an order suspending open-price provisions in all codes not yet approved, pending a study of their impact on the market. Almost immediately, he was deluged by protests from his deputy administrators and trade association leaders, who castigated him for yielding to "political expedience" and bringing about a "dangerous deviation" from established policy. Stung by their protests, Johnson backtracked, ruling that the order would apply only to provisions requiring "waiting periods" before price changes could take effect. Systems providing for revised prices to take effect at once would still be acceptable.

In February 1934, the Consumers' Advisory Board sent a report to Johnson stressing the undesirability of any open-price provision and urging their elimination. But Johnson was not moved. Angry over the board's continued "yapping" on prices, he scribbled on the report such comments as "Anonymous, indefinitive, and not fit for publication," "Appendix A is not evidence," "Nothing of this kind," "No general formula," "Read the Act," and "Balls—just the same." Although he eventually agreed to the publication of the report, Johnson was not amenable to any further change in open-price policy.[25]

THE OPPOSITION to the price-control devices from within the Roosevelt administration was matched by that from small businessmen and their anti-monopolistic Congressional supporters. In battling the code provisions that big business had drafted in its own favor, small business noted numerous non-price advantages that big business possessed, including advertising, brand names, access to credit, control of patents, ability to attract top managers, and the resources to conduct research and develop new products. Small firms, in contrast, often existed only because they offered lower prices than big businesses. These were often possible only because small employers could pay lower wage rates, position themselves conveniently for the customer, and specialize. Without the price and wage differentials, small firms lost the advantages that sustained them. Since the majority of the codes operated to equalize or eliminate these differentials, small businessmen viewed NRA as an effort to legislate them out of existence.[26]

Hugh Johnson rejected the charge that NRA was hurting the little fellow. He contended that the price-control devices actually helped him by preventing big business, which had larger financial resources, from underselling small firms and then establishing a monopoly.[27] Johnson's opinion was that NRA's small business critics were mainly sweatshop employers who were masking their true motivation for opposing the codes. "The only 'Little Fellow' complaint of wide application of which I have any knowledge," he later wrote, "is that the *Little Fellow does not want to pay code wages for code hours.*"[28]

Though he could not ignore its complaints, Johnson never retreated from his view that NRA was good for small business. Outcries against monopoly have had a powerful emotional appeal in this country's history, and the small business community had many vocal anti-monopolists in the Congress, most particularly Republican Senators William Borah and Gerald Nye. Agrarian progressives who feared that NRA threatened freedom by consolidating power in the hands of big business and big government, they believed freedom would be secure only as long as America remained in the hands of yeomen farmers and small businessmen. During the Senate debate over NIRA, Borah had strongly opposed the provision suspending the antitrust laws, while Nye had early warned that the "big fellows" intended to use the codes so that they could "consume the little boys for dessert."[29] When the Seventy-third Congress began its second session on January 3, 1934, the two men intensified their attack against NRA. Speaking before the Senate on January 18, Nye charged that NRA was breeding monopoly and predicted that the "plunderers" would "trample under heel" whatever remained of small business if present policy was continued. Borah reiterated Nye's message, adding that his office had already received 9,000 letters of complaint from small businessmen.[30]

Johnson viewed Borah's and Nye's incessant attacks with contempt. Considering anyone who failed to recognize the grandeur and nobility of NRA an unmitigated villain, devoid of honor, and destitute of shame, he went on a blistering counterattack, challenging the senators to offer remedies for alleged defects. In a January 18 speech before the National Retail Dry Goods Association in New York City, Johnson blasted his critics as "sideline beaters of the tom-tom of public incitement, and doers of nothing whatever except the composition of diatribe." They knew about as much about industry, he continued, as he knew about the "queer ichthyology of the great Pacific Deep."[31]

Johnson's blast surprised Borah and Nye, who had not realized that they were fighting with Johnson until he sprang on them. Yet they were prepared to take up the challenge. Nye dubbed Johnson a "Nero" who ranted and raved while the country burned; "but all the browbeating he may resort to will not destroy, though it may delay, knowledge of what NRA policy is doing." Borah was equally defiant. "Nothing," he said, "can dispose of the fact that many small firms are being driven out of business through the practices of combines and trusts. When these things are remedied, I will cease my efforts and not until then."[32]

His violent counterattack against Borah and Nye did not alleviate the growing pressure on Johnson to do something about prices and small business. The two senators were now joined by others. Johnson had to head them off or risk a Senate investigation of NRA, and he grudgingly gave ground. At his behest, Roosevelt issued an executive order on January 20, 1934, allowing any individual who believed that he was injured by unfair business practices under NRA to take his grievance to the FTC and the Department of Justice. The same day, Richberg issued a supplementary statement that the antitrust laws were not suspended in full and that NRA would not tolerate monopolistic practices not expressly approved by the administration.[33] Four days later, after a talk with Roosevelt and Senators Borah and Nye, Johnson announced that he planned to convene a special board of prominent persons to hear complaints. Finally, Johnson appointed Whiteside as his special assistant on credit and finance with responsibility for looking after the needs of "smaller business where the difficulty of obtaining credit may be one of the severest handicaps in competing with larger enterprises."

Johnson's concessions only whetted the appetites of Borah and Nye. After learning that the FTC had prepared a memorandum criticizing the steel code, Borah in early February authored Senate resolutions calling upon the FTC to probe price-fixing in the steel and oil industries.[34] Nye followed with a resolution of his own, calling on Johnson to provide the Senate with the names and business affiliations of all code authority members so that the extent of business control over NRA could be determined. And in an impassioned radio address on February 7 Borah, in discussing the plight of small business, scored Johnson's defense of NRA: "When these conditions are pointed out, someone goes into a trance and begins to ejaculate about how we cannot go back to rugged individualism; that we have arrived at a new era of planned industrialism." But whatever label the new industrial order carried, it brought domination by "combines, trusts, and monopolies" and was a "brutal indefensible system."[35]

Johnson decided, after Borah and Nye introduced their resolutions, that he must take the initiative away from his critics. If he failed to defuse them and shore up his support within the business community, he faced the unraveling of NRA. In a radio address on February 20, 1934, he called for a grand conference of the code authorities to convene on March 5 to review NRA policy. Prior to that he would arrange a "field day of criticism," beginning February 27, so that his critics could "blow off steam."[36]

Johnson opened the "field day of criticism" with a ninety-minute harangue before an overflow crowd in the Commerce Department auditorium. He flayed faultfinders in general, admitted some errors, and proposed a whole series of improvements that included better rules for working hours and wages, more adequate representation for labor and consumers, and stricter enforcement of code provisions. Two themes ran through the speech: first, NRA was putting men back to work and increasing purchasing power despite some shortcomings; second, NRA's enemies were basically those who opposed higher wages and shorter hours.[37]

Johnson's comments did nothing to lessen the ferocity of the attacks levelled against NRA during the four days of the "field day of criticism." By the time the critics finished, one observer noted, there was "left little that seemed desirable, or even decent, of the N.R.A." Johnson was disconcerted by the outpouring of criticism. He had naturally expected some and, in fact, had already made plans to use it during the March 5 meeting to persuade business to live up to NRA labor standards. But the critics' fierce indignation and ruthlessness showed how far the nation had traveled since August, when millions had hopefully marched behind the Blue Eagle. Johnson's army was deserting.[38] Yet summing up the results of the "field day of criticism" in a closing speech on March 2, he bravely put on the best face possible. He interpreted the four days of protests as unqualified support of NRA, saying that the criticism he had heard did not go beyond the program to which he had committed himself in his opening address.[39]

Three days later President Roosevelt opened the meeting of the 4,200 code authority representatives at Constitution Hall with a long speech echoing the thrust of Johnson's interpretation of the "field day of criticism" and calling for the adoption of the "Ten-and-Ten Plan" Johnson had presented then. It called for a 10 percent reduction in hours and a 10 percent increase in wages. Developed to appease NRA's labor critics, the Ten-and-Ten Plan was designed to spread work around and increase purchasing power. When Johnson had first proposed that Roosevelt endorse the plan in his speech, Secretary of Labor Perkins had vigorously opposed him on the grounds that he was "using the prestige of the White House to cover up shortcomings of the NRA." Arguing that he should not endorse any specific program before it had been fully studied, she persuaded Roosevelt to delete the plan and make only general statements of goodwill. But Johnson, in an emotional blowup, got Roosevelt to change his mind again. Roosevelt explained this reversal by saying to Perkins: "Oh, anything to satisfy Hugh." Several more times Perkins convinced Roosevelt to delete the plan, and each time Johnson got Roosevelt to put it back into the speech.[40]

Johnson's hope that he could use the pro-business gathering of code authorities to regain the initiative from NRA's critics was quickly dashed. To his bafflement, speaker after speaker damned the Ten-and-Ten Plan, claiming that any reduction of the forty-hour week "would bring a depression ten times worse" than the one the nation was enduring. Rather than concern themselves with the needs of labor and the consumer, the code authority representatives preferred talking about the trend toward "Bureaucracy" in the NRA organization—frequent shifts in NRA policy, overlapping codes, and the like—and the necessity for price-control devices. Confronted with this, the only specific action Johnson could take was to announce the formation of three study commissions—hardly necessary, given the studies already done by the Consumers' Advisory Board and the Research and Planning Division.

The "field day of criticism" and the gathering of the code authority representatives did not solve Johnson's problems with his critics. Instead, the new data stimulated an additional round of studies, debates, and divided councils. On the one hand, the pro-business elements within NRA continued to stress the importance of price stabilization through the price-control devices. On the other hand, the Consumers' Advisory Board and the Research and Planning Division stepped up their attacks against the price-control devices and called for prices determined either by free competition or an independent agency with more concern for consumer welfare. The critics of NRA received encouragement on March 19, when the FTC transmitted its report on the steel code to Roosevelt. FTC member James M. Landis later explained his agency's longtime wariness of Johnson and NRA: "what they were doing in these codes was legalizing, in many situations, practices upon which the FTC had already established a cease and desist order."[41] The FTC report charged that Bethlehem Steel and U.S. Steel absolutely controlled the Steel Code Authority and further noted that prices had advanced greatly since the code went into effect. It also singled out the basing-point price system, which was sanctioned in the code, as a violation of the NIRA and of an earlier cease-and-desist order issued by the commission. (Under the basing-point price system the manufacturer charged a price calculated by adding the freight charge from an agreed point, regardless of the actual point from which the product was shipped. It acted to minimize the geographical factor in competition.) Most ominously, the FTC proposed to proceed against the industry on that basis.[42] All this was bad enough for Johnson. But the newly created National Recovery Review Board was already at work on what promised to be a devastating analysis of NRA, adding one more major worry.

THE NATIONAL Recovery Review Board was conceived in December 1933 by Senator Nye. He suggested to Hugh Johnson that a board, made up of prominent anti-monopolists like Senators Borah; Robert LaFollette, Jr., Progressive from Wisconsin; and George Norris, Independent from Nebraska, be established to review NRA policies. Johnson, in turn, communicated the suggestion to Roosevelt with his cautious endorsement.[43] Favoring the idea because he had heard that the proposed board would head off a Senate investigation of NRA, Johnson expected the board to operate within NRA—under his thumb. Roosevelt was also favorably disposed toward the idea. He saw it as a way to bring progressive Republicans who had been critical of NRA into his New Deal coalition.[44] On December 29 Johnson conferred with Roosevelt, Nye, and Borah. The two senators declined board membership, as it would compromise their independence; and all then agreed that the board should not include any legislators. After a month of acrimonious negotiations, Roosevelt advised Johnson to make his peace with the senators. The result was an agreement framed by Nye and Johnson, under which the senators would suggest the board members.

Johnson and Nye at first wanted Samuel Seabury, widely known for his probe of corruption in New York City, to chair the recovery review board. When he demurred, Richberg proposed Clarence Darrow, the famed criminal lawyer and civil libertarian from Chicago. Like many Americans, Johnson was awed by Darrow's reputation and had "always admired his consistent intransigence and barnyard philosophy." In addition, Darrow was a noted liberal, and Johnson believed that NRA was a "liberal" program when compared to "cut-throat" competition. Although Johnson knew Darrow only by reputation, he thought him a wise choice. If Darrow found little wrong with NRA, it would be an invaluable boost to the agency's prestige, since this man was demonstrably not in the administration's hip pocket. And if Darrow proved troublesome, he was, after all, seventy-seven years old. Johnson was sure of his ability to persuade the elderly lawyer to produce a favorable report, directed by NRA itself. Johnson may also have counted on Darrow for an unorthodox, controversial report, one that would be easier to discredit than a moderate, conventional one conforming to the views of the mainstream critics of NRA.[45] Whatever his reasons, Johnson believed that he had nothing to fear from a recovery review board chaired by Darrow.

Johnson planned to place the Darrow Board under his own jurisdiction, and on March 6 he told the members in their first meeting that they could do some investigating and "let me know if the codes were all right." In this way he could keep any criticism inside NRA, where it could not be used by NRA's enemies to pillory him and the agency. Suppose "we find out the codes are not all right?" Darrow asked Johnson. "Then you report to me," replied Johnson. "I am the big cheese here." To facilitate his control, Johnson offered to have the NRA staff write the report.[46]

Darrow would have nothing to do with Johnson's plans. He had not come to Washington to wage what was probably his last big crusade just to be turned into a lackey. He declined the help of the NRA staff and abruptly marched over to the White House to complain directly to Roosevelt about Johnson's proposed line of authority. Not wanting to get off on the wrong foot with Darrow, Roosevelt, in his March 7 executive order formally creating the review board, stated that the board would report directly to the president.

The first of three reports prepared by the Darrow Board was sent to Roosevelt on May 1. Concentrating on eight codes, it was a scathing assault on NRA. The government, the report contended, had sanctioned monopolistic practices that were oppressing the little fellow. Only the cleaning and dyeing code was free of monopoly, the board said; and that code was not being enforced. To correct this situation, Darrow's board recommended the elimination of most price-control devices, major changes in the code authorities, and a return to the antitrust laws. In a brief supplement, Darrow and William O. Thompson, Darrow's former law partner and a member of the review board, postulated that recovery could only be achieved through the fullest use of productive capacity, which lay "in the planned use of America's resources following socialization."[47]

For the next seventeen days Washington was agog with excitement, awaiting the report. Instead of releasing it to the public immediately, Roosevelt had given it to Johnson so that the NRA staff could prepare an item-by-item rebuttal. This delay backfired. It only heightened public curiosity. Nye delightedly remarked, "If General Johnson wants to make an answer it will take him longer than a week to prepare it. If the administration had wished to make the Darrow report a best seller it could not have undertaken a better course than it has so far."[48] On May 20, already a tremendous sensation, the Darrow Board report, 155 pages long, was finally given to the press, along with NRA's 157-page rejoinder.

In his transmittal letter to Roosevelt, Johnson branded the Darrow Board report as the most "superficial, intemperate and inaccurate document" he had ever seen. Accurately viewing the supplementary report as a vulnerable target, he charged that Darrow's board gave Americans only a choice between "Fascism and Communism, neither of which can be espoused by anyone who believes in our democratic institutions of self-government." The review board, he urged, should be abolished immediately lest its continued existence impair "seriously the usefulness of the National Recovery Administration."[49] Johnson was even more biting in his memoir. "Bloody old Jeffries at the Assizes," he wrote, "never conducted any hearings equal to those for cavalier disposal of cases." The hearings, he added, were like "a Cave of Adullam to which every man who had a grievance, real or fancied, could come to the wailing wall and have his complaint avidly encouraged and promptly underwritten without the slightest inquiry into its merits."[50]

Johnson was correct in condemning the Darrow Board. Darrow's whole conception of liberty and economic well-being was rooted in nineteenth-century individualism—the very antithesis of NRA—and the board he directed made no effort to seek a cross section of small business opinion. Generally, it called witnesses it knew would condemn NRA. The board's report was based on selective evidence and included no statistical analysis determining the actual effect of NRA policy on small business. Consequently, it failed to prove either that the majority of small businesses opposed NRA or that NRA codes harmed small businesses. The report also blamed NRA for "unfair" practices such as basing-point pricing, which actually predated NRA, and contained numerous contradictions. Finally, the report portrayed monopoly as much more oppressive than evidence indicated. Johnson pointed out many of these weaknesses and was thus able to contain the damage done; he was even able to discredit the report among those readers inclined to give NRA the benefit of the doubt. Yet the report had a significant impact, demonstrating, as it did, the many monopolistic, questionable legal procedures in the codes. It certainly furthered debate over the merits of NRA policy.[51]

The release of the first Darrow Board report ignited a feud between Johnson and Darrow. The two began firing verbal barrages at each other, with a certain creative delight. Johnson spewed forth his characteristic invective, amply laced with picturesque language. Darrow retorted in simple prose. Although the feud generated considerable publicity, it failed to enlighten anyone about NRA. In fact, the two colorful characters had so many partisans and were able to be so intriguing as personalities that argument on the existence of monopoly was more or less the background to the Johnson-Darrow show.[52]

The last two Darrow Board reports were similar to the first and therefore aroused little in the way of interest or headlines; and as it developed, the board had little effect on the actual workings of the codes. Yet it played an important role in the history of NRA. It "brought violently into the open" the issues which had worried the Special Industrial Recovery Board and the Consumers' Advisory Board and "provided the perfect forum for the small business critics of the NRA." Johnson furiously inveighed against the Darrow Board, arguing that it had unfairly "traduced on the basis of erratic and *ex parte* hearings" the achievements of men like himself "who had worked long and hard to bring order out of industrial chaos." But whatever the merits of the Darrow Board, one thing was obvious: The Blue Eagle, as one editor pointed out, had "lost some feathers from the discharge of the Board of Review's shotgun."[53] Johnson's critics renewed their attack on his leadership with confidence and vigor.

IN THE spring and summer of 1934 the codes were daily subjected to criticism. The Consumers' Advisory Board, the Research and Planning Division, the Darrow Board, and others were all getting in their jabs, and they were now joined by pro–New Deal voices in the press and progressive reformers. At the same time, numerous government agencies persisted in their own questioning of the codes, and even Adolf Berle, a onetime supporter of industrial self-government, wrote Hugh Johnson that the codes hurt small business.[54] Johnson was nevertheless determined to ride out the storm. Convinced that NRA was a noble experiment in industrial self-government that would win the battle against the depression, he refused to buckle under to his critics. Since he retained Roosevelt's support, he was still able to win battles. But increasingly, the mounting criticism forced him to make concessions that presaged the end of large-scale price control.

Johnson won a major victory in the renewal of the steel code, which was scheduled to expire at the end of May 1934. Because the code contained the controversial basing-point price provision, Johnson wanted to circumvent the critics and renew it with as little fanfare as possible. Two problems emerged—the FTC and organized labor. Each was anxious to make an issue of the code. But in both cases Johnson was able to silence them and achieve his goal.

When the FTC report on the steel code was issued, Johnson took the position that it revealed nothing that he did not already know and that the code would be modified.[55] Negotiations for a revised code were carried on by NRA and American Iron and Steel Institute officials in late April and early May 1934. They agreed on several changes, although none greatly altered the pattern of trade and labor practices laid down the previous August. The FTC, however, was determined to be heard and informed Johnson that it intended to file suit against the steel industry. Johnson was appalled at the FTC stance. Not only did he resent its intrusion into his business, he feared that FTC action against the steel industry would undermine NRA. As he later wrote, "I admire the Federal Trade Commission, but at this crisis we must look facts in the teeth and by moving in to take over NRA it can only kill NIRA."[56]

Talks between Johnson and FTC officials failed to resolve the issue, and Johnson, now very angry over the prospect of FTC action against the industry, told Roosevelt that a suit would destroy NRA. Anxious to avoid a collision between NRA and the FTC and possibly wreck his entente with business, Roosevelt sided with Johnson. He persuaded the FTC not to take any immediate action and instructed Johnson and the FTC to continue negotiations to resolve their differences. They were still mulling them over when Johnson left NRA in October 1934.[57]

Unhappy over the labor provisions of the steel code, labor leaders wanted an open hearing to air their grievances. Johnson was not receptive and announced that an open hearing "on purely economic and technical corrections" would be counterproductive because of a threatened labor stoppage in the mills. Dissatisfied with Johnson's announcement, William Green recommended that the code be rejected, claiming that it had failed to relieve unemployment, increase purchasing power, or improve labor relations. But Johnson would not budge. On May 22 he sent the revised code to the White House for Roosevelt's approval without holding a hearing.

In his letter of transmittal, Johnson downplayed the complaints lodged against the code. They were "largely theoretical," he wrote, and based on the supposition that the code might encourage monopoly. In fact, he claimed, the industry was "highly competitive," and small firms had actually been helped by the code. He further stated that the basing-point price system should be retained "to maintain existing areas of production and channels of distribution and to prevent violent dislocations." While admitting that there were serious complaints emanating from the labor provisions, Johnson observed that workers were better off with the code. In his only concession to the critics Johnson suggested that Roosevelt should couple his approval with an order to

NRA and the FTC to conduct a joint study of the basing-point price system. Roosevelt accepted Johnson's recommendations, and on May 30 he issued an executive order approving the revised code. By standing together, Johnson and the industry had successfully maintained the basic fabric for the industry that they had established in the original code.[58]

Johnson's victory with the steel code was not matched by other triumphs. The general clamor against the codes was intensifying. Reluctantly, he again yielded to some of the critics' demands. After months of delay and over the strong opposition of industrial leaders he broadened the makeup of some of the code authorities to include non-industry representatives, whose role in the code authorities had sparked controversy for some time. Johnson was inclined to let industry run its own affairs, free from government intervention, as long as it did not abuse its power. In appointing the code authorities, therefore, he had largely drawn upon the business community for recruits and counted upon them to do the right thing. Labor and consumer groups, meanwhile, sought membership on code authorities in order to have a voice in the government of industry. Industry leaders strenuously objected to their admission to the code authorities; and Johnson, unwilling to see NRA disrupted by this question, had supported the businessmen.[59]

Beset by mounting complaints from non-industry groups, Johnson attempted to placate his critics by appointing government representatives to some of the code authorities in December 1933, but this action came too late. The government representatives usually came from the ranks of the industry and served "on a part-time, non-paid basis . . . with very little power, either to vote or to act on their own initiative." Unsatisfied by Johnson's action, his critics kept up their call for labor and consumer representatives on the code authorities. A despairing Johnson finally capitulated, though he was careful not to antagonize industry too much. Although they could have access to minutes and the right to speak before the authorities to make statements on specific subjects, the labor and consumer representatives were to attend code authority meetings only by invitation. Not surprisingly, these representatives had only negligible influence.[60]

In late May 1934, Johnson retreated from an area in which NRA was obviously overextended. Acknowledging criticism from small business, he eased the regulation of the service trades by granting exemptions from the trade practice provisions of the service codes for such groups as barbers, beauticians, and dry cleaners.[61] The cleaning and dyeing code had been particularly vexing. Johnson had approved price-fixing in it. But the atomistic structure of the industry made the code extremely difficult to enforce, and attempts to do so built up more consumer opposition to NRA than any of Johnson's other projects. Nothing had so disastrously symbolized NRA's alleged oppression of the little fellow than the dry cleaner in New Jersey drummed out for pressing suits at less than code price. By exempting the service trades from major code provisions, Johnson belatedly acknowledged that conditions in such businesses were not yet amenable to industrial self-government.[62]

Unable to escape the growing criticism of the codes, Johnson created NRA's Policy Group, which would assist in the long-neglected effort to produce clear-cut, written policy guidelines for NRA officials. Leverett S. Lyon of the Brookings Institution, a strong critic of NRA price-control devices, headed the group's trade practices division. During the last days of May 1934, he developed criteria by which code provisions could be judged and recommended the elimination or modification of many of the price-control devices that had been incorporated into the codes. His recommendations were the stimulus for Office Memorandum 228. Issued on June 7, 1934, it prohibited price-fixing, although Johnson diluted the prohibition to permit the setting of minimum prices in "emergencies."[63]

Office Memorandum 228 was one of the most controversial statements of NRA policy. Johnson's critics interpreted the memorandum as a major victory for their point of view, and the press proclaimed it as an abandonment of all price-fixing. But businessmen and code authorities howled in protest, and pro-business NRA officials threatened resignation. Faced with a revolt by his staunchest supporters, Johnson hastily retreated. Late in the afternoon of June 8, in a telephoned speech to the convention of the Ladies' Garment Workers Union in Chicago, he stated that

there has been some misunderstanding about a recently announced N.R.A. policy on prices. I cannot use too much emphasis in saying that this policy does not affect codes already approved. It is not a reversal of previous views. It was stated only for the sake of getting some uniformity in future codes.[64]

Johnson's point was that, with more than 90 percent of NRA-subject industries already codified, Office Memorandum 228 would have little practical effect. Price-control devices would certainly continue to be part of NRA. But the memorandum's importance was that it indicated, at least on paper, that large-scale price regulation was over and that future NRA price policy would direct itself toward strengthening, not limiting competition.

CHAPTER 11

LABOR POLICY

HUGH Johnson engendered as much controversy handling labor policy as he had done with the price problem. His attitude toward labor, rooted in his concept of it as a general producer interest, was complex and somewhat personal.[1] In his mind, labor was as much a part of the producer interest as management; and, facilitated by NRA, the two could work as a unit for the benefit of the industrial sector and ultimately the national welfare. Employers and workers had to be organized for this organizational vision to be realized. Johnson remarked to Frances Perkins that "if we didn't have these trade unions and trade organizations, we'd have to form them."[2]

Labor leaders were encouraged by Johnson's endorsement of unions. But his view of their role differed significantly from that of union members and leaders. They believed that a union should exist to get the best possible wages and working conditions for its members. Johnson, in contrast, believed that a union should function primarily to strengthen the economy of the nation and, in particular, to be supportive of the conditions of the industry in which it operated so that it could help develop its industry and move it into "its proper economic place in the whole sphere of the economy of the nation." Johnson often used the cotton textile industry to illustrate this concept:

The cotton textile industry is an old and declining industry. It has reached its peak long ago. It was the first industry that was affected by the industrial revolution with the introduction of machinery. It has reached its peak long ahead of the others and it never can hope to have the expansion, therefore the profits, therefore the wages, therefore the easy working conditions that other industries have. The people of the trade union of the cotton textile industry must contribute to this idea that the cotton textile industry in relation to the other industries of the country is of less importance and that the rewards will not be as great either in profits or in wages, as they were in other industries.

Frances Perkins's response to this was that cotton textile workers might not want to accept lower wages just because they worked in that industry, to which Johnson shot back:

Well, that's what they must learn. That's what the union should teach them. That's what the union should make possible for them. Their codes should reflect that. You can't expect the cotton textile industry to pay the same wages that are paid in a highly profitable manufacture of something new that has an enormous market like electrical machinery.[3]

Johnson elaborated on his ideas in a series of informal lectures given on Thursday evenings early in the life of NRA. The fifty to a hundred who attended came from employer and labor groups and the Department of Labor, and neither labor nor management was receptive to the ideas. The employers were startled by Johnson's suggestion that unions should have a definite voice in the affairs of an industry. They were convinced that unions had nothing to contribute to the economic thinking about an industry, and they could not conceive of a situation in which labor might have some prerogative in an industry's affairs. And most of the labor people were uninterested in the economics of industry, considering that the preserve of management. Their desires were for better wages and working conditions for their members. Both groups were suspicious of the role of government in Johnson's scheme of labor-management relations. The notion they had trouble with was that of labor and management taking orders from the government on questions of wages and working conditions, a frequent theme in the lectures.

Johnson not only believed unions to be a necessity; he had a genuine, if not consistent, sympathy for the plight of workers. He tended to be most cordial with workers who came to his office to air grievances and, in fact, often advised them to organize, in order to deal most effectively with their employers. In a code hearing once, disgusted when union officials were being outtalked by "high-priced industry lawyers," Johnson called for a temporary adjournment and instructed Leon Henderson to take the union men aside and give them better statistics and arguments.[4]

Johnson also liked many union leaders, especially John L. Lewis, head of the United Mine Workers, who shared his enthusiasm for military strategy, Napoleon, and, as Frances Perkins described them, "sad old songs." Once, returning to Washington from a NRA rally in Richmond, Virginia, the two sat in the backseat of Johnson's limousine warbling songs from the Great War for the entire countryside to hear. Lewis cultivated Johnson for practical reasons, of course, but he also liked Johnson and wanted to be "part of the glory" of NRA. For his part, Johnson believed that if he was friends with Lewis he could more easily win most labor leaders over to his ideas. There was no question in Johnson's view that Lewis was the best labor leader, one who he believed fought for the coal industry "just as hard as do its managers." With Lewis behind him, Johnson felt certain that other union leaders would fall into line. But other labor leaders, resenting what they saw as Lewis's blatant ambition, kept him at arm's length.[5] They were determined Lewis would not lead them.

Despite his sympathy with workers and despite his endorsement of unions, Johnson was never completely a labor man. Always opposed to strikes, he had been nurtured in the U.S. Army, which had suppressed labor disputes for the thirty years before he entered and whose officer corps shared the middle- and upper-class reverence for property and fear of anarchy and radicalism. Johnson's fellow officers had regarded collective bargaining and the closed shop as un-American and strikes, and the methods used to support them, as violations of property rights and the rights of non-strikers. They also believed strikes generally became riots and that unions, by resorting to the strike, were responsible for disorder.[6]

Johnson's opposition to strikes was also affected by his view of labor as a producer among producers. As strikes were counterproductive, producers never went out on strike, particularly in community crises. The final, and perhaps major, reason for Johnson's opposition to strikes—and for his ambivalent behavior toward labor—was his supreme confidence that he knew what was best for everybody. Since in his opinion NRA was doing a great deal for workers, he was the champion they should trust. If they failed to do so, this champion had to consider their strikes mutinies against his leadership.

The result was theoretical and practical chaos. Johnson supported labor's right to organize. But he viewed the unions' traditional weapon, the strike, as an obstacle to recovery. Strikers were at least public enemies; and strikes, therefore, had to be settled, regardless of the rights and wrongs in the dispute. The right formula was, simply, the one that would get labor back to work.

The government's World War I labor policies also shaped Johnson's perception of unions and strikes. The government had to avoid strikes and so encouraged workers to organize and prohibited businesses from discriminating between union and non-union workers. But the government never risked the wrath of business. The unions were granted no significant power, and the government did nothing to induce or compel companies to recognize unions or bargain with them.[7] As a war mobilizer, Johnson was familiar with these labor policies, and he believed that they had served the nation well. There had been no costly labor disturbances, and the pace of war production was only minimally disrupted by strikes. Johnson believed that similar policies would serve the nation equally well in its current crisis.

Johnson's experience as an executive also tempered his endorsement of unions. Where unions saw the nation's industrialists as ogres who oppressed the workers for the sake of one more cent of profit, Johnson naturally stood with industrialists. He saw them—many his good friends, whose problems he understood—as hardworking, well-intentioned men struggling to keep their enterprises afloat. They deserved support, not condemnation. Conversely, Johnson had little first-

RECOVERY ADMINISTRATOR CONFERS WITH LABOR LEADERS. In the first row, left to right, are Rose Schneiderman, Secretary Frances Perkins, General Johnson, Leo Wolman, John L. Lewis, and Francis Haas. Standing, left to right, are Joseph Franklin, John Frey, Edward McGrady, and Sidney Hillman. The Bettmann Archive, Inc.

hand knowledge of the problems of labor and had only recently made acquaintances with important labor leaders.

Finally, Johnson believed that organized labor was a secondary concern of NRA. As he read NIRA, NRA was specifically required to promote the organization of industry; in the case of labor, though, there was no such mandate. NRA had only to see that labor had absolute freedom to determine whether to organize and similar freedom to select the form of organization.[8]

The two foundations of Johnson's labor policy—first, that workers not only had the right to organize but, in fact, should do so in order to function effectively as partners of management in the general producer interest; and second, that workers should not strike—were unworkable. Management dissented with the first precept, labor leaders with the second. The result was widespread conflict to which Johnson responded by the issuance of numerous pronouncements on labor-management relations and repeated attempts to adjust labor disputes. He faced a knotty situation. The support of business was essential to the success of NRA; if Johnson alienated business, business could repudiate the recovery program. At the same time, costly strikes could scotch the recovery program almost before it was begun. Consequently, Johnson responded to specific labor matters in terms of conformity to actual power. This, combined with his identification with employers and his interpretation of NIRA, led him into a pro-management stance that earned him the enmity of labor.

HUGH Johnson's pro-management stance on labor matters emerged in the earliest stages of NRA. He would see to it that Section 7a of Title I, which granted workers the right to organize and bargain collectively, was respected. But he construed this right in such a way that it would not threaten the dominance of business over labor. In this way he would abide by the law and at the same time keep Section 7a from becoming a disruptive factor in the codification of industry. Johnson particularly feared that major industries might resist codification out of a concern that NRA would force them to allow their employees to organize and went out of his way in his initial statements on labor matters to allay their concerns. Even before he was appointed NRA administrator, he told reporters that NRA would not be "primarily interested in promoting trade unions or collective bargaining." His personal concerns, he continued, were wages and hours and the spread of employment, not the form of labor organization, and he would "not be disposed to disturb satisfactory relationships."[9] Johnson reiterated this position in the days immediately following his appointment. In a press conference on June 20, 1933, he stated that "this Administration is not going to be used as a means of unionizing any industry." And in a speech five days later, he said that "it is not the function or the purpose of the Administration to organize industry or labor."[10]

Nonetheless, many employers remained wary of Section 7a and decided that the best way to satisfy the law without upsetting their dominance over labor was to herd their workers into company unions, an effort they strengthened by appeals to patriotism and political loyalty (President Roosevelt was said to want them to join company unions) and by appeals to economic needs (this was the way labor could get a fair deal under NRA). Independent union organizers countered by telling workers that the only way to benefit from NIRA was to join them. Johnson regarded both interpretations as perversions of the law, and in a July 7 press release he berated labor and management for their self-serving propaganda. Their interpretations of Section 7a, he declared, were "incorrect," "erroneous," and intended to "foment misunderstanding and discord." Seeking the middle ground, he repeated his previous announcement that it was not his function or purpose "to organize either industry or labor."[11]

The July 7 press release failed to resolve the confusion about Section 7a. Johnson had said which interpretations were incorrect, but he had not stated a correct interpretation. The fact that negotiations for several major codes were bogged down because of uncertainty over Section 7a finally spurred Johnson's interpretation. It was shaped to a great degree by his experience in negotiating the auto code, where he had veered strongly toward support of management's view of Section 7a in order to get the reluctant auto industry codified. In a meeting with the Special Industrial Recovery Board on August 14 he advised that "it is not a condition [of the law] that a person shall belong, or shall not belong, to a union. This law should bring about open shops—shops where a man will be employed regardless of whether he belongs to any union or not." Perkins prodded Johnson into admitting that the law did not "force open shops." However, there could be no doubt about Johnson's position—open shops were not only permissible, they were desirable.[12]

A week later Johnson and Donald Richberg issued a statement purporting to outline "the plain meaning of Section 7(a)." The words "open shop" and "closed shop" were hereafter banned from the "dictionary of the N.R.A.," because they had "no agreed meaning." Section 7a, the statement continued, "can mean only one thing, which is that employees can choose anyone they desire to represent them, or they can choose to represent themselves." Employers, meanwhile, were free to "make collective bargains with organized employees, or individual agreements with those who choose to act individually." In other words, the representatives of the majority of workers would not speak for all the workers; individuals and minorities could do their own bargaining and make their own separate agreements. Johnson and Richberg stated, in addition, that Section 7a did not preclude the existence of company unions, as long as they were freely chosen by the employees.[13]

Johnson believed that the August 23 statement represented a neutral stance on labor policy. But in effect it placed him in the corner of management. Even though workers had the right to organize and bargain collectively, there was no obligation on the part of the employer to reach agreements with them. Further, the stand against majority rule in unionization undercut the benefits labor leaders expected Section 7a to yield. The sanctioning of company unions, of course, offered management an ideal opportunity to abide by the letter of the law while evading its spirit, at least in the view of labor people and their supporters, who believed the law's purpose was to foster and protect independent labor organizations.[14] When his position on multiple representation was later assailed, Johnson wrote in his own defense that he never regarded "a majority and a minority union in the same shop as practicable"; he was only "[carrying out] the law I had sworn to execute."[15] Many problems that NRA encountered, he continued, could have been avoided if only one union organization was recognized. Whatever his later opinion, however, Johnson never retreated from the August 23 statement while he was head of NRA.

The conflicting interpretations of Section 7a produced a rash of strikes, to Johnson's fury. Considering the strikes strictly as impediments to recovery, he wanted them settled quickly and was ready to rush in and do it himself if necessary. Johnson quotes Frances Perkins's joking observation that "the trouble with Hugh is that he thinks a strike is something to settle."[16] Indeed, Johnson was so incensed by the strikes that he privately suggested that "some very violent action of force" should be taken against the strikers. Informed that many of the strikes were really caused by employers who refused to bargain with unions, his thought was "to force the employer to do it." He spent a great many frustrated days, sometimes relieving his tensions by recalling the WIB days. Though he once said to Perkins, "I can stop them. I can deprive them of their supplies, cut off their raw materials," Johnson knew that he had no authority to deny anybody anything. He agreed in calmer times with Perkins and knew that strikes had to be settled through conciliation.[17]

Anticipating the possibility of numerous disputes, Johnson, even before NIRA was approved, had proposed the creation of a labor tribunal, modeled after the War Labor Board of the wartime mobilization.[18] He included such a body in the first organizational charts he prepared for NRA; however, Perkins, who saw the tribunal as a rival to the mediation service of the Department of Labor, spoke against Johnson's proposal, and Roosevelt refused to approve it.[19] A wave of strikes in the summer of 1933 and, more important, his own mediation efforts in the bituminous coal strike, prompted Johnson to renew his proposal. Perkins protested that the Department of Labor should continue to handle all conciliation efforts. Johnson replied that its efforts were too slow. He also argued that employers would never respond to the Department of Labor conciliators. The mandate of the Department of Labor, he wrote, was "to advance and advocate the cause of labor with a result that, if *that* Department were to act as arbitrators, management would regard itself as being forced before a partial judge and would not cooperate." Reluctantly, Perkins acquiesced and offered to assist Johnson in building up a labor mediation board in NRA.[20]

During late July and early August 1933, Johnson met with Roosevelt, Perkins, and other administrative officials to define the responsibility of the board and to recruit members. Believing that it should be headed by a big name, Johnson suggested that Senator Wagner, a strong supporter of NRA, be appointed chairman. Otherwise, he left the details to NRA's Industrial and Labor Advisory Boards. On August 5, Roosevelt approved, in the exact wording, their formal recommendation for a National Labor Board. It was to "consider, adjust, and settle differences and controversies that may arise through differing interpretations" of Section 7a. Labor and management were "to take no disturbing action pending hearings and final decision." However, lest he alienate industry by giving the board too much of a role in labor matters, Roosevelt, encouraged by Johnson, chose not to issue any executive order defining the mandate and procedures of the board or granting it specific authority to enforce its findings. The most it could do was to ask Johnson to remove a recalcitrant employer's Blue Eagle.[21]

During the winter of 1933–1934 Johnson's pro-management stance became more pronounced. In speeches he dutifully acknowledged labor's right to organize and bargain collectively. But his references to Section 7a were more than counterbalanced by some of his other statements, and many labor leaders became convinced that they would receive little sustenance from him. Speaking to the American Federation of Labor convention in Washington on October 10, 1933, Johnson insisted that strikes had been made superfluous by Roosevelt's creating the National Labor Board.[22] In a speech to labor officials in Philadelphia in December 1933, he forcefully restated his position on strikes. Responding to the questions of a crowd in the Mastbaum Theater, he said that while the "right to strike is inviolate like the law of self-defense," the day had arrived when it is "neither faithful nor fair to strike until the means provided under the law have been pursued."[23] And in a speech to a meeting of the National Association of Manufacturers later that month he clearly spelled out his priorities as NRA administrator: "We have a mandate under this act—positive and direct—to foster the organization of industry for cooperative action among the trade groups," he proclaimed. "But we have no such mandate as to labor. The only thing that labor gets here is a right to organize (if it desires) and to bargain (as it may elect) either individually or collectively—without employer interference."[24]

Johnson's position on the makeup of code authorities also indicated a pro-management bias. He continually talked about NRA's creation of a partnership between industry and labor. Yet when it came to appointing representatives to code authorities, he consistently refused to include any labor representatives. Labor leaders were infuriated by Johnson's procrastination, and for a time this dispute between labor and Johnson smoldered beneath the surface of NRA-labor relations. It came to a head in November 1933, in a fight over the composition of the National Bituminous Coal Industrial Board. Perkins and Lewis wanted labor represented on the board; Johnson stalled, not wanting to set a precedent for all code authorities. As time passed, several angry NRA labor advisors threatened to resign if he continued to ignore labor in his appointments to code authorities. In a heated, hour-long telephone conversation with Johnson, Perkins backed labor's demand.[25] Under Perkins and Lewis's concerted pressure, Johnson, in December 1933, agreed to the appointment of labor representatives to some code authorities. Yet industry's strong opposition kept him from real implementation of this policy.

His decisions on matters affecting specific codes gave further evidence of Johnson's pro-management stance. This was particularly the case with the automobile code. In the fall of 1933 the National Automobile Chamber of Commerce requested that the code, which was scheduled to expire on December 31, 1933, be extended without change until September 1934. Labor spokesmen immediately demanded public hearings and the removal of the infamous merit clause. Johnson, however, was willing to give the auto chamber whatever it wanted. Payrolls and production in the industry were climbing, and work hours were decreasing—signs, in Johnson's opinion, that the code was working. He did not want to do anything that would disrupt the industry's contribution to the recovery program. Thus, William Green's protest over the continuation of the merit clause met Johnson's cold reply that it was "a matter of complete indifference" to him. As justification, he cited a letter Roosevelt had sent him on October 19, 1933, in which the president had decreed that future code should not interpret Section 7a.[26] Johnson felt Roosevelt's letter had disposed of the merit issue; therefore, he did not need to remove the clause, which became "a purely academic issue." On December 18 the code extension was approved, and no one could sensibly doubt that labor had suffered a defeat at Johnson's hands.[27]

Shortly afterward, the auto workers suffered another setback at Johnson's hands. When he had negotiated the auto code with the National Automobile Chamber of Commerce, Johnson had apparently promised the auto makers that at some future time he would permit them to raise the average workweek for most employees from thirty-five to forty hours. About a week after Johnson approved the extension of the code, the auto chamber asked Johnson to cash his promise, and Johnson, now irrevocably committed to the industry, felt he had no alternative but to comply. He justified the upward revision of the workweek on the grounds that skilled workers were in short supply and that the anticipated spring production upsurge would otherwise attract workers to Detroit who would lose their jobs once the spring peak ended. The only authority he cited for the alleged shortage of workers was the auto industry itself, even though a spokesman for the United Auto Workers Federal Union, speaking against the increase in hours on the famed "field day of criticism," reported 128,000 unemployed workers as of February 15.

None of Johnson's other pro-management actions had as much significance as his differences with the National Labor Board. Despite the vagueness of its mandate and authority, the board evolved a policy on Section 7a in the fall of 1933. The crux of its position was the "Reading Formula," which it successfully put forth in August 1933 to end a union recognition strike in Reading, Pennsylvania, hosiery mills. The Reading Formula called for an immediate end of the strike, reinstatement of all strikers, the holding of an election under the board's auspices to choose representatives for collective bargaining, and an agreement to submit differences to the board for final adjudication. Although it was not made explicit at the time, the National Labor Board operated on the assumption that the representative chosen by a majority of the workers would act as the bargaining agent for all workers.

The National Labor Board's endorsement of majority rule ran counter to Johnson's support of multiple representation; it was also less tolerant of company unions than he was. Hesitant to use the NIRA-prescribed sanctions against employers, Johnson was inclined to look the other way when a company drew its workers into a company union, even when there was good evidence of coercion. The labor board, in contrast, threatened the existence of such unions by insisting on its right to poll workers on their preferences in confidence if a challenge to a company union had been made.

In the winter of 1933–1934, Weirton Steel and the Budd Manufacturing Company, in noncompliance with National Labor Board rulings, conducted elections to sanction company unions. Johnson was drawn into the disputes since the board depended on NRA to force compliance with its rulings, but in both cases his support was so half-hearted that it did little to shore up the board's position.

The Weirton Steel Company, of Weirton, West Virginia, was controlled by Ernest Weir, "an old-fashioned paternalist" who was strongly anti-union. Faced with the possibility of unionization, Weir opted for a company union in July 1933. In September 1933, more than 10,000 of his workers struck in protest against the company-dominated union. In October, the National Labor Board arranged a settlement under the Reading Formula, and an election was scheduled for the second week of December to determine whether the workers preferred the company union or an independent one.[28]

In early December, Weir indicated that the only election he would permit would be one in which the workers would choose their representatives under the company-union plan. At Wagner's instigation, Johnson wired Weir on December 14, stating that "in my opinion you are about to commit a deliberate violation of federal laws." In the same telegram he also warned that Weir's further conduct of the election would result in the removal of his Blue Eagle and a request that the attorney-general begin prosecution immediately. Johnson's heart was not in this warning. Fearing that the removal of this Blue Eagle would be a toothless act, he preferred to arrange a compromise with Weir that would save face for NRA without frightening business. According to Weir, he and Johnson agreed in a telephone conference that the question of the election should be decided by the courts, a solution that could take years. Because of Johnson's reluctance to remove the Blue Eagle, the labor board had to resort to its only other option, court proceedings to force compliance. During the time this took, the board had to stand helplessly by while Weir proceeded with his election.[29]

Like Weir, E. G. Budd, the owner of the company, was vehemently anti-union. Installing a company union, he refused to recognize the United Auto Workers, which had organized some of his workers. A strike ensued, and within days Budd replaced the strikers with new employees. In December 1933, the National Labor Board ruled that the strike should be called off, that the strikers should be reinstated, and that an election should be held under its direction to determine whether the workers wanted to be represented by the company union or the United Auto Workers. But Budd refused to hold an election and agreed to rehire strikers only as business improved.

On January 11, 1934, the National Labor Board turned the Budd case over to Johnson. Angered that it had again placed him in a position that might cause embarrassment for NRA, Johnson, in a slight to the board, directed the Compliance Division of NRA to make its own investigation of the facts. A month later the Compliance Division recommended that an election be held, supervised by NRA, and that Budd rehire all strikers still out of work and available for reemployment. Prepared by William Davis, the recommendations clearly favored Budd: They did not require Budd to give the strikers priority in reemployment; nor did they unequivocally grant the suffrage in the proposed election to those still on strike.

Over the protests of the United Auto Workers local, Davis scheduled the election for March 9, 1934. The protests grew so vocal, however, that on March 8 he postponed the election for ten days to give Johnson an opportunity to reevaluate the situation. But Budd would not wait. The election was held as scheduled, and the company union won an easy victory.

Johnson was indignant over the election. In the eyes of the old cavalryman, Budd had done the unthinkable; he had disobeyed orders. Johnson promptly denounced the election and sent Bob Lea to Philadelphia to get Budd to agree to a second election, in which strikers could vote. March 20 was the agreed-upon date. The substance of Johnson's statement ordering the election, however, all but endorsed Budd; for he had no intention of alienating Budd. After a slap on the wrist for his defiance of Johnson, Budd—in Johnson's opinion—needed to be placated and not bullied. Johnson opined that Budd had acted "in complete good faith" and had complied with the law; new elections were desirable not because there was doubt that the employees favored the company union but only because "there was some doubt as to whether in arriving at this state of the law" all workers had been accorded their rights. As a result, while decreeing that strikers who had not been rehired could participate in the new election, he ruled that the company-union plan would remain in effect unless a majority voted in favor of the United Auto Workers.

Johnson's statement shocked the United Auto Workers, and even his advocates, putting the most charitable light on Johnson's evaluation of Budd and the outcome of the election, had to admit that his conclusion was at best questionable. More important, the stipulations that Johnson laid down for the election presaged the outcome. The strikers would be voting, but so would the workers who had taken their places. There was extremely little chance that the United Auto Workers could secure a majority. The UAW decided, therefore, to sit out the election. In view of the UAW boycott, the company union decided that its supporters should stay home too; nothing was to be gained or lost. To Johnson's embarrassment, only fifty or so workers voted in the election.

Johnson now considered the Budd case a closed incident. The workers had been given the opportunity to select their own representatives, and the company union had prevailed. The requirements of the law had been satisfied. The strike, however, had been an utter defeat for the United Auto Workers and a serious setback for the National Labor Board.[30]

Even before the Weirton Steel and Budd cases were well under way, Wagner realized that the National Labor Board was in trouble. Taking his concerns to the White House, he easily persuaded Roosevelt to strengthen it. The president took the most important step on February 1, 1934, when he granted the labor board specific authority to conduct representation elections when requested by a "substantial number" of employees and to refer noncompliance cases to NRA. As expected, businessmen objected to Roosevelt's action, prompting Johnson and Richberg to reassure them. In a February 3 statement the two NRA officials reaffirmed their commitment to multiple representation and insisted that company unions were permissible as long as they were freely chosen by the workers.[31]

The Johnson-Richberg statement, besides being patently anti-union, placed Johnson in open opposition to the National Labor Board. Unless repudiated by Roosevelt, the statement destroyed the board's principle of majority rule and enabled business to bargain with company as well as independent unions. Labor groaned, but Roosevelt was silent, again caught with Johnson in a by-now familiar trap—wanting to deal better with labor disputes but wanting at least equally not to alienate business. Still committed to business's solution to the depression, he was unprepared to risk upsetting the status quo in labor-management relations. A month later the National Labor Board, which had been rather in the background for a time, reemerged, firmly rejecting Johnson's interpretation of Section 7a. The board also ruled that the union selected by a majority of workers should bargain for all the employees. With the board and Johnson now in open conflict for jurisdiction over Section 7a, a frustrated Roosevelt severed the board's link with NRA, made its findings final, and increased its membership in order to expedite action. But these governmental processes took too much time and interfered too greatly with labor solutions to labor problems. By the time the board gained position, labor had put its faith in strikes.[32]

Johnson's pro-management stance infuriated organized labor. Yet just when it seemed that he was the captive of business, he appeared to waver. Organized labor was determined to make the most of the New Deal, and Johnson felt he had to pay attention to its pleas. He still waxed sympathetic toward the workers, and in a speech before the meeting of the code authorities on March 7, 1934, he praised the leaders of organized labor and called on the nation's industrialists to work with them. "Take it from a wealth of experience," he stated, "their interests are your interest and under the law and in this modern day, it is the best and quickest way to economic peace."[33] It is an indication of Johnson's complexity—and of his extraordinary way with people—that he remained good personal friends with many labor leaders and that John P. Frey, head of the Metal Trades Department of the American Federation of Labor and a member of the Labor Advisory Board of NRA, could still laud him for his vigor and broad-minded purpose in carrying out the "most tremendous undertaking assigned to one man since modern industry emerged."[34]

IN THE spring of 1934 the nation was threatened by labor disputes in major industries that had the potential for wiping out whatever gains had been made in the recovery program. Maintaining that strikes were "unnecessary" and "unpatriotic" because NRA stood ready to adjudicate labor disputes, Hugh Johnson rushed into the fray to bring labor peace.[35]

The first dispute was in the automobile industry. In early March 1934, union leaders in several plants announced that workers would strike unless they received a 20 percent wage increase, reinstatement of men discharged for union activity and agreements by the companies to bargain collectively with the United Auto Workers. Knowing the damage to recovery that a long strike in this industry could do, Roosevelt, through the National Labor Board, persuaded the union to postpone the strike, pending a hearing into industry conditions. On March 13, sixty union leaders arrived in Washington for the hearing, bringing with them warnings of widespread strikes if the government did not bring the auto companies into line and support the union demands. The auto makers were unmoved. In their testimony before the labor board on March 14 and 15 they defiantly rejected the union demand for elections under the Reading Formula and refused to recognize the authority of the National Labor Board or confer with the union officials present.[36]

After leaving the labor board hearing, William S. Knudsen, executive vice-president for General Motors and a spokesman for the industry, saw Johnson, who gave him "more than a little hell" for the views he had expressed. Knudsen replied that his views were consistent with the interpretation of Section 7a that Johnson had approved when the auto code was drafted, and the trapped Johnson lamely conceded that NRA would not attempt to force anything on the industry that it did not want. His only purpose, he told Knudsen, was to see that the dispute was settled "square."[37]

This meeting with Knudsen convinced Johnson that the National Labor Board would not be able to obtain a settlement. Therefore, he decided that he had to intervene. During the afternoon of March 15 he conferred in his office with union organizer William Collins and Knudsen and made a series of telephone calls to auto officials in Detroit. Late in the evening he presented Knudsen with a proposal from Collins calling for the establishment of an impartial grievance committee and an election to determine the actual representation of labor in the industry.[38] In order to give Johnson time to arrange a settlement, the union officials asked their locals to defer strike action until March 21. The auto men, however, responded indifferently to Johnson's mediation. On March 19, Collins told Johnson that a strike could be avoided only by direct presidential intervention. The following day, at Roosevelt's request, Johnson invited a committee of auto manufacturers to Washington, while Roosevelt personally wired Collins, asking him to keep the workers on the job until he had a chance to talk to both labor and industry leaders.

Discussions dragged on for several days, with Johnson and Roosevelt meeting frequently with both groups and serving as go-betweens because of the auto industry's refusal to meet the union representatives face-to-face. All the while auto workers were holding angry meetings in various cities to support their union representatives in Washington. At one point the mayor of Detroit phoned Leo Wolman of the National Labor Board and suggested that the situation in Detroit might be defused if Johnson would come to speak at a mass meeting. Wolman thought the meeting would serve no purpose and killed the idea on the spot. When he later learned of the incident, Johnson exploded. Ever since the Blue Eagle campaign, he had seen himself as a leader of masses who could sway audiences with his oratory. "If there was something nobody else could handle, he could handle it he thought," Wolman recalled. Thereafter, Johnson resented Wolman for denying him the opportunity to rush to Detroit on a charger and pacify the rebellious workers.[39]

The dispute now centered on two issues: discrimination against workers for union activity and the form of employee representation. Throughout the tense negotiations the industry had the upper hand. It was determined to stand by its position and was not afraid of a general strike. Johnson and Roosevelt, meanwhile, were worried about the potentially negative consequences of a strike and were disposed to avoid it at almost any cost. When the industry presented its terms for a settlement in the manner of an ultimatum, Johnson and Roosevelt endorsed it and convinced the union leaders to accept it by appeals to patriotism and reminders that they owed it to the president. They stated, somewhat beside the point, that he was, after all, the first president in recent years to welcome union leaders to the White House.

Roosevelt announced the settlement on March 25, declaring that it laid the foundation for a just and comprehensive system of labor conditions. But hopeful words could not change reality; the settlement was a crushing defeat for labor. It provided for a tripartite board, independent of the pro-labor National Labor Board but part of the NRA structure, to deal with charges of discrimination for union activity. Known as the Automobile Labor Board, it quickly disappointed workers. It had no power to enforce its decisions and dealt with grievances on a case-by-case basis rather than formulating general principles; consequently, it was helpless in protecting labor on any significant scale. That part of the settlement that dealt with worker representation was even more harmful to labor. Employers agreed to bargain with freely elected representatives of worker groups. However, the settlement did not specify which groups, saying only that "the government makes it clear that it favors no particular union or form of employee organization of representation." In this respect, the agreement completely ratified the industry's position on Section 7a. The company unions in the industry were now afforded legal sanction, and multiple representation, as opposed to majority rule and exclusive representation, was legally acceptable.[40]

The automobile dispute was also a defeat for the National Labor Board. By creating a new labor board to adjudicate the grievances of workers in the auto industry, Johnson destroyed what was left of the effectiveness of the National Labor Board. The settlement further repudiated the position of the board on representation, rendering useless previous decisions by the board calling for majority rule and exclusive representation. Johnson had triumphed over the National Labor Board, which soon receded into oblivion.

Elated by his victory, Johnson moved quickly to expand his authority. Four days after Roosevelt announced the auto settlement, Johnson, with much fanfare, issued an administrative order calling for the establishment of NRA labor-adjustment boards in every codified industry. The Labor Advisory Board of NRA opposed Johnson's power play, largely because it questioned the establishment of boards in non-unionized industries, where they would presumably be dominated by employers. For months Johnson and the Labor Advisory Board feuded over the makeup of the boards. The Labor Advisory Board demanded the privilege of nominating the members of the boards, a demand that rankled Johnson. If you nominate the boards, he growled, "you'll pack this thing with AF of L men" and lose any semblance of impartiality. Eventually Johnson agreed that the advisory board could nominate board members, but he would do the selecting. By this time, though, Johnson's order was a "dead letter."[41]

The second of the major disputes was in the bituminous coal industry. In negotiations with the Appalachian operators that began on February 28, 1934, the United Mine Workers' John L. Lewis demanded that miners be given a six-hour day, a five-day week, higher wages, and a reduction in the wage differential between northern and southern mines. Northern operators were receptive to a reduction in the wage differential, on the grounds that they could compete more successfully with the southern mines. But the southern operators were reluctant to give up their competitive advantage. Some walked out of the negotiations; other refused even to take part. In retaliation Lewis threatened a nationwide strike if a new agreement had not been reached by March 31 and petitioned Johnson to make any settlement part of the bituminous coal code. Since the United Mine Workers was a potent force in the industry, Johnson agreed. Rather than risk a strike and possible federal intervention, the northern and many of the southern operators accepted a wage agreement on the eve of Lewis's deadline that raised wages from $4.60 to $5 a day in Ohio and Pennsylvania and from $3.40 to $4.60 a day in Alabama.[42]

Charles O'Neill of Peacock, Peale, and Kerr, Inc., promptly presented the fruits of the negotiations to the code authority, which was holding wage hearings concurrently with the negotiations. Because it drastically narrowed the wage differential, mine operators from Alabama, Georgia, and western Kentucky vigorously condemned the agreement; and Lewis let Johnson know that the United Mine Workers would strike any area which refused to comply. Fifty thousand southern workers were likely to be affected. Ballooning the danger of the walkout sevenfold (to 350,000 miners), Johnson later portrayed the situation as a "thriller because we were within a few hours of a general walkout from every Bituminous mine in the country." Convinced that the nation could not afford a coal strike, Johnson hurried to the rescue. Late in the evening of March 31, the eve of the strike deadline, he arbitrarily issued an executive order making the new Appalachian agreement part of the coal code.

This action embroiled the government in the biggest conflict in the history of the coal code. The industry's publication, *Coal Age*, called it "lynch law in Washington," while southern operators attacked "military ringmaster" Johnson and compared NRA to Sherman's march to the sea. On April 6, Alabama operators closed their mines in defiance of Johnson's edict, putting 15,000 miners out of work. In protest against the lockouts, miners in neighboring states went on strike. The unrest, combined with pressure from important southern figures in Congress and Roosevelt, who did not want to antagonize his southern supporters, forced Johnson to lower the basic wage to $3.80 for Alabama and

Georgia, which brought an end to the strife. By modifying his edict, Johnson tarnished the victory Lewis had won at the negotiating table, although coal miners and the United Mine Workers were still in a better position than they had been in 1933.[43]

The cotton textile industry had yet another labor dispute. Codification of this industry had improved cotton textile workers' working conditions very little. The minimum wage prescribed by the code quickly became the virtual maximum, so that many workers were actually earning less in 1934 than they had in 1932. Moreover, management exerted every effort to frustrate the intent of Section 7a, refusing to negotiate with the United Textile Workers of America and systematically discriminating against union members. These conditions produced a wave of wildcat strikes in the South in late 1933 and early 1934. Invariably the workers lost, and their discontent naturally increased. The framers of the code had provided for a tripartite board to settle disputes. But the Cotton Textile National Industrial Relations Board, known as the Bruere Board after its chairman, economist Robert W. Bruere, was under the control of the code authority and strongly biased in favor of management.

During the winter of 1933–1934 the question of production curtailments exacerbated labor-management hostility. Because of bulging warehouses, Johnson in December 1933, granted the code authority's request for a 25 percent reduction in machine hours, from eighty to sixty hours per week. Inventories declined, but at the expense of employment and weekly earnings. Johnson removed the restriction in early 1934; however, by spring, the industry was pressing for its reimposition on the grounds that almost every firm had large quantities of unsold stock on hand. The textile workers' union bitterly protested the industry's request. Thomas McMahon, union president, argued that it would reduce the minimum wage in the south from $12 to $9 per week and asked Roosevelt to intervene and stop the curtailment. Failing that, he demanded that wages be increased to offset the hour reduction. At the same time, Francis J. Gorman, vice-president of the union, threatened to call a general strike of 300,000 workers if Johnson approved the curtailment.[44]

Johnson was not so quick to act on the industry request as he had been the previous December. Growing Congressional pressures, the strong opposition to production controls within NRA, and the threat of an industry-wide strike persuaded him to stall the request, channeling it through Leon Henderson's office. The code authority, however, would not be put off. Its president, George Sloan, bluntly told Johnson that the industry's future support of NRA depended on his decision; either Johnson would approve the request or the cotton textile industry would pull out of NRA. Out of philosophy and fondness, even before Sloan's threat, Johnson was inclined to grant the industry's request. He was a dedicated proponent of industrial self-government, and the industry's request epitomized what industrial self-government was about. If that was not enough, Sloan was a good friend; and Johnson was confident that he would never ask for anything that was not absolutely necessary. Predictably, on May 25, 1934, Johnson signed an order approving a temporary 25 percent curtailment for June, July, and August.[45]

The United Textile Workers, which had not been consulted by Johnson before he approved the curtailment request, strongly protested the order. While expressing a willingness to negotiate, it renewed its threat to strike to achieve the workers' goals. Since the workers had no faith in the Bruere Board, Johnson jumped in to head off the strike. He arranged for a June 1 conference in his office, with McMahon representing the union. Sloan refused to attend as a representative of the code authority, attending in a personal capacity. Johnson also took the somewhat unorthodox step of outlining what would occur even before the conference was held. In his mind, the real reason for the strike threat was the failure of the industry to recognize the United Textile Workers as a bargaining agent and the union's hope of increasing wages, not curtailment. So he announced that the curtailment order would go through. In return for not striking, the union would be granted concessions.[46]

The negotiations proved difficult. Since the industry refused to recognize the United Textile Workers as a legitimate bargaining agent, Johnson had to put the union men in one room, Sloan in another, and rush back and forth between the two with proposals and counterproposals. Sloan had the upper hand. The industry was not afraid of a strike; in fact, Sloan thought a strike might even be beneficial, because it would solve the industry's problem of overproduction. The union, uncertain of its strength, was reluctant to risk what it had in a losing effort. No settlement was reached on June 1, but on the next day Johnson finally got the two sides to agree. The United Textile Workers countermanded the strike order without relinquishing the union's future right to strike, while the curtailment order would go in effect as planned. The concessions granted to labor included the appointment of one more labor representative to the Labor Advisory Board of NRA; the appointment of two additional members to the Bruere Board, one representing labor and one, industry; the designation of a representative from the United Textile Workers to advise the NRA members on the code authority; and an investigation by NRA of the ability of the industry to pay higher wages and of various questions relating to wage differentials and machine-hour limitations. It was assumed that the investigations would serve as the basis for changes in the code.[47]

In a statement issued after the conference and in his comments on the dispute in his memoir, Johnson left no doubt about where he stood on the questions and personalities involved in the dispute—the United Textile Workers had no cause to threaten a strike, and the industry had acted in good faith. The curtailment order, he stated, was necessitated by conditions in the industry, and "no argument against either the wisdom or the equity of this order has been presented." Even if labor had a legitimate argument against the order, "all that was necessary was to apply for an open hearing and amend the code (if amendment was warranted), as the code was made—in the Goldfish Bowl." To strike on the basis of the curtailment order was to *"strike against the code, which is a strike against the government."* Johnson went on to score the union for asking for a wage increase and statements declaring that workers were in a more depressed condition than before the code had been formulated. The industry, he contended, could not afford the wages demanded by the union, nor could the nation and still maintain "any balance or cohesion in the fundamentals on which NRA was moving." Wages and employment had improved under the code, he asserted, and "the improvement of labor conditions . . . surpasses that in any other industry." Credit for these improvements belonged to NRA, Johnson proclaimed, and Sloan and the Cotton Textile Institute, which went more than halfway to meet every grievance of labor. For these reasons, Johnson concluded, "strictures on the good faith of that industry are unwarranted and unjust."[48]

Both labor and management proclaimed victory in the dispute. But there could be no doubt that management had prevailed. By accepting the need for a temporary curtailment, Johnson acknowledged that the industry's position had been correct all along. No move had been made to recognize the United Textile Workers as a bargaining agent, and nothing was said about maintaining wages during the period the curtailment order was to be in effect. Finally, there was no guarantee that Johnson would heed the reports of the investigations that had been ordered, even if they indicated that changes were needed. Johnson, in other words, had extracted from the industry only the barest concessions necessary to avoid the strike.[49]

The final dispute in which Johnson intervened was in the steel industry. Organized labor was pathetically weak in this industry, even after codification. The principal union was the Amalgamated Association of Iron, Steel and Tin Workers, a desultory craft union whose leader, Michael F. Tighe, was a superannuated, grandfatherly figure with little interest in expanding membership beyond the 5,000 or so members already in the union before codification. But younger, less patient union members were determined to make the union a force in the industry. At the national convention in May 1934, the rebellious rank-and-file seized control of the resolutions session and pushed through a motion demanding that employers immediately bargain with the union. They set June 16 as the strike date if the demand was not met.

The steel companies adamantly refused to bargain with the union or even to receive union representatives requesting recognition. Determined to forestall a strike, Roosevelt announced on May 30 that he would call for representation elections in the steel mills under the supervision of the National Labor Board. The workers' representatives were not appeased. They knew from the experience of unions in other industries that administration promises of elections were just so much bunk. The National Labor Board could not force an election; even if it could, there was no guarantee that the union would be recognized. Frustrated by Roosevelt's tepid support, the rank-and-file representatives demanded a six-hour-day, a five-day week, a dollar-an-hour minimum wage, and union recognition.[50]

In a replay of his role in the automobile and cotton textile disputes, Johnson became the administration's principal mediator. Between June 4 and 6, he held conferences with steel executives and union representatives in an effort to avert the strike. The talks did not go well. The steel executives remained firm in their opposition to union recognition, while Johnson's relations with the union representatives were strained because they believed that he did not appreciate the harsh conditions under which steel workers toiled. After an unproductive meeting in Johnson's office, William J. Spang, president of the Duquesne, Pennsylvania, lodge of the Amalgamated and a leader among the rank-and-file militants, said of Johnson, "We'd like to see him walk up to an open hearth furnace and get his pants scorched for $21.84 a week." Johnson let the steel workers know that he could take anything they could dish out, and more. Referring to Spang's barb a few days later, he recalled his past days as a cavalryman: "I have worn enough skin off the part of me that fits into a saddle—or used to—riding over the flat lands of Texas and the hills of Arizona to make a half dozen critics such as they."[51]

Harking back to the auto dispute, Johnson proposed that the steel dispute be settled by the creation of a special labor relations board. Neither side showed interest. The union representatives believed that it would do no more for them than the Automobile Labor Board had been able to do for the auto workers. The steel executives, on the other hand, did not want to take any step that even suggested that something was less than satisfactory with the company union system. In an effort to persuade the steel executives to change their stance, Johnson, Frances Robinson, and Richberg flew to New York City late in the afternoon of June 6 to confer with officials of the American Iron and Steel Institute. Meeting late into the evening with sixteen institute officials in its headquarters on the thirty-third floor of the Empire State Building, Johnson pleaded with the steel men for two and a half hours to be conciliatory toward the workers.[52] Eventually, he convinced them that a strike would harm the recovery program and that the industry had little to lose by making a symbolic compromise with the union. Although reaffirming their commitment to the open shop, enough of the steel officials reluctantly agreed to his plan that Johnson felt confident in proposing it again to the workers.

On June 8 Johnson met with the steelworker representatives in Washington. He offered them a tripartite industrial relations board that would conduct elections but not force recognition. Since the industry was amenable to the board, Johnson argued that the Amalgamated's acceptance of it would give the union a chance to become the bargaining agent for workers where it could command the support of a majority of the workers. But Amalgamated turned Johnson down. There were too many unanswered questions. How would grievances be handled? Who would enforce the board's decisions? And what would happen if a company defied the board? Declaring that they had "had nine months of stalling and we're not going to stand for any more," the rank-and-file representatives left Washington on June 10, calling Johnson's proposed settlement "an insult to every worker in this country."[53]

Johnson was furious with the workers. He had fought hard to win the American Iron and Steel Institute over to his plan, only to see the workers contemptuously reject it. He vented his anger in a speech delivered on June 8 to the International Ladies' Garment Workers Union convention. While taking care to condemn extremists on both sides in the recent labor disputes, he singled out the steelworkers for particular criticism. He implied that the rank-and-file representatives were Communists and warned the workers that they risked punishment at the hands of the American people for their irresponsibility.[54]

Eventually, a solution was devised, and on the eve of the deadline the Amalgamated called off the strike; but Johnson did not play a direct part in the frantic negotiations that led to the settlement, which was part of a larger administration effort to blunt complaints that it was ignoring the interests of labor. The administration, however, did not fare much better than Johnson. The settlement included the creation of the National Steel Labor Relations Board. As things developed, however, it proved ineffective in helping the steelworkers.[55]

Johnson said he was "unhappy" and "bewildered" after his interventions in the labor disputes of the spring of 1934. He had intervened in the belief that he would be the impartial third party who expedited settlements, and in his own mind he had satisfied this objective. Disruptive strikes had been averted and the recovery program kept on course. But his interventions earned him the enmity of labor. Throughout the disputes, Johnson's primary concern had been to avert strikes, not to alleviate the legitimate grievances of labor. Moreover, except in the coal industry, where it was already a significant factor, he had been unwilling to support labor. Sorely disappointed in Johnson, labor leaders denounced him as a tool of management and demanded the creation of labor mediation facilities separate from NRA. For his part, Johnson, stung by the attacks of labor and wearied by the continual crises of the disputes, privately vowed that he would never get involved in another labor dispute.[56]

THE IMPOTENCE of the National Labor Board in 1934 persuaded Senator Wagner that a new labor relations board, with broad enforcement powers, should be established by statute. On March 1, he introduced legislation in the Senate providing for a permanent labor relations board. It would hold elections to determine representation for collective bargaining; it would mediate labor disputes; and, most importantly, the board would possess enforcement powers. The legislation also outlawed certain coercive practices used by employers to keep unions weak.[57] Wagner's proposal evoked a tremendous protest from industry. The National Association of Manufacturers organized trade associations against the legislation and orchestrated a massive propaganda campaign to defeat it in the Congress.

Except in the debate over where the new labor board should be located, Hugh Johnson played almost no role in the early stages of Wagner's bill. Wagner, who considered Johnson a pawn of industry, conceived of the board as an independent agency, while Johnson was adamant that it should be within NRA. He wanted nothing outside his control that could affect NRA. On the day before Wagner introduced the legislation in the Senate, Secretary Perkins summoned Johnson and Richberg to her office to meet with Wagner and her assistants; they agreed not to leave until they had made a decision. After hours of repetitious debate about the location of the board, and with no resolution, Johnson jumped up and said, "I can't stand this any longer. I have too much to do. I can't stay here and fiddle around about a thing like this. I don't know what you are talking about. I don't know what your objections are." Reminded that he had promised to stay and settle the matter, Johnson bounded away, saying he would abide by whatever arrangement Richberg found acceptable. This impatience cost him: Once Johnson had left, the group agreed that the board should be independent of NRA.[58]

Publicly, Johnson adopted an equivocal position on the Wagner bill. In theory he supported it, and during the auto dispute he used it as a stick to prod the industry to accept the Automobile Labor Board as part of the settlement. Convinced that Johnson's support would be a key element in getting the bill through Congress, Wagner set aside two separate days for him to testify before the Education and Labor Committee. Johnson, in a letter made public on April 10, advised Wagner that "a series of misadventures" made it impossible for him to appear. He went on to damn the bill with faint praise. Johnson was committed to a policy of NRA cooperation with business, and once business had marshaled its troops against the bill, he judged that he should tred warily. In all probability his initial indications of support for Wagner's bill were motivated by the need to mend fences with labor, not a strong belief in Wagner's proposal. Johnson's letter stated that "we must have a supreme court of industrial relations." But he refused to endorse the bill's provision outlawing company unions and put forth a proposal on them that would be practically impossible to implement. Since the "government should not favor any particular form of labor organization," he stated, an employer should be permitted to initiate a company union; however, he should not "finance, foster, nor direct what the men do" once the company union plan was put into effect. Johnson did not explain how the government could compel an employer to stop his involvement at the initiation of a company union.[59]

Wagner announced that Johnson's letter amounted to an endorsement of his bill. Most congressional leaders, however, saw it as the coup de grace for the section outlawing company unions. Wagner, they thought, was now whistling in the dark if he expected the bill to pass as he had proposed.[60] The concerted campaign by business against the bill was causing whatever support it might have had to slip away, and most congressmen and senators had little interest in the bill once Johnson failed to lend administration backing to the section outlawing company unions.

During the next week Wagner worked with administration figures to amend the bill and make it more acceptable. At Johnson's suggestion, he removed the ban against employer initiation of company unions.[61] On May 26, the Education and Labor Commitee reported out an amended version of Wagner's bill. It permitted employers to initiate company unions and pay company-union representatives; it also authorized the proposed labor relations board to use either majority rule or multiple representation as the basis for selecting employee representatives. Johnson endorsed the bill without reservation. But he was quick to remind reporters that it was not a panacea and would not necessarily protect workers from coercion, saying:

I lived in a town [Moline] that called itself an open-shop town. . . . They never refused a man employment in those plants in that town because he had a union card in his pocket; but they damned well saw to it that he was fired for dropping a monkey wrench a couple weeks after he was employed, or something like that.[62]

Despite the amendments, Roosevelt remained noticeably unenthusiastic about the Wagner bill. With his recovery program based on the courting of business, strong administration support for Wagner's bill could hurt. Congress, meanwhile, weary and ready to go home for a rest, had no greater taste for a prolonged, bitter debate on a controversial bill. The threatened steel strike finally propelled the government into action. Bypassing the Wagner bill, Roosevelt proposed a congressional resolution authorizing him to set up labor boards empowered to conduct elections and investigate disputes arising out of Section 7a. The resolution—Public Resolution 44—was railroaded through the Congress to head off the steel strike, and Roosevelt signed it on June 19. Ten days later, he abolished the National Labor Board and created the National Labor Relations Board to investigate and mediate labor disputes and hold elections.

The passage of Public Resolution 44 clearly indicated that New Deal labor policy was entering a new phase. For a year Johnson had been dominant in the jurisdiction of Section 7a and in the settlement of disputes. But his pro-management stance had so aroused labor and its supporters that by the spring of 1934 he was a target. He had to be removed from power, and the enactment of Public Resolution 44 and the creation of the National Labor Relations Board made it appear that labor had at least relegated him to a secondary position.[63]

CHAPTER 12

PECK'S BAD BOY

B Y T H E spring of 1934 Hugh Johnson was on the verge of mental and physical collapse. Overwork and unrelenting criticism sapped his self-control, which was never notable; and the years of heavy drinking had taken their toll. Deep pouches under bloodshot eyes, a bulbous red nose, guzzled hair, disheveled clothing, and a sagging, weighty paunch told much of his life story. Minor ailments and nervous exhaustion forced his hospitalization in February, May, and June of 1934. Frequently overwrought from job pressures, he reacted to problems with furious outbursts of work that more often than not avoided basic issues and furthered incessant arguments with his critics. Because of his growing bad press, Johnson, who had once held press conferences almost daily, shunned reporters, often going weeks without meeting the press. When he did meet reporters, he glowered over his glasses at them, resisted photographers' efforts to take his picture, and rarely smiled for the few shots that were snapped. Increasingly, he was suspicious of everyone around him, save for Frances Robinson.[1]

The pressure of running NRA was now regularly pushing Johnson to excess in language and drink. He had talked too loud and too often from the day he was appointed NRA administrator. But as the attacks against him mounted, he increased the volume of his baritone voice, unleashing a wave of invective that appalled the capital and embarrassed the administration. In one speech he paid his doubtful respects to Ogden Mills by denouncing the former secretary of the treasury as "the little son of the rich." In describing criticism of NRA, he used such words as "impertinence," "impudent," and "sleazy deception."[2] In another speech he described the author of a series of *Washington Post* articles critical of him as one "in whose veins there must flow something more than a trace of rodent blood." This author and *Post* owner Eugene Meyer, he continued, were contemptible:

"By their fruits ye shall know them," and these are the Dead Sea apples of envy, futility and frustration. They are financed and procured by sharpshooting interests of the Old School, who never used the cream, shrewdly skimmed from the efforts of other men, to produce results constructive for the public good. They are produced at this behest and for the shekels by some mercenary character-assassin firing, masked, from ambush without the courage common to 90 per cent of men to step out into the open and meet his adversary eye to eye.[3]

Many administration figures believed that Johnson's scattergun attacks were disproportionate to the seriousness of the criticism and potentially harmful to the administration; they seemed virtual gifts of publicity. Roosevelt, however, claimed to be unconcerned, philosophizing to his cabinet after the attack on Meyer that every administration must have "a Peck's Bad Boy."[4]

Spewing forth invective somewhat relieved the tension churning inside Johnson, and he took pride in the knowledge that Washington considered him a master in gouging an opponent. But Johnson also lost stature in the public view. At first his biting phrases were entertaining and novel. But the public quickly wearied. Like everything else about Johnson, his language was just too much. Interest in his invective turned to boredom, and, when Johnson increased the tempo, resentment.

Invective alone could not ease Johnson when things got tough. Only alcohol could do that. In his heavy drinking during the spring of 1934, Johnson consumed so much that it was hard to know whether he knew what was taking place. At meetings he reeked of whiskey. He did not reel or stagger, but his eyes had a glassy look, and there was a vagueness about his manner. Sometimes he simply disappeared for a day or two; he would return looking like a hobo, and there were no explanations from this public man as to his whereabouts during these absences.

Heavy drinking led Johnson into some classic alcoholic behaviors. He would make impossible promises and preposterous statements, run out on engagements, and enter into agreements he had no intention of keeping. Sobered up later, he would deny that he had ever made the promise or statement or committed himself to the engagement or the agreement. Not surprising, people found it nerve-wracking to do business with him.

Frances Perkins provided a vivid example of the difficulty in dealing with Johnson at this time. It became obvious in the meeting to decide the location of Wagner's proposed labor relations board that Johnson had been drinking. He paid little attention and left despite the agreement not to leave, promising to abide by the arrangement Richberg found acceptable. Shortly after the meeting, Robbie and son Pat hustled Johnson to Walter Reed Hospital to dry out. Once he had regained control of himself, Perkins and Wagner visited the hospital to show him the draft of the bill calling for the board. When Johnson realized that the labor board would not be under his control, he turned reddish purple and yelled that the bill was unacceptable. Reminded that he had promised to abide by any arrangement Richberg accepted, Johnson bellowed irrationally at Perkins and Wagner: "I never agreed to anything. You know I never agreed to anything. What are you trying to put over on me? I wouldn't have thought it of you, Frances, to put something over on me. If you tell me Richberg has agreed to this, he's putting something over on me." Robbie and Pat tried—and failed—to talk sense to him. Johnson regained his wits and dropped his opposition, but Frances Perkins recalled this as "the most painful experience we had with him."[5]

The problems created by Johnson's mental and physical state were compounded by his administration of NRA. Unwilling to delegate authority, Johnson tended to run a one-man show.[6] Building on his military background, he had intended to create an agency in which function and authority were clearly delineated. But once NRA was under way, he got so caught up in the drama of the recovery program that he put off bureaucratizing the organization of NRA, which was growing rapidly in size. He tried to take part in every major NRA function and make every important decision. There was little time or energy for the administration of NRA and cool thought about its organization. Often staffers had to wait weeks before Johnson made a decision because of the self-imposed pressures he worked under. Friends and advisors warned that he must delegate authority and streamline the organization. Johnson refused; and as a result, his subordinates were never sure of the extent or limits of their own authority, and new agencies were thoughtlessly superimposed on the existing organizational structure.[7]

In early 1934, with staff morale terrible, and administrative collapse seeming like a real possibility, Johnson finally gave serious consideration to the administration of NRA. Revised rules, regulations, charts, and delegations of authority now flowed out of Johnson's office so fast that even insiders could hardly keep up with developments. Moreover, most of the changes, which Johnson made without consultation with advisors, were knee-jerk reactions to specific criticism of NRA policies and organization, not parts of a well-thought-out administrative plan; and usually they were more gesture than substance. In March, Johnson decided to lighten the load on himself by naming a "few pinch hitters" whom he would "ask to undertake and carry through specific instructions." Apparently, he hoped that the pinch hitters would evolve into a general staff. But that was in the future, for, as he declared, he preferred "to feel my way toward that." In the meantime, it was better "to suit necessity unto occasion."[8]

Amid much publicity, Johnson on April 9, 1934, announced a plan to decentralize authority in NRA and delegate many powers formerly exercised by himself. The whole organization, he told Richberg, needed "a dose of salts." Lea, McGrady, Robbie, and Pat were to be his personal staff, "shock troops" to be thrown into emergencies and to assist him in any other way he deemed necessary. He also provided for an eight-man administrative staff whose principal members would be Alvin Brown and Colonel George A. Lynch, a West Point classmate. Brown would be responsible for reviewing all documents before they were presented to Johnson and for maintaining consistency in all actions, documents, and orders. Lynch was to have an even more important role. Detailed to NRA by the army at Johnson's request only two weeks previously, Lynch was given complete authority to approve codes, orders, amendments, and modifications in Johnson's name; he also had authority to sign codes which did not require presidential signature and authority over the organization and office management of NRA.[9]

Despite the changes, Johnson still tried to do too much himself, and confusion reigned in the NRA organization. Many staffers were virtually sick over what he was doing to himself and the agency.[10] Others were angered by Johnson's administration of the agency. The changes of the spring of 1934 had not made matters better, only more complex. "Without odds this is the damnedest mess it has ever been my misfortune to be connected with," bewailed one disgusted deputy administrator. Frances Perkins went even further. Under Johnson's alcoholic direction, she later wrote, it seemed as if NRA "would blow up by internal combustion" at any time.[11]

THE SPRING of 1934 brought a growing consensus that NRA had to be remodeled. Criticism of its policies abounded, and its administration cried out, in Perkins's memory, for "intelligent, consecutive, logical, stable leadership."[12] There was also a growing consensus that policies would be unaltered and NRA would be a melodrama starring Hugh Johnson as long as Johnson was at its helm. Since the previous August, rumors had circulated that he would soon resign from NRA, either because of health or feuds. Most of the rumors originated with Johnson's critics and were based on hope rather than fact. He was determined to see the experiment in industrial self-government through and could not conceive of NRA without himself at its head.

In public Johnson implied that his only real enemies were chiselers, reactionary industrial plunderers trying to turn the clock back to the nineteenth century, and Republicans wanting to discredit a Democratic administration In private, however, he readily acknowledged that many critics within the administration wanted him out. Because of his policies, some had vocally opposed him from the inception of NRA; others had joined in because they thought he had become a liability and was dragging down the administration with him. The latter group now included two influential figures who had previously been crucial allies—Donald Richberg and Frances Perkins.

Johnson had worked closely with Richberg in defining NRA labor policy and considered him a good friend. He enjoyed Richberg's company, and the two had even talked about practicing law together after they finished their work with NRA. But their friendship had its stress points. Philosophically, Richberg became increasingly concerned that Johnson was permitting the most powerful economic interests in the country to use the power of government to enforce economic decisions in their favor. This was particularly the case, in his thinking, in their use of NRA authority to restrict production and fix prices. It was better, Richberg contended, for NRA to pull back from such matters, except in extreme cases, and concentrate instead on basic standards of fair competition in regard to labor practices. Differences over personnel were another of the growing strains between the two men. Very early, Richberg made it clear that he regarded Frances Robinson as a disruptive factor in NRA. In addition, Richberg craved order and liked to make careful decisions. He found Johnson's work habits disconcerting and often complained to friends about Johnson's penchant for ignoring channels in dealing with subordinates. Temperamentally, the two men could not have been more different. Johnson talked loud, while Richberg talked little. Johnson overworked and lunched at his desk, while Richberg went out to lunch and home for dinner. A grave problem was that Richberg never regarded himself as Johnson's subordinate and was frankly ambitious for a more responsible role in NRA. When Richberg had joined NRA, Roosevelt had confided to him that he needed a watchdog on Johnson; he expected Richberg to fill the role. Richberg interpreted Roosevelt's remarks to mean that he had a special relationship with the president and that actual power in NRA was to be shared between Johnson and himself—at least unofficially. Johnson, with his reliance on a boy's-book concept of loyalty, appeared oblivious to Richberg's resentments. "I had no secrets from him," he later wrote, "and I trusted him as I would have trusted my own brother."[13]

By May 1934, Richberg was telling friends that working with Johnson was "a living hell." He confided to David Lilienthal, a member of the board that oversaw the Tennessee Valley Authority, that "Johnson has worn himself out, to the point where he doesn't want to work"; and "the whole thing is built up so that only he can decide." His resentments and a growing belief that Johnson was no longer fit for the job convinced Richberg that he should move against Johnson before NRA was wrecked. In meetings with Roosevelt he made certain that the president was apprised of Johnson's incapacity and the deteriorating situation in NRA. For his part, Johnson grew suspicious of Richberg. He came to believe his old friend was disloyal, conniving for Johnson's job. Richberg used all his skills of intrigue to try to alleviate Johnson's suspicions, wanting to avoid a break before he had marshaled his forces.

But Johnson was not deceived, and their relationship became one of rivalry and distrust.[14]

Relations between Johnson and Perkins had been particularly cordial. From the earliest days, when she had supported his codification of industry over opposition by some members of the Special Industrial Recovery Board, Perkins was so effective in dealing with Johnson's emotional ups and downs that many people in the administration came to regard her as his "special guardian."[15] In the spring of 1934, however, their relationship changed. Perkins increasingly doubted Johnson's labor policy, and she deeply resented the way he shouldered aside the Department of Labor when he charged into labor disputes. More important, she concluded that Johnson's drinking was so serious that he no longer could function rationally and that he should be replaced.

Not wishing to hurt Johnson and anxious to minimize any adverse publicity that his departure might cause, Perkins searched for some way to ease him out of NRA so that both he and the administration could save face. In March 1934, she proposed that Johnson be named head of the National Emergency Council's Modernize America movement.[16] When nothing came of her proposal she turned to Baruch for advice. If anyone could apparently resolve the Johnson problem, it was Baruch. Johnson had been a Baruch man for years, and he spoke constantly of his admiration and friendship for the Chief. But the Hugh Johnson of 1934 was not the Johnson of 1933. He had fashioned an independent identity for himself and was no longer the Chief's tool. In both policy and personal matters, Johnson ignored the Chief's advice, prompting Baruch to complain that Johnson had become too "bullheaded" and that he no longer had control over him.

The Chief had been in agreement with the basic concept of NRA; it represented the philosophy of industrial self-government that he had championed for years. But as the months passed, Baruch grew concerned that Johnson was "losing sight of the forest for the trees." Johnson, in his estimation, was trying to regulate too much, and the Chief now feared that Johnson and NRA would go under because, ironically, they had succeeded in making too many codes, which might lead toward "a regimented and bureaucratized economic system operating under government control."[17]

In November 1933, Baruch began to bombard Johnson with unsolicited advice. He harked back to the way "we" had handled matters during the "war days" and repeated his verities many times, and loftily. NRA was getting away from its original goal of industrial self-government, he told Johnson, for it was seeking to direct the activities of industries that had not asked for government intervention: "I think you should clearly define how the Industrial Recovery Act was started and what object . . . you have in mind," stating clearly "that your object was not government control of industry except where so requested by industry." Baruch also reminded Johnson that capital and labor should be protected, but never at the expense of the public. Any increase in prices, he added, "must be examined most carefully to see if it is justified by the facts"; if not based on higher wages or material costs, the "higher prices" must be fought on the "ground of improper and unwise profits."[18] Johnson graciously thanked the Chief for his advice on NRA policy and at every turn bemoaned that the nation did not have the benefit of his wisdom. Otherwise, he tended to ignore the advice.

The same was true of Baruch's advice on personal finances. Johnson's $6,000-a-year salary did not meet his obligations. In addition to his fixed charges, he had assumed obligations for several members of his family. Pat, for example, could not make it on his $143 monthly army pay, and Johnson, wanting his son at his side, had to give him a fair amount of money. Lacking collateral to borrow from a bank, Johnson turned to Baruch. By the fall of 1933 he was borrowing heavily from the Chief—$4,000 in October 1933; $6,000 in February 1934; $6,000 in May 1934; and $15,000 in September 1934. Baruch provided the money with no strings, although he did scold Johnson, advising that he be more diligent, "cutting your suit to fit your cloth" and not permitting family members to be so "dependent upon you." If not, Baruch warned, "when you leave Washington you will . . . be in such debt that will prove an embarrassment."[19] Johnson brushed aside these admonishments, confident that when he returned to private life, he would have no difficulty again making "one hundred thou" a year.[20]

With such changes in the Johnson-Baruch relationship, the meeting between Perkins and Baruch had little chance of success. When Perkins detailed Johnson's drinking bouts and their impact on NRA, Baruch replied to her astonishment, "Of course I'm not surprised. Hugh has done this a great many times. He goes along for a while and then he goes all out on a terrific bout. He has gone very, very low at times." Perkins angrily asked why Baruch had not mentioned this disability in May 1933, when he had simply characterized Johnson as "a number-three man." His reply only partially satisfied her: "Well, . . . at that time Hugh was straightened out and I thought he might be all right. He was riding fine then, and I thought perhaps all he needed was public attention, that it would make a good man of him, that it would help him get his strength together." But perhaps without realizing it, Baruch seemingly offered Perkins an out, saying, "I've stood by Hugh. I like him. I'm fond of him. I'll always see that he has work to do and a salary coming in one way or another. He can earn money when he's in good shape, if somebody keeps watch over him and stands over him, telling him what to do."

Taking her cue from Baruch's comment, Perkins asked him "to say to Hugh that you need him badly and want him back. . . . Tell him you need him and have a good post for him." She also asked for publicity,

LIEUTENANT KILBOURNE JOHNSTON AND GENERAL HUGH S. JOHNSON. Historical Pictures Service, Chicago

"so that it will appear like an important promotion for him." Without even a pause to consider, Baruch turned down the request, saying, "I couldn't do that. I couldn't do that under any circumstances." Perkins was mystified. Johnson had worked for him for years and apparently had flowered under his direction. "Why," she asked, "couldn't he come back and do just the same thing?" Baruch was ready for her question:

Hugh's got so swell headed now that he sometimes won't even talk to me on the telephone. I've called him up and tried to save him from two or three disasters that I've heard about. People have come to me because they knew that I knew him well, but sometimes he won't even talk to me. When he does talk to me, he doesn't say anything, or he isn't coherent.

Perhaps he was only drinking at the time, she suggested. "No, I know the difference," Baruch retorted:

He's just pushing off. I never could manage him again. Hugh has got too big for his boots. He's got too big for me. I could never manage him again. My organization could never absorb him. He's learned publicity too, which he never knew before. He's tasted the tempting, but poisonous cup of publicity. It makes a difference. He never again can be just a plain fellow working in Baruch's organization. He's now the great General Hugh Johnson of the blue eagle. I can never put him in a place where I can use him again, so he's just utterly useless.

The only help Perkins got from Baruch was a suggestion that she get Walter Chrysler to offer Johnson a job, since he was a good friend of Johnson and knew his limitations. But Chrysler gave Perkins the same response and reasons as Baruch's. "I can't manage him," he told Perkins.[21]

Notwithstanding Johnson's numerous critics and the calls for his removal, Roosevelt continued to support him. For one thing, he personally liked Johnson, whose charm and exuberant humor touched "a responsive cord in the President." Roosevelt got "a tremendous kick" out of the stories, variegated cusswords, and turbulent life of the ex-cavalryman.[22] He did not want to hurt him by forcing him to resign or firing him, and Johnson's frequent rushes to the White House to seek reassurance (i.e., to be told he was doing a good job) did not make matters easier. There were also political considerations. If Roosevelt removed Johnson because of the avalanche of criticism, he would open himself to direct attack, admitting that his recovery program was not working. If something had to be done about Johnson, it was better to wait until after the fall elections. In the meantime, Johnson was playing a useful role. He was a lightning rod, attracting criticism that would otherwise be directed at the White House.

In May 1934, Johnson gave further evidence that he had become an embarrassment to the administration. In a speech before the American Trade Association Executives on May 2, he called for a new full-blown Blue Eagle campaign because of "a lapse of public enthusiasm over the codes."[23] Many administration figures believed that the speech demonstrated that Johnson was out of touch with the reality of public sentiment. The public had felt a great sense of letdown after the first campaign, and a new set of brass bands and hoopla could not be expected to make the eagle soar again; they were of the opinion, in fact, that such a campaign would lead to an even bigger letdown. On May 4, speaking to a mass meeting in the State Fair Stadium in Columbus, Ohio, Johnson delivered a slashing attack against the critics of NRA, replete with the flamboyant phrases and characterizations that the public now expected from him.[24] Roosevelt, finally concerned that Johnson's sledgehammer tactics were becoming counterproductive, expressed dismay about the speech; and columnist Arthur Krock reported that it sparked a new round of talk about turning NRA over to someone else.[25]

Gradually, Roosevelt came to the realization that Johnson had to go. But he could not stir himself to take action. He always tended to avoid difficult decisions that had a personal side to them, and Johnson was a special case, the highest-ranking figure to leave his administration. Instead, Roosevelt, as Lilienthal recorded in his diary, sat back and prayed that "some eleventh hour miracle would intervene to save him the painful necessity of pulling Johnson out" or, better yet, that Johnson would see the difficulty he was creating and make things easy by resigning on his own initiative.[26]

Throughout the brief history of NRA, Johnson had always professed his readiness to resign "any time this despicable thing becomes too much for my self respect to bear."[27] Confronted with the ever-enlarging circle of resistance, however, he would not consider resignation. In fact, all the talk seemed only to stiffen his resolve to stay. He swore to Matthew Josephson that he would "not go until this thing has jelled a damn sight more than it has yet." And in a conversation with a friend at the end of May 1934, he stated that the opposition was having no effect on him. "They can't kill a Johnson," he bragged.[28]

Not only was Johnson unwilling to resign, he was actually looking to enhance his own power. In May 1934, he asked Roosevelt to transfer to him the power vested in the president by NIRA "to make rules and regulations" to carry out the purposes of the act and "to amend or cancel all codes, rules, orders" and the like issued under Title I. Several cabinet members neared the exploding point at this proposal, and Perkins advised Roosevelt that giving Johnson this power would create chaos. She stated:

New problems are constantly arising, often intimately affecting labor. . . . If past experience is any criterion, those new problems would be disposed of by rules promulgated by General Johnson with a minimum of study, thought and discussion. The parties most vitally concerned might not even hear about it until after the regulation had come into effect.[29]

Faced with the opposition of his cabinet, Roosevelt rejected Johnson's proposal.

By June 1934, both Johnson and Richberg were discussing a major reorganization of NRA, although for different reasons. Johnson believed that reorganization was the logical step as NRA evolved from a code-drafting to a code-administering body. In marked contrast, Richberg saw reorganization as a way of removing Johnson from the scene. During their discussions, Johnson's mistrust of Richberg prompted him to bring up the possibility that both of them might resign, "so the President could go ahead with a new management" of NRA. He added on reflection that he could not yet leave because too much was yet to be done, but he implied that Richberg's immediate resignation would be no problem.[30] Though he had no intention of resigning completely from the recovery program, on June 26 Richberg submitted an official resignation to Roosevelt and Johnson,[31] using the resignation as a lever

to compel Roosevelt to choose between himself and Johnson and to prepare for a reorganization of NRA in which he would play an enlarged
role.

Along with his letter of resignation, Richberg submitted his own
plan for the reorganization of NRA. Johnson and Frances Robinson, he
stressed, must be required "to take a *complete rest* for thirty to sixty
days" and Johnson *"himself"* should appoint a three-man "Acting
Board of Administration" to guide NRA in his absence. Richberg also
called for Roosevelt to suspend the National Emergency Council for
ninety days and transfer its function to a proposed Industrial Council,
made up of three Cabinet members, two top recovery administrators,
and a director. The council would carry out the instructions of the
president "in approving codes or prescribing regulations" and in exercising other powers not previously delegated to the NRA administrator. Finally, Richberg proposed that he be named head of the new Industrial Council.[32]

In the meantime, Johnson was finishing work on his plan. The principal feature was a recommendation that the administrator be replaced
by a board of directors. It would act as a "High Court of Economic Relations . . . and pass finally on or create, all N.R.A. policy and administration." Johnson included in his plan the observation that implementation of his proposal would make him "superfluous." But he was vague
as to whether he would be resigning at any specified time. In all probability, Johnson was trying to avoid the public humiliation that would
come if Roosevelt removed him from NRA. Roosevelt appeared open to
Johnson's recommendation. However, when Johnson brought up the
subject of his resignation in a meeting in the White House, Roosevelt,
to his relief, waved his hand and said, "Later perhaps, but not now."[33]

For the time being, Roosevelt opted for Richberg's plan. He prevailed
on Baruch to ask Johnson to accompany him to Europe for a month or
so. With Johnson gone, Roosevelt planned to name a committee, which
would include Wallace, Perkins, Ickes, and Richberg, to run NRA.[34]
Baruch "laid it on heavily with Johnson," and for a time he seemed
amenable to the request. But after Robbie convinced him that it was all
a Richberg plot to push him out of NRA, Johnson balked. If anybody
should be going to Europe, he told Perkins, it should be Richberg.
"Richberg," he said, "can't do the things I can do for the NRA."[35]
Roosevelt, however, was not stymied. On June 30, 1934, he granted
Richberg a leave of absence from NRA and appointed him director of
the newly created Industrial Emergency Committee and executive director of the National Emergency Council. Two days later Roosevelt
sent Johnson a letter asking him to stay out of the office for at least a
month of well-deserved rest so that he would be "in racing trim to carry
on with me to the finish."[36]

Roosevelt's actions left Johnson's status as NRA administrator intact and convinced the general that he retained the confidence of the White House. In a press conference on July 10 he told reporters that he would ultimately be replaced by a board and that he hoped "to avoid" becoming a member of that board. But taking care to tell reporters that his upcoming vacation should not be construed as evidence that he was "getting out," Johnson also said that his only specific plans were to return to Washington after his vacation and stay with NRA "just as long as the President needs me."[37] Johnson, however, was only deceiving himself. Summarizing Roosevelt's maneuvering, Rexford Tugwell noted in his diary at the end of June that "it was well known that Johnson's days were numbered."[38]

HUGH Johnson's vacation, which was supposed to relieve the controversy surrounding him and provide some respite for the administration as well, only occasioned more controversy and more resentment. Several months earlier, Johnson had scheduled a speaking tour of the Midwest and the Pacific Coast for July 1934. It included a speaking engagement at his alma mater, the University of California, where he was to be awarded a Phi Beta Kappa key. After receiving Roosevelt's orders to take a vacation, Johnson decided to combine the vacation with his tour. Because of the various problems, White House staffers Louis Howe and Marvin McIntyre warned Roosevelt, who was vacationing aboard the cruiser USS *Houston*, that the speaking tour was ill-advised and that Johnson needed to concentrate on rest. "We all think speeches highly undesirable and vacation essential," McIntyre wired Roosevelt. Their warnings impressed Roosevelt, and with his backing the White House staffers urged Johnson to cancel his speeches. He refused, telling Roosevelt that the cancellations would be personally embarrassing. But to assure Roosevelt that he would create no problems, Johnson promised to take a two-week vacation with his mother while on the tour and to keep his speeches on a "purely noncontroversial and constructive basis." Satisfied with Johnson's assurances, Roosevelt overruled his staff.[39]

Accompanied by Frances Robinson and Bob Lea, Johnson left Washington on July 11. After a speech at Waterloo, Iowa, they went to the Pacific coast. It could not have been a more volatile spot for the tempestuous general. On May 9, 1934, the International Longshoremen's Association went on strike in demand for the union hiring hall, a wage increase, a thirty-hour week, and union recognition, closing down the entire coast. A federal mediating team, led by Edward McGrady, worked out a compromise. Joseph P. Ryan, international president of the union, accepted it; but the local rank and file, influenced by the Australian Marxist Harry Bridges, rejected it. After the passage of Public Resolution 44, Roosevelt created the National Longshoremen's Board, which was empowered to investigate the causes of the strike and, if both parties agreed, to arbitrate the differences. Nothing had come of the action, for the employers were not interested in arbitration. They intended to break the strike.

By early July the struggle had become explosive. In San Francisco the vehemently anti-union Industrial Association, an organ representing the city's leading industrial, banking, shipping, railroad, and utility interests, decided to open the port by force. Violence resulted, spurring the other unions in San Francisco to action; and on July 13, 1934, the San Francisco Central Labor Council voted for a general strike, which was in force by July 16. The passionately anti-union newspaper publishers of California quickly branded the strike as Communist-inspired and, at the instigation of John Francis Neylan, chief counsel for the Hearst Corporation, took upon themselves the mission of seeing that it was crushed.

Heading west from Waterloo, Johnson resolved to remain above the dispute. He knew "only in a casual way" about its background, and McGrady had already strongly urged him not to stick his neck out on this one. In the morning of July 16 Johnson arrived in San Francisco. His only purpose was to visit McGrady and other old friends and to give his speech at the University of California. What Johnson saw in the city, however, stunned him. As he later wrote, "I did not know what a general strike looked like and I hope that you may never know. I soon learned and it gave me cold shivers." San Francisco's economic life was being strangled, and there was fear that the power, light, and water supply would be shut off. "A foreign enemy could scarcely threaten more than that," Johnson commented.[40]

Although conditions in San Francisco were distressing, the situation was not as desperate as Johnson perceived. No essential services had been curtailed. Food was available, and one observer noted that "about the only real deprivation endured by the general public was the inability to go to the theater, eat at a hotel dining room, ride in a taxi or a Market St. Railway car, get clothes cleaned or washed, and get a hair cut."[41] Most important, the strikers instigated no violence; when Johnson arrived, the city was calm.

The newspaper publishers were initially anxious about Johnson's arrival. While they had busied themselves calling for the suppression of the strike as "a Red revolution," the federal government had given no credence to their claims, and some federal officials had even ridiculed them. "If General Johnson took a similar stand it would put a pretty sharp pin in their red balloon," one writer later noted. Yet if Johnson's visit provided cause for nervousness among the newspaper publishers, it also provided an opportunity. They planned to break the general strike by splitting the ranks of the strikers. Newspaper stories and editorials repeatedly distinguished between "conservative leaders" and "radicals," in order to scare and shame the conservative membership of many of the city's unions, which could assert its considerable influence and call off the strike. Although some of the other publishers' representatives were skeptical, Neylan believed Johnson could be persuaded to their position; if so, some people might infer that the publishers' line had the approval of Washington. With that thought in mind, the publishers greeted Johnson with a blare of publicity and hustled him off to the Palace Hotel, which was serving as their strike headquarters.

Many labor leaders and local government officials became wary of Johnson's scheduled speech at Berkeley. Fearful that Johnson's habit of shooting from the hip would only make matters worse, they urged university officials to cancel the speech. On the pretext that they could not provide adequate police protection, university officials tried to call it off. But Johnson would "not stand for that." When university officials were not moved by his protests, Johnson raced to Neylan, who persuaded them to drop their objections.[42]

Johnson worked on his speech until three o'clock in the morning of July 17, with Neylan and associates at his side. In the early stage of their discussion, Johnson urged Neylan to support the International Longshoremen's Association's position on hiring halls. But Neylan vigorously rejected Johnson's proposal, arguing that it would be a compromise with revolution. Continuing this theme, Neylan and the others saturated Johnson with anti-union sentiment and convinced him that the general strike was a revolutionary communistic attack against law and order. Once the Communists were eliminated, they told him, the dispute could be easily settled; and Johnson, they indicated, was in a unique position to help end the strike. He was the unbiased outsider, they preached, who could get calmer heads to prevail and bring both sides together. His resolve to remain aloof forgotten in the face of this appeal to his ego and sense of values, Johnson once more interjected himself into a major labor dispute.

The whole story of why Johnson changed his mind and involved himself is unclear. According to some contemporary accounts, the publishers "asked" him to leave town unless he changed his mind. Others attributed his change to confusion brought on by heavy drinking. There is no reason to believe, however, that either factor had any significant effect; and in reality, Johnson's change is not surprising. He had consistently opposed the closed shop; if Neylan or anyone in the meeting had told him that the net result of a union hiring hall would be to sanction a closed shop in all but name, that alone could have convinced him to change his mind about the docks strike. In addition, Johnson had never approved of the general strike, and after the publishers' representatives began to work on him and refer to his duty to help end the strike, he had no doubt about what he should do.[43]

On July 17, Johnson traveled across the Bay to Berkeley to speak in the university's open-air Greek theater before an overflow crowd of some five thousand. Officially, the occasion for the speech was the awarding of his Phi Beta Kappa key. But as he crossed the Bay, Johnson had something else in mind. After his session with Neylan, he believed that he could use his speech to separate the moderate labor people from the extremists and in this way hasten an end to the labor strife. Johnson began his speech, which was broadcast locally, by blandly recalling his days as a student at Berkeley and spelling out the rights guaranteed by Section 7a. Taking care to strike an evenhanded pose, he pointed out that the right to bargain collectively had not been "justly accorded" the dockworkers and suggested that "if the shipping industry does not fully and freely accord these rights, then on its head will lie every ounce of responsibility for whatever may happen here."

Johnson then shifted direction. Pumped up by the long session with Neylan, he let his emotions get the better of him. Growing more animated, he lashed out belligerently at the general strikers, echoing the publishers' sentiments. "There is another and worse side to this story," he yelled into the microphone. "You are living here under the stress of a general strike," and "it is a threat to the community. It is a menace to government. It is civil war." A heated Johnson called for an end to the strike:

When the means of food supply—milk to children, necessities of life to the whole people—are threatened, that is bloody insurrection. . . . I am for organized labor and collective bargaining with all my heart and soul and I will support it with all the power at my command, but this ugly thing is a blow to the flag of our common country and it has got to stop.

Without mention of the factors that brought on the general strike, Johnson called upon "responsible labor organizations" to "run these subversive influences out from their ranks like rats" if they wanted to retain the respect and support of the American people. He concluded with these words:

Insurrection against the common interest of the community is not a proper weapon and will not for one moment be tolerated by the American people who are one—whether they live in California, Oregon or the sunny South. It would be safer for a cotton-tail rabbit to slap a wildcat in the face than for this half of one per cent of our population to try to strangle the rest of us into submission by any such means as this. Let's settle this thing and do it now.[44]

In more normal circumstances, Johnson's speech might have been received as just another forgettable example of his verbal excess. But San Francisco in July 1934 was a pressure cooker on the verge of exploding. Even as Johnson spoke, vigilante groups took to the streets in San Francisco and eleven other towns in northern California. Left-wing union offices and meeting halls were raided, equipment and other property destroyed, and Communists and suspected Communists were beaten up and manhandled. Johnson had spoken as the highest-ranking administration official in the region. Although he had intended his words to be taken figuratively and probably knew nothing of the plans of the organized vigilante groups, he had seemed to bestow the sanction of the New Deal on some of the worst instincts of the community.[45]

Johnson's involvement in the dispute did not end with the speech. Following telephone discussions between Johnson and Marvin McIntyre and between Johnson and herself in the evening of July 17, Perkins reluctantly approved the National Longshoremen's Board's suggestion that Johnson be named official spokesman for the board. The circumstances surrounding this move are murky, especially since McGrady, a board member, had previously indicated that Johnson should not be involved, and Perkins had long resented his role in mediating labor disturbances. But by his own action Johnson was now involved; and most likely the board felt, and Perkins agreed, that if Johnson was made an official spokesman, he would be forced to exercise more restraint in his comments.[46]

Caught up in the excitement of being at the center of the dispute, Johnson quickly lost control of himself. As part of his plan to orchestrate the end of the general strike, Neylan had arranged for Johnson to meet with John McLaughlin, the secretary of the San Francisco Teamsters Union, on the afternoon of July 18. Before a bevy of reporters and photographers, Johnson, in the name of the government, was to appeal to the unions to call off the strike in return for his promise to use his office to resolve the issues. McLaughlin, in turn, was to agree to Johnson's pledge and call upon other union leaders to comply. By this time, however, the excited Johnson was near a breaking point. He showed up at the meeting drunk, and instead of following the prepared script, made a violent attack on labor that left McLaughlin dumbfounded and "convinced that he had been made into a fool." Fortunately for Johnson's reputation, Neylan prevailed upon the press to kill the stories on the incident.[47]

Johnson was not so drunk, however, that he could not issue a statement in his official capacity making it clear that the general strike must be ended before the dockworkers' grievances could be settled. "I am here," he said, "to do what the federal government can do to aid these coast committees to settle this trouble. . . . But the federal government cannot act under the continuing coercion of a general strike. The first step to peace and agreement is to lift that strike. Until this is done, I have nothing to offer."[48] Regaining some of his balance, Johnson also cautioned the governor of California not to accede to the employers' request to declare martial law. They only wanted to use martial law as a cover to break the dockworkers' strike and reopen the waterfront, he advised, a move that would inevitably lead to more violence.

By the time Johnson issued his statements, the general strike was fizzling. Feeling that they had made their gesture toward labor solidarity, the more conservative union leaders in the city were anxious to end it. In addition, Johnson's actions had erroneously persuaded the strikers that the administration was better inclined toward management than at any other time since the docks strike began. After hearing of Johnson's remarks at Berkeley, even Bridges felt pessimistic. In the evening of July 17, the General Strike Committee voted to recommend the arbitration of all the issues still in dispute in the docks strike. Union restaurants and butcher shops reopened on July 18. And on July 19 the General Strike Committee voted to end the general strike. Johnson was overjoyed, and on July 19 he sent a buoyant wire to Roosevelt, whose ship was now in Hawaiian waters: "General strike called off by splendid patriotic attitude of regular labor leaders. . . . Hurrah for Roosevelt."[49]

Press accounts praised Johnson for quickening a settlement. His speech and follow-up "crack-down" statements, they emphasized, "hit the bullseye of independent and moderate public opinion" and coalesced it against the "extremists of both sides."[50] Others, however, were not so enthusiastic about his involvement. Many leaders of organized labor and their liberal supporters believed that Johnson did nothing to hasten a settlement and that his Berkeley speech was a calculated appeal to mob violence against peaceful strikers. "Crack Down on the General" before he totally destroys the New Deal, the *New Republic* lectured Roosevelt. Some labor elements in San Francisco were reportedly so angered by Johnson's speech that they demanded that officials in Washington cancel his remaining speeches and get him away from the Bay area as soon as possible.[51]

Johnson had certainly antagonized labor; but for his own security, it was much more important that he had infuriated Labor Secretary Perkins.[52] In her opinion, Johnson had no business butting into the dispute when he did. Its settlement was entrusted to the Department of Labor and the National Longshoremen's Board; and she, for one, had McGrady and others in San Francisco working to restore peace. There was no need for Johnson to stick his nose in. As she saw it, he had naively permitted himself to be used by the anti-union elements, making the administration appear the tool of the employers, and then, through his reckless speech, had sanctioned a new wave of violence. If that was not enough, he in effect made it appear that major labor disputes could only be settled by the nation's number-one crack downer. This was the very notion she had been working to dispel. These actions were intolerable in her eyes, and she now adamantly insisted that Johnson must go.[53]

Johnson was oblivious to the antagonism and resentment aroused by his actions in San Francisco. He saw himself as a Sir Lancelot who had charged heroically to the rescue of the beleaguered city. Boasting to friends that he had taken command of the situation when it was most desperate, he was certain that he had induced labor leaders to call off the strike through a deft strategy of condemnation and persuasion.

As soon as the strike was settled, Johnson flew to Los Angeles, where on July 20 he delivered another speech in which he denounced left-wing labor leaders in vitriolic terms.[54] Following other stopovers in California and a stay in Okmulgee, Oklahoma, to visit his mother, Johnson went to Chicago on August 2 for another round of speeches. Compared to some of the other speeches on the tour, Johnson's remarks were noncontroversial. Nevertheless, during his time in Chicago he managed again to antagonize Perkins by involving himself in a labor dispute centering on a strike in the stockyards. Previously, the concerned parties had agreed to let a federal judge settle the issues; but that agreement broke down. A strike was called, and the regional labor board was unable to effect a settlement. Johnson later claimed that his involvement was literally forced on him. In actuality, however, he needed little pushing. After being approached by both sides to help move the negotiations, he eagerly stepped forward to mediate. In "forty-eight hours of the usual sort of horse trading," he wrote, they agreed to submit the dispute to a federal judge.[55]

Johnson received a cool reception when he returned to Washington at the end of the first week of August. Perkins made it plain that she was displeased by his involvement in the San Francisco and Chicago strikes. McIntyre, Howe, and other White House staffers were bitter about the embarrassment he had caused the administration with some of his remarks. And Richberg was telling anybody who would listen that Johnson's actions in San Francisco proved what he had been saying all along—Johnson was no longer fit to run NRA. Roosevelt, though, had not yet decided what to do with Johnson. Henry Morgenthau told Roosevelt on August 8 that Johnson was the worst situation in Washington and that he should be removed from NRA and given a job in the Reconstruction Finance Corporation. Roosevelt agreed that something had to be done, but he stated that getting Johnson out of NRA was several steps down the road.[56]

HUGH Johnson had no sooner returned to the new, cooler Washington than he was involved in an acrimonious feud with the National Labor Relations Board. In part, the feud grew out of Johnson's handling of a labor relations spat in his own organization. Early in June 1934, Nancy Luke, a stencil cutter in the Mimeograph Division, was dismissed from her job with NRA for insubordination. The American Federation of Government Employees took up her case, and Johnson, wanting to avoid a squabble in his own backyard at a time when organized labor was questioning his commitment to Section 7a, tried to push the whole affair under the table by reinstating Mrs. Luke. The affair, however, did not end with the reinstatement, for John Donovan, the local president, regularly showed up at Johnson's office and demanded to see him about the details of her case. Since the woman had been reinstated, Johnson could see little reason for these meetings and increasingly questioned Donovan's motives. He came to view Donovan as an uppity employee taking up time with only one goal in mind—administration baiting for the purpose of impairing NRA's standing with labor. Fed up, Johnson fired Donovan from his position with the Labor Advisory Board for "inefficiency, insubordination, and absence for days without leave." Two days later, on June 20, 1934, Johnson hinted to union officials that Donovan was a "leftist."

Johnson insisted that Donovan was fired only because he was a bad employee, not because he was a local union president. Others saw the Donovan affair in a different light. Labor leaders, many of them long-standing opponents of Johnson who were anxious to jab at him, thought Donovan was fired because of his activities as a union leader. Before long Johnson was "given a severe jolt, and the nation some much-needed humor," when picket lines were thrown up around NRA headquarters. Marchers tromped around carrying banners and placards proclaiming Johnson "Chiseler No. 1" and declaring that "This Concern Is Unfair to Organized Labor."[57]

Following his dismissal, Donovan took the matter to the National Labor Relations Board. In this respect, Johnson later lamented, he "knew his garden products."[58] Still feeling its way, the labor relations board was determined that it would not go the way of the National Labor Board and was most anxious to prove that it could stand up to any employer, including Johnson. Disdaining an appearance before the board, Johnson dispatched two subordinates to the Donovan hearing and sent a letter explaining the facts to Chairman Lloyd K. Garrison. Garrison refused to accept the letter and said that Johnson should personally appear so that he could be cross-examined. An infuriated Johnson rejected any suggestion that he was obliged to appear. Garrison, he felt, had to accept in good faith his denial that he had fired Donovan for union activity. Garrison accepted the letter as the extent of Johnson's testimony with such obvious displeasure that from that point on, Johnson expected an adverse ruling.

On August 21, 1934, the National Labor Relations Board ruled against Johnson, holding that he had violated Section 7a and rebuking him for "unjustified interference" in union activity. The ruling forced Johnson to take Donovan back, but he steadfastly refused to concede that he had erred and charged that the ruling was "absolutely inconsistent" with the evidence and that it was handed down for the purpose of "discrediting" NRA. Like so many other men and agencies that had differed with him, the National Labor Relations Board was "a rink-stink."[59]

The Donovan affair blended into an even more important controversy

THE NRA BLUE EAGLE: "I invented him, have kept him aloft. . . ."

between Johnson and the National Labor Relations Board. The case of the Chicago Motor Coach Company, which the Chicago regional labor board had in April 1934 found guilty of firing employees for union activity, was unresolved. NRA did nothing to enforce the decision and turned the case over to the labor relations board after its formation. The National Labor Relations Board reviewed it in July 1934 and on August 2 ruled that the company had violated Section 7a. Garrison then referred the case to the NRA Compliance Division for immediate removal of the Blue Eagle and possible prosecution, announcing that he believed Johnson would act quickly.

To that date Johnson had failed to act in every case in which the labor relations board had recommended withdrawal of the compliance symbol, and he balked at Garrison's request as well. Still fuming over the Donovan affair, he resented Garrison's announcement that NRA would automatically fall in line behind the National Labor Relations Board. To do so would be to admit that NRA took second place to another agency. But there was more at work than Johnson's spite. Johnson's study of the case led to his conclusion that removal of the Blue Eagle would be ineffective and a risk to support for NRA in the Chicago area. For many of the city's suburbanites, the bus company was the sole means of commuting to Chicago. Johnson could readily see that they would undoubtedly ignore his action and continue to ride the company's buses, Blue Eagle or no Blue Eagle. Moreover, the Chicago newspapers were uniformly hostile to NRA; if he took away the Blue Eagle, they would make the most of a new chance to denigrate NRA. Following the precedent he had adopted in the Budd case, Johnson announced that NRA would have to make its own investigation of the case before acting on the National Labor Relations Board's recommendation.[60]

In an effort to avoid a break with the National Labor Relations Board, Johnson sent A. R. Glancy, chief of the NRA Compliance Division, to explain his reasoning to Garrison and seek his assent to the NRA investigation. Garrison rejected Johnson's arguments and rushed off a letter to him in which he practically lectured the NRA chief on how to do his job. Johnson, enraged by Garrison's letter, quickly replied in a scathing letter overflowing with melodramatic invective. In his view, Garrison was a "Johnny come lately" to the problems growing out of Section 7a, and for Garrison to say that he might better know how to handle the Chicago bus case was poppycock. "It is like a boy who had ridden a raft out of Johnstown flood lecturing Noah about the Ark," he wrote. Johnson went on to say that he would not be stampeded into removing the Blue Eagle. To do so in this case was to risk killing it. The eagle was his bird, and he alone would decide when it should fly and when it should fall to earth: "I invented him, have kept him aloft so far, and shall not let anybody pull him down while I have responsibility for the job."[61]

Garrison refused to budge from his position that Johnson should accept the board's findings. But he had no authority to force it upon him. Soon afterward Johnson announced that NRA was not "obliged" to follow the labor relations board's findings and in all cases would decide itself whether it was appropriate to remove the Blue Eagle.[62] His announcement pulled the teeth of the National Labor Relations Board. It was now in the position of hearing cases and making decisions without any certain way of punishing those who disobeyed its orders. The chasm between NRA and the National Labor Relations Board could not have been wider.

The Johnson–National Labor Relations Board feud caused many administration figures to question the wisdom of Roosevelt's approach to dealing with Johnson. Organized labor and its supporters had interpreted the creation of the labor relations board as an administrative move away from Johnson's pro-management stance in labor matters. By refusing to accept the findings of the board, however, Johnson clearly signaled that he intended to keep control of labor matters in his own hands. Many of Johnson's critics saw this as rank sabotage of administration policy, and they were apprehensive that if Roosevelt did not move quickly to check Johnson, the administration would lose the support of organized labor. In their thinking, in other words, this feud was another reason for Roosevelt to remove Johnson as NRA administrator as soon as possible.

CHAPTER 13

EXIT JOHNSON

THE month of August 1934 was a disspiriting time for Hugh Johnson. His policies were being relentlessly shelled by opponents within the administration and by countless individuals in Congress, in business and labor organizations, and in the general public. In addition, his personal life was growing more troublesome. His wife, Helen, was seriously ill and required the attention of two private-duty nurses, an expense Johnson could not support. Within NRA many officials resented Frances Robinson's power, and Robert Straus reported to Adolf Berle that as many as half of the men in the agency would resign "because of the affair between Johnson and 'Robby.'"[1] Straus's report was grossly exaggerated. Yet there was no doubt that Johnson's relationship with Robbie had become an embarrassing public scandal. Reporters were scrambling around Washington to discover another tidbit of juicy gossip about the mystery woman behind the general. Marvin McIntyre regularly warned Roosevelt about the hazard of keeping Johnson on in the administration, pointing out that voters would likely resent the president's apparent tolerance of Johnson and Robbie's relationship, especially since both were paid with public money. Nor would Johnson's drying-out stays at Walter Reed strike the voters well. Likewise, Morgenthau, Tugwell, Wallace, Perkins, Richberg and other administration figures told Roosevelt he could no longer afford Johnson. His leadership at NRA was drowning the recovery program and alienating important groups, they reported, while his personal excesses had become nothing less than disgraceful. The pressure from his administration convinced Roosevelt that he had to remove Johnson. As he told Perkins, "It's really worse than you knew or said, and we really have to do it."[2]

FOLLOWING his return to Washington from his western speaking tour-vacation, Hugh Johnson made plans for "a real vacation" at the end of August at Bethany Beach, Delaware. At the same time, Richberg speeded up his campaign to unseat Johnson. On August 14 he visited

Roosevelt and explained his concerns about the organizational chaos in NRA. Over the next several days he told McIntyre that the Johnson situation was "much more acute than I realized" and emphasized the need for quick action on several grounds: (1) "Major matters of policy are pressing so for decision that the alternative is confusion and disintegration for lack of decision, or a grave risk of decisions which will cause increased difficulty"; (2) "Distrust and dissatisfaction throughout the country are increasing daily the resistance to the program"; (3) "The quality of N.R.A. personnel is steadily declining. Important officials are leaving"; and (4) "The General himself is, in the opinion of many, in the worst physical and mental condition and needs an immediate relief from responsibility." Hinting that he would leave the administration unless something was done soon, Richberg made it clear that he thought everything would work out once Johnson was gone.[3]

Impelled by Richberg's scheming and the recommendations of others in his administration, Roosevelt made his move to ease Johnson out. It had to be done gently. Tugwell and others were cautioning him that Johnson could not be fired abruptly because of his "cantankerousness and volubility."[4] Tugwell, like many, expected Johnson would rant and rave and bring down NRA with him.

With this thought in mind, Roosevelt met with Johnson on August 18. This Saturday meeting was their first in nearly seven weeks, and when Johnson entered the White House, newspapermen on the presidential beat speculated that Roosevelt intended either to fire him or give him a different job. The meeting lasted for more than an hour. After praising Johnson for his work, Roosevelt tried to explain to him, without actually saying so, that he had become a definite liability at NRA and that he should take a rest as a prelude to accepting a new and more important assignment. He told Johnson that he was thinking of a mission in which Johnson would study the progress of economic recovery in Europe. Johnson lost patience. "If you want to fire me, say so. Don't beat around the bush," he yelled.[5] Johnson's outburst surprised and dismayed Roosevelt. The last thing he wanted was for Johnson to stomp out of his office in a huff and tell the waiting reporters that he had been fired. Turning soft, he decided it was better to calm Johnson down and bring up the matter of his status at NRA at a later time. According to Johnson, Roosevelt then said that he did not want him to leave NRA and, in fact, insisted that he stay until the reorganization of the agency was completed. "I need you," he said very flatteringly, "and the country needs you." Elated by the president's remarks, Johnson marched out of the White House with his red face glowing and his head held high. The newspapermen immediately swarmed around him and asked, "Are you going out?" Shutting them off with a wave of his hand, Johnson answered that Roosevelt wanted him to stay: "The President told me that I could not get away from the NRA or the administration. He wants me right here with my feet nailed right down on the floor. And of course I'm staying."[6]

Neither Johnson nor Roosevelt was satisfied with the meeting. For his part, Johnson wanted to stay with NRA. But his wife's mounting medical expenses were pressing hard on him, and he was not at all sure that he had handled the meeting correctly. After he had time to reflect on it, he concluded that it might have been better for him to have tendered his resignation so that he could return to private life. Reporting on the meeting to Baruch, who was vacationing in Europe, Johnson expresed doubt about the wisdom of remaining with the administration in light of his financial circumstances and the possibility that he might end up little more than "a dead cock in the pit."[7] Roosevelt, meanwhile, knew that his softhearted remarks had only delayed the inevitable, and Johnson had made matters more difficult by his comments to the press. Johnson had told the press that Roosevelt wanted him to stay with NRA, which was not the case. Instead, Roosevelt had intended to say that he wanted Johnson to stay with the administration but that others would take care of NRA.[8] From the president's viewpoint, Johnson either misunderstood his intent or deliberately perverted it in order to stay with NRA. Whatever happened, Roosevelt realized that he must set Johnson straight, even if it meant having it out with him.

Roosevelt quickly asked Johnson to return to the White House for a meeting at ten o'clock in the morning of the following Monday, August 20. He also asked Perkins and Richberg to report at the same time, although he gave them no indication of the agenda. The two arrived at the White House a few minutes before Johnson and were ushered into Roosevelt's office. Without his normal ice-breaking chat, Roosevelt, obviously braced for something quite serious, sternly beckoned them to sit and kept his thoughts to himself. The unhappy outcome of their meeting the previous Saturday had convinced Roosevelt that Johnson just could not take a hint. He would have to be more forceful, and he had to have witnesses so that Johnson could not misunderstand or pretend to. As he later told Perkins and Richberg, "I knew I had to have witnesses. Hugh would not understand or believe that I did ask him" to leave. "You can tell him if he asks you, because I expect that he'll be confused again by tonight and not know whether he's been told to stay with his feet nailed down, or to go."[9]

Exactly at ten o'clock Johnson was also ushered into Roosevelt's office. Although he did not know what to expect, he felt something was wrong when he saw that Perkins and Richberg were present and that *"neither of them looked up"* to acknowledge his presence. Instantly, there flashed in his mind the memory of "two peons who were skinning a cow at the barred gates of San Rosalita Rancho" during the Pershing punitive expedition into Mexico. George Patton had been leading a patrol in search of one of Villa's lieutenants; and as they approached the ranch, they instinctively realized that they "had cornered" their quarry "because neither peon raised his eyes." Johnson later wrote that "without rhyme or reason that incident flashed back to me when Mr. Richberg and Madam Secretary did not look up. They too had been skinning a cow."

Roosevelt began the meeting by announcing that "I am going to explode a bomb-shell." Recounting how he had previously asked him to go to Europe and make a report on European recovery, Roosevelt again asked Johnson to accept the assignment. Sweetening his proposal, Roosevelt told him he could keep his title as NRA administrator and that he could take anybody he wanted with him. He even suggested that Baruch or Gerard Swope might be good choices. Sensing that this was "the sugary lipstick smeared over the kiss of death," Johnson interrupted and asked suspiciously about the fate of NRA in his absence. Roosevelt paid little heed to Johnson's question, replying merely that he need not concern himself with NRA; it was only a detail. Taken aback by Roosevelt's cavalier comment, Johnson replied: "Mr. President, of course there is nothing for me to do but resign immediately." Not wanting Johnson to leave the administration on a sour note, Roosevelt told him that he did not want him to resign. He only wanted him to take a new assignment.

The meeting continued for some time, with the discussion centering around the makeup of the committee that would run NRA while Johnson was abroad. Richberg argued that the small committee which Johnson intended to have run NRA while he was at Bethany Beach was the worst committee that he could have selected and should be replaced by a completely new one selected from a list of names drawn up by him. Johnson's committee included Alvin Brown, who had never gotten along well with Richberg; and his name was conspicuously absent from Richberg's list, as were the names of other Johnson loyalists. In Johnson's mind Richberg's comment was just further evidence that Richberg was out to dethrone him. Attempting to get a commitment from Johnson, Roosevelt reiterated that Johnson "did not realize the importance of what he wanted" him to do and stated that he was growing weary of "all this pulling and hauling" and the constant publicity about the reorganization of NRA. Not knowing what to do, Johnson broke off the meeting and asked for time to consider Roosevelt's proposal. Shortly afterward, Johnson left the White House, his eyes glaring and his brow furrowed. To waiting reporters he only growled that he "wanted less responsibility" under the new plans being made for NRA.[10]

Johnson was in a daze for the remainder of the day. For months he had been convinced that Richberg was out for his job and that Perkins was "sore" about his role in settling labor disputes; he was certain that the morning's meeting was the capstone of their conspiracy to oust him. In his words: "Both of these officials had just demonstrated an ability to change the situation of NRA without according me a hearing, or even raising with me a single point for discussion or even according me the courtesy of a word." Johnson never "suffered more" than he did in the next few hours. In utter despair he tried to call Baruch, who was in Prague, for advice. But he could not reach the Chief. Shoring himself up, Johnson concluded that there was no need to consult anybody. NRA was not his personal property, and "it was better" for the president and the "whole enterprise" for him to resign with as little fuss as possible.[11]

Once he had made the decision, Johnson dashed off a three-page letter of resignation and had it delivered to the White House that evening. In the "long and overwrought" letter he reviewed his relationship to the president and NRA and reaffirmed his affection for Roosevelt the man. At the same time, though, he chastized Roosevelt for the un-chivalrous act of bringing him "into the company of those two without warning" and for humiliating him in their presence. He also used the letter to vent his bitterness against Richberg and exhort Roosevelt to be wary of his NRA associate. "I was completely fooled by him until recently," Johnson told Roosevelt, "but may I suggest to you that if he would double-cross me, he would double-cross you." In summary, Johnson stated that

I am leaving merely because I have a pride and a manhood to maintain which I can no longer sustain after the conference of this afternoon and I cannot regard the proposal you made to me as anything more than a banishment with futile flowers and nothing more insulting has ever been done to me than Miss Perkins' suggestion that, as a valedictory, I ought to get credit for the work I have done with N.R.A. Nobody can do that for me. To use your own phrase *Res Ipsa Loquitur*.[12]

Roosevelt replied with his own handwritten letter within an hour—a reply, Johnson remembered, that was "so affectionate, kind, considerate, understanding, and long suffering, that I felt lower and more ashamed of myself than ever." Not yet willing to break with Johnson and anxious not to hurt him, Roosevelt tried to patch things up. He told Johnson that "it is just as true today as last Saturday or 1933 or 1932 that 'I need you and the country needs you.'" Rejecting Johnson's contention that the president was trying to banish him, Roosevelt declared that "I am too fond of you and too proud of all you have done to offer you 'futile flowers'—I want you for work which *tonight* you cannot see as bigger for the Nation than what you are now doing." Forget the letter of resignation, he ordered Johnson, adding that he wanted to speak with Johnson in the White House the following Friday. In a final effort to reassure Johnson he concluded the letter with the gentle admonishment: "Your quotation of 'Res Ipsa Loquitur' is rotten—it should be 'No word is the last between friends.'"[13]

Moved by Roosevelt's letter, Johnson decided that he should remain with NRA. In all probability he had not been completely serious with the resignation anyway. His rational side told him that he had lost Roosevelt's confidence and should resign. Yet his sentimental side told him that he should stay, and in August 1934 that side was dominant. Serving as NRA administrator had been the biggest event of his life, and in his view leaving NRA under the present circumstances would be a humiliating defeat. It would also thrust him into a void. He had often talked about going back to his "hundred thou a year." However, in reality he had no idea of what he would do. It was better to stay with NRA and hope for the best, he thought, then to leave the job like a whipped dog.

If Johnson was not serious about leaving NRA, why did he submit his resignation? Most likely it was a theatrical ploy, used to reassure himself of Roosevelt's support. Earlier that day Roosevelt had said that he wanted him to stay, and Johnson, now a jumble of emotions, desperately wanted more reassurance. If Roosevelt really wanted him to stay, he would again say so. And if Roosevelt wanted him out, he could accept the resignation and save Johnson the embarrassment of being fired.

On Friday, August 24, Johnson had another meeting with Roosevelt. This time the two men talked alone, in a meeting that was at first strained. Still smarting from the Monday meeting, Johnson again spoke against Roosevelt's proposal to send him to Europe. Using all his charm, Roosevelt calmed Johnson down and got him to agree to stay with NRA and work out his reorganization plan. In the meantime, however, he told Johnson that he wished to take over NRA personally "so that he could see at first hand what its problems were."[14]

From that time on Johnson was, in effect, through as NRA administrator, "practically hermetically" sealed off from the agency he had hatched and raised to maturity. At a press conference that same day Roosevelt told reporters that Johnson would be devoting most of his time to the reorganization of the agency, not to the "actual details of administration."[15] Without informing Johnson, he instructed Blackwell Smith, acting general counsel for NRA, and Colonel Lynch to run NRA in direct contact with him and not to talk to anyone else, particularly Johnson.[16]

Notwithstanding Roosevelt's announcement, Richberg and Tugwell maintained the pressure on him over the next weeks to resolve the Johnson situation. On September 5 Richberg sent a memorandum to McIntyre describing the disintegrating condition of NRA. None of the four key men in the organization (Lynch, Smith, Henderson, and Glancy) would continue on their job under Johnson's leadership, he told McIntyre, and it was no longer possible to recruit able men to join NRA. The administrative divisions had been reduced "to hot beds of petty politics, jealousies and fears, which are destructive to any reasonable efficiency." And "the people intimately concerned with the situation" were "struggling against inclinations to hysteria" and talking to their superiors "with tears in their voices and sometimes actively in the eyes." Here Richberg revealed his own tensions and nervousness as much as the actual situation in NRA. As long as Johnson was around, he emphasized, "it is not worthwhile to waste time upon any plans, because no plan can be made effective so long as the obstacle remains." In his most telling statement, Richberg noted that "a team of horses can't be driven in harness with a wild bull." In summary, if Roosevelt really wanted to rehabilitate NRA, he had to stop wasting time waiting for Johnson to map out his plan; instead, he had to remove him and implement Richberg's plans.[17]

Unwilling to base his action only on Richberg's estimate, Roosevelt ordered Tugwell to sample the opinions of administration figures. His survey reinforced Richberg's dismal picture. Harry Hopkins, who had been in charge of the Federal Emergency Relief Administration and the Civil Works Administration, advised that probably 145 out of 150 of the highest officials in the government believed that Johnson's usefulness was at an end and that he should be retired. "Everyone," Tugwell wrote, "agrees that Johnson cannot muster any support from business, provided that he is not given a policy platform. He has alienated them by temperamental changes, uncertain policy, and devious procedure." Perkins told Tugwell that Johnson might still command some support "from old-line labor," but others believed this support was "completely dependent on an administration connection." If Johnson was not in office, this support would dissipate. "All agree," Tugwell stated, that the removal of Johnson "will be highly popular, that the weight of danger lies in Johnson's remaining." Almost as if in a postscript, Tugwell also reported that he found an "extraordinary vindictiveness" about "Miss Robinson." "Many feel that she has caused a good share of the trouble," he concluded.[18]

On September 9 Johnson met with Roosevelt at Hyde Park. He spent the whole evening with Roosevelt and returned the next morning for further discussion. During their talks Roosevelt continually referred to his personal affection for Johnson, so ensuring that the general would stay calm. The basis for discussion was the plan for reorganizing NRA that Johnson had framed. Like Richberg's plan, it called for a board to replace the single administrator. It also called for NRA to relinquish its legislative and judicial functions and confine itself to administrative matters.[19] Roosevelt, however, had no real interest in Johnson's plan. The meetings were a charade—a face-saving gesture for Johnson. The Richberg and Tugwell assessments had convinced Roosevelt that Johnson must not only be replaced but that his removal would entail little political risk. Moreover, Roosevelt had decided Johnson could best be removed in two steps. He would first be appointed to the new NRA board; later, he would be granted a leave of absence until December 1934, at which time Johnson would be given another job outside NRA.

ROOSEVELT's plan to ease Hugh Johnson out of NRA was dashed before he had an opportunity to set it in motion. On leaving Hyde Park, Johnson went to New York City for a September 14 speech in Carnegie Hall before metropolitan code authorities from over 400 industries. In what was the most controversial speech of his career, he reinjected himself into the labor dispute in the cotton textile industry and made "tasteless and unwarranted references" to Justice Louis Brandeis. In so doing, he cut himself off completely from any further dealings with labor and prejudiced NRA's standing before the Supreme Court. The speech sparked a storm of protest and made Johnson an even more unbearable burden for the administration.

The settlement that Johnson had arranged in the cotton textile labor dispute of June 1934 had quickly broken down. The industry went ahead with the temporary curtailment; at the same time, the NRA research project on wages prescribed by the settlement concluded that the industry was in no position to grant wage increases. In addition, George Sloan effectively neutralized the only tangible gain the United Textile Workers had achieved in the settlement, a seat on the Bruere Board. He persuaded Johnson to appoint a young and inexperienced union organizer and then refused to enter the same room with this individual on the grounds that the young man's presence on the board constituted a conflict of interest. In September the textile workers went out on strike; and on September 5, Roosevelt created a three-man board of inquiry, headed by John G. Winant, governor of New Hampshire, to arbitrate any issues submitted to it by both the industry and the union. The Winant board, however, was of little immediate value, for Sloan advised it that the code authority could handle all labor problems without any outside help.[20]

Despite the prominent role he had played in arranging a settlement in June 1934, Johnson was conspicuously absent from the negotiations in September. NRA organizational matters were occupying much of his time, and both Perkins and the National Labor Relations Board had requested him to mind his own business. Johnson, however, got itchy sitting on the sidelines. As the strike neared the end of its second week, he was anxious to rush in and arrange a settlement. He boasted to presidential press secretary Steve Early that "he could guarantee the President settlement of the strike within twenty four hours if he were given the job of handling it."[21] Thinking that he might be of some help, Johnson got in touch with the White House and asked whether he should make any statements in his Carnegie Hall speech. The White House, in turn, referred him to Winant, who told Johnson that it would be better to say nothing. After their conversation Winant was quoted as saying that Johnson had promised not to mention the strike, though Johnson later denied this allegation.[22] But when the White House inquired about the report, Johnson told Early that he was not planning to say anything about the strike and that he probably would clear the general outline of the speech with Roosevelt.

In the meantime, Sloan pressured Johnson to intervene, although in deference to his "orders" not to take part in the dispute, Johnson tried to hide out and avoid him. Unable to put off Sloan, Johnson met him in the evening of September 13, and the cotton textile executive proceeded to inundate him with reports of violence allegedly instigated by the strikers. He also pushed the industry's line that the United Textile Workers had violated the June 2 settlement and that the strike was illegal; in effect, it was a strike against the federal government, since the workers were striking against the code. Johnson needed little convincing. By the end of the evening, Sloan had persuaded him to speak out against the strikers in his speech the next evening. Ignoring his promise to clear his remarks with Roosevelt, Johnson gave the White House no indication of what he was going to say or even that he intended to discuss the strike.

Speaking before an enthusiastic and predominantly anti-labor gathering in Carnegie Hall, Johnson denounced the strike by the United Textile Workers as a breach of faith with him. It was, he said, an "absolute violation" of the agreement he had arranged in June. If that is the way organized labor honors its agreements, he declared, "then that institution is not such a responsible instrumentality as can make contracts on which this country can rely." Continuing his near hysterical tirade against the union, Johnson resurrected the red-baiting technique he had used in his Berkeley speech. He accused Norman Thomas, the leader of the Socialist party, of inspiring the strike at the special United Textile Workers convention in mid-August 1934 by circulating among the delegates and assuring them that "the government would feed the strikers." Thomas's involvement, he editorialized, made the strike political in motivation rather than an attempt to improve economic conditions. "Whatever there is of economic doctrine in the Socialist party, it is political first and economic afterwards," he concluded.

Johnson finished his remarks on the strike by avowing that no group of workers had less reason to strike than those in the cotton textile industry. Hourly wages had increased by 70 percent and employment by one-third, he stated; and any further increase would unreasonably increase the price of cotton goods. Labor had prospered, Johnson reiterated, and yet it repaid the industry and NRA by striking. For this reason

Johnson made it clear that he had no sympathy for the strikers. Instead, Johnson's sympathies went out to old friend Sloan. As Johnson declared:

When I think of George Sloan my heart weeps. I knew what kind of opposition he went up against. He overcame it all and got these concessions for labor which were at first opposed by practically the whole industry. It is a pity that he now has to take the rap in the dissension between labor and management on this proposition.[23]

Johnson's discourse on the cotton textile dispute was laced with inaccuracies. The charge that Thomas had inspired the strike was without foundation. Johnson's charge that the strike was illegal was patently false. In accepting the June 2 agreement the United Textile Workers had specifically stated that the union accepted the agreement "without prejudice to the right to strike." More important, Johnson's remarks betrayed a complete lack of impartiality on labor conditions in the industry. He offered no appraisal of the effectiveness of the June 2 agreement and ignored the widespread violations of the code, the prevalence of the stretch-out, and arguments over wage differentials, all major abuses which had fueled the strike.[24]

The controversy aroused by the speech did not end with Johnson's anti-labor remarks. After completing his diatribe against the United Textile Workers, Johnson turned to the topic of the evening—NRA reorganization. Although he avoided the details of the scheme he had proposed to Roosevelt, he mentioned that NRA needed to be scaled back and that power in the agency should be shifted so that it was not concentrated in one man's hands. In justification of these views, Johnson dragged in the name of the aged Justice Brandeis. "During the whole intense experience I have been in constant touch with that old counselor, Judge Louis Brandeis," he told the audience. "As you know, he thinks that anything that is too big is bound to be wrong. He thinks NRA is too big, and I agree with him."

Like many of his remarks in regard to the cotton textile dispute, this statement lacked foundation. Johnson's contact with Brandeis had been limited since he was appointed NRA administrator—one face-to-face meeting and three phone calls—and while they had discussed NRA in very general terms, Brandeis had never specifically criticized the agency or indicated how he would vote when NRA came before the Supreme Court. But Johnson's comments on September 14 created the impression that Brandeis had been his intimate counselor as NRA developed and that the justice approved of Johnson's policies. Worse, Johnson had implied that one of the nation's most respected jurists had prejudged NRA even before the Supreme Court had ruled on its constitutionality.

His use of Brandeis was stunning evidence of the lengths Johnson would go to in order to hold on to his job. Many of the liberal critics of NRA were followers of Brandeis, and Johnson believed that by linking his policies to the justice he could mute their criticism. It was the strategy of a desperate man, whose sense of reality had been warped by mental and physical exhaustion; and it had no chance of success.[25]

Johnson's specific remarks were quickly forgotten. Within days the cotton textile strike ended in a total defeat for the United Textile Workers. Johnson's anti-union outburst played a role only in the sense that it gave added weight to the industry's claim that the strike was illegal and reinforced the employers' belief that they could win the strike.[26] In public, Johnson's references to Brandeis meant little, for the justice prudently remained silent. Nevertheless, his friends and associates privately pressed Roosevelt to do something about Johnson before Brandeis's reputation was seriously damaged by public speculation.[27] Johnson steadfastly maintained that his remarks on the cotton textile dispute were the "literal truth," although he quickly realized the error of his remarks about Brandeis and apologized to the justice for any embarrassment he might have caused him.[28]

Not surprisingly, Johnson's speech delighted Richberg. Here, finally, was the proof he needed to get Roosevelt to act quickly to remove Johnson. For weeks he had been nudging Roosevelt to do something. Now, he believed, he had all the ammunition he needed. Shortly after hearing reports of the speech, Richberg wrote McIntyre that he "assume[d] that in view of the General's radio speech of last night with its blazing indiscretions, the President will be very anxious to act as soon as possible." "Insanity in public performances, added to insanity in private relations," he noted, "is pretty dangerous." Putting Johnson in the worst possible light, Richberg also mentioned that he had discussed the negative effects of Johnson's "explosion" with Winant and, rather piously, that "I only hope it does not produce an outbreak of violence paralleling the one he helped to produce by . . . [his] speech in San Francisco." If that was not enough, Richberg concluded by informing McIntyre that "one of the press association men called me up last night within ten minutes after the General's speech and asked 'For God's sake how long is the President going to let him perform?'"[29]

Richberg's bludgeoning of Johnson was unnecessary. The speech had destroyed whatever remained of Johnson's standing with Roosevelt.[30] In his opinion, Johnson had obviously lost control of himself. His comments on the strike showed an utter disregard for the facts, while the references to Brandeis seemed little more than the ramblings of a man furiously searching for any crutch to prop him up. Roosevelt, now sure that he could no longer delay action on Johnson, decided to remove him.

ONCE he had finally steeled himself to the necessity of removing Hugh Johnson, Roosevelt acted rapidly. Yet he could not do the deed himself. He feared a Johnson tantrum if the two of them met, and he just was not up to the ordeal. As a result, Roosevelt enlisted Baruch to prevail upon Johnson. He hoped that the Chief would deal better with Johnson if he acted up and also thought Johnson might take the medicine better if it came from an old friend. After a conference with Roosevelt, Baruch contacted Johnson and bluntly told him he must resign. Johnson kicked up a bit, but the Chief made it clear that he had no choice. "When the Captain wants your resignation," he lectured Johnson, "you better resign."[31] On September 24, 1934, Johnson submitted another letter of resignation, effective October 15. Roosevelt promptly accepted it and in a letter of September 25 thanked him for his service to the nation and expressed the hope that Johnson would get a good rest so that he would then be able to "help me further in new duties and new tasks of public service."[32]

Like so many other aspects of his tenure at NRA, Johnson's departure was marked by melodrama, only more. On October 1 hundreds of NRA employees crowded into the auditorium of the Commerce Department to hear his swan song. The speech could not have been more emotional. With tears in his eyes he told NRA employees that "you can treasure in your hearts your part in as great a social advance as has occurred on this earth since a gaunt and dusty Jew in Palestine declared, 'The Kingdom of Heaven is within you,' the Sermon on the Mount, and the Golden Rule." NRA, he continued, even if it were "regarded as nothing more than a practical school of economic and philosophical theory, . . . has been the greatest educational force that has ever existed." Reaching almost unparalleled heights of hyperbole, even for himself, Johnson climaxed his talk by telling his troops that the "last words of Madame Butterfly engraved on the haft of her Samurai dagger" expressed his feeling toward his resignation. After quoting them first in Italian, he translated her words with great deliberation: "To die with honor when you can no longer live with honor." As he neared the end of his speech, sobs could be heard in the auditorium. Johnson himself was so overcome with emotion that he could not "go on with the beautiful Mosaic benediction" with which he wished to finish the speech. Faltering badly, he merely said, "God bless you."[33]

Johnson spent the next several days receiving friends and employees who came to his office to say goodbye. Contrary to what many of his friends expected, Johnson was not plunged into depression by these farewells, and on October 8 Baruch informed Roosevelt that he did not have to worry about Johnson. "Johnson situation is all right," he wrote to Roosevelt.[34] In all probability his swan song had served as a catharsis for his pent-up emotions, enabling him to accept his departure.

Liberal organs like the *New Republic* bid good riddance to Johnson.

JOHNSON DELIVERS FAREWELL ADDRESS. The Bettmann Archive, Inc.

His policies had rendered his leadership of NRA bankrupt, they opined, while his intervention into labor disputes and his intemperate speeches had created "a stomach ache in the affairs of state."[35] Other commentary was devoted to itemizing Johnson's personal failings and to playing up the dominant role of Frances Robinson.[36] Some of the private comments were downright nasty. Columnist Frank Kent, who strongly disliked Johnson, gave Baruch the following summary of Johnson's NRA stint on the day the general bade his farewell: "Now really, Bernie. Think of this big slob putting this sort of stuff over on us. What a humbug he is—and what suckers the people are."[37] Most commentary, however, generally found good in Johnson's work with NRA. An editorial in the *Philadelphia Record* spoke for many when it suggested that Johnson had served the country well in the summer of 1933 and could have left the job with honor and acclaim if he had only left at the one-year mark. His mistake was to overstay his usefulness.[38] No major publication bemoaned Johnson's departure. But *Commonweal* perhaps best summed up the opinion of those who were friendly toward him. While recognizing his mistakes, the magazine stated that Johnson had made "his prodigious job a great success." Because of his efforts, "the basic idea of the true representation and vital cooperation of capital, management, labor and consumers in the nation's industrial system had been actually introduced, and put into operation." In its most laudatory comments the magazine proclaimed that Johnson had provided the nation with a dramatic example of the "spirit of a soldier—the true, the ideal fighting man: courageous, frank, bold and supremely loyal."[39] No postmortem appraisal could have been more satisfying to the old cavalryman.

BY THE time Hugh Johnson left NRA, the recovery agency had lost most of its popularity and support. In its early months NRA helped check the deflationary spiral by providing a temporary psychological stimulus. Even more important, it consolidated many social innovations by bringing them to the national scene. These included the abolition of child labor, the recognition of labor's right to organize, the elimination of unfair trade practices, and the share-the-work idea. Whatever its accomplishments, however, the minuses of NRA outweighed its pluses. It hindered recovery; it failed to advance significantly the position of labor except in those industries where it was already strong; and if it had endured, the most likely result would have been "economic stagnation, permanent unemployment, and the perpetuation of a depression standard of living, at least for the great majority of the people."[40]

What went wrong? In 1918, despite considerable difficulties, industrial self-government worked as a relatively effective mechanism for mobilizing the economy for war. Backed up by an element of coercion, it had been implemented by the WIB in such a way that business served its own ends and the common good. In 1933 supporters of industrial self-government argued that it could bring recovery by eliminating destructive competition, insuring profits, raising wages, and improving labor standards. But in 1933 and 1934 industrial self-government as implemented by NRA failed to fulfill its promise. For industrial self-government to succeed, the various segments of the economy had to look beyond their own interests and exhibit a concern for the national welfare; and this approach did not prevail. Each group had its own objectives, and in the absence of coercion Johnson had to reconcile these often conflicting objectives through economic and political bargaining in which the advantage lay with the most highly organized group, the one that possessed "a specific and well-articulated set of demands." More often than not, this group was organized business, which by and large shaped the codes to restrict production, raise prices, and thwart labor's aspirations.[41]

Historians have generally concluded that Johnson's performance as NRA head contributed to the failings of industrial self-government. He was an atrocious administrator; he was pro-business; and he let code making become an end in itself. As a result, organized business was able to do much as it pleased. These deficiencies, historians add, were compounded by his emotionalism and inability to work harmoniously with others.[42]

One must be careful, though, not to overlook Johnson's achievement as NRA administrator; it is also inappropriate to attribute too much of the blame for the failings of industrial self-government to him. For all practical purposes, NRA owed its being to Johnson. Although many in the spring of 1933 had advocated industrial self-government as the solution to recovery, none did so as forcefully or effectively as Johnson. Then as head of NRA he mobilized the nation behind industrial self-government and made it the center of the early New Deal recovery effort. Throughout, he helped articulate a vision of industrial enlightenment that has continued to have a significant influence on the American political economy to this day. That industrial self-government proved to be a disappointment does not discredit Johnson. In hindsight it is questionable whether anyone could have made NRA a success, given its "confusing welter of contradictions and conflicts."[43]

CHAPTER 14

A GOOD SOLDIER

THE YEAR following his resignation from NRA was most eventful for Hugh Johnson. After several months of multifarious endeavors, he embarked upon a new career. He also remained a fervent New Dealer, loyal to the president and willing to do whatever was necessary to help the cause. He battled some of Roosevelt's most dangerous enemies; he labored to salvage NRA; he accepted a new job in the administration; and he desperately tried to return the New Deal to the principles of the 1933–1934 period. Johnson's successes were limited; however, his flair in carrying out his duties preserved a prominent spot for him in the national limelight.

WHEN he left NRA, Hugh Johnson had no long-term plans. Job offers abounded, including an offer to manage industrial and labor relations for a group of eighty midwestern industrial concerns. There was also a rumor that he would soon reenter public service to oversee the federal government's unemployment programs.[1] Johnson, however, preferred a job where he could be his own boss and recoup his finances and so decided to be an advisor to industry. In mid-October 1934, he opened an office on F Street in Washington and let businessmen know that he was available to advise them in their dealings with NRA.[2] But he lacked enthusiasm for the work. Although it was obvious that most of his clients would be those who thought he had influence in the capital, Johnson did not want to be known as a "fixer." The very thought of getting this reputation, he later stated, "gives me a faint nausea."[3] Instead, Johnson concentrated his energies on writing.

His first major project was his memoir. He started it in August 1934, while vacationing in Delaware, and went to Okmulgee in October for an extended writing session. With Frances Robinson at his side, he wrote at a frantic rate. In one week he averaged 6,000 words a day. Usually, he worked all day and well into the early hours of the morning. Speaking rapidly and working without an outline, he paced the room like a "caged lion," dictating to Robbie and littering the floor with crumpled newspapers and discarded cigarette packs.[4]

Despite his absence from Washington, Johnson remained a controversial figure. In November 1934, retired Marine Corps Major General Smedley D. Butler disclosed to the House Special Committee on Un-American Activities that a group of Wall Street plotters was planning a coup d'etat to unseat Roosevelt and that either Douglas MacArthur or Johnson was earmarked for the post of dictator. All those mentioned as conspirators denied Butler's allegations. Johnson, for example, growled that Butler "had better be pretty damn careful. Nobody said a word to me about anything of this kind, and if they did I'd throw them out the window." Butler was quickly discredited, and Matthew Josephson spoke for many when he dismissed the whole affair as "a cocktail putsch."[5]

The winter of 1934–1935 brought further controversy. In December 1934, Roosevelt announced the appointment of a special commission, under the chairmanship of Baruch, to formulate plans for mobilization in time of war. Johnson was among the commission's members. Baruch and Johnson went to Hobcaw to plan for the commission and soon issued a report incorporating their well-known ideas on mobilization and stabilization. In January 1935, the report was put into legislative form by the chairman of the House Military Affairs Committee, J. J. McSwain, Democrat of South Carolina.[6]

The Baruch commission aroused the ire of Gerald Nye, who was heading a special Senate investigation of the munitions industry. Nye correctly saw Baruch's commission as a Roosevelt ploy to check his investigation, and he and his supporters counterattacked, with the intent of undermining the commission by stigmatizing its members. Nye Committee sources leaked stories that both Baruch and Johnson had profiteered during the war and that the committee might inquire into their incomes for the years 1917 and 1918. For the record, Nye charged that Baruch and Johnson were too compromised by their business connections to deal with mobilization legislation. "Just watch Baruch and Johnson devising ways and means that won't take the profit out of war," he told reporters. Any legislation, he observed, should "be written by disinterested persons."[7]

Nye's strategy worked. The furor sparked by his charges impelled Roosevelt to retreat. After assuring the senator that he wanted the investigation of the munitions industry to proceed, Roosevelt pushed Baruch's commission into the background. There is no record that the commission held any formal meetings after its organization. In early March 1935, Baruch and Johnson, preparatory to disbanding it, made an oral report to Roosevelt and submitted some written material, which was filed and soon forgotten. Nevertheless, Nye continued his attacks against Baruch and Johnson. He encouraged witnesses before his committee to criticize the two men and wherever possible got in his own licks.[8]

As Johnson did the Baruch commission work, he also moved ahead with his literary endeavors. In December 1934, new editions of his boys' books were released.[9] A month later, the *Saturday Evening Post* serialized part of his memoir, sparking a new round of controversy with Richberg. Hearing that Johnson dealt harshly with him, Richberg sent a letter to the magazine's editor threatening legal action if Johnson made any derogatory statements. Somehow, Richberg's letter became public, leading Johnson to scowl to the *Post* editor that Richberg's threat was groundless and that he "merely has in his pants the ants of conscience."[10]

The *Post* series drew a mixed response. Frank Kent was most critical. Judging it to be of "terrible length" and plagued by "general lousiness," he asserted that it showed Johnson to be "a wonderful piece of cheese." Others were more generous. They were amused by Johnson's pithy expressions and his "violently partisan" account of NRA. One commentator noted that the series made it seem that Johnson would like to change the meaning of the letters NRA to "No Richberg Around." Another was saddened: Johnson "will go down in history," he wrote, "as the guy who put 2,785,000 men in jobs and lost his own."[11]

During February 1935, Johnson and Robbie finished the proofs of his memoir. It was published by Doubleday, Doran on March 29 under the title *The Blue Eagle from Egg to Earth*. The book provided an informative and lively insider's look at the recovery program. But as a literary and historical work it was deficient. Too hastily prepared, it abounded with misspelled names, factual errors, and abstruse sentences. It also slurred chronological detail and, as expected, overstated Johnson's role in the great events in which he was a participant. "I was wholly and personally responsible for the N.R.A.," he trumpeted. Repelled by Johnson's boasting, Richberg remarked that the book might better be entitled "The Blue Eagle from Egg to Egomania." Not to be outdone, Johnson growled that Richberg "once had ants in his pants. Now he has tarantulas."

Contrary to expectations, the thrusts at Richberg in *The Blue Eagle* were interesting but mild. Otherwise, the book was vintage Johnson. He attacked those who had differed with him and wrote with certitude that he and his intimate associates had been fair, if not always correct, in their actions. Peyton March, Frances Perkins, Donald Richberg, and a host of others were "rink-stinks." Bernard Baruch and Franklin Roosevelt were paragons of virtue. Unintentionally, Johnson provided some ammunition for the critics of NRA by recommending that a specific interpretation of Section 7a, the prohibition of child labor, and the minimum wage and maximum hours provisions be written into the law and not left to the codes. Critics of NRA had been vigorously urging this step since the inception of NRA, while Johnson and his cohorts had just as vehemently opposed it. Now Johnson was prepared to support this step, which would leave only the price-control devices in the codes. In the opinion of John T. Flynn, one of Johnson's most strident critics, this recommendation was "the most powerful argument that can be advanced for the complete abandonment of the N.R.A." After calling everybody "who had disagreed with him . . . a rink-stink," the general has "about come around to where his critics stood eighteen months ago."[12]

While completing *The Blue Eagle*, Johnson pursued other writing opportunities. During 1934 he had contributed articles to the *American Magazine*. Their favorable reception prompted him to consider writing a political column on a regular basis. Robbie approached Roy W. Howard, head of the Scripps-Howard newspaper chain, with the idea and piqued his interest. Howard shared many of Johnson's political views and believed that his "gift of phrase and his strong opinions" would make him popular with Scripps-Howard editors and the customers of United Features, the press syndicate controlled by the Scripps-Howard chain. On March 8, 1935, Johnson contracted to write 500 words of comment on current affairs six days of the week. He was given complete freedom to say whatever he pleased.[13] At the time, Johnson was not certain he could meet the syndicate's requirements. As it developed, however, the column evolved into a full-fledged career. It first appeared on March 15, 1935, and appeared regularly for the next seven years.

HUGH Johnson's sortie into journalism was prefaced by a controversy that captivated the nation for several weeks in March 1935. It grew out of Johnson's attack against Senator Huey Long and Father Charles Coughlin and degenerated into a war of words that had few parallels in contemporary American politics. Before it was over, the controversy again made Johnson's name a household word and solidified his reputation as "an orator, hammerer, demonstrator, [and] lambaster" who stirred up his countrymen.

The "Kingfish," as Long liked to call himself, was a rising political star in the winter of 1934–1935. Relying on an effective political style—using ridicule to belittle his opponents and cultivating the impression that he himself was an ignoramus—Long had made himself a force to be feared. He loudly attacked Roosevelt, Baruch, and many New Deal measures and built a national political organization around the slogan Share Our Wealth, by which he meant tax the rich and give the money to the poor.

Father Coughlin reinforced Long's barrages. A parish priest in Royal Oak, Michigan, Coughlin began giving radio sermons in 1926. By 1934 he had a weekly audience numbering 30 to 45 million. Coughlin told his listeners what they already half believed: bankers had caused the depression; Communists and bankers were equally bad; and there was magic in silver. Originally, Coughlin endorsed Roosevelt's program. But in the winter of 1934–1935 he turned against the New Deal and formed the Union for Social Justice to press for his own vision of a just society. Roosevelt, he told his audience, was "still in love with the international bankers" who were interested only in keeping America safe for the plutocrats.[14]

In the face of the popularity of Long and Coughlin, Roosevelt and other administration figures were conspicuously silent. Some took the position that their remarks should not be dignified by replies. But this does not fully explain the silence. Just as important was Roosevelt's uncertainty over where to take the nation. Several of his advisors wanted him to continue the policies initiated in 1933; others wanted to follow a more pro-labor policy and one that clearly subordinated business to government. Not knowing which route to adopt, Roosevelt drifted—and thus incited Long and Coughlin to new heights. Privately, Roosevelt recognized that something had to be done to counter them. But publicly he and his people said nothing. Only Hugh Johnson was prepared to speak out.[15]

Reports later circulated that the administration encouraged Johnson to take on Long and Coughlin. Moreover, a correspondent for the *Providence Journal* privately wrote that Charles Michelson, a White House speech writer, was with Johnson both on the day before and the day after he first spoke out against the two and that Michelson told him that "he had considerable to do with it." If Michelson did encourage Johnson to speak out, however, there is no evidence that he was acting as an agent for Roosevelt. The president had already made it clear to his advisors that the administration should not be associated with anything that Johnson had to say, and Johnson later denied that he had consulted anybody in the administration about his intention.[16] Johnson stated he had talked with some friends at Catholic University and that he received no other encouragement from anyone. In his words: "I . . . advised . . . with my best and wisest friends—New Dealers, Old Dealers, and Coughlinites. Without . . . exception they advised against it."[17] Baruch, for one, warned that if he spoke out against the two demagogues he risked being accused of demagogy himself. Johnson, however, was not swayed and determined to go ahead with his attack.[18]

The most compelling reason for Johnson to make war against Long and Coughlin—perhaps aside from his loyalty to the administration, whose members did not encourage the struggle—was his need for attention. In view of the demeaning circumstances surrounding his departure from NRA, he needed to feel important again. Renewed public attention would restore his deflated ego; it would also publicize his column and, he hoped, boost the sales of *The Blue Eagle*. Johnson was also motivated by other factors. Regarding Long and Coughlin as the agents of fascism, he felt obligated to warn the American people about the evil they represented. In the same manner, he felt obligated to defend the policies he had implemented and the two men he admired—Baruch and Roosevelt—against the denunciations of Long and Coughlin. Loyalty to his former commanders required no less. Someone had to climb "down in the sawdust" to wrestle with the pair, he remarked. It was "time for somebody to get up on his legs and howl."

Johnson launched his attack in a speech at a banquet given for him by *Redbook* magazine on March 4, 1935, in the Waldorf-Astoria Hotel in New York City. Since it was also broadcast over a nationwide radio hookup, the speech would clearly attract attention. Entitled "The Pied Pipers," it was masterful. After reviewing the accomplishments of the Roosevelt administration, Johnson excoriated Long and Coughlin as "a couple of Catilines." "You can laugh at Father Coughlin—you can snort at Huey Long—but this country was never under a greater menace," he declared. Johnson did not mince words in ridiculing Long's economic ideas. His platform of "'ev'ry man a king' and $5,000 a year for every-body . . . is no less ridiculous than . . . 'two cars in every garage,'" Johnson thundered—"or 'two chickens in every pot' which turned out to be two chickens in every garage." He judged Long "a dictator by force of arms" and opined that "Adolf Hitler has nothing on him any way you care to look at both." With great delight Johnson mimicked the King-fish: "Ahm not against the Constitution. Ahm fo' de Constitution. Ahm not against p'ivate p'ope'ty. Ahl mah plan says is tax 'em down—till nobody has mo' dan six million dollahs capital an' one million dol-lahs income."

Johnson was just as caustic in discussing Coughlin. Proclaiming that Coughlin derived much of his appeal from his priestly office, he point-edly directed the cleric to get out of politics if he wanted to remain in the priesthood and made references to Coughlin's citizenship:

There comes burring over the air the dripping brogue of the Irish Canadian priest. . . . Musical blatant bunk from the very rostrum of religion, it goes straight home to simple souls weary in distress and defrauded in delay. . . . We can neither respect nor revere what appears to be a priest in Holy Orders entering our homes with the open sesame of his high calling and there, in the name of Jesus Christ, demanding that we ditch the President for Huey Long.

Johnson particularly emphasized that an unholy alliance had been forged "between the great Louisiana demagogue and this political padre" and that it was a deadly peril to the American people:

Between the team of Huey and the priest we have the whole bag of crazy or crafty tricks possessed by . . . Peter the Hermit, Napoleon Bonaparte, Sitting Bull, William Hohenzollern, the Mahdi of the Soudan, Hitler, Lenin, Trotsky, and the Leatherwood God—here they are—all boiled down to two with the radio and the newsreels to make them effective, and if you don't believe they are dangerous you must haven't thought much about it or you don't know the temper of this country in this continued moment of distress.[19]

The White House, on whose behalf Johnson seemed to be speaking, reacted to the speech with "a chilly silence," and the partisans of Long and Coughlin were infuriated by Johnson's broadside. In letters and telegrams to Roosevelt and Johnson they branded him "a bigoted, venal under-strapper" and "a silly ass" braying for the administration. Even many who were favorable toward Roosevelt and the New Deal were critical, believing that Johnson's "disgraceful phraseology" and his association with the unpopular NRA made him a poor defender of the administration. One writer told Roosevelt that most of the common people "hate the name of Johnson." They "think of him as an army mule driver," "a bluffer and a bulldozer" who is "not smart enough to cope with Father Coughlin or Huey Long." Others believed that Johnson was well-intentioned but that his sledgehammer tactics had the effect of further advertising Long and Coughlin. For the most part, however, the public response was positive. Letters and telegrams supported Johnson in a ratio of seven to one. One individual even implored Roosevelt to use every means to let Johnson "be heard by every red-blooded American."[20]

The press response to Johnson's speech was mixed. The *Detroit News* and the *Chicago Journal of Commerce* questioned the propriety of the attack, while the *Kansas City Star* labeled Johnson's fear of political extremists "just a bit overdrawn and premature." But in general the press was behind Johnson. The *New York World-Telegram* called him a "D'Artagnon with a Dictionary"; the *Louisville Courier-Journal* editorialized that the "General did the country a service"; the *New York Times* praised him "for taking his courage in both hands and refusing to subject himself to two of the would-be political tyrants of the hour"; and both Arthur Krock and Walter Lippmann judged that Johnson, "with unerring accuracy," had challenged the leaders of both political parties to take a stand on Long and Coughlin.[21]

During the next week both Long and Coughlin responded to Johnson's attack with their own fusillades against him. Amused by the scorn of the three men for one another, the public looked forward to a lengthy exchange of epithets that would provide some late winter–early summer entertainment.[22] But the exchange soon came to an end. Johnson moved on to other interests, advised by friends that further attacks against Long and Coughlin would be counterproductive.

Johnson's attack on Long and Coughlin had results beyond entertainment. For one thing, his spunk spurred others, who had hung back, to stand up to them. No longer did Long's attacks on the New Deal go unanswered in the Senate. There were also reports that Johnson's speech may have inspired some senators, fearing they would be accused of helping the two demagogues destroy Roosevelt, to support the administration on an important amendment to a public works bill.[23] However, Johnson's attack did not seriously damage Long or Coughlin. In reality, they probably benefitted; for it secured them a much greater hearing than they might have otherwise commanded. In a sense, Roosevelt and the nation also benefitted. Despite his own silence, Roosevelt recognized that in light of the upcoming 1936 election, the shootout was long overdue. As he wrote Colonel Edward M. House, "It was vastly better to have this free side show presented to the public at this time than later on when the main performance starts."[24]

Some of Johnson's critics suggested that his blast drove Long and Coughlin closer together. Radio commentator Raymond Swing claimed that Johnson's polemic had "joined in holy matrimony two movements which had only reached the stage of flirtation." This charge lacked foundation. In his speech Johnson emphasized the likelihood of an alliance between the priest and the senator. On the surface his claim was credible. But in actuality, the probability of an alliance was slight, although Johnson's speech helped to link the two in the public's mind. For one thing, Coughlin was personally repelled by Long. Even more important, the two men had adopted different political stances. Long had completely broken with Roosevelt, while Coughlin was careful to distinguish between his criticism of the New Deal and his basic support of Roosevelt. In fact, Johnson's attack spurred Coughlin to reaffirm his support for the president and to reiterate that he was concerned only about the influence of the moneychangers on the administration. Whether intentionally or not, Johnson had helped scotch any prospect of a consolidation between the priest and the senator.[25]

HUGH Johnson found the renewed public attention to his liking. But he hankered for a more active role in Washington. Encouraged by his brother Alex, he contemplated running for political office. He was especially interested in one of the U.S. Senate seats from Oklahoma. It would give him two benefits—another forum from which to propound his views and firsthand involvement in what was happening in the nation's capital. The time seemed propitious to embark on a political career. He still retained some popularity from the Blue Eagle campaign, and his column was keeping his name before the public's eye. As an extra, Democrat Thomas P. Gore, an inviting target, was up for reelection in 1936. He lacked a solid political base in the state, and his preachments about the virtues of rugged individualism were conspicuously out-of-date in a state that had been hit hard by the depression.[26]

As early as 1933 Alex Johnston had sounded out Democratic party officials in Oklahoma about a Johnson run for Gore's seat. They expressed little interest. But Alex was not deterred, and in the winter of 1934–1935 he again tested the water. The response, while not greatly encouraging, was positive enough to convince Johnson that he could unseat Gore in the primary. With his encouragement, Johnson's friends in the press speculated about a Johnson-Gore campaign and suggested that Johnson would be a formidable foe for the veteran senator.

In late March 1935 Johnson went to Oklahoma, ostensibly to visit his mother in Okmulgee and his brother in Tulsa. However, Johnson also intended to see as many political figures as possible and get his name in local papers. Wherever he went, Johnson was received favorably. Elated by his reception, he announced that he intended to live again in Oklahoma, although he was coy about the race against Gore. That was something he would have to think about, he barked to reporters, and he reserved the right to make up his mind "any damn time I please."[27]

When Johnson returned to Washington in April, friends were confident that he would announce his candidacy. But after reflecting on what he heard in Oklahoma and estimating the expense of a campaign, Johnson gave up the notion of running for the Senate. Gore was vulnerable, as events would show in 1936 when he was defeated for renomination. However, Johnson recognized that too many roadblocks faced his own candidacy. First, he was an outsider to Oklahoma politics, and the state's major figures were not among his boosters. Second, NRA had never been popular in Oklahoma, and he could expect to be constantly defending himself against charges that he had caused farmers to pay higher prices for goods, that he had fostered monopoly, and that he was a tool of Wall Street. Finally, Long and others were prepared to aid Gore, thereby compelling Johnson to fight a host of ruthless opponents. Even though Johnson continued to talk about returning to Oklahoma to live, there was no more serious talk about a Senate seat. Johnson's political career was over before it started.[28]

HUGH Johnson's departure from NRA did not lessen his interest in the agency. Convinced that it still offered the best hope of recovery, he met with Roosevelt on December 10 at the White House to discuss improvements in the administration of NRA. Two months later, on February 10, 1935, the two men had another meeting to discuss NRA, when Johnson stopped in at the White House to inquire about the health of the ailing Louis Howe.[29]

In these meetings Johnson informed Roosevelt that any problems confronting NRA would work themselves out if he staunchly supported its basic principles and got rid of Richberg. Others, however, were not so sure about what needed to be done. Some believed that NRA was bankrupt and should be allowed to expire in June 1935, when its two-year charter was scheduled for renewal. Others concluded that the wisest course would be to let the agency die in peace and preserve its best features through separate enactments.

During the winter of 1934–1935 Roosevelt and his advisors weighed their options. Should they renew NRA without substantial change? Should they seek major modifications? Or should they let it die a natural death? At Richberg's urging, Roosevelt, on February 20, 1935, asked Congress to renew NRA for two years. Included in his request were recommendations for the retention of Section 7a, restriction of price and production controls, and application of the antitrust laws against monopolies and price-fixing. Roosevelt also dropped the Johnson policy of delaying a court test of NRA in the belief that its constitutionality must be confirmed if local enforcement of codes was not to collapse. When a federal judge in Alabama ruled that NIRA was unconstitutional in a case involving a lumber mill operator who had not abided by NRA labor standards, the administration made plans to appeal immediately to the Supreme Court.

Johnson was not directly consulted on either action. But he approved of both, although with two caveats. Refusing to retreat from his original position on the antitrust laws, he warned against an antitrust crusade. The "anti-trust acts and NIRA can't stand side by side," he chortled. He also warned that no code should be imposed on industry. The Blue Eagle was the only force necessary to make the program work. In a turnabout, though, Johnson now looked forward to a Supreme Court ruling on NRA. Many constitutional experts were confident that it could survive a court test, and so far NRA had a good record of success in the courts. As a result, Johnson optimistically wrote in March 1935 that "the rock of our deliverance is the Supreme Court," especially the case involving the lumber code. It truly represented "the real Constitutional issues" in "a great natural resource industry of national extent."[30]

Roosevelt's proposal ran into a hornet's nest in the Senate. For some time Borah, Nye, and others had been pressing for a full-blown investigation of NRA, and in 1935 they finally pushed through an investigation by the Finance Committee.[31] For six weeks a steady stream of witnesses appeared before the committee in a replay of the "field day of criticism." The high point came on April 18, 1935, when Johnson testified. Several hundred people crowded into the marble caucus room of the Senate Office Building to hear him defend NRA. They were not disappointed. In December, Johnson had said to a reporter that NRA was "as dead as a dodo." But now he beseeched the senators not to throw his NRA baby "down the drain with the dirty water." Fidgeting constantly in his chair, he opened by reading an eighty-eight-page statement he had prepared the previous night. He admitted that progress under NRA had not been as rapid as he had hoped, that "rotten provisions" found their way into some codes, and that the administration of the codes needed to be streamlined and strengthened. Adopting the pose of the martyr, he pleaded that "such faults as arose were due to my bad administration rather than bad law." For this reason, he admonished the committee, "to destroy N.R.A. because there are these creaky joints in its structure would be like burning down your house to get rid of a few rats in the attic."

Then Johnson took the offensive. He recommended the elimination of many codes and the consolidation of others and declared that NRA had checked the concentration of industry which threatened to destroy small business. Denying that big business had shaped the codes to the detriment of small business, he insisted that "the most persistent . . . opponents of codes have been the big interests, while the most zealous advocates . . . have been small business men." Near the end of his testimony Johnson solemnly told the committee that "we must take our capitalistic system in hand. . . . To my mind we should not go back to what has failed, we should not go forward to communism or fascism, but we must do something, and let us stick to this middle of the road."[32]

Johnson's loyal and picturesque defense of NRA was applauded by many of the spectators; but it had little effect on the committee, which was stacked with opponents of NRA. In addition, a damaging report on NRA prepared by the Brookings Institution was handed to reporters at the close of the hearing. It practically extinguished whatever attention Johnson's testimony claimed. The first independent study to be made of the impact of the NRA codes, the report praised NRA for the "psychological lift" it had provided in 1933 and then went on to damn the agency for retarding recovery, injuring the wage earner, and diminishing the volume of production.

Coming after all the negative testimony of the previous six weeks, the Brookings report shattered the remnants of NRA support on Capitol Hill. In the meantime, the Department of Justice had decided not to pursue the case involving the Alabama lumber operator. The lumber code contained a provision for production controls, and the administration was no longer willing to defend these devices. On the recommendation of Richberg, the administration turned to a case involving the Schechter brothers of Brooklyn, who had violated the live poultry code by disregarding wage and hour regulations, filing false sales and price reports, and selling diseased poultry. For this reason Johnson called it the "sick chicken" case. Johnson doubted that the Schechter case offered the best opportunity for a favorable ruling. The live poultry trade was a petty trade and thus one in which it would be hard to justify constitutional innovation; if that were not impediment enough, the Schechter brothers were not directly engaged in interstate commerce. Yet administration legal officers believed that a court ruling was a necessity and that the Schechter case was the best available to elicit a favorable ruling.

Johnson's concern about the Schechter case proved correct. On May

27, 1935, the Supreme Court ruled that NRA was unconstitutional. Speaking for the Court, Chief Justice Charles Evans Hughes stated that Title I of NIRA was an invalid delegation of legislative power to the president and an unconstitutional regulation of intrastate commerce. Arguments could be raised about the Court's reasoning; but it was clear that NRA as put together in 1933 was dead.

In the days before the Court handed down its ruling, Johnson devoted much of his time to drumming up support for his offspring in the press and in an appearance before the House Ways and Means Committee. Hearing of the Schechter decision while riding the train from Washington to New York City, he told reporters that he had predicted the outcome. The Schechter case was a manifestly "rotten" case in which to seek a favorable decision, he roared. Seeing a chance to blame Richberg for the downfall of NRA, he suggested that one could only wonder why "Richberg some time ago referred to it as the 'perfect case.'"[33]

Johnson was back in Washington the following day to talk with Roosevelt about the decision. On the night of May 29, Johnson spoke over the Columbia Broadcasting System radio network, passionately defending NRA and calling for a continuation of its principles. The court's action had brought NRA to a "temporary halt," he conceded; but it "hadn't wrecked it." Employers and employees must do everything possible to save the good in NRA, he pleaded, or else they would go back to the old days and their ghoulish orgy of wage slashing.[34]

During the last days of May a gaggle of New Deal personalities visited the White House for hectic conferences on the administration's next step. Johnson stopped by so often that reporters suspected that Roosevelt was about to appoint him to another job in the administration. In their meetings Johnson told Roosevelt that it was possible to devise new legislation that would take into account the court's objections to NRA and assured him that he could draft the legislation. It would call either for a voluntary or a state system of codes that would be enforced by contract and by public opinion. Roosevelt, in turn, had Johnson meet with Felix Frankfurter to discuss the matter in depth.

Frankfurter and Johnson met several times on May 29 and 30. In their discussions the law professor strove to curtail Johnson's enthusiasm for new NRA legislation. Because of his comments on the Schechter case, Frankfurter was convinced that Johnson did not "understand what the Supreme Court had really decided and the Supreme Court barriers to what he was trying to do." But Johnson was not dissuaded. The two men met with Roosevelt on the afternoon of May 30, and Johnson won "the President to new NRA legislation." Frankfurter's warnings about "the unwisdom and difficulty of sponsoring any jerry-built, over-night legislation in the face of the Schechter decision" were brushed aside.[35] That night Johnson put his ideas into bill form, and the following

morning he phoned Frankfurter to tell him that he was prepared to review his draft with him.

Despite the encouragement he gave to Johnson, Roosevelt was listening to other voices. Richberg agreed with Johnson's assessment that it
was possible to draft legislation for a new NRA with more carefully
defined powers, while Raymond Moley, Vice-President John Nance
Garner, and Senators James Byrnes and Robert LaFollette, Jr., all advocated a constitutional amendment to enlarge the powers of Congress
over the economy. Frances Perkins, in contrast, argued that at least part
of NRA could be salvaged through a "public contracts" bill that would
require all firms engaged in public business to adhere to NRA labor standards. Attorney General Homer Cummings, meanwhile, told
Roosevelt that he should let the whole issue slide and "get rid of the
present membership of the Supreme Court."

In his "own mysterious way," Roosevelt proceeded to a decision. At a
news conference on May 31 he denounced the Schechter decision for
pushing the nation back to "the horse and buggy days" in its definition
of interstate commerce and openly wondered if the federal government
could now do anything to deal with the economic and social conditions
affecting the nation. On June 4 he told congressional leaders that for all
practical purposes he was giving up the fight for NRA.

Dumbfounded by Roosevelt's decision, Johnson instinctively blamed
Frankfurter for turning Roosevelt against his recommendation. But the
decision was hardly as simple as Johnson made it out to be. Roosevelt
was convinced that NRA had done about all it could do, and he was
skeptical that Johnson's plan for a voluntary or a state system of codes
would work. His reasoning was compelling. In his words: "If ninety per
cent of industry honestly works for social betterment and ten per cent
pulls the other way, we get nowhere without some form of government
enforcement. Secondly, if forty states go along with adequate legislation and eight do not—again we get nowhere." Personal and political
factors also came into play. In recent months, business had stepped up
its attacks against the New Deal and Roosevelt. Personally, Roosevelt
could not help but resent these attacks, particularly since he had generally followed a conservative pro-business policy. Politically, Roosevelt's
progressive supporters were pushing for a more pro-labor policy and one
aimed at breaking up concentrated economic power. He could hardly
ignore them if he expected to command their support in 1936. As a result, Roosevelt let NRA, the symbol of his pro-business policy, die and
embarked upon a new program centering around social security, pro-
labor legislation, economic decentralization, and soak-the-rich taxes.[36]

Although Roosevelt had all but repudiated NRA, Johnson refused to
give up the fight without some final words. In speeches during June
1935, he argued that NRA was necessary to bring about recovery and

that the Court's ruling should not be regarded as the death sentence for the Blue Eagle. There was nothing wrong with the principles of indus-trial self-government, he stated. "All that we are faced with is errors in a statute written under stress, mistakes in application, and selecting a bad case for the Court test." In a sense Johnson was justified in his view that the Court had not totally eliminated the possibility for a revised NRA. In a series of decisions in the spring of 1937 it retreated from its reasoning in the Schechter decision. Commenting on these decisions, Johnson wrote Roosevelt: "I was taken for a ride on a chicken truck in Brooklyn two years ago and dumped out on a deserted highway and left for dead. It seems this was all a mistake."[37]

HUGH Johnson's contact with Roosevelt in the spring of 1935 was not limited to the rearguard fight to save NRA. At the same time he lobbied hard to have Roosevelt name Malin Craig as Douglas MacArthur's suc-cessor as army chief of staff.[38] He also pestered Roosevelt to give him a job in the administration, for he missed the excitement of making things happen. His eyes were set on the Federal Trade Commission's in-vestigation of the American Telephone and Telegraph Company. Want-ing the job badly, he bragged to Roosevelt that he "could do as good a job as anybody and better than most." As evidence he explained that "in-vestigating industrial companies was my job with Bernie for several years and I know enough about that one to start with and to believe that I can make somebody jump through hoops." Johnson likewise asked friends to push him for the job. Roosevelt, however, was not inter-ested.[39] He already had Johnson in mind for another job—head of the Works Progress Administration in New York City.

WPA was a massive public works project designed to provide emer-gency public employment, and Roosevelt's choice of Johnson to head the project in New York City was surprising. He had already strongly criticized federal relief and expressed a preference for private relief. "I have no way to prove it," he stated in a speech in late May 1935, "but I honestly believe that Federal relief is the most expensive and wasteful sharing that we could devise." Instead, he suggested, the nation should rely on agencies like the Salvation Army. They were able to make the money go further, and there was no political fear or favor, no wrangling ambition or ponderous bureaucracy, and no "official disdain" or "cold waiting." Johnson voiced an equally adverse opinion of WPA in his col-umn on the same day that his appointment as a WPA director was an-nounced. "The new Works Relief program is not public works," he wrote; rather, it "is part of a new, if more ambitious kind of leaf raking."

Besides expressing negative views about federal relief, Johnson had never worked well with Harry Hopkins, the head of WPA. As head of the Federal Emergency Relief Administration and the Civil Works Ad-ministration, Hopkins had been a trenchant critic of NRA codes, and in December 1933, he and Johnson had feuded over CWA wage rates. Hopkins set CWA rates at a higher level than NRA code wages, particularly for textile workers in the South. Textile producers protested that the CWA rates threatened to plunge them into bankruptcy, a charge Johnson believed to be correct. The feud, however, represented more than a clash over wage rates. On the one hand, it reflected different views on the best way to achieve recovery. Johnson held that any increases in purchasing power must come from productive activity, while Hopkins was primarily interested in getting money into circulation. On the other hand, it also reflected Johnson's petulance. Hopkins had acted without seeking his approval at a time when Johnson believed that all initiatives should begin with himself. This record of discord hardly augured well for the two men to work together, especially with Johnson in a subordinate role.[40]

The notion of appointing Johnson as head of WPA in New York City apparently originated with Mayor Fiorello LaGuardia, who believed that the city's work relief program, already under heavy attack from aldermen for inefficiency and ineffectiveness, desperately needed "a strong captain." In his opinion, Johnson was that captain. Impressed with Johnson's reputation for energy, drama, and decisiveness, LaGuardia was hopeful that these qualities would pacify the restless aldermen. Moreover, LaGuardia hoped that Johnson would appeal to the predominately Democratic New York congressional delegation, which would have to approve him if he was to be appointed. In this respect LaGuardia's hope was well founded. Because of his active role in New York state politics in the 1928 and 1932 campaigns, Johnson was on good terms with many members of the delegation.

Other elements were also at work in LaGuardia's scheme of things. Since he had been a key administration figure and was close to Roosevelt, Johnson could undoubtedly use his connections in Washington to cut through red tape and open important doors. Finally, LaGuardia surmised that Johnson's considerable experience in dealing with labor problems made him a good choice to handle the city's fractious building trades unions should trouble develop. Hopkins was cool to the appointment of Johnson. But after some badgering the mayor prevailed and convinced him that Johnson could do the job.[41]

Like Hopkins, Roosevelt was initially cool to making Johnson a WPA director. Besides the state of Pennsylvania, New York City had the largest relief load in the nation, and after the problems with NRA Roosevelt was skeptical that Johnson could cope with the administrative responsibilities that went with the job. LaGuardia, however, would not be put off, and Roosevelt finally consented. In all probability he concluded that Hopkins could succeed where the Special Industrial Recovery Board had failed in keeping Johnson under control.

Johnson was in Indianapolis, Indiana, when Hopkins and LaGuardia telephoned from Hopkins's Washington office and offered him the job. He heard them out but replied that he would have to consult some of his friends before he could give them a final answer. The friends gave Johnson little encouragement. They warned that the city's work relief program was beset with mammoth problems that would overwhelm him. He recalled in October: "They kept the long distance telephone busy for several hours imploring me to go on further west as promptly as possible."[42]

Disregarding all the red flags, Johnson accepted the job. Asked why, he told reporters, "My feeling is that I was educated by the government, that I have served it for twenty years, and that I should do everything I am told to do in the way of public service, whether I want it or not."[43] This statement only partly explained Johnson's motivation. He was fearful that if he did not take it, Roosevelt would not offer him any of the more desirable assignments he wanted in the future. These included arguing the cases involving AAA and the oil code before the Supreme Court and keynoting the 1936 Democratic convention.[44] Even so, Johnson negotiated for two weeks before accepting the offer, and he drove a hard bargain. He would receive no compensation except for expenses and would leave as soon as the relief project was on its feet. Johnson tentatively set October 1, 1935, for his departure. With these conditions Johnson hoped to avoid some of the wrangling that had bedeviled him in NRA. Moreover, Johnson insisted that he should be responsible to Hopkins alone and have a free hand to pick his assistants. Last, Johnson demanded that he be permitted to depart from the $1,100 per worker project limit laid down by the law creating WPA, take a census of the city's unemployed, and hire men who were not on relief rolls.[45]

Johnson began work as head of WPA in New York City on June 26, 1935. During the next several days he surveyed the operations of the city's Emergency Relief Bureau and put together his own staff. It included his son Pat, Frances Robinson, and Alvin Brown.

Johnson's first responsibility was to absorb the workers on the rolls of the Emergency Relief Bureau. Initially, he hoped to do this by July 15. But as it turned out, his scheduling was too optimistic. He had to examine the proposals for work relief that had already been drawn up by the city and forward them to Washington for final approval, a requirement that consumed a month's time.[46] The time required to get approval for the relief bureau's projects was magnified by uncertainty over the availability of funds. More than $100 million was needed to complete these projects. Yet it was halfway through July before Johnson had any federal funds to spend, and even these funds represented only a minimal commitment by Washington. Consequently, Johnson had to make emergency arrangements with the city to avoid laying off thousands of workers. Eventually, Comptroller General McCarl released $40 million to the city, and on August 26, Johnson was cleared to spend the funds to complete the projects. Even then, however, money remained a nagging problem, for Johnson had enough funds to carry WPA only through mid-January 1936.[47]

On August 1, Johnson commenced the takeover of work relief from the Emergency Relief Bureau. Involving more than 88,000 workers, it proved most difficult. New methods of accounting and purchasing had to be implemented, as well as new standards for hours and wages. Under the relief bureau, common laborers had worked ninety-six hours a month. Hopkins's office, however, ordered Johnson to install a 120-hour month. This order decreased the need for workers, forcing Johnson to create 22,267 new jobs "so that every worker on the rolls on July 31st could be continued."[48]

Payroll problems added to the difficulty. The Emergency Relief Bureau had paid workers weekly; but Johnson, despite his "repeated and vigorous" protests, was instructed to pay workers semimonthly. Apparently, the decision resulted from the determination of Hopkins to emphasize the work, rather than the relief, side of WPA. By treating the WPA labor force like regular federal employees, he hoped he could minimize the criticism that WPA was a virtual dole. The new payroll schedule created great hardships for many workers. They received their last relief bureau check on August 7, and under the federal regulation they would not receive their first WPA check until they had been on the job for fifteen days. The red tape involved in preparing checks and getting them to the workers added to the delay.

Johnson responded by getting the city to pay $13 each to 93,000 people who had previously worked for the Emergency Relief Bureau; the federal government reimbursed the city for the funds. This action was only a stopgap. Large numbers of workers were still unpaid at the end of August, forcing the Salvation Army to set up mobile kitchens in park areas to give food to relief workers. Gradually, the payroll delays were shortened, and in October 1935, they stopped when Washington, after strong lobbying by LaGuardia and Johnson, permitted Johnson to make weekly payments. Nevertheless, the dispute left Johnson discouraged. He had alerted Hopkins to the problem in shifting to a semimonthly payment as early as July 19 and thereafter had bombarded him with warnings about the dire consequences of moving away from the city's practice of paying workers on a weekly basis. Hopkins ignored the warnings, spawning "unpleasantness and criticism" that could have been easily avoided if Johnson's recommendation had been accepted.[49]

Johnson's second responsibility was to expand work relief so as to cut deeply into the number on the city's home relief rolls. He was never given specific instructions as to how many people he should put to work, although through conversations with Hopkins the figure of 220,000 was eventually set. Since approximately 100,000 people were already on work relief rolls, Johnson had to create and man 120,000 new jobs.[50]

On August 1, Johnson pledged to meet this goal by October 1, 1935. Skeptics viewed the pledge as just so much NRA-style ballyhoo, and for a time it seemed they were correct. Johnson's instructions compelled him to place his requisitions for workers with the National Reemployment Service, which, in turn, received names from local relief authorities. This procedure was too cumbersome. The reemployment service lacked the personnel to handle the enormous number of WPA referrals and did not have direct access to those on home relief. For three weeks Johnson fretted and fumed while waiting for the National Reemployment Service to provide the workers he needed; and when he decided that he could wait no longer, he publicly charged, on August 20, that the reemployment service was undermining his efforts by furnishing less than a quarter of the 28,000 workers he had requisitioned. Intending to smooth matters over, LaGuardia and officials in Washington brought Johnson and William Lange, director of the reemployment service in New York City, together in a meeting on August 23. After a sharp exchange, peace was momentarily restored when Lange convinced those present that he could produce the workers. His persuasiveness did not keep Johnson from taking the matter into his own hands. Before the meeting adjourned, he got the participants to agree that WPA would go to the National Reemployment Service only when it required skilled workers who could not be recruited from the home relief rolls.[51]

Plans called for Johnson to give jobs to 20,000 people within the first week. But the number who showed up for placement swamped WPA. On some days as many as 20,000 people stormed his offices. WPA took on 13,000 workers in ten days of feverish work, and by the second week of September it was hiring workers at the rate of around 5,000 a day. The huge numbers naturally led to initial job assignments that were haphazard at best. However, the priority was to put people to work. All things considered, as one historian of the city's WPA later wrote, "one is amazed at how much was accomplished. The defects pale almost into insignificance in contrast."[52]

WPA's high-geared hiring practices enabled Johnson to meet his pledge on new jobs. By the first week of September almost 130,000 workers were on the rolls; at the end of the month there were 170,000. Two weeks later, on October 15, there were 208,000 workers and enough openings to raise the total to 220,000 by November 1.

Johnson's success in putting so many people to work in such a short time was remarkable, especially considering that it was accomplished in the face of an eight-week strike against WPA. The dispute predated Johnson's appointment. In proposing WPA, Roosevelt had insisted that workers receive a "security wage," which would vary according to skills and regions. It would be greater than welfare but less than the prevailing wage in private industry. New York City wage rates would run from $55 to $94 for 120 to 140 hours of work a month. When Roosevelt announced the wage scales on May 20, 1935, the city's strong building trades unions protested immediately. The monthly remuneration for work relief would be greater than that paid by the Emergency Relief Bureau. However, the number of hours lowered the rate of hourly pay. In the case of plumbers the union rate was $1.50 per hour. Under the security wage, though, they would work 140 hours a month for $85, or slightly more than 63 cents an hour. Because many skilled workers had hardly worked enough to earn even the security wage in recent years, it seemed surprising that the unions would complain. But labor leaders were convinced that they must fight for the prevailing wage or see wages in the private sector driven down to the security-wage level.

When he arrived in New York City, Johnson moved quickly to settle the dispute. He pinned his hopes on a private meeting with George Meany, president of the New York State Federation of Labor. With McGrady at his side, he met with Meany on July 2 at the St. Regis Hotel. At the outset, Johnson was sanguine and conciliatory. Conversations with Hopkins had convinced him that McGrady could talk to Meany and straighten everything out. In the July 2 discussions, McGrady suggested that everybody should receive $75 for 130 hours of work a month. Meany rejected the proposal and adamantly stated that "I will not go along with anything which requires members of our unions to work for below the prevailing scale of wages." Johnson, who had been silent, was stunned by Meany's reply. Up to this point he had expected that McGrady could head off trouble. Slamming his fist down on the desk, he bawled: "Goddammit, I knew there was a catch here. I knew I was getting myself in for some trouble."[53]

As the meeting continued, Meany hammered home labor's position, but Johnson needed little persuading. Even before he had taken the job, he had realized that the security wage would be a problem. It may be sound in theory, he had told Hopkins; however, it put labor at a disadvantage in dealing with private employers. It also seemed certain, he had added, that Washington would ultimately accept labor's viewpoint if sufficient pressure was brought to bear. "I thought it wiser gracefully to accede from the beginning," he later wrote Hopkins, "before the pressure had been applied than to capitulate under strike and turmoil."[54] At the end of the meeting, Johnson sent mixed signals. He told Meany that "I've been given a job to do, and I've got to do it according to the rules." Yet he indicated to reporters that he was sympathetic to labor's position and that he wanted to make modifications in the security wage. In speaking of it he stated, "Labor doesn't like it and I don't like it. It is going to give me a lot of headaches."[55]

On July 12 the prospect of a settlement darkened when the Central

Trades and Labor Council announced that organized labor would work on relief projects only for the prevailing wage. If this wage were not paid, union members would return to home relief rolls. Attempting to placate labor, Johnson used the authority available to him to alter wages and hours. He reduced WPA hours to the minimum 120 and instituted a 10 percent wage increase. He also took Meany to Washington to see Hopkins. Neither action, however, had any effect on labor's position.

Realizing that Meany was deadly serious about a strike, Johnson pressed Hopkins to accept the principle of the prevailing wage. But Hopkins would not yield. He argued that workers would be better off under the security wage than they were under home relief and that they had no reason to complain. The controversy soon took on national significance. Many people regarded WPA as nothing more than a make-work program, and Hopkins feared that they would turn against the administration if WPA paid union wages. Meany, meanwhile, was determined to stand firm. He believed that construction workers in New York City were fighting a battle that would affect union men everywhere and that he was obligated to fight the good fight.[56]

As WPA took over Emergency Relief Bureau projects, Johnson was in agony. The impending strike threatened to bring his operation to a halt before it had a chance to get underway. He was also in the unenviable position of defending what he had "condemned in independent opinion."[57] Grasping for a solution, he made an uninvited visit on August 5 to a meeting of the Executive Council of the American Federation of Labor in Atlantic City, New Jersey, in a fruitless effort to solicit its help. The same day, union workers struck work relief projects. Johnson promptly declared that those who failed to return to work the next day would lose their jobs. Taking care to preserve his standing with labor, however, he also announced that strikers who were fired might be re-hired in the future. It was a more liberal position than the one adopted by Hopkins and Roosevelt.[58]

Desperate to keep the strike from spreading, Johnson made a last-minute appeal to a meeting of the trade and labor council on August 8. With Meany's consent, Johnson entered the meeting just after the council had voted to strike all WPA projects and pleaded with the unions to remain on the job. His "intended clincher" was the reading of the radio address he was to deliver that evening. Made up of "solid economic argument" and "sheer political nonsense," it was vintage Johnson. He argued that the security wage would give workers more money per month than they had earned during the previous period of five years, that the security wage would not lead to the lowering of wages by private industry, and that New York City workers were being given "the best of the deal" and should repay the government by "comradeship in a great effort." If Johnson had stopped with these comments, he may have had "considerable impact upon rank-and-file members as well as the public." But in a replay of his speeches during the San Francisco general strike and the cotton textile dispute he descended into red baiting. Overwrought from the weeks of tension, he launched into a tirade, charging that the unions were being seduced into a strike by a small minority of Communists who were out to destroy WPA in its infancy and fan the flames of class warfare. "Don't do it, boys," he yelled to the audience. "Don't let yourself be used to foul your own nest and play a sucker's game." Labor's position, he panted, was "so sickly that it couldn't get a night's lodging in a leper colony."[59]

Johnson was interrupted by catcalls and howls of protest, and his response was to shout back and pound the table with his fist. Immediately after Johnson's performance, the council reaffirmed its commitment to strike. On the following day Meany denied Johnson's charges that the union men were Communist dupes and predicted that ten to fifteen thousand skilled workers would soon be on the picket lines. The war between Johnson and the building trades unions was under way.

The very existence of a strike became a disputed issue. Only about 15,000 of the more than 200,000 WPA workers belonged to building trades unions, and Johnson insisted that the number of strikers never exceeded 1,157 men. For this reason, he argued, there never was a strike—or if there was, it failed. People off the job steadily drifted back to work, he pointed out; and work on major projects generally continued without serious interruptions.[60] Not surprisingly, Meany made a different claim. According to him, the union men on the picket lines were the supervisors of the unskilled workers. The work crews might show up for work, but with no supervisors on the job there was nothing they could do. After several days of these claims and counterclaims, Johnson called Meany and said, "Georgie Porgie . . . your strike is a failure. They're coming in ninety per cent." Said Meany: "But General, they're not working."[61]

In the end, Johnson's position in the dispute was undermined by Lange. Johnson planned to defeat the strike by hiring additional skilled workers to take the place of those who were off the job. Rejecting Johnson's claim that there was no strike, Lange, following the procedures of the Wagner-Peyer Act of 1933, refused to refer workers to jobs where a strike was in progress unless they signed a waiver acknowledging that they knew of the existence of the strike. Under these circumstances, union members would not sign the waiver for fear of losing their union cards. In effect, Lange was blacklisting WPA and making it impossible for Johnson to get the skilled labor he needed.

In September, negotiations for a settlement intensified. Conferences between Johnson, city officials, and union leaders were held regularly. But little was accomplished. Simultaneously, there were outbreaks of violence at the Astor Housing Project and additional work stoppages. On September 17, LaGuardia, Governor Herbert Lehman, and Johnson met with Roosevelt at Hyde Park. Johnson bluntly stated that the dispute was keeping him from getting the skilled workers he needed to expand the city's WPA work force to the number the administration wanted. Anxious to have as many people as possible working, Roosevelt told Johnson to make peace with Meany. The next day Johnson announced that he favored reducing the number of hours for skilled workers from 120 to 80 hours, with no change in the remuneration. Meany, however, was cool toward this proposal; for it still did not bring WPA workers up to the prevailing wage. Thereupon, Hopkins issued an order granting Johnson authority to make whatever adjustments he deemed necessary. With this grant of authority Johnson held several conferences with Meany and ironed out a settlement. On September 26 Johnson cut the hours of skilled labor to 60 hours per month; total remuneration remained unchanged. The strike was over and resulted in a total victory of the building trades unions. Meany's only concession to Johnson was to agree not to "shout victory."[62]

Johnson was roundly censured by the press for surrendering to Meany. Critics argued that he only had to stand firm to defeat the unions. But Johnson never considered his action a capitulation. From the outset he had been sympathetic with labor on this issue, and he regarded the settlement as nothing more than frank recognition of a step that should have been taken weeks earlier. As he said to Hopkins, "It would have been wiser if I had been allowed to do this in the beginning as I requested."[63]

Like his other career stopovers, Johnson's tenure with WPA was marked by a bitter feud, in this case with Robert Moses, commissioner of parks for New York City. As Johnson well knew from his experience with the National Transportation Committee, Moses was a difficult man to work with. He had an explosive temper and reveled in bullying people and quarrelling in the limelight. He seemed, in fact, to initiate trivial and unnecessary fracases for no other reason than to get press attention. Moreover, Moses was a master at protecting and expanding his bureaucratic turf. Under the Emergency Relief Bureau, projects were sponsored by city departments, which were responsible for plans and specifications, while the work relief agency was responsible for wages, hours, assignment of workers, labor relations, and supervision of the actual work. Using all his guile and bluster, Moses carved out a favored position for himself. Unlike the situation with other city departments, parks projects were essentially under the control of the Parks Department, not the relief bureau. After his arrival, Johnson indicated that he intended to follow federal regulations, which called for a sharing of power between the sponsoring department and WPA. This position, combined with Moses's character, ensured bickering between the two men.

The trouble was not long in coming. Moses insisted that his department must retain complete control over all projects, including the conditions of work. In this respect he was disregarding instructions from LaGuardia to all department heads and borough presidents to cooperate thoroughly with Johnson. Whatever the legitimacy of Moses's claim, Johnson could not afford an open break with him. As a result, he announced on August 5 that Moses could continue to operate as he had done under the relief bureau through the month of August.[64]

The feud between the two strong-willed men heated up in September. Because of the size of its operations, the Parks Department was expected to use a large number of relief workers. Moses, however, was not happy with the people Johnson sent him. He was a perfectionist, known for getting things done and getting them done right; and a key to his success was having people he could count on to do the work. Not surprisingly, he resented being forced to take anybody that Johnson sent. On September 9, Moses said he needed more supervisors and foremen and that many of the relief workers sent him were "bums." The next day he charged that WPA was "stupid" and that Johnson was inefficient. Johnson struck back by charging that Moses was in defiance of federal regulations regarding the administration of WPA projects and was the one really guilty of inefficiency. Moses threatened to oust 10,000 WPA workers unless he was supplied with more foremen to supervise the WPA people, while Johnson threatened to take away all 36,000 WPA workers assigned to Moses and assign them to other projects.[65]

Johnson's feud with Moses went beyond words. During its most bitter phase the two men met in Baruch's New York City apartment. Needled by Johnson's comments, Moses started swinging at Johnson and landed a punch before they were pulled apart. At the time, Johnson was eight years older than Moses, more than twenty pounds lighter than the hefty parks director, and "exceedingly drunk."[66]

Contending that Moses's demand for additional foremen was merely a smokescreen, Johnson argued that the real issue was the question of who was going to run park projects—Moses or WPA. After all, he later wrote Hopkins, "I thought that out of 60,000 to 70,000 relief workers he ought to be able to find supervisors of all classes, especially labor foremen." But in the end Johnson had to accede to Moses's demand or risk seeing WPA fail to meet its employment commitments. For all his tough talk, Johnson agreed to provide Moses with all the foremen he needed, taking them in many cases from other projects.[67]

In September 1935, Johnson made plans to leave WPA. When he had accepted the job, he had told Roosevelt that he would take it only for three months. The three-month period was up on October 1, and Johnson was determined to leave by that date or October 15 at the latest. Nothing had happened since to cause him to change his mind. New York's building trades unions and city officials like Moses were as taxing to deal with as the United Mine Workers and the coal barons, and Johnson no longer had the physical and emotional strength to keep up the pace. Equally compelling, Johnson did not relish his subordinate position. As head of the largest work relief program in the nation, he was the single most important director in WPA; yet he had to take directions from Washington, often from unnamed bureaucrats he had never met. Deeply resenting the intrusion of the bureaucrats, Johnson declared his independence in September after the Central Statistical Board of WPA turned down several projects. "I can't and won't have any authorities beside myself running this job here," he told Hopkins, "especially without the courtesy of so much as a consultation with me." In the future, he proclaimed, his organization would have no further administrative contact with the board unless "there is final consultation with me by them before action in Washington."[68]

The factor that most influenced Johnson's decision to leave WPA, however, was his opinion that WPA was "boon-doggling." Opposed to a spending approach to the depression, he was convinced that a balanced budget and a continuation of NRA principles were the keys to recovery. WPA, with its big price tag and its hastily put together projects, hardly fit this prescription. In a letter to Roosevelt on September 13, 1935, Johnson spelled out some of his impressions of WPA. "The danger is in letting this work go forward at all," he told the president. No one knew how much the projects would cost, nor did anyone know how much money would be available. "Now that just *can't be done* in emergency work."[69]

Johnson wrapped up his WPA work with a final report on his service, which he submitted to Hopkins on October 26. It included trenchant comments on the role of the bureaucrats in Washington and policy recommendations. Because of its critical tenor, Hopkins did not give it publicity. In April 1936, however, the press acquired the report, which had been buried in WPA files, and published it with much fanfare. For several days it was front-page news and an embarrassment to the administration and the supporters of work relief. Johnson, also embarrassed by the unauthorized release, moved quickly to contain the problem. He told reporters that it only "covered the early experimental phase of WPA" and that "many of the things criticized have now been corrected." These comments helped silence the furor. But Johnson never changed his opinion that WPA was too expensive and less desirable than direct relief.[70]

Despite his personal reservations about WPA, Johnson served the work relief program well. In less than three months—and with "color and zest"—he moved the new federal agency in New York City from the planning stage to one of the largest single employers in the nation. Johnson also served WPA well by leaving after three months. What WPA needed by the fall of 1935 were organizational refinements, the tightening up of practices, careful review of projects, and the reassignment of workers to jobs that best suited them. These tasks were too prosaic for Johnson's temperament.[71]

IN THE early years of the Roosevelt administration, the New Deal had no more loyal and outspoken champion than Hugh Johnson. By 1935, however, Johnson had doubts, shared, to a greater or lesser degree, by Raymond Moley, George Peek, and Donald Richberg, among others. For the most part these people refrained from criticizing the administration for fear of weakening it. This was not the case with Johnson. To his way of thinking, he was required as a good soldier to do everything possible to set the New Deal back on course, even if it meant publicly criticizing the administration: "I feel that a constructive public criticism of the weak spots of the New Deal will work for the success of its fundamental principles."[72]

Above all else, Johnson was disturbed by the failure of the administration to balance the budget. In 1932 he had pressed on Roosevelt the need for fiscal conservatism. Roosevelt had made gestures toward this objective in 1933 and 1934, but in 1935 he opted for more spending as a solution to the problem of recovery. To Johnson, this was rank heresy. A balanced budget and removal of the fear of inflation, he argued, would do more to hasten recovery than any spending program. In his column Johnson issued repeated warnings about the threat of inflation and bemoaned the fact, as he saw it, that "the financial and fiscal affairs of the United States are in the worst mess in our history."[73]

Johnson was also disturbed by the administration's failure to make its future course clear. Business needed signals so that it could plan; yet the administration was either unable or unwilling to spell out where it intended to take the nation. This failure, in Johnson's view, was unfair to business and an ultimate harm to the nation. "Business might get better if it were relieved of uncertainty," he commented. "It ought to be relieved of that."[74]

Finally, Johnson was concerned about the administration's unemployment and agricultural policies. He was certain that "the combined WPA-PWA program of made-work was a fantastical flop." It was "accomplishing next to nothing, satisfying nobody and at a cost of billions, making no improvement whatever in the underlying causes of unemployment." Johnson was equally caustic in evaluating agricultural policies. In 1933, he wrote, the administration faced two choices in dealing with the farm problem—implementing the McNary-Haugen program or restricting production. It chose the latter, which partly did "the job of increasing both farm prices and farm income." But the cost—in lost export trade, havoc in some industries, and the continued existence of the surplus—was massive. "It would be much simpler to compute a fair price relation between farm and other products on the domestic market and pay, out of a general manufacturers' tax, a direct subsidy equal to the difference between that and the actual price," he suggested. Doing so "would not cost the public one cent more. It would preserve our foreign trade. It would increase the farmer's net income by his return for his surplus. It would do away with 90 per cent of present administrative difficulties."[75]

Johnson's disenchantment grew out of his belief that incompetents and anti-business advisors and administrators had twisted the ideals of the New Deal. Roosevelt had permitted himself to be influenced by radicals like Hopkins and Tugwell, "Hop-Tugs" as Johnson dubbed them, who knew nothing about business and agriculture. Then, to make matters worse, Roosevelt had fallen under the sway of Frankfurter and his "Happy Hot Dogs." Novices to Washington and often disdainful of the business point of view, the Hot Dogs were recent graduates of the Harvard Law School whom Frankfurter had placed in government jobs and who, in Johnson's opinion, acted as if they had all the answers. These anti-business and know-it-all elements, he felt, had persuaded Roosevelt to remove every "important official with first-hand information or knowledge of business—or sympathy with it." They were driving business to chaos. If something was not done about them, the result would be "to wreck the New Deal."[76]

Johnson was quick to point out, however, that his criticism of the New Deal extended only to administration policies, not to the president himself. He still believed that Roosevelt was the ideal leader for the nation and that he sincerely wanted to solve the nation's economic mess. Anxious to make this point, Johnson wrote the president in September 1935 to pledge his eternal loyalty. "If anybody has taken it more on the chin for you and without hope or realization of anything but grief for myself I haven't heard the name suggested," he protested. "I shall support you as long as I have a voice."[77]

Johnson's belief that he could publicly criticize the administration and still remain an insider with Roosevelt reflects a political naiveté. Criticism in private was one thing; criticizing the New Deal in his column and speeches was quite another. Johnson, however, could not see the difference. He knew he was loyal to Roosevelt and was certain that his criticism could only be for the best. It apparently never entered his mind that Roosevelt might see it otherwise and push him completely out of his circle of advisors.

Soon after he left WPA, Johnson undertook a coast-to-coast speaking tour. It lasted through January 1936 and included visits to forty-one states. Throughout the tour he emphasized the theme of "Back to the New Deal." He was a friendly critic of the administration and devoted much of his rhetoric to the evil of unbalanced budgets, the inadequacies of the relief system, and the efficacy of industrial self-government. For the most part, administration officials publicly ignored Johnson's speeches so as to stop, or at least minimize, controversy. Privately, however, they were troubled by his personal attacks on individuals and his frequent references to Frankfurter and his Hot Dog Group, language they feared for its anti-Semitic overtones.

Although Johnson's writings and speeches further alienated the administration, he still regarded himself as a member of Roosevelt's team and sought again to be a first stringer. In early 1936, when the Supreme Court declared the Agricultural Adjustment Act unconstitutional, he quickly wired Roosevelt with advice on what steps he should take to minimize the Court's action. Do not make a constitutional issue out of the decision, he lectured; instead, amend the original act to satisfy the Court's objections. More important, Johnson took this opportunity to let Roosevelt know that he still was a good soldier and available whenever he was needed. In his boys' book manner he told Roosevelt, "Gosh I'd like to be able to fight for you again."[78]

CHAPTER 15

IN OPPOSITION

THE LAST years of Hugh Johnson's career were marked by disappointment. Although his column and speeches kept him in the national spotlight, he was no longer in government service; and his role in policy matters was reduced to that of a propagandist who was increasingly opposed to those in power. Thus, even as millions of Americans read and heard his views, he became less and less a factor in policy equations. In addition, his relationship with Roosevelt steadily deteriorated so that by 1940 the two were bitter enemies.

IN 1935 Hugh Johnson's writing career followed a rocky path. Propelled by the controversy with Senator Long and Father Coughlin, his column was "hot for the first few days." Usually writing while lying on the floor of his Washington office, Johnson minced few words in identifying the heroes and villains in the New Deal drama. If he thought someone was haywire, Johnson was quick to say so. He once wrote of an opponent's proposals, "If I think its a bunch of tripe, I can't call it ravioli." Rarely did Johnson pull his punches. His way was to hit and keep on hitting until the opponent was down for the count. Reflecting on this side of his personality, Johnson commented, "It's all right to lift the living hide off an opponent, and boy how I like to do it." Letters, many of them of the dead-cat variety, flowed in to newspaper editors, and Johnson himself received so many that they seemed to stack to the "height of an elephant." Johnson took pleasure in this response and measured his effectiveness by the number of dead-cat letters. The more dead-cat letters, the greater his impact, at least in his mind.

After this flying start, Johnson's column sputtered. He found the task of meeting the 5:00 P.M. deadline to be a full-time job in itself; if that were not enough, he was also committed to producing one magazine article a month. Johnson compounded his difficulty by immersing himself in the struggle to save NRA and by accepting the WPA assignment. These responsibilities left precious little time for work on his column. Critics soon noted that he "seemed to be writing with his elbows." His constant use of the word "guy" irritated many people; his numerous testimonials to the great wisdom of Baruch smacked of sycophancy; and his practice of referring to Baruch as Bernie became tiresome. So hastily did Johnson put his column together that at times it was little more than a hodge-podge of disconnected ideas. It was little wonder, as columnist Westbrook Pegler recalled, that editors in the fall of 1935 began to move Johnson "back toward the goiter cures and electric belts."[1]

During the winter of 1935–1936, Johnson "found his stuff again." No longer burdened by the WPA job, he devoted more time to the column. Always a master of the striking epithet, he gleefully sailed into arguments and, as Pegler said, tackled "those still straight-up-and-down stylish debators who use fancy words." Sometimes Johnson's biting remarks were downright cruel; but the public took to them nevertheless. The popularity of his column may also have been enhanced by its sharper focus. He had settled on a theme—the need for the New Deal to return to first principles—and he hammered away at it as if he was a repentent sinner.

The comeback of Johnson was underscored when the *New York World-Telegram*, the flagship paper of the Scripps-Howard chain, put his column between those of the chain's two stars, Pegler and Heywood Broun. In a memo to Scripps-Howard editors, Roy Howard emphasized that Johnson's "increasing importance" could be easily deduced from "his relative position on the page."[2] Johnson's opinions, which closely paralleled the political line of the Scripps-Howard papers, carried no particular weight in Washington and were predictable; and he never attained the stature of such journalistic giants of his age as Walter Lippmann and Arthur Krock. But his hard-hitting style set him apart from other columnists and earned him many loyal readers.

Johnson's journalistic success did not bring any immediate improvement to his personal finances. Despite the $25,000 salary he received for his column and the fees for speeches, articles, and occasional odd jobs for Baruch, his finances were in disarray. He was still in debt, and only a $15,000 loan from Baruch in the fall of 1935 saved his Long Island property from foreclosure.[3] His situation improved gradually, largely because of a $40,000 fee he received from the Radio Corporation of America in 1936 for helping to mediate a labor dispute.

Centering around RCA's Camden, New Jersey, plant, the dispute grew out of a company effort to keep out an independent union. Attempting to assert itself, Local 103 of the United Electrical and Radio Workers in May 1936 demanded a closed shop, abolition of the company union, a twenty percent pay increase, and the right to overrule the dismissal of employees by the company. The local management rejected the union's demands; and in early June, David Sarnoff, president of RCA, took over the negotiations.

One of Sarnoff's first steps was to bring in Johnson. He had little firsthand experience in labor matters, and at the suggestion of John L. Lewis he retained Johnson to handle the negotiations with the union and to try to head off a strike. As Johnson later explained, "Sarnoff came to me on a basis of personal friendship. He said he was much disturbed by the appearance of labor trouble in his Camden plant and that since he had no experience with such matters felt uncertain what to do." Johnson's initial move was to recommend that Lewis be brought into the negotiations, apparently in the belief that Lewis would support RCA and counsel the workers against a walkout. However, Lewis backed the union's demand for exclusive representation; and when RCA failed to yield, Local 103 went out on strike on June 23, 1936.

Things soon got nasty. RCA recruited strikebreakers to run the plant, and management goons beat up the union men. Johnson raced back and forth between union leaders and Sarnoff with proposals and counterproposals until Sarnoff decided that it was fruitless to continue the fight. On July 21, at the Bellevue-Strateford Hotel in Philadelphia, Sarnoff, with Johnson and Lewis looking on, agreed to terms with the union. The key provision called for the National Labor Relations Board to hold an election to determine which union—Local 103 or the company union—would be the sole bargaining agent for the workers. The winner was to be the union "receiving a majority of all those eligible to vote in such an election."

The Bellevue-Stratford agreement ended the strike, but it did not end the trouble at Camden. The company union boycotted the election; when it was held, in October 1936, the United Electrical Workers received 3,016 votes to the company union's 51. However, the total received by the electrical workers' union was far short of a majority of the 9,752 eligible to vote. The matter then went to the labor relations board, whose chairman had already indicated that the provision requiring a majority of those eligible to vote was probably a violation of the National Labor Relations Act, also known as the Wagner Act. Despite this opinion, Johnson went to National Labor Relations Board member John M. Carmody and pestered him to give RCA a break. The board ignored Johnson's request and ruled on November 9, 1936, that Local 103 was the sole bargaining agent at Camden, basing its ruling on the theory that the Wagner Act required "merely a majority of those voting." Thereupon, Johnson advised RCA to ignore the board's ruling.

Labor peace eventually came to Camden in 1939, long after Johnson had severed his involvement with the affair. His role in Camden, like so many aspects of his career, was controversial. In March 1937, the Senate Civil Liberties Committee disclosed that Johnson had received $45,654 in salary and expenses from RCA. The fact that he had been on RCA's payroll in 1936 was not widely known, for Johnson had led the press to believe that he was serving as an impartial mediator out "of pure public service." When his salary became public knowledge, many people concluded that he had been nothing more than a company hired gun who was continuing the pro-management stance he had adopted while NRA head. This attitude all but destroyed whatever effectiveness Johnson might have retained with organized labor and removed any likelihood that he would again be called upon to help end a labor dispute.[4]

Throughout this phase of Johnson's career Frances Robinson remained at his side. Fiercely loyal, she zealously used her contacts in the press to polish his image. She also helped write his column, managed his business affairs, and generally took care of him. Robbie's pervasive presence and influence put a tremendous strain on Johnson's relations with his family. Johnson's son, Pat, thought she was a con artist who was milking Johnson of his earnings; he did not believe she was needed. But out of concern for Johnson's emotional peace, he kept his opinion to himself. Johnson liked to think that Pat and Robbie got along well, and Pat, knowing that Johnson would not tolerate any criticism of her, never confronted his father with their friction.

Robbie's presence had a devastating effect on Helen Johnson. At a loss over what to do with herself for years, she detested Robbie and resented the manner in which she herself was shut out of her husband's life. Her physical and mental condition steadily declined. She totally disregarded his financial affairs and was completely averse to signing any papers, whether it was a check that had been sent to her or a property deed that required her signature. Doubting that her affairs could ever be put in order, Johnson turned them over to Helen's brothers and sisters and to Pat, all of whom had better luck than he.[5]

ANOTHER separation in Johnson's life after 1935 was the fundamental transformation of his relationship to Roosevelt and the New Deal. The ardent New Dealer and Roosevelt supporter became an impassioned opponent of the New Deal who condemned Roosevelt's leadership. In the process he lost Roosevelt's goodwill and, inevitably, any opportunity ever to serve again in a government position.

In the presidential campaign of 1936, Johnson steadfastly adhered to the course he had charted for himself the previous year—criticism of the New Deal and support for Roosevelt. He caustically denounced administration policies and waxed indignant over Roosevelt's departure from the policies of the 1933–1934 period. Notwithstanding these vehement denunciations, Johnson remained a Roosevelt man. Coming out for the president's reelection in January 1936, he praised Roosevelt's courage and humanitarianism. Johnson saw no inconsistency between his stances on the New Deal and Roosevelt. The New Deal as it stood was bad; the Republican party was even worse; and Alfred E. Landon, the Republican standard bearer, was unfit for the office. Johnson stated that "regardless of all the false starts and errors of the recovery effort in a time of unprecedented turmoil, it is the conviction of this writer that the second four years of Roosevelt will be the ablest national administration of our time."

In addition to criticizing the New Deal, Johnson lambasted the Republicans. Chafing at being on the outside and desperately wanting again to be a team member, he hoped that these attacks would provide the opportunity for him to return to the Roosevelt fold. So that he would be "identified" with the "cause," Johnson prepared a vitriolic attack on Hoover during the spring of 1936 and then asked Roosevelt to endorse it. Aside from James Farley, who thought his "picturesque language" would be helpful, no one in the Roosevelt circle cared to have Johnson identified with the administration. The risk that he might say something that could be turned against Roosevelt was just too great. When his offer was spurned, the resilient Johnson, in May 1936, told Roosevelt that leaders like Baruch, Walter Teagle, and Roy Howard were favorably disposed toward the administration and hinted that he might be a good go-between in helping the president to prepare an industrial reemployment plan in cooperation with business leaders.[6]

Nothing came of Johnson's efforts to be an insider in the Roosevelt campaign. Yet he never wavered in his support of Roosevelt and effectively employed his prickly pen and the radio mike to pillory the Republicans. Next to Landon, the individual who received the fullest gust of Johnson's wrath was onetime friend George Peek. After an unhappy sojourn at AAA and a major disagreement with Roosevelt over tariff policy while serving as the president's special advisor on foreign trade, Peek fell out with Roosevelt; and in 1936 he endorsed Landon. Johnson was appalled by Peek's action. For years he and Peek had fought the Republican Old Guard over equality for agriculture, and now Peek had gone over to the enemy. During the summer of 1936 Johnson pressed Peek not to support Landon. He argued that Roosevelt was the only candidate who would give the farmer a square deal and that Peek was acting more out of anger over his own personal treatment by Roosevelt than a rational assessment of the facts. Peek was not impressed. He replied that "I haven't the same confidence you seem to entertain in getting a square deal for agriculture from those whom you yourself have branded Communists."[7]

In September 1936, Peek blasted Roosevelt in a radio address. Peek had this time gone too far, Johnson thought; and in a September 30 speech over radio station KYW in Philadelphia he laid into his former associate. Deriding Peek's argument that the Republicans were now the salvation of farmers, Johnson scored Peek's ingratitude. Pointing out that Peek had gotten nowhere trying to sell his ideas to the Republicans in the 1920s and had made headway only because of Roosevelt, he decried Peek's wish to scuttle Roosevelt over a personal spat. "Farmers," he snarled, giving full vent to his anger, "will not go from the man who rescued them back to the men who ruined them—no, not even to grat-ify the wounded pride of a man who once served them valiantly."[8]

In passing out plaudits after his avalanche victory in the November election, Roosevelt praised Johnson for his good work during the cam-paign. Baruch likewise believed that Johnson had performed admirably and urged Roosevelt to reward Johnson by appointing him chairman of the United States Maritime Commission. Roosevelt conceded that Johnson had said only positive things about him and that there were no recent reports of him having problems with booze. But he wanted nothing more to do with Johnson in an administration job. No longer considering him trustworthy, he told his cabinet that Johnson was "a confirmed toper."[9]

Through the winter of 1936–1937, Johnson continued to defend Roosevelt. When Roosevelt sent his design for restructuring the federal judiciary to Congress on February 5, 1937, Johnson sprang to his side. An outgrowth of the Supreme Court action that declared major New Deal legislation unconstitutional, the plan included a provision en-abling the president to appoint additional justices to the Court. In his column of February 6, Johnson wrote that Roosevelt's plan was clearly constitutional. And in a nationwide radio address the next day he as-serted that the results of the November 1936 election had been a clear signal from the public to do something about the Court. Roosevelt was only doing "what he was elected to do," and Johnson was confident that he was doing the right thing. Roosevelt was moved by Johnson's vig-orous defense of his plan and praised him for the "real contribution" he had made with his broadcast. He added that "I may use some of the lan-guage. I myself prefer yours 'at its luridest' to the 'language of legal opinions.'"[10]

The fight over the Court plan dominated Congress for months, as op-ponents effectively mobilized to stop Roosevelt. Still Roosevelt would not retreat; and despite personal doubts, Senator Joseph Robinson, majority leader and a prominent Baruch man in the Senate, loyally struggled to line up enough votes for Roosevelt. In July 1937, Robin-son's sudden death from a heart attack angered many who were close to events in Washington; for they were convinced that Roosevelt, pushing too hard for a bill that had no chance of passing Congress, had contrib-uted to his death. Johnson shared this belief and said so in his column.

Shortly afterward, Roosevelt invited Johnson to visit the White House. On his appearance, Roosevelt castigated him for his column on Robinson: "If Joe Robinson should walk into this room and read this column, he would say that the man who wrote it was a cad and a cow-ard." Johnson was astonished by Roosevelt's remark, but as usual he was not at a loss for words. His face livid and his pugnacious spirit aroused, he gazed sternly at Roosevelt and replied, "If Joe Robinson said that, I would smash him on the nose"—even, he added, "if he were

President of the United States." For some time Roosevelt laid Johnson out, without one word of regret from Johnson. The acrimony ended only when they happened to begin to argue over the meaning of the word "bagnio," which Johnson had used in describing Roosevelt's palace guard. Roosevelt said that he understood the word to mean "a house of ill fame," while Johnson asserted that it "merely meant the group of advisers that gathered about an oriental monarch and the place where they assembled." Before this argument ended, Roosevelt, with his formidable sense of timing, switched to his soft approach and appealed to Johnson "on the basis of old friendship." This "broke the dykes" of Johnson's sentimentality, and he was soon in tears as he reavowed his support of Roosevelt. The visit ended with the two men expressing mutual love and friendship and patting each other on the back.[11]

These expressions of goodwill meant little. Johnson was an avowed critic of the New Deal, and, if anything, his attacks on the administration were marked by "mounting intensity." In some respects the message was the same he had been delivering since 1935. The men around Roosevelt were left-wing experimentalists. The administration had turned its back on the fundamental principles of the Democratic party. Business was beset by uncertainty because of blatantly anti-business administration policies. And the administration's fiscal, agricultural, and unemployment policies were mistaken. But to these charges, he added a more powerful and personal line of attack—Roosevelt was leading the nation in the direction of personalized government that could only result in "as rigid a dictatorship as there is on earth."

Prior to the summer of 1937 Johnson had scrupulously avoided personal attacks on Roosevelt. He was the Boss, the commander-in-chief; and a soldier was required to be loyal to his superiors. The West Point code allowed nothing less. Recognizing the apparent contradiction between his loyalty to Roosevelt and his attacks on the New Deal, Johnson told his readers that there was no inconsistency: "My stock answer to people who pan this column for sticking up for him and at the same time being highly critical of some things that have been done or are planned is—'what is the alternative?'."[12]

In the summer of 1937, Johnson changed his tune. He now saw a dangerous pattern in Roosevelt's recent proposals dealing with the federal judiciary, wages and hours, executive reorganization, additional TVA's, farm policy, and Social Security. In his opinion, the effect of these proposals would be a diminution in the powers of Congress, the courts, the regulatory commissions, and the states and a concomitant increase in the powers of the executive. These proposals, to his way of thinking, constituted a thinly disguised Mussolini-style attempt by Roosevelt to undo the Constitution and make himself "minister of everything." Loyalty to the commander-in-chief was dear to Johnson; but he believed his higher loyalty was to the nation, whose Constitution he was sworn to uphold. This was what commanded him to speak out against Roosevelt. Bit by bit Johnson moved away from Roosevelt in his column. In a speech in Chicago on September 14, 1937, he finally attacked Roosevelt directly, declaring that Roosevelt was leading the nation "away from the democracy imagined by the Constitution" through "the seduction of ballyhoo, bribery and charm."[13]

One cannot escape the conclusion that Johnson's attack against Roosevelt was motivated at least partly by personal animus. Next to Roosevelt, he had been the nation's number-one depression fighter in the early New Deal. But in 1934 Roosevelt had cast him aside. Brash young men with what seemed to him no practical experience came to have more influence with the White House than a veteran who had been at the president's side since the first shot. This point was driven home to him in 1936 and 1937, when Roosevelt rejected his proposal for repeal of the excise tax on imported copper and publicly derided his call for a census of the unemployed.[14] Thereafter, Johnson harbored no illusions that his opinions carried weight with the administration. He would still lobby for promotions and choice assignments for army buddies, but he did not expect anyone to pay much attention. The realization that his judgment did not count with the White House was the end of his bond with the president. Humiliated, he struck out at Roosevelt like a hurt child, venting his anger in his column and speeches.

Johnson's critics condemned him for letting personal feelings color his opinion of Roosevelt. But in this case they were too critical, for his feelings were not the only reason for his break with Roosevelt. Equally important was his heightened concern over the direction in which Roosevelt was taking the nation. According to Johnson, the early New Deal attempted to overcome the depression through the traditional American system. The idea was to raise the low places in the economy—agriculture, labor, and unemployment—and curb the unfair advantages of big business and the abuses in securities, banking, and public utilities. All of this was done without changing the form of the system. By 1937, however, Roosevelt had moved on to a different New Deal, one that entailed revolutionary changes and undermined the chance for recovery. Johnson saw this as the Third New Deal, not the New Deal. (In his scheme, the First New Deal covered the years 1933 and 1934 and included AAA and NRA. The Second New Deal covered 1935 and 1936 and included WPA, Social Security, and the Wagner Act. The Third New Deal covered the period beginning January 1937 and included all the measures scheduled to take effect in 1937 or proposed by Roosevelt since his reelection.) The Third New Deal meant concentrated power in the White House, more spending, and more taxes. It had nothing to do with the nation's economic malaise and, if anything, exacerbated it.[15]

The Third New Deal disillusioned Johnson. NRA had epitomized his concept of what the New Deal should represent. Washington would stimulate recovery through industrial self-government and eschew the heavy hand of federal regulation. The private rather than the public sector would be the fulcrum of recovery, and massive government spending and welfare programs would only undermine the efforts of businessmen to restore prosperity. But in 1935 Roosevelt had abandoned these principles and opted for the very policies Johnson disdained. Despite misgivings over his policies, Johnson supported Roosevelt in 1936 in the belief that he would eventually return to the policies of the early New Deal. However, the Third New Deal showed that Roosevelt, instead of retreating from the ill-founded policies urged by his anti-business advisors, was moving further to the left. Business would no longer be safe, and Johnson's vision of industrial self-government now seemed a chimera.

No measure of the Third New Deal infuriated Johnson more than the undistributed profits tax, which seemed to represent everything that was wrong with the direction in which Roosevelt was taking the nation. It placed a levy on surplus corporate profits not distributed to stockholders. Because it threatened to deprive them of their beloved venture capital, the tax aroused the collective ire of businessmen. Mirroring their attitude, Johnson branded the tax an impediment to reemployment and the repayment of debt. One can surmise that Johnson was probably most concerned about the debt aspect when he criticized the tax, particularly in writing about its impact on his own company, Lea Fabrics:

I know a small company that was started with adequate capital in 1929. The crash hit it just as it was getting under way. By some miracle of management it was kept alive through the long valley of the shadow of industrial death from 1929 to 1935. . . . In 1936 for the first time it made money—enough money to pay off its debts. Can it do so now? On its life it cannot. If it did the new law would assess on it a confiscatory tax almost as large as its debt, and that would bankrupt it—prosperous though it now is.[16]

Johnson's violent attacks on the New Deal and Roosevelt did wonders for his column. Initially, it was carried only by thirty or so papers. United Features salesmen had little success in expanding his string, probably because many publishers remembered his belligerent attitude during the squabble over the newspaper code. In the fall of 1937, however, salesmen were able to add thirteen new papers to his string in just sixty days, thanks in large measure to his anti-Roosevelt stance. When the *Philadelphia Inquirer* signed on as Johnson's forty-ninth paper, United Features proudly announced that it was "proof that he had journalistically arrived." In 1935 the arch-Republican *Inquirer* would not have printed a column by Johnson if he had been "the last columnist on

Earth." Johnson's string did not remotely approach the more than 500 papers that carried some of the nation's most popular columnists. But it was now strong enough to earn him about $50,000 a year.[17]

Throughout 1938 and 1939 Johnson battered away at the New Deal and Roosevelt. Little about his litany of charges and complaints was original. Conservatives had been charging Roosevelt and the New Deal with the same crimes ever since they realized that they were not in control of the administration. Yet Johnson's assault stands out for its ferocity. Spewing forth denunciations was not enough for him. Frustrated by his exile status and incapable of doing anything in moderation, he unleashed a torrent of verbal abuse. Johnson frequently engaged in red-baiting and, using his knack for coining a catchy phrase, branded the New Dealers as "economic pansies," "breast-beating prophets of disaster," a "cock-eyed non-Democratic crew of wand-waving wizards," "drunken sailor spenders," and "termites." He especially liked to use nicknames for the New Dealers. Harry the Hop (Harry Hopkins), Fanny the Perk and Muddum Perkins (Frances Perkins), Henry the Morgue (Henry Morgenthau, Jr.), Tommy the Cork (Thomas Corcoran), Benny the Cone (Benjamin Cohen), Leon the Hen (Leon Henderson), Danny the Rope (Daniel Roper), and Harold the Ick (Harold Ickes) all appeared regularly in his column.[18] Many readers found Johnson's word plays humorous, but to others they were merely personal and puerile.

Johnson's onslaught caused Roosevelt to lose all tolerance for him. Not only was it in bad taste, it showed a lack of gratitude. He had given Johnson a major post in his administration and had stood by him for months when everybody else was yelling for his scalp. Hurt, even saddened, by Johnson's attacks, Roosevelt sought revenge by denigrating Johnson and letting it be known that he was persona non grata in the White House. When Baruch in September 1938 proposed the creation of a "defense coordination board" that would include Johnson, Roosevelt testily told him that he believed in the army tradition that a man ought to be an officer and a gentleman and that Johnson was no longer an officer and had never been a gentleman. As it developed, the board never came into being, largely because Baruch had put forth for membership old WIB retreads like Johnson who were now opponents of the New Deal. Later, in 1940, when a magazine article suggested that "Hell hath no fury like Hugh Johnson scorned," Roosevelt laughingly told a press conference, "I love that. It rather implies he is a superannuated female."[19]

HUGH Johnson's attacks on Roosevelt were not confirmed to his New Deal policies. Devoting a large number of his writings and speeches to the nation's foreign and defense policies, Johnson also emerged as one of the most rabid non-interventionists and critics of Roosevelt's neutrality policies. Early in the life of his column, Johnson expressed a strong concern about events in Europe and warned that they "could bring down on the world a new 1914 or worse."[20] He coupled this warning with calls for preparedness and measures to keep the United States out of war.

In these respects Johnson voiced the sentiments of a significant minority of the American people. This minority was never strong enough to prevail in policy matters, but it did impel Roosevelt to follow a cautious course in dealing with the Axis threat in the period before 1941.

Beginning in 1908 with his article "The Lamb Rampant," Johnson had preached the doctrine of preparedness, emphasizing in articles and speeches that the weak state of America's defenses invited attack. Once established as a columnist, he increasingly harped on the need for proper measures to insure the nation's security and the likelihood that a strong defense would enable America to stay out of Europe's wars. Included in his list of necessary defense items were the stockpiling of strategic materials, modernization of the army and the navy, fortification of air bases in Alaska, Hawaii, and Panama, and an end to government belaboring of businessmen and coddling of labor so that industry could get on with the job of producing for the armed forces. Only by relying on its own strength, he preached, could the nation be sure of keeping out of war.[21]

Johnson matched his calls for preparedness with proposals to keep the United States out of war. Such measures, he wrote, should assume the form of legislation to take profits out of war and the relinquishment of the Philippines to Japan. Johnson also advocated the abandonment of some of the traditional neutral rights that the nation had taken up arms to protect in 1812 and 1917. For example, in September 1936, he suggested:

How about saying to our foreign traders something like this; "Travel and ship as you will, but if you travel and ship into war zones you do so at your peril. It is better that you lose a little trade than that your country suffer the mass madness of another war?"

Johnson's belief that the United States should stay out of war led him to oppose any embargoes. In response to those who urged that the United States should flex its economic muscle to prevent war or punish aggressors, Johnson voiced skepticism and argued that economic sanctions would probably have the opposite effect and increase the prospect of American involvement in war.[22]

Like most non-interventionists, Johnson based his views on several assumptions. Although he detested Hitler and was appalled by the Japanese actions in China, he could not see that the turmoil in Europe and Asia involved any interests vital to the United States. In his eyes it was rooted in economic rivalry and the jockeying for power inherent in the nation-state system. Arguments that ideological considerations were just as important and that there were fundamental moral issues at work did not impress him.[23] Working from this framework, Johnson argued that any estimate of the American interest in the turmoil must be judged by economic and security considerations.

In the case of trade, Johnson contended that an Axis victory did not portend the economic strangulation of the United States. Foreign trade, he pointed out, was only 6 percent of the nation's trade, and its loss was hardly worth a war. Moreover, Johnson was not frightened by the possibility of Europe and Asia coming under the control of the Axis. There was no question in his mind that the United States was safe from attack regardless of what happened elsewhere. It had nothing to fear, for geography (the Atlantic and Pacific Oceans, which served as giant moats) had made it an impregnable fortress.[24]

Aside from economic and security considerations, Johnson's non-interventionism was conditioned by two other factors. Johnson distrusted the English. He believed that their failure to make war debt payments demonstrated that they were ungrateful for American help in 1917 and 1918. He also contended that Britain's survival was not at stake and insisted that its sole war aim was "to maintain her dominant Empire position with her own kinsmen and also over black, brown and yellow conquered and subject peoples in three continents." Nothing could be more foolhardy than for the United States to be caught in Britain's web. If would spread American strength too thin; it would enable Britain again to play America for a sucker; and, he wrote in a December 1939 *Reader's Digest* article, it would "possibly wreck what we now laughingly call 'Western Civilization'—no matter who wins."

In addition, Johnson was concerned about the long-range effect of American involvement in a war. Undoubtedly, it would augment presidential powers to the detriment of the free enterprise system. This had been the case during the previous war, "and if we get in" another war, he wrote, "it is doubtful whether our free economic system could survive the necessary war dictatorship." It was rather a strange position to take for one who had done so much in 1917 and 1918 to increase the government's powers over its citizens; but then, Johnson now knew there would be no place for him in Washington if the nation again found itself in war, and a different role can alter perspective.[25]

Before 1939 Johnson generally gave high marks to Roosevelt for his defense and foreign policies. On several occasions he praised Roosevelt for doing more for American defense than any president since Wilson and bestowed similar praise on his foreign policies. In 1939, however,

Johnson changed his stance. Previously, he had been convinced that Roosevelt intended to keep the nation out of war. Now he was not so certain. To him, Roosevelt's repeated talk about the threat of war sounded more and more like propaganda to prepare the nation for war. Even more threatening in his mind was Roosevelt's call for modification of the neutrality laws to permit the United States to aid the victims of aggression. It was a roundabout step to bring the nation into war without going through the constitutional process, he postulated. Throughout the spring and summer of 1939, Johnson denounced proposals to repeal the arms embargo and to exert economic pressure against aggressors. At the same time, he urged Congress to adopt a law stating that any American ships or nationals would do business or travel in danger zones at their own risk.

When full-scale war broke out in Europe in September 1939, Johnson favored letting the participants settle their own problems. Seeing no overriding issue involving the United States, he derided the idea that the nation could not keep out of war. Yet in Johnson's estimate Roosevelt's actions in pushing for repeal of the arms embargo indicated that the administration intended to follow a course that could have no other outcome but American entry into war. The only hope for the nation, he wrote, was "the overwhelming popular American determination against getting into a new war. As long as that popular opinion remains, I think there will be no dangerous move." Hugh Johnson intended to use all of his energies to keep that opinion in place.[26]

HUGH Johnson's stature as a columnist and his strong opinions gave him a prominent role in the 1940 presidential election campaign. He pounded away at the anti-business character of the New Deal, WPA, the caliber of the president's cabinet, the problem of preparedness, and the danger of American involvement in the European and Asiatic catastrophes. For Johnson, all of these matters centered on one overriding issue—the reelection of Franklin D. Roosevelt. In 1932 and 1936 Roosevelt had had no more loyal supporter than Johnson. But now he was convinced that the reelection of Roosevelt would be an unmitigated disaster, and in 1940 Roosevelt had no more outspoken opponent than Johnson.

As early as February 1938, Johnson predicted that Roosevelt would make another try for the White House. He found the prospect odious. In summarizing his objections to Roosevelt, he wrote, "Mr. Roosevelt's principal duties and policies lie in the fields of agriculture, labor, industry, American finance, foreign relations, and, more recently, national defense. His performance in each field is a heap of complete and utter wreckage." Nevertheless, Johnson also predicted that Roosevelt would be reelected and, prophetically, laid out the scenario for his renomination. Roosevelt, he surmised, would not try for renomination before the Democratic convention. Then, at the convention, "someone will make a 'cross of gold and crown of thorns' speech and he will be nominated by acclamation."[27]

The prospect of Roosevelt's renomination and reelection did not lessen Johnson's opposition to his return to the White House. But he was uncertain that there was any candidate who could successfully challenge Roosevelt. He personally favored a conservative like Cordell Hull, John Nance Garner, or James Farley. None of these men, however, commanded a large following; and all were stymied by Roosevelt's refusal to state his intentions for 1940.

Unintentionally, Johnson boosted the candidacy of another man who was a novice to national politics—Wendell Willkie. In early 1939, a group of Republicans began to beat the drums for Willkie, even though he was a lifelong Democrat who had voted for Roosevelt in 1932 and had only recently switched his party affiliation. Willkie was president of the Commonwealth and Southern Corporation, a utility firm, and had made a name for himself fighting TVA in the courts and on the public platform. He presented himself as a business victim of the New Deal and impressed many New Deal critics with his down-home style and debating ability. Johnson, for example, was attracted to Willkie because the utility executive labeled himself "a Bill-of-Rights Democrat, in rebellion against the New Deal not because of its aims but because of its arbitrary exercise of power." Johnson could not have described himself any better. But there were bigger names in the Republican party than Willkie who desired the nomination, and during 1939 Willkie's candidacy was on the back burner while public attention focused on others.

The situation changed on November 21, 1939, when Johnson spoke to a large gathering of the Bund Club in New York City. After his speech, a member of the audience asked if Willkie would make a good president. Having mentioned Willkie in his column as a presidential possibility earlier in the year, Johnson retorted that Willkie was "a very strong candidate" and an ideal businessman for the White House. "I have seen that guy in pretty tough circumstances," Johnson added, "and he always came out with his head above water." Johnson made it clear, though, that he did not think Willkie could get the nomination. There was nothing prearranged about Johnson's remarks. He had not seen Willkie for months before, nor would he see him for weeks afterward. He was simply talking off the top of his head in response to a question. But from that point Willkie's candidacy mushroomed.

After hearing Johnson's remarks, an enterprising reporter telephoned Willkie in Atlanta, Georgia, and asked for his reaction. Willkie replied that "in view of the speed with which the federal government is taking over my business, shortly I'll have to be looking around for a new job. General Johnson's is the best offer I've had thus far." Johnson's remarks and Willkie's reply incited the public's interest in a Willkie candidacy. He became hot property, and he owed much of this success to Johnson. Others had suggested Willkie's name in talking about presidential possibilities, but Johnson's remarks and Willkie's reply had gone over all the country. Johnson had planned none of this; and, seeing the Willkie balloon launched, he moved to disassociate himself from it to retain his options. "All this," he wrote on November 24, 1939, "impells me to hasten to say that this column has no pre-convention candidate for President in either party."[28]

Johnson rushed to disassociate himself from the Willkie boom because he did not think Willkie had a chance to win the Republican nomination. Willkie was a newcomer to the party, and Johnson knew that political parties tended to shun latecomers as nominees. In his opinion, the Republicans would probably nominate a Landon-like candidate and repeat their 1936 campaign of "criticism plus imitation New Deal." This approach, he postulated, was a sure formula for defeat; and he wanted nothing to do with it. Instead, Johnson believed it was best to place his bet on a conservative Democrat who might, albeit very unlikely, wrestle the Democratic nomination from Roosevelt.

During the spring of 1940, Johnson looked for a conservative Democrat to emerge who could challenge Roosevelt. The most amazing occasion during his search was a speech he delivered on April 6, 1940, before the National Democratic Club at the Hotel Commodore in New York. The occasion, the annual Jefferson dinner, gave Johnson the opportunity to expound his views before the leading Democratic club in the nation. That Johnson would even be invited to address this group was a surprise. Johnson was an outspoken critic of the New Deal, and most of those in attendance believed it was time for party harmony, not discord. But it was discord they received from Johnson, who had been scheduled for the speech by Farley, chairman of the dinner committee and a presidential aspirant.

Johnson devoted much of his speech to elaborating the complaints that conservative Democrats like himself had against Roosevelt and the New Deal. Condemning the spending programs enacted by Roosevelt as the harbinger of national disaster, he called for a return to the policies of the early New Deal and praised the conservatives for keeping the faith: "It is these veteran Democrats who have borne the heat and the burden of all these close contests. . . . They have carried the fight and torch and all too often gotten kicks in the pants for their pains." Perhaps with himself in mind, he implied that they deserved better from the party they had served so faithfully. Johnson left no doubt about what should be done with those who were now in charge of the New Deal:

Let's get rid of the interlopers and usurpers in the Democratic party. Let's throw out these strange doctrines which have defiled the temples of our political religion. Let's return to the faith and house of our fathers and let us, the Democrats, and not strangers, be masters in that house.[29]

Predictably, his heated plea for a purge of the current crop of New Dealers from the Democratic party fell on deaf ears. Roosevelt and his people were in control of the party, and few doubted that he would receive the nomination unless he specifically took himself out of the race. As a result, Johnson increasingly looked to the Republicans as the nation's salvation, with the provision that they nominate Willkie.

In the months preceding the Republican convention, Johnson turned himself into a publicist for the utility executive. The high point of his pre-convention campaign for Willkie came on June 22, when the anti-Roosevelt *Saturday Evening Post* practically came out with a special Willkie issue. Included was a brilliant pro-Willkie article by Johnson entitled "I Am Not Nominating Him." Johnson was careful to point out that Willkie faced difficulties in getting the nomination and that his only chance to win the party's nod depended on a deadlock among the Big Names and his selection as "the compromise in sight." But Johnson left no doubt that Willkie was the best man for the job and took particular care to dispel any notion that Willkie might be an Old Dealer because of his business background. Instead, Johnson presented Willkie in much the same light as he perceived himself—a businessman who recognized that there were abuses in the American capitalistic system that needed government regulation and one who was not afraid to tell off the reactionaries to their face. Willkie understood, Johnson preached, that there were abuses that were "long overdue for regulations" and "that any attempt to frustrate or prevent these corrections would be both futile and disastrous."[30]

Although two weeks before the convention he did not have the vote of a single state delegation, the Republicans nominated Willkie at the end of June. A combined professional-amateur team of operators overwhelmed the convention and engineered Willkie's nomination on the sixth ballot. Willkie owed his nomination to international events, particularly the German victory over France that same month, the weakness of his rivals, the work of the dedicated professionals and amateurs who inundated the delegates with Willkie propaganda and chants of "we want Willkie," and a well-orchestrated publicity campaign to present him as a viable and winning candidate. Many individuals contributed to his publicity campaign, not the least of whom was Johnson. Through his columns, articles, and speeches, Johnson publicized Willkie as the man to challenge Roosevelt and put the nation on a straight course. Though others said much the same, Johnson's voice boomed across the nation and was heard by as many people as any

Willkie publicist. It is not possible to know how much credit to attribute to Johnson for the emergence of Willkie. However, one contemporary, with perhaps not an excessive amount of exaggeration, wrote that

Johnson, in his lifetime, never had the credit for this job of super-selling but everyone remembers how Willkie suddenly burst on the national picture, . . . how Johnson himself catapulted Willkie in the political arena in the *Saturday Evening Post*. . . . The basic framework of the whole building—a necessary factor in American politics on occasion—was Johnson's. A good buildup, inevitably appears to be the result of a spontaneous public interest, *and* this was a good buildup.[31]

Although no longer close to the center of power, Johnson was still hoping to be a kingmaker.

Privately, Johnson was noncommittal about Willkie for the November election. The Democrats were not holding their convention until the middle of July, and he wanted to see whom they nominated before cutting his ties with the party. Johnson prayed that the Democrats still might come to their senses and nominate a conservative. But after Roosevelt feigned lack of interest in a third term, the convention went ahead and drafted him, to his contentment. Johnson was disgusted at this charade. Bewailing Roosevelt's renomination, he wrote that "this thing in Chicago seems to me enough to nauseate a large pack of cast-iron hyenas plus a couple of flights of copper-lined turkey buzzards." Roosevelt's renomination, he charged, was based on a "Hitlerized vote" and foreordained the doom of democracy if the people did not do something about it in November.[32] Despite his bitterness, Johnson wavered before he decided to abandon the Democratic party and endorse Willkie. Writing to Peek in late July, he stated, "I don't know if I am going to vote for Willkie. I've got to see what he will really stand for."[33]

On August 12 Johnson had a long meeting with Willkie at Colorado Springs, Colorado, to discuss a wide range of domestic and foreign policy issues.[34] The meeting firmed up his inclination to support Willkie. Although Willkie was more interventionist on foreign policy issues than he would have preferred, Johnson found Willkie's views generally compatible with his own. Moreover, Johnson realized that he really had no choice. He had been blasting the New Deal and Roosevelt for years and had been one of Willkie's most prominent promoters. To turn around and support Roosevelt for reelection would cause him to lose all credibility.

Sounding more anti-Roosevelt than pro-Willkie, Johnson plunged into the fall campaign "with roars against White House vacillation and Palace intrigues." He viciously attacked Ickes and other administration stalwarts with such venom that Baruch and other friends who were reluctantly supporting Roosevelt had to disassociate themselves from him for fear that they would have the White House door closed on them. A kind of anti-Semitism crept into his comments, particularly when he noted that 95 percent of "non-Christians" were going to vote for Roosevelt because they thought he would lead the nation into war against Hitler.[35]

His obsession with the defeat of Roosevelt led Johnson to link himself with groups he otherwise would have avoided. In September 1940, he made a national broadcast to help launch the America First Committee, which quickly emerged as the nation's most powerful anti-interventionist group. By itself the address contained little that Johnson had not said previously. But it associated him with what would prove to be an extremely controversial organization and put him in league with a disparate group of anti-Roosevelt people. Drawing its strength from the so-called Chicago *Tribune* belt, the America First Committee was chaired by one of the old Purchase, Storage and Transportation gang from World War I, Robert Wood, now of Sears, Roebuck and Company. It included other such respectable people as Mrs. Alice Roosevelt Longworth, Chester Bowles, Philip Jessup, and John T. Flynn, who had regularly scathed Johnson and NRA in his column in the *New Republic*. However, America First also attracted Coughlinites and pro-German elements with whom Johnson felt extremely uncomfortable. He first rationalized his involvement on the grounds that the defeat of Roosevelt was the paramount issue, but in late 1941 he changed his mind. The Coughlinites and pro-German elements in America First evidenced sufficient anti-Semitism to spark a rush by the more respectable members to repudiate them and keep their organization from being totally discredited. Johnson went a step further. Judging that any association with these elements would kill his column in the major eastern cities, he severed his ties with America First with a blast at the anti-Semites.[36]

In the last weeks of the campaign, Johnson plugged away for Willkie. He praised Willkie's "simple homespun honesty"; he damned Roosevelt's "cleverness, slickness and guile." Two days before the election Johnson flatly predicted that Willkie would win. But on the day of the election he hedged and bemoaned the terrible future under Roosevelt:

If this kind of political urge [the Willkie campaign] can be stopped by any kind of political jim-cracks and finagling even by the billions of dollars in New Deal spending, we might as well write democracy off as an American tradition. The people no longer rule, the janissariat does.[37]

Johnson's prediction that Willkie would triumph was far wide of the mark. The New Deal was just too popular to beat, and the American people also wanted Roosevelt's experienced hand at the helm as they headed to the brink of war and beyond. The outcome left Johnson demoralized, who could look forward only to the isolation that awaits those who supported the loser. Yet he thought there could be the possibility, slight though it seemed, that Roosevelt might let bygones be bygones now that the election was over. On November 6 Johnson wired Roosevelt that he was again ready to serve. Calling Roosevelt the Boss, he stated that "I fought you but the American people thought otherwise. We must all now get together. I am still a soldier and you are my commander in chief."[38] Roosevelt never answered Johnson's telegram.

THE YEAR 1941 brought little cheer to Hugh Johnson. His contract with United Features was scheduled to expire in March, and a hitch developed in the negotiations for its renewal. A number of the syndicate's customers had complained that Johnson's outspoken opposition to Roosevelt had little appeal to their many readers who were "have nots" and saw Hitler as a real threat. Some wanted the right to edit his column, while others decided to stop taking it altogether. In all, Johnson lost about 10 percent of his string in the months following the election. Typical of the papers that dropped him was the Tyler (Texas) *Morning Telegraph*. Said the *Telegraph* in an editorial explaining its action: "The General . . . has allowed his personal animosity for President Roosevelt to cause him to oppose every defense measure undertaken by the present administration without regard to fact or expert opinion."

In light of these developments, several United Features executives questioned the wisdom of continuing Johnson's contract. After consultations with Roy Howard, they decided that it should be renewed only if severe conditions were attached. Johnson knew that there had been grumbling about his column. But he never anticipated what took place on February 20 when he met with three syndicate executives to discuss his contract. The three unleashed a torrent of criticism that flabbergasted Johnson. They contended that his column provoked less discussion than any of the other syndicate's major columns, that he was too strident, that he engaged in too much nostalgia about the World War I mobilization, that he was using his column as a vehicle to get back into government, that he lacked even a semblance of objectivity, that he came across as "an anti-Roosevelt heel," and that he was so unpopular that many papers had dropped his column. So great were Johnson's faults, they indicated, that his column would be continued only if he publicly pledged to tone down his remarks and if he went through a six-month probationary period.

Convinced that he was being treated unfairly, Johnson rushed off a long letter to Howard defending his column. He was ready to grant that he might have written too intemperately on occasions. However, he believed that most of the other criticism was unjustified. He had received numerous testimonial letters from editors praising him for provoking more discussion than any other columnist, and his anti-Roosevelt thrust was hardly worthy of criticism—his views had generally coincided with those of Howard and the editorial policies of the Scripps-Howard newspapers. Johnson also attacked the contention that he was losing his popularity. For every paper that dropped him, he argued, there was another anxious to pick him up. And if that was not enough proof of his popularity, two other syndicates had expressed interest in his column; and his speaking engagements were as numerous as ever.

Refusing to admit that the syndicate might have legitimate concerns, Johnson concluded that some of the executives had always resented his quick rise to prominence and were just trying "to do a job" on him. Others, he deduced, were being stampeded into getting rid of him as a result of a floodtide of complaints trumped up by the Roosevelt camp to punish him for his role in the 1940 campaign. Fair play, Johnson pleaded, demanded that he not be ejected "as a sort of heave offering at the horns of the altar to appease the Washington Cammora."

For a brief moment, Johnson was so disconcerted by the attack against him that he considered accepting the syndicate's terms. But on second thought he decided that a six-month stint in purgatory was personally and professionally degrading. It would only postpone an inevitable "witch burning," with him as the main attraction. Consequently, Johnson severed his ties with United Features and in March 1941 joined Hearst's King Features. His column, however, continued to appear in a number of Scripps-Howard papers, including the *Washington Daily News* and the *New York World-Telegram*.[39]

Johnson had no sooner weathered this storm when he received a blow from which he never completely recovered. In the summer of 1940, the War Department advised Johnson that his commission in the Officers' Reserve Corps would expire in April 1941 and that he must undergo a physical examination if he desired reappointment. Because of his break with Roosevelt, Johnson did not anticipate a call to active duty, although he understood that his name was at the head of army lists for the recall of reserve officers to assist in both manpower and industrial mobilization. Nevertheless, he was anxious to renew his commission. The army had been his life, and he cherished the honor that went with the commission. But a physical examination was a stumbling block. He was forty pounds overweight, and his blood pressure was elevated. Knowing that he could not pass the physical, Johnson decided to postpone it in the hope that the requirement would be waived or that he could lose the excess poundage.

During the winter of 1940–1941 Johnson struggled to lose weight. He had little success and on March 28, 1941, asked Chief of Staff General George C. Marshall to waive the physical examination. Marshall quickly acceded to his request. Other reserve general officers in similar circumstances had been granted waivers, and Johnson would have to pass a physical examination before being called to active duty. In Marshall's opinion, as long as Johnson remained on the inactive list there was no need to worry about his weight or blood pressure. The following day Johnson formally applied for renewal of his commission.[40]

Unknown to Johnson, Roosevelt was determined not to submit his name to the Senate for reappointment. Evidencing a seldom-displayed vindictive side, he had resolved that Johnson must pay for his "ungentlemanly" attacks on the New Deal and its supporters and his treasonous support of Willkie. Such opportunities to accord punishment were few, so when Johnson's commission came up for renewal, Roosevelt could not let such a golden one pass. What better way to punish the old cavalryman than to drum him out of his beloved army?

Johnson's commission expired on April 10, 1941, without any indication from the War Department on the status of his application. Concerned about the holdup, Johnson contacted Major General Edwin M. "Pa" Watson, the White House military secretary, to determine whether there was any problem. From Watson he learned that Roosevelt had decided not to renominate him. Devastated, Johnson wrote to plead with Roosevelt for reappointment on the basis of what "used to be a very close and precious friendship." "I am sure that you don't like me any more—and I don't blame you," he told the president. "But I am equally sure that you know in your heart, more confidentially, perhaps, than about some other people that in whatever you might ask me to do, I would serve faithfully and loyally—as I have always done."[41]

Roosevelt was not moved. He had made up his mind not to renominate Johnson, and on April 17 he instructed Watson to inform Johnson that the administration preferred to reappoint officers to the reserves "only in the event they are able, prior to reappointment, to pass a physical test." The head of the Personnel Division in Marshall's office strongly rejected this approach. He argued that it was the practice to reappoint reserve officers even when there was no intention to call them to active duty or there was question about their physical condition. These appointments were understood to be "more as a recognition of past service than as to eligibility for call to active duty." Johnson, he contended, was entitled to the same treatment as other reserve officers. As he told Marshall, "from the viewpoint of the War Department there is no other defensible procedure."[42]

Despite the War Department's position, Roosevelt was adamant in his opposition to the renomination of Johnson. Basing his reply to Johnson on the grounds of physical condition, Watson wrote Johnson that Roosevelt preferred to renominate only officers who were physically fit and whose recall could be anticipated. In view of these circumstances, he told Johnson, "your reappointment would be of no purpose." He added that "personalities had no place" in the decision.[43]

Johnson was not surprised by Watson's letter. Still the rejection hurt.

In a return letter he quarrelled over the reasons given for the denial of his renomination and then pledged not "to make any issue out of this." His prime purpose in writing, however, was to let Watson know that, in his opinion, Roosevelt was a hypocrite: "You can't support what you say in the President's assurance that there is no personal angle here," he sermonized. "On the face of the record there is only one answer to that and the answer is NUTS."[44]

Realizing that a cashiered officer was expected to go quietly and bring no embarrassment to the army, Johnson planned to put the affair to rest with his letter to Watson. The press, however, made a cause célèbre out of it and reported that Johnson was sulking and was "sore as hell" at Roosevelt. In an effort to put himself in the best possible light, Johnson went public with his side of the story, issuing a press release on April 30 and devoting his May 2 column to it. In both cases he denied that he was mad at anybody and stated that he had been "treated with remarkable fairness," but he let the public know that the reasons given for Roosevelt's refusal to renominate him were inaccurate and intolerable in his view. His message was clear. Roosevelt may have been acting within his prerogative in refusing to renominate him; however, there was no justification for his action. Like so many others who had parted ways with him, Roosevelt was a "rink-stink."[45]

Many people agreed with Johnson. Newspaper editorials opined that he had been shabbily treated; and even Eleanor Roosevelt, the president's wife, questioned Johnson's "dismissal." In a letter to her husband she wrote: "I wish I knew more of what really led to your refusal to renew Johnson's appointment. . . . I suppose there is some valid reason, but to a great many people it looks as though you had simply indulged in annoyance because Johnson had been attacking the administration."[46] Johnson, meanwhile, tried to put the best face forward. "It's all water over the dam," he wrote. "There are too many more important things to think about."

Privately, Johnson was heartbroken. The army had given him his college and legal educations, the chance to prove himself, and lifelong friends. He took pride in the right to use the title of general. Now Roosevelt's spite severed all his ties with the army. What especially dismayed Johnson was his conviction that Roosevelt used the army to punish a political enemy. In his belief, that action was unthinkable. The army should always be above politics. Johnson was also dismayed by Roosevelt's hostility toward him. Even though he had been in the forefront of Roosevelt's opponents, Johnson believed that their differences were purely political and that they were still joined by a bond of friendship. He likewise believed that their military relationship had remained intact. Roosevelt was commander-in-chief and could always count on him to serve loyally in national emergencies. Johnson could not understand why Roosevelt failed to see that he remained a friend and loyal soldier. Bemoaning his treatment at Roosevelt's hands, he wrote to Steve Early, "I only wish the Boss were a bit more realistic. He ought to know that I would go to hell if necessary for him as President."[47]

The flap over his reserve commission paralleled some of Johnson's fiercest attacks on Roosevelt's foreign policies. Certain that Roosevelt was deliberately leading the country into war against the desire of the American people to remain neutral, he hotly condemned lend-lease and warned that Roosevelt was planning to have the navy convoy ships to Britain. Johnson made his supreme effort to alert the nation to the perils of Roosevelt's policies in a book he published in the late spring of 1941. Entitled *Hell-Bent for War*, it represented his most complete statement on foreign policy. Two ideas predominated. First, Roosevelt was leading the American people into a war for which they were not prepared and which they did not want. Second, the United States should concern itself primarily with the defense of the Western Hemisphere and aid Britain only to the extent that it would not involve itself in the war or impair hemispheric defense. Underpinning these ideas was the assumption that if the United States armed itself to the hilt, no nation would dare challenge it in the Western Hemisphere.

Throughout the summer and fall of 1941, Johnson excoriated Roosevelt's policies, but with a growing realization that he was losing the battle. Like many Americans, Johnson was not surprised when war came on December 7, 1941; however, like most Americans, he was surprised that it came at Pearl Harbor. On that day, though, Johnson was engaged in a struggle for his own life.

IN LATE November 1941, Hugh Johnson was hospitalized in Walter Reed for a kidney ailment compounded by influenza and cirrhosis of the liver. His condition was so serious that at one point doctors cautioned Frances Robinson that he might never leave his bed. On their recommendation Johnson had round-the-clock nurses, which imposed a heavy financial burden on him. Not wanting his old friend to worry, Baruch generously paid the nursing bills.[48] Johnson was not so ill, however, that he was unable to work on his column. He never missed a deadline, although some of his columns were written by Robbie.

Hearing of Johnson's illness, Roosevelt sent a cheery get-well note at Christmas. "You must get back among us very soon," he bade Johnson, "for there is work for all of our fighting men to do." Johnson's instinctive reaction was to murmur to son Pat that "the son of a bitch doesn't really mean it. He knows I'll never leave here." On second thought, he decided that Roosevelt was sincere. His spirits perked up, and on the day after Christmas he penned a moving letter to Roosevelt in which he downplayed his health problems and reported that he was ready for the president's call to duty. "You must know that I would give my right arm to be in there trying to help in any capacity and that my services are always at your disposal," he wrote. Expressing remorse about all of their differences, he told the Boss that "if I ever again permit a personal difference with an old friend to hurt such a kindly relationship, it will be in another incarnation."[49]

On January 8, 1942, Johnson got out of bed for the first time in weeks, and on January 13 he went home to his apartment in the Wardman Park Hotel in Washington. Before long, however, he was back in Walter Reed, and his spirits quickly sank to low ebb. The loss of his commission had been an even deeper wound than those around him had imagined. And with the nation now engaged in another world war, the heartache of being on the sidelines had intensified. Johnson gave the public a hint of his torment when he wrote in January 1942 that "I do know what it is like for an ex-soldier to be told in time of war that there is no place for him. It is like hell."[50] Hoping to "buck him up," Robbie asked James Byrnes to intervene with Roosevelt and see if Johnson's commission could be restored. But nothing came of these efforts, for the administration quietly let it be known that it considered Johnson's case closed.

In early April, Johnson improved enough that the doctors permitted him to return home. Loss of weight and frequent blood transfusions, however, left him weak and led to pneumonia. At first, no one thought it was very serious, least of all Johnson. But after finishing his next day's column on the morning of April 14, Johnson became noticeably listless. His strength "failed visibly and rapidly," and he lapsed into unconsciousness shortly after midnight. He died at 4:45 A.M. on April 15, 1942, from massive internal hemorrhaging. Johnson was buried with full military honors at Arlington National Cemetery.[51]

The public comment on Johnson's death praised his many accomplishments, his personality, and his character. The *New York Times* called him "an original" and thanked him for bringing cheer to the nation at a time when it was "short of milk and honey." The *Chicago Daily News* editorialized that "few Americans of his era have been called on to undertake a more varied array of difficult and thankless tasks in the service of his country; and few served their country more conscientiously or efficiently." Old friend Bernard Baruch, though, summarized most poignantly and succinctly what Johnson's death meant to the nation. After attending Johnson's funeral he wrote General Pershing: "As I left him on the hillside in Arlington Cemetery I thought of how useful that brain, his courage and facility of expression could have been in the present circumstances."[52]

NOTES

Abbreviations Used in Notes and Bibliography

COHC   Columbia Oral History Collection, Columbia University,
          New York City
GC   General Correspondence
NA   National Archives, Washington, D.C.
OF   Office File
PPF   President's Personal File
RG   Record Group
SC   Selected Correspondence
WHAF   White House Alphabetical File
WNRC   Washington National Records Center, Suitland, Maryland

On Citation of Sources

In order to avoid an excessively large number of notes, I have sometimes collected the references for one or even several paragraphs in a single note. Sources in each note are generally given in the order in which the information or quotation under citation appears.

Chapter 1

1. Hugh S. Johnson, *The Blue Eagle from Egg to Earth* (Garden City, N.Y.: Doubleday, Doran and Company, 1935), 8.
2. Ibid., p. 6.
3. Ibid., p. 2.
4. Kilbourne Johnston, interview with Ralph F. de Bedts, Hamilton, Ohio, August 28, 1965 (cited hereafter as Kilbourne Johnston interview, August 28, 1965).
5. B. B. Chapman, "The Land Rush of 1893, As Seen at Kiowa," *Kansas Historical Quarterly* 31 (Spring 1963): 67–75; Joe B. Milan, "Opening of the Cherokee Outlet," *Chronicles of Oklahoma* 9 (September and December 1931): 268–86, 454–75. The Milan work continued in *Chronicles of Oklahoma* 10 (March 1932): 115–37.
6. Edward C. McReynolds, *Oklahoma: A History of the Sooner State* (Norman: University of Oklahoma Press, 1964), 302; *Evening Star*, Washington, D.C., December 18, 1934.
7. Johnson, *Blue Eagle*, p. 13.
8. Frances R. Newman, interview with Ralph F. de Bedts, Winter Park, Florida, June 14, 1965; *Washington Daily News*, March 14, 1935. (The interview with Mrs. Newman is cited hereafter as Frances R. Newman interview, June 14, 1965.)

9. Record of Hugh M. [*sic*] Johnson, Office of the Registrar, Northwestern Oklahoma State University.

10. Johnson, *Blue Eagle*, p. 15; James E. Ament to F. D. Roosevelt, May 20, 1933, Roosevelt Papers, WHAF; *Washington Daily News*, October 11, 1933.

11. Allan R. Millett, *The General: Robert L. Bullard and Officership in the United States Army, 1881–1925* (Westport, Conn.: Greenwood Press, 1975), 29.

12. Johnson, *Blue Eagle*, p. 21.

13. Academic Record of Hugh Samuel Johnson, USMA 1903, United States Military Academy Library and Archives.

14. Stephen F. Ambrose, *Duty, Honor, Country: A History of West Point* (Baltimore: Johns Hopkins University Press, 1966), 222–30; Thomas J. Fleming, *West Point: The Men and Times of the United States Military Academy* (New York: William Morrow and Company, 1969), 270–78.

15. Matthew Josephson, "The General—I," *New Yorker*, August 18, 1934, p. 21.

16. Johnson, *Blue Eagle*, p. 21.

17. D. Clayton James, *The Years of MacArthur: 1880–1941* (Boston: Houghton Mifflin Company, 1970), 82–83.

18. Johnson, *Blue Eagle*, p. 34.

19. Barbara Tuchman, *Stilwell and the American Experience in China, 1911–1945* (New York: Macmillan Company, 1970), 17.

20. Johnson, *Blue Eagle*, p. 34.

21. Kilbourne Johnston interview, August 28, 1965.

22. Johnson, *Blue Eagle*, p. 35.

23. H. S. Johnson to The Military Secretary, June 29, 1906, General Correspondence File, RG #94, NA.

24. H. S. Johnson to The Adjutant General, September 13, 1906, ibid.

25. Johnson, *Blue Eagle*, pp. 35–36.

26. H. S. Johnson to F. D. Roosevelt, n.d., Roosevelt Papers, PPF 702; Frances R. Newman interview, June 14, 1965.

27. Military Record of Hugh S. Johnson, General Correspondence File, RG #94, NA.

28. Johnson, *Blue Eagle*, p. 40.

29. H. Duane Hampton, *How the U.S. Cavalry Saved Our National Parks* (Bloomington: Indiana University Press, 1971), 139–63.

30. H. S. Johnson to The Adjutant General, August 31, 1913, General Correspondence File, RG #94, NA.

31. E. H. Crowder to N. D. Baker, September 11, 1916, Pershing Papers.

32. *New York Herald Tribune*, July 15, 1934.

33. Allan Nevins, *Herbert H. Lehman and His Era* (New York: Charles Scribner's Sons, 1963), 58.

34. *Washington Post*, April 16, 1942.

35. Kilbourne Johnston interview, August 28, 1965.

36. H. S. Johnson to N. D. Baker, January 27, 1920, Baker Papers; H. S. Johnson to F. D. Roosevelt, April 30, 1935, Roosevelt Papers, OF 1332.

37. John Kennedy Ohl, "Tales Told By a New Dealer—General Hugh S. Johnson," *Montana: The Magazine of Western History* 25 (Autumn 1975): 66–77.

38. *New York Times*, December 20, 1936.

39. Hugh S. Johnson, "How Caldwell 'Made Good,'" *Appleton's Magazine*, December 1906, p. 695.

40. Hugh Johnson, "Lascar," *Scribner's Magazine*, August 1907, p. 175.

41. Lieut. Hugh Johnson, "The Lamb Rampant," *Everybody's Magazine*, March 1908, pp. 291–301.

42. Lieutenant Hugh Johnson, "The Mission of the Service Magazines," *Cavalry Journal* 19 (October 1908): 301–8.

43. "Hugh Samuel Johnson," *Current Biography, 1940* (New York: H. W. Wilson Co., 1941), 431.

44. Johnson, *Blue Eagle*, p. 47.

45. *New York Times*, December 20, 1936.

46. Johnson, *Blue Eagle*, p. 47.

47. David A. Lockmiller, *Enoch H. Crowder: Soldier, Lawyer and Statesman* (Columbia: University of Missouri Press, 1955), 147–48.

48. E. H. Crowder to J. J. Pershing, June 8, 1916, Pershing Papers.

49. Johnson, *Blue Eagle*, p. 61.

50. E. H. Crowder to J. J. Pershing, June 8, 1916, and E. H. Crowder to N. D. Baker, September 11, 1916, both in Pershing Papers.

51. H. L. Scott to B. I. Wheeler, June 29, 1915, Chief of Staff Correspondence File, 1907–1916, RG #165, NA.

52. J. J. Pershing to E. H. Crowder, June 15, 1916, Pershing Papers.

53. Kilbourne Johnston interview, August 28, 1965.

54. Johnson, *Blue Eagle*, p. 71. An untitled copy of the study is included in the Johnson Papers.

55. Lockmiller, *Enoch H. Crowder*, p. 150, n. 25.

56. Crowder to Baker, September 11, 1916, Pershing Papers.

57. Pershing to Crowder, June 15, 1916, Pershing Papers; R. L. Owen to W. Wilson, August 17, 1916, General Correspondence File, RG #94, NA.

58. H. S. Johnson to J. J. Pershing, September 27, [1916], Pershing Papers.

59. E. H. Crowder to J. J. Pershing, September 19, 1916, and J. J. Pershing to H. S. Johnson, September 30, 1916, both in Pershing Papers.

CHAPTER 2

A version of this chapter has been published as John Kennedy Ohl, "Hugh S. Johnson and the Draft, 1917–1918," *Prologue: The Journal of the National Archives* 8 (Summer 1976), 85–96.

1. Johnson's account of this episode can be found in Brig. Gen. Hugh S. Johnson, "Draft Problems" (lecture delivered at the Army War College, Washington, D.C., December 22, 1924), pp. 1–2; and Brig. Gen. Hugh S. Johnson, "Selective Service" (lecture delivered at the Army War College, Washington, D.C., October 20, 1939), pp. 3–4. Also see *New York Times*, February 2, 1931; and Johnson, *Blue Eagle*, p. 73.

2. E. H. Crowder to Mr. Keith and accompanying drafts, February 23, 1917, Crowder Papers.

3. Daniel R. Beaver, *Newton D. Baker and the American War Effort, 1917–1919* (Lincoln: University of Nebraska Press, 1966), 25–32; John Whiteclay Chambers II, "Conscripting for Collossus: The Progressive Era and the Origins

of the Modern Military Draft in the United States in World War I," in *The Military in America: From the Colonial Era to the Present,* ed. Peter Karsten (New York: Free Press, 1980), 275–96; David M. Kennedy, *Over Here: The First World War and American Society* (New York: Oxford University Press, 1980), 145–49.

4. E. H. Crowder to H. L. Scott, March 21, 1917, Crowder Papers; House Committee on Military Affairs, *Selective Service Act, Hearings,* 65th Cong., 1st sess., 1918, 26–27; I. B. Holley, Jr., *General John M. Palmer, Citizen Soldiers, and the Army of a Democracy* (Westport, Conn.: Greenwood Press, 1982), 260–67; John Kennedy Ohl, "'Old Iron Pants': The Wartime Career of General Hugh S. Johnson, 1917–1918" (Ph.D. diss., University of Cincinnati, 1971), p. 18.

5. H. S. Johnson to J. J. Pershing, May 29, 1925, Pershing Papers.

6. H. S. Johnson to E. H. Crowder, n.d., Crowder Papers.

7. H. S. Johnson to Mrs. Rogers, June 4, 1918, Office File, RG #163, WNRC.

8. Johnson, *Blue Eagle,* p. 75.

9. H. S. Johnson to E. H. Crowder, November 29, 1921, Crowder Papers.

10. Johnson, *Blue Eagle,* p. 75.

11. House Committee on Military Affairs, *Taking the Profits Out of War, Hearings,* 74th Cong., 1st sess., 1935, 111; Senate Committee on Military Affairs, *To Prevent Profiteering in Time of War, Hearings,* 75th Cong., 1st sess., 1937, 94, 119.

12. Johnson to Crowder, November 29, 1921, Crowder Papers.

13. H. S. Johnson to C. Hayden, June 4, 1918, Crowder Papers; Seward W. Livermore, *Politics Is Adjourned: Woodrow Wilson and the War Congress, 1916–1918* (Middletown, Conn.: Wesleyan University Press, 1966), 41, 44; Beaver, *Newton D. Baker,* pp. 34–36; Kennedy, *Over Here,* pp. 155–57.

14. J. E. Kuhn to H. L. Scott, April 5, 1917, War College Division, RG #165, NA; J. E. Kuhn to H. L. Scott, April 19, 1917, General File, RG #163, WNRC.

15. B. M. Chiperfield to P. C. March, March 29, 1932, March Papers.

16. A Plan for Execution of a Draft, Historical File, RG #163, WNRC.

17. H. S. Johnson to E. H. Crowder, n.d., Crowder Papers.

18. Lockmiller, *Enoch H. Crowder,* p. 165.

19. H. S. Johnson to G. C. Henry, April 28, 1917, General File, RG #163, WNRC.

20. William H. Crawford, "He Risked Disgrace to Speed the Draft," *New York Times Magazine,* June 9, 1918, pp. 4–6.

21. E. H. Crowder to H. S. Johnson, May 12, 1917, Office File, RG #163, WNRC; E. H. Crowder to E. A. Kreger, October 30, 1930, Crowder Papers.

22. Ray Stannard Baker and William E. Dodd, eds., *The Public Papers of Woodrow Wilson,* 6 vols. (New York: Harper and Brothers, 1925–1927), 5:39.

23. E. H. Crowder to J. J. Pershing, August 16, 1917, Pershing Papers.

24. Johnson, *Blue Eagle,* p. 88; Johnson to Crowder, November 29, 1921, Crowder Papers.

25. Crowder to Pershing, August 16, 1917, Pershing Papers.

26. J. J. Pershing to T. H. Bliss, October 2, 1917, Papers of John J. Pershing, RG #200, NA.

27. Johnson, *Blue Eagle,* p. 81.

28. Marvin A. Kreidberg and G. Merton Henry, *History of Military Mobiliza-*

tion in the United States Army, 1775–1945 (Washington, D.C.: Department of the Army, 1955), 266.

29. E. H. Crowder to N. D. Baker, June 26, 1917, Historical File, RG #163, WNRC; Johnson, *Blue Eagle*, p. 81.

30. Edward M. Coffman, *The War to End All Wars: The American Military Experience in World War I* (New York: Oxford University Press, 1968), 43.

31. E. H. Crowder to N. D. Baker, September 12, 1917, General File, RG #163, WNRC.

32. Johnson, *Blue Eagle*, p. 82.

33. *New York Times*, October 18, 1917.

34. John Dickinson, *The Building of an Army: A Detailed Account of Legislation, Administration and Opinion in the United States, 1915–1920* (New York: Century Company, 1922), 147.

35. Johnson, *Blue Eagle*, p. 83.

36. H. S. Johnson to E. H. Crowder, March 8, 1918, Reference Library Files, National Headquarters of the Selective Service System.

37. Kreidberg and Henry, *History of Military Mobilization*, p. 250.

38. Johnson to Crowder, March 8, 1918.

39. E. H. Crowder to H. S. Johnson, March 8, 1918, Reference Library Files, National Headquarters of the Selective Service System.

40. Johnson, *Blue Eagle*, p. 84.

41. Resolution of the War Council, March 20, 1918, General File, RG #163, WNRC.

42. E. H. Crowder to H. S. Johnson, March 15, 1918, Reference Library Files, National Headquarters of the Selective Service System.

43. Johnson, "Selective Service," p. 8; *Second Report of the Provost Marshal General, 1918* (Washington, D.C.: Government Printing Office, 1919), 86.

44. *New York Times*, June 9, 1918.

45. *Report of the Provost Marshal General, 1917* (Washington, D.C.: Government Printing Office, 1918), 10.

46. E. H. Crowder to T. H. Bliss, October 3, 1917, Office File, RG #163, WNRC.

47. Johnson, *Blue Eagle*, p. 89; Johnson to Crowder, November 29, 1921, Crowder Papers.

48. Johnson to Crowder, November 29, 1921, Crowder Papers.

49. *New York American*, December 18, 1917; Peyton C. March, *The Nation at War* (Garden City, N.Y.: Doubleday, Doran and Co., 1932), pp. 239–40.

50. H. S. Johnson to the Editor of the *New York American*, December 18, 1917, and Johnson to Hayden, June 4, 1918, both in Crowder Papers; *New York Times*, October 9, 1932.

51. Johnson, *Blue Eagle*, p. 74.

52. Lockmiller, *Enoch H. Crowder*, p. 181.

53. Johnson to Crowder, November 29, 1921, Crowder Papers.

54. W. G. Murdock to E. H. Crowder, August 23, 1920, Crowder Papers.

55. H. S. Johnson to E. H. Crowder, January 25, 1918, Crowder Papers.

56. J. J. Pershing to J. Biddle, February 20, 1918, Papers of John J. Pershing, RG #200, NA.

57. J. J. Pershing to N. D. Baker and P. C. March, March 4, 1918, Papers of John J. Pershing, RG #200, NA.

58. E. H. Crowder to J. J. Pershing, February 25, 1918, Pershing Papers.

59. H. S. Johnson to E. H. Crowder, March 8, 1918, Office File, RG #163, WNRC.

60. J. J. Pershing to E. H. Crowder, March 24, 1918, Papers of John J. Pershing, RG #200, NA.

61. Alvin Brown, interview with Ralph F. de Bedts, Washington, D.C., June 29, 1965 (cited hereafter as Brown interview, June 29, 1965).

62. *New York Times*, January 16, 1919.

CHAPTER 3

A version of this chapter has been published as John Kennedy Ohl, "General Hugh S. Johnson and the War Industries Board," *Military Review* 55 (May 1975): 35–48.

1. Robert D. Cuff, *The War Industries Board: Business-Government Relations during World War I* (Baltimore: Johns Hopkins University Press, 1973), 1–12; Ellis W. Hawley, *The Great War and the Search for a Modern Order: A History of the American People and Their Institutions, 1917–1933* (New York: St. Martin's Press, 1979), 6–11, 23; Jordan A. Schwarz, *The Speculator: Bernard M. Baruch in Washington, 1917–1965* (Chapel Hill: University of North Carolina Press, 1981), 50–52; Stephen Skowronek, *Building a New American State: The Expansion of National Administrative Capacities, 1877–1920* (Cambridge: Cambridge University Press, 1982), 236–37.

2. Samuel P. Huntington, *The Soldier and the State: The Theory and Practice of Civil-Military Relations* (Cambridge: Harvard University Press, 1957), 267–69; Paul A. C. Koistinen, "The 'Industrial-Military Complex' in Historical Perspective: World War I," *Business History Review* 41 (Winter 1967): 402–3.

3. Statement of General Hugh S. Johnson, pp. 2–5, Baruch Papers; Daniel R. Beaver, "The Problem of Military Supply, 1890–1920," in *War, Business, and American Society: Historical Perspectives on the Military-Industrial Complex*, ed. Benjamin Franklin Cooling (Port Washington, N.Y.: Kennikat Press, 1977), 77–78.

4. James L. Abrahamson, *America Arms for a New Century: The Making of a Great Military Power* (New York: Free Press, 1981), 153–62; Paul Y. Hammond, *Organizing for Defense: The American Military Establishment in the Twentieth Century* (Princeton, N.J.: Princeton University Press, 1961), pp. 10–38; James E. Hewes, Jr., *From Root to McNamara: Army Organization and Administration, 1900–1963* (Washington, D.C.: Center of Military History, 1975), 21–31; Otto L. Nelson, Jr., *National Security and the General Staff* (Washington, D.C.: Infantry Journal Press, 1946), 73–217; Dickinson, *The Building of an Army*, pp. 279–87.

5. Beaver, *Newton D. Baker*, pp. 93–96; Skowronek, *Building a New American State*, pp. 237–40.

6. Robert D. Cuff, "Bernard Baruch: Symbol and Myth in Industrial Mobilization," *Business History Review* 43 (Summer 1969): 115–33; Kennedy, *Over Here*, pp. 126–38; Schwarz, *The Speculator*, pp. 50–108; Skowronek, *Building a New American State*, pp. 241–42.

7. E. H. Crowder to H. S. Johnson, n.d., and H. S. Johnson to E. H. Crowder, n.d., Crowder Papers.

8. H. S. Johnson to N. D. Baker, January 31, 1918, Baker Papers.

9. Edward M. Coffman, *The Hilt of the Sword; The Career of Peyton C. March* (Madison: University of Wisconsin Press, 1966), 119–21.

10. March, *The Nation at War*, pp. 239–40.

11. Statement of General Palmer E. Pierce, pp. 24–26, and Statement of General Hugh S. Johnson, p. 4, both in Baruch Papers.

12. E. R. Stettinius to B. Crowell, April 2, 1918, Purchase, Storage and Traffic Division, RG #165, NA; Beaver, "American Military Supply," p. 79.

13. H. S. Johnson to B. M. Baruch, November 28, 1919, Baruch Papers, GC.

14. Statement of General Hugh S. Johnson, p. 3, Baruch Papers.

15. H. S. Johnson to P. E. Pierce, April 2, 1918, Purchase, Storage and Traffic Division, RG #165, NA.

16. Dickinson, *The Building of an Army*, p. 279.

17. Report of the Committee Appointed by the Assistant Secretary of War to Plan an Organization for the Office of the Director of Purchase and Supplies, Purchase, Storage and Traffic Division, RG #165, NA; *War Department Annual Reports, 1919* 4 vols. (Washington, D.C.: Government Printing Office), 1 : 349.

18. Johnson, *Blue Eagle*, p. 89; *Evening Star*, Washington, D.C., April 16, 1918.

19. On hearing of the promotion, Douglas MacArthur's mother wrote a biting letter to Pershing protesting that her son—the number one cadet in the 1903 class and the current chief of staff of the 42d Division in France—was still only a colonel in the National Army (James, *The Years of MacArthur: 1880–1941*), pp. 169–71. See also Martin Elumenson, ed., *The Patton Papers, 1885–1940* (Boston: Houghton Mifflin Company, 1972), 548–49.

20. Goethals Desk Diary #1, April 16, 1918, Goethals Papers; C. Day, T. N. Perkins, and H. S. Johnson to B. Crowell, April 18, 1918, Purchase, Storage and Traffic Division, RG #165, NA.

21. Statement of George N. Peek, pp. 16–18, Baruch Papers.

22. G. W. Goethals to G. R. Goethals, May 10, 1918, Goethals Papers.

23. Statement of George N. Peek, p. 17, Baruch Papers.

24. G. N. Peek to C. D. Velie, May 6, 1918, Peek Papers.

25. H. S. Johnson to G. W. Goethals, August 21, 1918, Purchase, Storage and Traffic Division, RG #165, NA; *War Department Annual Reports, 1919*, 1:355–77.

26. House Committee on Expenditures in the War Department, *War Expenditures, Hearings*, 66th Cong., 1st sess., 1921, 523–27.

27. H. S. Johnson to C. C. Williams, June 6, 1918, Chief of Ordnance Correspondence File, 1915–1931, RG #156, WNRC; H. S. Johnson to Chief of Procurement of Each Supply Bureau, June 22, 1918. Quartermaster General Correspondence File, 1917–1922, RG #92, WNRC.

28. Reminiscences of Gerard Swope, pp. 84–85, COHC.

29. G. W. Goethals to P. C. March, July 18, 1918, Purchase, Storage and Traffic Division, RG #165, NA.

30. Goethals Desk Diary #3, July 30–August 24, 1918, Goethals Papers.

31. Daniel R. Beaver, "George W. Goethals and the Problem of Military Supply," in *Some Pathways in Twentieth-Century History: Essays in Honor of Reginald Charles McGrane*, ed. Daniel R. Beaver (Detroit: Wayne State University Press, 1969), 103–4.

32. Statement of General Hugh S. Johnson, pp. 2–3, Baruch Papers.

33. Grosvenor B. Clarkson, *Industrial America in the World War: The Strategy behind the Line, 1917–1918* (Boston: Houghton Mifflin, 1923), 131.

34. Minutes of Meeting of Commodity Chiefs, July 13, 1918, Quartermaster General Correspondence File, 1917–1922, RG #92, WNRC.

35. Bernard M. Baruch, *Baruch: The Public Years* (New York: Holt, Rinehart and Winston, 1960), 53; Margaret L. Coit, *Mister Baruch* (Boston: Houghton Mifflin, 1957), 166, 334.

36. Statement of George N. Peek, p. 17, Baruch Papers.

37. Reminiscences of Frances Perkins, vol. 5, p. 495, COHC.

38. Johnson, *Blue Eagle*, pp. 90–91.

39. G. W. Goethals to P. C. March, May 13, 1918, Chief of Staff Correspondence File, 1917–1921, RG #165, NA; H. S. Johnson to J. G. Harbord, January 28, 1919, Harbord Papers; H. S. Johnson to J. J. Pershing, September 29, 1930, Baruch Papers, SC.

40. Program for 1918–1919, Purchase, Storage and Traffic Division, RG #165, NA.

41. Baruch, *Public Years*, p. 53.

42. Johnson, *Blue Eagle*, p. 91; Johnson to Harbord, January 28, 1919, Harbord Papers; Goethals Desk Diary #2, May 21–22, 1918, Goethals Papers.

43. Statement of General Hugh S. Johnson, p. 9, Baruch Papers.

44. P. C. March to G. B. Clarkson, February 21, 1921, March Papers.

45. Coffman, *Hilt of the Sword*, p. 74.

46. Senate Special Committee to Investigate the Munitions Industry, *Minutes of the War Industries Board from August 1, 1917, to December 19, 1918*, Senate Committee Print 4, 74th Cong., 1st sess., 1935, p. 287.

47. H. S. Johnson to P. C. March, August 1, 1918, Chief of Staff Correspondence File, 1917–1921, RG #165, NA.

48. *WIB Minutes*, pp. 402, 406.

49. H. S. Johnson to C. C. Williams, August 6, 1918, Chief of Ordnance Correspondence File, 1915–1931, RG #156, WNRC.

50. Statement of George N. Peek, p. 9, Baruch Papers; Clarkson, *Industrial America in the World War*, pp. 129–32.

51. *War Department Annual Reports, 1919*, 1:365–67 and 370–72.

52. Bernard M. Baruch, *American Industry in the War: A Report of the War Industries Board*, ed. Richard H. Hippelheuser (New York: Prentice Hall, 1941), 109–16; Clarkson, *Industrial America in the World War*, pp. 299–314; Cuff, *The War Industries Board*, pp. 150–82.

53. Statement of General Hugh S. Johnson, p. 5, and Statement of George N. Peek, pp. 23–24, both in Baruch Papers.

54. War Industries Board Commodities Committees, April 23, 1918, Chief of Ordnance Correspondence File, 1915–1931, RG #156, WNRC. Statement of General Hugh S. Johnson, pp. 5–6, Baruch Papers.

55. H. S. Johnson to C. C. Williams, June 4, 1918, Chief of Ordnance Correspondence File, 1915–1931, RG #156, WNRC.

56. Memorandum, Purchase and Supply Branch, May 31, 1918, General Johnson's Papers, Minutes of the Superior Board of Review, August 14, 1918, and Supply Bulletin #8, July 23, 1918, Purchase, Storage and Traffic Division, all in RG #165, NA.

57. H. S. Johnson to G. N. Peek, August 16, 1918, in *WIB Minutes*, pp. 427–28.

58. Supply Bulletin #22, August 28, 1918, File #1-C2, RG #61, WNRC.

59. G. N. Peek to Commodity Section Chiefs, September 25, 1918, and replies, File #21A–A2, WNRC; Cuff, *The War Industries Board*, pp. 167–68.

60. Koistinen, "The 'Industrial-Military Complex': World War I," p. 401.

61. Summary by General Johnson of Tasks Accomplished and Tasks to Be Accomplished by the Purchase and Supply Branch, *Appendix II, Exhibits to Accompany Section Relating to Purchase and Supply Branch, History of Purchase, Storage and Traffic Division*, War Department Historical File, RG #165, NA.

62. Goethals Desk Diary #3, June 25–July 5, 1918, Goethals Papers.

63. P. C. March to N. D. Baker, October 19, 1932, and P. C. March to J. Cabell, July 10, 1933, both in March Papers. The quotation is from March to Cabell.

64. Johnson to Harbord, January 28, 1919, Harbord Papers; H. S. Johnson to N. D. Baker, January 27, 1920, Baker Papers; H. S. Johnson to R. L. Owen, January 7, 1920, Pershing Papers; Johnson to Crowder, November 29, 1921, Crowder Papers.

65. H. S. Johnson to G. W. Goethals, July 5, 1918, Goethals Papers.

66. Goethals Desk Diary #3, July 5, 1918, Goethals Papers.

67. H. S. Johnson to J. J. Pershing, July 23, 1918, Pershing Papers.

68. J. G. Harbord to J. J. Pershing, September 10 and 23, 1918, Harbord Papers.

69. Goethals Desk Diary #3, August 27–28, 1918, Goethals Papers. Wood had been an upperclassman at West Point during Johnson's plebe year.

70. Ibid., August 28, 1918; Reminiscences of Gerard Swope, pp. 84–85, COHC.

71. Johnson, *Blue Eagle*, p. 97. H. S. Johnson to J. G. Harbord, January 28, 1919, Harbord Papers.

72. Johnson, *Blue Eagle*, pp. 99, 101–2; "Hugh Samuel Johnson," *Assembly*, April 1943, p. 12.

73. H. S. Johnson to G. N. Peek, November 21, 1918, Peek Papers.

74. J. G. Harbord to J. J. Pershing, December 7, 1918, Harbord Papers.

75. B. M. Baruch to G. N. Peek, November 24, 1919, and H. S. Johnson to B. M. Baruch, November 28, 1919, both in Baruch Papers, GC.

76. Senate Special Committee to Investigate the Munitions Industry, *Final Report of the Chairman of the United States War Industries Board to the President of the United States, February 1919*, Senate Committee Print 3, 74th Cong., 1st sess., 1935, 50–51. In 1935 the Senate Committee to Investigate the Munitions Industry secured galley proofs of this report and printed it. After some confusion, Baruch informed the committee "that these galleys do not constitute my report and the assembly of them under the title of 'Final Report of the War Industries Board' is wholly unwarranted" (Senate Special Committee to Investigate the Munitions Industry, *Munitions Industry, Hearings*, 74th Cong., 1st sess., 1935, 6393–94, 6642). Also see Otis L. Graham, *Toward a Planned Society: From Roosevelt to Nixon* (New York: Oxford University Press, 1976), 15–16.

77. Johnson, *Blue Eagle*, p. 102.

CHAPTER 4

1. Robert F. Himmelberg, "Business, Antitrust Policy, and the Industrial Board of the Department of Commerce, 1919," *Business History Review* 42 (Spring 1968): 1–23; Melvin I. Urofsky, *Big Steel and the Wilson Administration: A Study in Business-Government Relations* (Columbus: Ohio State University Press, 1969), 308–24.

2. G. N. Peek to G. E. Tripp, April 18, 1919, Peek Papers.

3. L. B. Reed to G. N. Peek, June 26, 1919, Peek Papers; J. H. Scobell to W. S. Peirce, March 31, 1919, Chief of Ordnance Correspondence File, 1915–1931, RG #156, WNRC.

4. L. B. Reed to G. N. Peek, June 27 and 28, 1919, and G. N. Peek to L. B. Reed, June 28, 1919, both in Peek Papers; H. S. Johnson to E. H. Crowder, July 5, 1919, Crowder Papers; Brown interview, June 29, 1965.

5. H. S. Johnson to E. H. Crowder, July 8 and 22, 1919, and E. H. Crowder to H. S. Johnson, July 30, 1919, Crowder Papers; Lockmiller, *Enoch H. Crowder*, p. 224.

6. Johnson, *Blue Eagle*, p. 103.

7. G. N. Peek to B. M. Baruch, July 21, 1919, Baruch Papers, GC.

8. G. N. Peek to B. M. Baruch, February 24, 1919, and G. N. Peek to A. H. Wiggins, March 14, 1919, Peek Papers.

9. G. N. Peek to R. Colton, March 1, 1919, Peek Papers.

10. G. N. Peek to H. S. Johnson, November 29, 1918, Peek Papers.

11. Gilbert C. Fite, *George N. Peek and the Fight for Farm Parity* (Norman: University of Oklahoma Press, 1954), 21–37.

12. Johnson, *Blue Eagle*, pp. 103–4; Brown interview, June 29, 1965.

13. James H. Shideler, *Farm Crisis: 1919–1923* (Berkeley: University of California Press, 1957), 1–52.

14. Johnson, *Blue Eagle*, p. 104.

15. H. S. Johnson to J. J. Pershing, April 21, 1921, and J. J. Pershing to H. S. Johnson, June 29, 1921, Pershing Papers.

16. Fite, *George N. Peek*, p. 74.

17. G. N. Peek to B. M. Baruch, January 22, 1923, Baruch Papers, GC.

18. F. O. Wetmore to Holders of Debenture Bond Participation Certificates, February 20, 1923, and G. N. Peek to B. M. Baruch, February 27, 1923, Baruch Papers, GC.

19. H. S. Johnson to G. N. Peek, February 25, 1924, Peek Papers.

20. Johnson, *Blue Eagle*, p. 108.

21. Reminiscences of Eugene Meyer, Jr., p. 419, COHC.

22. Johnson to Peek, February 25, 1924, Peek Papers.

23. H. S. Johnson to G. N. Peek, January 20, 1924, Peek Papers.

24. G. N. Peek to B. M. Baruch, October 3, 1923, Baruch Papers, GC.

25. Reminiscences of Jerome N. Frank, pp. 57 and 60, COHC.

26. Johnson to Peek, February 25, 1924, Peek Papers.

27. Johnson, *Blue Eagle*, p. 104.

28. An Analysis of Present Day Agricultural Problems, August 1920, Peek Papers.

29. Fite, *George N. Peek*, p. 43.

30. Donald L. Winters, *Henry Cantwell Wallace as Secretary of Agriculture, 1921–1924* (Urbana: University of Illinois Press, 1970), 249.

31. Reminiscences of Chester C. Davis, p. 190, COHC; Reminiscences of Jerome N. Frank, p. 55, COHC.

32. *Equality for Agriculture* (Moline: H. W. Harrington, 1922).

33. Gilbert C. Fite, "The Farmers' Dilemma, 1919–1929," in *Change and Continuity in Twentieth-Century America: The 1920s*, ed. John Braeman, Robert H. Bremner, and David Brody (Columbus: Ohio State University Press, 1968), 84.

34. Brief Report on What Took Place in Washington—January 20–February 15, February 20, 1922, Peek Papers.

35. Johnson, *Blue Eagle*, p. 106.

36. Fite, *George N. Peek*, pp. 47–48.

37. Brief Report on What Took Place in Washington—January 20–February 15, February 20, 1922, Peek Papers.

38. H. C. Taylor and G. N. Warren to H. C. Wallace, February 5, 1922, quoted in Winters, *Henry Cantwell Wallace*, p. 254.

39. H. S. Johnson to H. C. Hoover, January 10, 1922, Peek Papers.

40. Joan Hoff Wilson, *Herbert Hoover: Forgotten Progressive* (Boston: Little, Brown and Company, 1975), 102–8; Shideler, *Farm Crisis*, pp. 212–13; Winters, *Henry Cantwell Wallace*, pp. 252–53.

41. Johnson, *Blue Eagle*, p. 105.

42. Quoted in Fite, *George N. Peek*, p. 51.

43. H. C. Taylor to G. N. Peek, December 14 and 24, 1922, Peek Papers; Winters, *Henry Cantwell Wallace*, pp. 256–57.

44. G. N. Peek and H. S. Johnson, *To All Who May Be Interested in Equality for Agriculture*, Peek Papers.

45. T. J. Walsh to G. W. Norris, December 27, 1923, quoted in Fite, *George N. Peek*, p. 55.

46. Edward L. Shapsmeier and Frederick H. Shapsmeier, *Henry A. Wallace of Iowa: The Agrarian Years, 1910–1940* (Ames: Iowa State University Press, 1968), 67–76; Shideler, *Farm Crisis*, pp. 260–68; Winters, *Henry Cantwell Wallace*, pp. 254–67.

47. H. C. Wallace to H. S. Johnson, October 2, 1923, and H. S. Johnson to H. C. Wallace, October 2, 1923 (both in Secretary of Agriculture Correspondence File, RG #16, NA); H. S. Johnson to H. C. Wallace, n.d., Peek Papers; Donald R. McCoy, *Calvin Coolidge: The Quiet President* (New York: Macmillan Company, 1967), 165.

48. H. S. Johnson to G. N. Peek, n.d., Peek Papers.

49. Ibid.

50. Johnson to Peek, February 25, 1924, Peek Papers.

51. H. S. Johnson to F. Woods, February 11, 1924, and H. S. Johnson to G. N. Peek, February 13, 1924, Peek Papers.

52. Fite, *George N. Peek*, p. 74.

53. G. N. Peek to H. S. Johnson, February 12 and 23, 1924, and G. N. Peek to J. B. Blunt, Jr., February 26, 1924, Peek Papers.

54. H. S. Johnson to G. N. Peek, February 25 and 26, 1924, Peek Papers.

55. G. N. Peek to H. S. Johnson, March 2, 1924, Peek Papers.

56. H. S. Johnson to G. N. Peek, March 3 and June 5, 1924, Peek Papers.

57. H. S. Johnson to G. N. Peek, December 13, 1924, and January 20, 1925, and G. N. Peek to H. S. Johnson, December 21, 1924, and February 1, 1925, all in Peek Papers.

58. J. J. Pershing to H. S. Johnson, May 1, 1924, Pershing Papers.

59. Johnson, *Blue Eagle*, p. 115.

60. Reminiscences of Jerome N. Frank, pp. 58–60, COHC.

61. H. S. Johnson to B. M. Baruch, July 7 and November 25, 1924, and n.d., Baruch Papers, GC; Johnson, *Blue Eagle*, p. 108.

62. *Moline Dispatch*, August 7, 1951.

63. Johnson, *Blue Eagle*, pp. 194–95; Brown interview, June 29, 1965.

64. Johnson, *Blue Eagle*, p. 109.

65. H. S. Johnson to B. M. Baruch, October 29, 1925, Baruch Papers, GC; H. S. Johnson to B. M. Baruch, February 12, 1934, Baruch Papers, SC.

66. Johnson, *Blue Eagle*, p. 109.

67. Merlo J. Pusey, *Charles Evans Hughes*, 2 vols. (New York: Macmillan Company, 1951), 1:374.

68. H. S. Johnson to B. M. Baruch, April 20, 1927, Baruch Papers, GC.

69. *Moline Dispatch*, August 7, 1951.

70. H. S. Johnson to B. M. Baruch, September 7, [1927], Baruch Papers, GC.

71. Johnson, *Blue Eagle*, pp. 106–7, 115.

CHAPTER 5

1. Schwarz, *The Speculator*, pp. 31–35, 206, and 287.

2. Ibid., pp. 334–36.

3. E. J. Kahn, Jr., *The World of Swope* (New York: Simon and Schuster, 1965), p. 395.

4. B. M. Baruch to H. S. Johnson, May 4, 1921, Baruch Papers, GC.

5. Baruch, *American Industry in the War*, pp. x–xl, 37.

6. Johnson to Pershing, May 29, 1925, Pershing Papers; Johnson to Pershing, September 29, 1930, Baruch Papers, SC.

7. For examples, see H. S. Johnson to B. M. Baruch, May 1, 1929, Baruch Papers, SC, and "Speech by Mr. Bernard M. Baruch," delivered at West Point, New York, May 4, 1929, Baruch Papers, Public Papers.

8. B. M. Baruch to H. S. Johnson, May 5, 1925, Baruch Papers, GC.

9. Brig. Gen. Hugh S. Johnson, "Industrial and Man-Power Mobilization," lecture delivered at the Army War College, December, 1922; Hugh S. Johnson, "Fallacies of 'The Universal Draft,'" *Army Ordnance* 10 (November–December, 1929): 155–57.

10. H. S. Johnson to B. M. Baruch, n.d., Baruch Papers, SC.

11. Schwarz, *The Speculator*, p. 337.

12. Paul A. C. Koistinen, "The 'Industrial-Military Complex' in Historical Perspective: The Interwar Years," *Journal of American History* 56 (March 1970): 825.

13. Schwarz, *The Speculator*, p. 356.

14. General Hugh S. Johnson, "Feasible Peacetime Approaches to Industrial Mobilization," lecture delivered at the Army Industrial College, February 2, 1940.

15. Quoted in Schwarz, *The Speculator*, p. 359.

16. H. S. Johnson to B. M. Baruch, n.d., Baruch Papers, SC.

17. Harold Epstein, interview with Ralph F. de Bedts, New York City, July 15, 1965.

18. House Committee on Military Affairs, *Taking the Profits Out of War*, pp. 97–124; Senate Committee on Military Affairs, *To Prevent Profiteering in Time of War*, pp. 85–99.

19. Koistinen, "The 'Industrial-Military Complex': The Interwar Years," p. 835.

20. H. S. Johnson to B. M. Baruch, May 11, 1925, and October 25, 1926, both in Baruch Papers, GC.

21. Johnson, *Blue Eagle*, p. 110.

22. Carter Field, *Bernard Baruch: Park Bench Statesman* (New York: McGraw-Hill Book Company, 1944), 85; B. M. Baruch to H. S. Johnson, May 20, 1927, and H. S. Johnson to B. M. Baruch, n.d., both in Baruch Papers, GC.

23. "Bernard Mannes Baruch," *Fortune*, October, 1933, p. 37.

24. H. S. Johnson to B. M. Baruch, August 8, 1931, Baruch Papers, GC.

25. Johnson, *Blue Eagle*, p. 116.

26. H. S. Johnson to B. M. Baruch, November 25, 1930, Baruch Papers, GC.

27. Johnson to Baruch, February 12, 1934, Baruch Papers, SC.

28. Field, *Bernard Baruch*, p. 85.

29. Baruch, *The Public Years*, p. 200; Schwarz, *The Speculator*, p. 252; Johnson, *Blue Eagle*, pp. 114.

30. Johnson to Baruch, September 7, [1927], Baruch Papers, GC.

31. James Grant, *Bernard Baruch: The Adventures of a Wall Street Legend* (New York: Simon and Schuster, 1983), 223–53.

32. Johnson, *Blue Eagle*, p. 114.

33. H. S. Johnson to B. M. Baruch, August 12, 1929, Baruch Papers, GC.

34. Johnson to Baruch, June 23, 1930, Baruch Papers, GC.

35. Memorandum on Lea Fabrics, January 2, 1931, Baruch Papers, GC.

36. H. S. Johnson to B. M. Baruch, January 22, 1931, Baruch Papers, GC.

37. H. S. Johnson to D. Cates, August 7, 1931, Baruch Papers, GC.

38. B. M. Baruch to H. S. Johnson, June 29, 1935, Baruch Papers, SC.

39. H. S. Johnson to E. K. Files et al., November 21, 1936, and H. S. Johnson to D. Cates, August 10, 1939, both in Baruch Papers, GC.

40. H. S. Johnson to B. M. Baruch, July 5, 1935, Baruch Papers, SC.

41. G. N. Peek to H. S. Johnson, October 4 and 9, 1928, Peek Papers.

42. Reminiscences of Chester C. Davis, p. 247, COHC.

43. H. S. Johnson to G. N. Peek, September 24, 1928, Peek Papers.

44. G. N. Peek to H. S. Johnson, October 3, 1928, Peek Papers.

45. Fite, *George N. Peek*, pp. 219–20.

46. H. S. Johnson to B. M. Baruch, July 7, 1930, Baruch Papers, GC.

47. H. S. Johnson to M. A. Boyle, July 27, 1931, and Johnson to Baruch, August 7, 1931, both in Baruch Papers, GC; Johnson to Baruch, August 3, 1931, Baruch Papers, SC.

48. Schwarz, *The Speculator*, pp. 260–62.

49. Eliot A. Rosen, *Hoover, Roosevelt, and the Brains Trust: From Depression to New Deal* (New York: Columbia University Press, 1977), 278, 285–89.

50. Schwarz, *The Speculator*, p. 261.

51. Baruch, *The Public Years*, p. 228.

52. Jordan A. Schwarz, *The Interregnum of Despair: Hoover, Congress, and the Depression* (Urbana: University of Illinois Press, 1970), 114–15.

53. Rosen, *Hoover, Roosevelt, and the Brains Trust*, p. 311.

54. H. S. Johnson to B. M. Baruch, February 2, 1932, Baruch Papers, SC.

55. O. L. Mills to H. S. Johnson, May 30, 1932, Mills Papers.

56. Matthew Josephson, "The General—II," *New Yorker*, August 25, 1934, p. 25.

57. Schwarz, *The Speculator*, p. 262.

58. Johnson, *Blue Eagle*, pp. 123–33.

59. H. S. Johnson to G. N. Peek, May 11, 1932, Peek Papers.

60. Rosen, *Hoover, Roosevelt, and the Brains Trust*, pp. 245–47; Field, *Bernard Baruch*, p. 32.

61. Raymond Moley, *After Seven Years* (New York: Harper and Brothers, 1939), 32; Raymond Moley, *27 Masters of Politics in a Personal Perspective* (New York: Funk and Wagnalls, 1949), 166. R. G. Tugwell, *The Brains Trust* (New York: Viking Press, 1968), 34.

62. Baruch, *The Public Years*, p. 229; Johnson *Blue Eagle*, pp. 134–40.

63. Beatrice Bishop Berle and Travis Beal Jacob, eds., *Navigating the Rapids, 1918–1971: From the Papers of Adolf A. Berle* (New York: Harcourt Brace Jovanovich, 1973), 51–52; Rexford G. Tugwell, *In Search of Roosevelt* (Cambridge: Harvard University Press, 1972), 135–36.

64. R. C. Moley to F. D. Roosevelt, July 16, 1932, Baruch Papers, SC.

65. Rosen, *Hoover, Roosevelt, and the Brains Trust*, pp. 311–12.

66. Charles Michelson, *The Ghost Talks* (New York: G. P. Putnam's Sons, 1944), 194.

67. Tugwell, *The Brains Trust*, p. 461; Tugwell, *In Search of Roosevelt*, p. 136.

68. Rosen, *Hoover, Roosevelt, and the Brains Trust*, p. 315; Tugwell, *In Search of Roosevelt*, p. 136.

69. Robert F. Himmelberg, *The Origins of the National Recovery Administration: Business, Government, and the Trade Association Issue, 1921–1933* (New York: Fordham University Press, 1976), 183–84; Schwarz, *The Speculator*, p. 269.

70. Theodore Saloutos, *The American Farmer and the New Deal* (Ames: Iowa State University Press, 1982), 65; Bernard Sternsher, *Rexford Tugwell and the New Deal* (New Brunswick, N.J.: Rutgers University Press, 1964), 45 and 281.

71. Moley, *27 Masters of Politics*, pp. 167–68.

72. H. S. Johnson to M. A. Boyle, September 8, 1932, Baruch Papers, GC.

73. Moley, *27 Masters of Politics*, pp. 168–69.

74. Rosen, *Hoover, Roosevelt, and the Brains Trust*, pp. 341–42.

75. The text of the Johnson draft can be found in the Moley Papers.

76. Rosen, *Hoover, Roosevelt, and the Brains Trust*, pp. 345–47.

77. Rexford G. Tugwell, *Roosevelt's Revolution: The First Year—A Personal Perspective* (New York: Macmillan, 1977), 60.

78. H. S. Johnson to R. C. Moley, September 15, 1932, Moley Papers.

79. Moley, *After Seven Years*, p. 59, n. 7.

80. H. S. Johnson to R. C. Moley, September 27, 1932, Moley Papers.

81. Alfred B. Rollins, Jr., *Roosevelt and Howe* (New York: Alfred A. Knopf, 1962), 359–60; Tugwell, *Roosevelt's Revolution*, p. 60.

82. Frank Freidel, *The Triumph*, vol. 3 of *Franklin D. Roosevelt* (Boston: Little, Brown and Company, 1956), 362.

83. Samuel I. Rosenman, ed., *The Public Papers and Addresses of Franklin D. Roosevelt*, 13 vols. (New York: Random House, 1938–1950), 1:795–814.

84. H. S. Johnson to G. N. Peek, October 31, 1932, Peek Papers.

85. Berle, *Navigating the Rapids, 1918–1941*, ed. Berle and Beal, pp. 74–75.

86. Schwarz, *The Speculator*, p. 287.

87. H. S. Johnson to R. C. Moley, December 21, 1932, Moley Papers.

88. Schwarz, *The Speculator*, pp. 265–66.

CHAPTER 6

1. Schwarz, *The Speculator*, pp. 284, 287–88.

2. B. M. Baruch to G. N. Peek, June 13, 1932, Peek Papers.

3. Reminiscences of M. L. Wilson, p. 804, COHC.

4. H. S. Johnson to G. N. Peek, July 2, 1932, Peek Papers.

5. G. N. Peek to H. S. Johnson, July 3, 1932, Peek Papers; B. M. Baruch to G. N. Peek, July 15, 1932, Baruch Papers, GC.

6. Frank Freidel, *Launching the New Deal*, vol. 4 of *Franklin D. Roosevelt* (Boston: Little, Brown and Co., 1973), 88.

7. H. S. Johnson to R. C. Moley, November 29, 1932, Moley Papers.

8. R. C. Moley to H. S. Johnson, December 20, 1932, Moley Papers.

9. Freidel, *Launching the New Deal*, p. 100.

10. Raymond Moley, *The First New Deal* (New York: Harcourt, Brace and World, 1966), 253.

11. Van L. Perkins, *Crisis in Agriculture: The Agricultural Adjustment Administration and the New Deal* (Berkeley: University of California Press, 1969), 39.

12. Johnson, *Blue Eagle*, p. 192.

13. H. S. Johnson to L. M. Howe, March 24, 1933, Roosevelt Papers, PPF 702; H. S. Johnson to H. A. Wallace, n.d., Secretary of Agriculture Correspondence File, RG #16, NA; H. S. Johnson to F. D. Roosevelt, March 30, 1933, Peek Papers.

14. F. D. Roosevelt to H. S. Johnson, March 31, 1933, Roosevelt Papers, PPF 702.

15. H. S. Johnson to R. C. Moley, March 30, 1933, Moley Papers.

16. Johnson, *Blue Eagle*, pp. 191–92; Peek Diary, March 14–16, 20, and 27, and April 13, 1933, Peek Papers; Schwarz, *The Speculator*, pp. 282–85, 287–88. The quotation is from the Peek Diary, March 27.

17. Moley, *The First New Deal*, p. 283.

18. Ibid. Moley dates the encounter with Johnson on April 25. James P. Warburg, in a diary that is included in his reminiscences, indicates that Johnson was working on industrial recovery as early as April 4, 1933 (Reminiscences of James P. Warburg, pp. 369–70, COHC). Warburg was undoubtedly errant in preparing his diary. Others were at work on an industrial recovery bill during April, and evidence indicates that Johnson did not become aware of their efforts

until the end of April. To accept Warburg's dating is to accept the notion that Johnson could be at work on the bill for nearly a month without being aware of them.

19. Himmelberg, *Origins of the National Recovery Administration*, pp. 181–96.

20. Charles Frederick Roos, *NRA Economic Planning* (Bloomington, Ind.: Principia Press, 1937), 37.

21. Johnson, *Blue Eagle*, pp. 186–87.

22. Schwarz, *The Speculator*, pp. 79–88.

23. Reminiscences of Frances Perkins, vol. 5, pp. 50–51, 301, COHC.

24. Roos, *NRA Economic Planning*, p. 37.

25. Reminiscences of Frances Perkins, vol. 5, pp. 32–36, COHC.

26. Reminiscences of James P. Warburg, p. 618, COHC; Johnson, *Blue Eagle*, pp. 164, 196–200.

27. J. Joseph Huthmacher, *Senator Robert F. Wagner and the Rise of Urban Liberalism* (New York: Atheneum, 1968), 146–47; Himmelberg, *Origins of the National Recovery Administration*, pp. 196–205.

28. Moley, *After Seven Years*, p. 188; Himmelberg, *Origins of the National Recovery Administration*, pp. 217–18; Freidel, *Launching the New Deal*, pp. 423–24.

29. Johnson, *Blue Eagle*, p. 204; Moley, *After Seven Years*, pp. 188–89; Frances Perkins, *The Roosevelt I Knew* (New York: Viking Press, 1946), 198–99.

30. Reminiscences of Frances Perkins, vol. 5, p. 70, COHC.

31. Tugwell Diary, May 30, 1933, Tugwell Papers; Sternsher, *Rexford Tugwell and the New Deal*, p. 158.

32. Bernard Bellush, *The Failure of the NRA* (New York: W. W. Norton, 1975), 13–14; Huthmacher, *Senator Robert F. Wagner*, pp. 147–48.

33. Reminiscences of Jerome Frank, p. 28, COHC.

34. As Warburg summed it up, "I don't know how Douglas did it, but it was only common sense to get rid of it" (Reminiscences of James P. Warburg, pp. 369–70, 605, 768, COHC).

35. Reminiscences of Frances Perkins, vol. 5, pp. 18–22, 93, and 99, COHC.

36. Johnson, *Blue Eagle*, p. 185; Bellush, *The Failure of the NRA*, pp. 18–24; Ronald L. Feinman, *Twilight of Progressivism: The Western Republican Senators and the New Deal* (Baltimore: Johns Hopkins University Press, 1981), p. 63.

37. Bellush, *The Failure of the NRA*, pp. 25–29; Ellis W. Hawley, *The New Deal and the Problem of Monopoly: A Study in Economic Ambivalence* (Princeton, N.J.: Princeton University Press, 1966), 31–34; Albert U. Romasco, *The Politics of Recovery: Roosevelt's New Deal* (New York: Oxford University Press, 1983), 189–90.

38. *New York Times*, May 19, 1933.

39. Reminiscences of Frances Perkins, vol. 5, p. 74, COHC.

40. Schwarz, *The Speculator*, p. 270.

41. Reminiscences of Henry A. Wallace, p. 299, COHC; Larry G. Gerber, *The Limits of Liberalism: Josephus Daniels, Henry Stimson, Bernard Baruch, Donald Richberg, Felix Frankfurter and the Development of the Modern American Political Economy* (New York: New York University Press, 1983), 273–74; Tugwell, *Roosevelt's Revolution*, p. 118.

42. Johnson, *Blue Eagle*, pp. 114–15.

43. Ibid., p. 208.

44. *New York Times*, May 19, 1933.

45. Tugwell Diary, May 30, 1933, Tugwell Papers.

46. Reminiscences of Jerome Frank, pp. 28–29, COHC.

47. Bellush, *The Failure of the NRA*, p. 21.

48. Perkins, *The Roosevelt I Knew*, pp. 200–201.

49. Reminiscences of Frances Perkins, vol. 5, pp. 98–100, COHC; Schwarz, *The Speculator*, p. 289.

50. Reminiscences of Frances Perkins, vol. 5, pp. 50, 111, and 145–49, COHC.

51. A. Sachs to H. S. Johnson, June 10, 1933, in Roos, *NRA Economic Planning*, pp. 533–36.

52. D. C. Roper to F. D. Roosevelt, June 16, 1933, General Correspondence File, 1933–1937, RG #40, NA; Bellush, *The Failure of the NRA*, p. 34.

53. Saul Alinsky, *John L. Lewis: An Authorized Biography* (New York: Vintage Books, 1970), 66–67; Gerber, *The Limits of Liberalism*, p. 277; Johnson, *Blue Eagle*, pp. 205–6.

54. M. McIntyre to H. S. Johnson, May 27, 1933, and E. Hurja to M. McIntyre, June 3, 1933, Roosevelt Papers, OF 466; Harold L. Ickes, *The First Thousand Days, 1933–1936*, vol. 1 of *The Secret Diary of Harold L. Ickes* (New York: Simon and Schuster, 1953), 48.

55. Donald R. Richberg, *My Hero: The Indiscreet Memoirs of an Eventful but Unheroic Life* (New York: G. P. Putnam's Sons, 1954), 165–67; Thomas E. Vadney, *The Wayward Liberal: A Political Biography of Donald Richberg* (Lexington: University Press of Kentucky, 1970), 120–21; F. Frankfurter to A. E. Cohn, October 30, 1935, in *Roosevelt and Frankfurter: Their Correspondence, 1928–1945*, annotated by Max Freedman (Boston: Little, Brown and Company, 1967), 288–91.

56. Reminiscences of Frances Perkins, vol. 5, p. 357, COHC.

57. Reminiscences of Frances Perkins, vol. 5, 360–62, COHC; Kilbourne Johnston interview, August 28, 1965; Frances R. Newman interview, June 14, 1965.

58. Johnson, *Blue Eagle*, pp. 205, 213–19; Kilbourne Johnston interview, August 28, 1965.

59. A. Sachs to H. S. Johnson, May 20, 1933, in Roos, *NRA Economic Planning*, pp. 530–32.

60. Reminiscences of Jerome Frank, pp. 27–28, COHC.

61. Johnson, *Blue Eagle*, pp. 209–10; Ickes, *The First Thousand Days*, pp. 53–56; Perkins, *The Roosevelt I Knew*, pp. 201–3.

Chapter 7

1. Hawley, *The New Deal and Monopoly*, pp. 38–39, 69–70; Himmelberg, *Origins of the National Recovery Administration*, pp. 221–22.

2. Arthur M. Schlesinger, Jr., *The Coming of the New Deal*, vol. 2 of *The Age of Roosevelt* (Boston: Houghton Mifflin Company, 1958), 110; Theda Skocpol and Kenneth Finegold, "State Capacity and Economic Intervention in the Early New Deal," *Political Science Quarterly* 97 (Summer 1982): 265–67, 277–78.

3. Johnson, *Blue Eagle*, pp. 246–47.

4. Ibid., p. 235; Minutes of the Special Industrial Recovery Board, June 19, 1933, Series #39, RG #9, NA (hereafter cited as SIRB Minutes); *Wall Street Journal*, June 15, 1933.

5. Louis Galambos, *Competition and Cooperation: The Emergence of a National Trade Association* (Baltimore: John Hopkins University Press, 1966), 209–12.

6. Ibid., p. 212.

7. Bellush, *The Failure of the NRA*, p. 44.

8. Johnson, *Blue Eagle*, p. 233.

9. Galambos, *Competition and Cooperation*, p. 219.

10. J. Dickinson to M. H. McIntyre (with enclosed memorandum), June 23, 1933, Roosevelt Papers, OF 466.

11. Galambos, *Competition and Cooperation*, p. 220.

12. Ibid., pp. 221–22.

13. NRA Release #25, June 30, 1933, Marshall Coles Files, RG #9, NA.

14. F. Frankfurter to H. S. Johnson, July 6, 1933, Frankfurter Papers.

15. Galambos, *Competition and Cooperation*, p. 225.

16. William G. Robbins, "The Great Experiment in Industrial Self-Government: The Lumber Industry and the National Recovery Administration," *Journal of Forest History* 25 (July 1981): 128–43.

17. Johnson, *Blue Eagle*, pp. 207, 235.

18. David Brody, *Steelworkers in America: The Nonunion Era* (Cambridge: Harvard University Press, 1960).

19. Jesse Carroll Moody, Jr., "The Steel Industry and the National Recovery Administration: An Experiment in Industrial Self-Government" (Ph.D. diss., University of Oklahoma, 1965), pp. 108–22.

20. Cuff, *The War Industries Board*, pp. 125–28; Urofsky, *Big Steel and the Wilson Administration*, pp. 207–19. Also see John K. Ohl, "The Navy, the War Industries Board, and the Industrial Mobilization for War, 1917–1918," *Military Affairs* 40 (February 1976): 17–22.

21. Moody, "The Steel Industry and the National Recovery Administration," pp. 123–26.

22. Schlesinger, *Coming of the New Deal*, p. 117.

23. Moody, "The Steel Industry and the National Recovery Administration," pp. 128–29.

24. SIRB Minutes, August 21, 1933.

25. Donald R. Brand, "Corporatism, the NRA, and the Oil Industry," *Political Science Quarterly* 98 (Spring 1983): 106–12; Linda J. Lear, "Harold L. Ickes and the Oil Crisis of the First Hundred Days," *Mid-America* 63 (January 1981): 3–17; Norman E. Nordhauser, *The Quest for Stability: Domestic Oil Regulation, 1917–1935* (New York: Garland Publishing, 1979), 96–115.

26. Gerald D. Nash, *United States Oil Policy, 1890–1964: Business and Government in Twentieth-Century America* (Pittsburgh: University of Pittsburgh Press, 1968), 115–36; Brand, "Corporatism, the NRA, and the Oil Industry," pp. 113–14; Nordhauser, *The Quest for Stability*, pp. 117–19.

27. SIRB Minutes, July 31, 1933; Johnson, *Blue Eagle*, p. 245.

28. Nash, *Oil Policy*, p. 138.

29. Johnson, *Blue Eagle*, p. 246; Nordhauser, *The Quest for Stability*, pp. 122–24.

30. Johnson, *Blue Eagle*, p. 246.

31. Schlesinger, *Coming of the New Deal*, p. 116.

32. Johnson, *Blue Eagle*, p. 246; Nash, *Oil Policy*, pp. 138–39; Nordhauser, *The Quest for Stability*, pp. 124–28.

33. SIRB Minutes, June 26, 1933; Ickes, *The First Thousand Days*, pp. 72–73; Johnson, *Blue Eagle*, p. 235.

34. Nordhauser, *The Quest for Stability*, p. 129.

35. Sidney Fine, *The Automobile under the Blue Eagle: Labor, Management and the Automobile Manufacturing Code* (Ann Arbor: University of Michigan Press, 1963), 46–54.

36. Johnson, *Blue Eagle*, p. 236.

37. *New York Times*, July 28, 1933; *Detroit Times*, July 28, 1933.

38. Cuff, *The War Industries Board*, pp. 204–19; Schwarz, *The Speculator*, pp. 84–86.

39. Fine, *The Automobile under the Blue Eagle*, pp. 55–56.

40. Johnson, *Blue Eagle*, p. 238; Fine, *The Automobile under the Blue Eagle*, pp. 55–56.

41. Fine, *The Automobile under the Blue Eagle*, p. 57.

42. Ibid., p. 60.

43. Ibid., p. 68.

44. Ibid., pp. 69–71.

45. Bellush, *The Failure of the NRA*, p. 96.

46. F. Frankfurter to H. S. Johnson, September 7, 1933, Frankfurter Papers.

47. SIRB Minutes, October 9, 1933.

48. Johnson, *Blue Eagle*, p. 243.

49. Johnson Speech, June 16, 1933, Johnson Papers.

50. S. Early to F. Walker, August 1, 1933, Roosevelt Papers, OF 466.

51. SIRB Minutes, August 7, 1933; Johnson, *Blue Eagle*, p. 314.

52. *Philadelphia Record*, August 3, 1933.

53. James P. Johnson, "Drafting the NRA Code of Fair Competition for the Bituminous Coal Industry," *Journal of American History* 53 (December 1966): 530.

54. Roosevelt Press Conference, August 5, 1933, Roosevelt Papers.

55. SIRB Minutes, August 21, 1933.

56. Johnson, "NRA Code for the Coal Industry," p. 534.

57. L. Stark to F. D. Roosevelt, August 23, 1933, Roosevelt Papers, OF 175.

58. SIRB Minutes, August 21, 1933; Johnson, "NRA Code for the Coal Industry," p. 531.

59. *Washington Post*, September 9, 1933.

60. Johnson, "NRA Code for the Coal Industry," p. 536.

61. Ibid., pp. 536, 541.

62. Ibid., pp. 539–41; H. S. Johnson to F. D. Roosevelt, October 2, 1933, Roosevelt Papers, OF 175.

63. *Philadelphia Public Ledger*, October 4, 1933.

64. Melvyn Dubofsky and Warren Van Tine, *John L. Lewis: A Biography* (New York: Quadrangle, 1977), 194–96; Johnson, "NRA Code for the Coal Industry," p. 540.

65. Bellush, *The Failure of the NRA*, p. 48; Himmelberg, *Origins of the National Recovery Administration*, pp. 211–12, 222.

CHAPTER 8

1. *Boston Post*, August 25, 1933.

2. Johnson, *Blue Eagle*, pp. 250–51.

3. Gerber, *The Limits of Liberalism*, p. 282; Schwarz, *The Speculator*, p. 289; Goldthwaite Dorr, interview with Ralph F. de Bedts, New York City, August 2, 1966.

4. Roos, *NRA Economic Planning*, p. 88, n. 6.

5. Johnson, *Blue Eagle*, pp. 251–52.

6. Robert S. McElvaine, *The Great Depression: America, 1929–1941* (New York: Times Books, 1984), 160; Roos, *NRA Economic Planning*, pp. 88–89.

7. Bellush, *The Failure of the NRA*, p. 49.

8. Gerald D. Nash, "Experiments in Industrial Mobilization: WIB and NRA," *Mid-America* 45 (July 1963): 164, 173; William E. Leuchtenburg, "The New Deal and the Analogue of War," in *Change and Continuity in Twentieth-Century America*, ed. John Braeman, Robert H. Bremner, and Everett Walters (Columbus: Ohio State University Press, 1964), 121, n. 127.

9. *Washington Post*, July 29, 1933.

10. *Kansas City Times*, August 14, 1933.

11. Johnson, *Blue Eagle*, pp. 255–56.

12. Reminiscences of Henry A. Wallace, p. 246, COHC.

13. Johnson, *Blue Eagle*, p. 258.

14. SIRB Minutes, July 17, 1933; Johnson Reference File, Clapper Papers.

15. Tugwell Diary, July 16, 1933, Tugwell Papers.

16. Himmelberg, *Origins of the National Recovery Administration*, p. 210.

17. SIRB Minutes, July 18, 1933.

18. Ibid., July 17 and 18, 1933.

19. Ibid., July 19, 1933.

20. Schlesinger, *Coming of the New Deal*, p. 127.

21. Peek Diary, July 19, 1933, Peek Papers.

22. Johnson, *Blue Eagle*, p. 259.

23. Andrew Davis Wolvin, "The 1933 Blue Eagle Campaign: A Study in Persuasion and Coercion," (Ph.D. diss., Purdue University, 1968), pp. 8–10.

24. Schlesinger, *Coming of the New Deal*, p. 116; Elisha Hanson, "Official Propaganda and the New Deal," *Annals of the American Academy of Political and Social Science* 179 (May 1935): 182.

25. Johnson, *Blue Eagle*, p. 226.

26. Josephson, "The General—II," p. 27.

27. *Washington Daily News*, June 5, 1935.

28. Johnson Speech, July 25, 1933, Marshall Coles Files, RG #9, NA.

29. Johnson Speeches, August 23 and 29, 1933, Marshall Coles Files, RG #9, NA.

30. *New York Times*, September 5 and 13, 1933.

31. Johnson, *Blue Eagle*, p. 267.

32. Rosenman, ed., *Public Papers of Franklin D. Roosevelt*, 2:345.

33. *Brooklyn Eagle*, June 17, 1933.

34. *New York Times*, August 5, 1933; Matthew Josephson, "The General—III," *New Yorker*, September 1, 1934, p. 23.

35. *Washington Daily News*, October 11, 1933.

36. George Creel, *Rebel at Large* (New York: G. P. Putnam's Sons, 1947), 274.

37. Reminiscences of William H. Davis, pp. 40–42, COHC.

38. Ickes, *The First Thousand Days*, pp. 71–72.

39. Clapper Diary, July 13, 1933, Clapper Papers.

40. *New York Times*, August 15, 1933.

41. Ibid.

42. *Evening Star*, Washington, D.C., September 3, 1933.

43. *Washington Times*, September 26, 1933; Johnson, *Blue Eagle*, p. 244.

44. Clapper Diary, July 13, 1933, Clapper Papers.

45. Reminiscences of William H. Davis, p. 67, COHC.

46. Reminiscences of Frances Perkins, vol. 5, pp. 496–98, COHC.

47. Ibid.

48. Matthew Josephson, *Infidel in the Temple: A Memoir of the Nineteen-Thirties* (New York: Alfred A. Knopf, 1967), 273–75; *Charlotte Observer*, August 13, 1933; Johnson, *Blue Eagle*, p. 267; Reminiscences of William H. Davis, p. 67, COHC.

49. *Evening Star*, Washington, D.C., September 3, 1933.

50. *Washington Herald*, June 28, 1933; *Roanoke Times*, May 21, 1941.

51. Johnson Press Conference, April 2, 1934, Marshal Coles Files, RG #9, NA.

52. Clapper Diary, July 13, 1933, Clapper Papers.

53. Jonathan Mitchell, "The Versatility of General Johnson," *Harper's Magazine*, October 1934, pp. 588–90.

54. *Birmingham Post*, September 6, 1933; Reminiscences of Milton Handler, p. 15, COHC.

55. Johnson, *Blue Eagle*, pp. 305, 309–10.

56. Margaret A. Blanchard, "Freedom of the Press and the Newspaper Code: June 1933–February 1934," *Journalism Quarterly* 54 (Spring 1977): 40–49; Clapper Diary, August 6, 1933, Clapper Papers; Johnson, *Blue Eagle*, pp. 303–4; *New York Times*, April 21 and June 9, 1934; *Washington Post*, April 21, 1934.

57. *New York Times*, October 15, 1933.

58. *New York Times*, October 18, 1933; *New York Herald Tribune*, October 18, 1933.

59. H. S. Johnson to B. M. Baruch, January 3, 1930, Baruch Papers, GC; Clapper Diary, July 13, 1933, Clapper Papers.

60. Reminiscences of Frances Perkins, vol. 5, p. 506, COHC.

61. Clapper Diary, February 24, 1934, Clapper Papers.

62. *New York Herald Tribune*, November 4, 1933.

63. Reminiscences of Frances Perkins, vol. 5, p. 506, COHC.

64. Frances R. Newman interview, June 14, 1965.

65. Reminiscences of Frances Perkins, vol. 5, pp. 362–63, COHC.

66. *Rochester Democrat and Chronicle*, September 3, 1934.

67. *Philadelphia Record*, December 8, 1933.

68. Johnson Reference File, Clapper Papers.

69. Reminiscences of Frances Perkins, vol. 5, pp. 362–63, COHC.

70. "Mixed Doubles," *Time*, September 10, 1934, p. 6.

71. Johnson Reference File, Clapper Papers.

72. *New York Daily News*, September 7, 1934; Schlesinger, *Coming of the New Deal*, p. 153.

73. Raymond Moley, interview with Ralph F. de Bedts, New York City, July 16, 1965; Reminiscences of Henry A. Wallace, p. 298, COHC.

74. Reminiscences of Frances Perkins, vol. 5, pp. 362–63, COHC.

75. Clapper Diary, November 15, 1933, Clapper Papers.

76. George Martin, *Madam Secretary: Frances Perkins* (Boston: Houghton Mifflin Company, 1976), 329; Vadney, *The Wayward Liberal*, p. 137.

77. Kilbourne Johnston interview, August 28, 1965.

78. Reminiscences of Frances Perkins, vol. 5, pp. 366–67, 373–74, COHC; Kilbourne Johnston interview, August 28, 1965.

79. Reminiscences of Frances Perkins, vol. 5, p. 366, COHC.

80. Ibid., vol. 5, pp. 373–74; *Philadelphia Public Ledger*, August 10, 1933.

81. Martin, *Madam Secretary*, p. 329.

82. *Washington Herald*, February 2, 1934.

83. Johnson Press Conference, December 7, 1933, Marshall Coles File, RG #9, NA; Schlesinger, *Coming of the New Deal*, p. 153.

84. "Man of the Year," *Time*, January 1, 1934, pp. 8–9.

CHAPTER 9

1. Johnson, *Blue Eagle*, pp. 269, 366–67.

2. D. Cates to H. S. Johnson, August 2, 1933, Peek Papers.

3. D. Cates to H. S. Johnson, August 28, 1933 (two letters), and H. S. Johnson to D. Cates, August 28, 1933, all in Peek Papers.

4. *New York Times*, September 1, 1933.

5. Johnson, *Blue Eagle*, p. 248.

6. *Washington Herald*, September 2, 1933.

7. *Washington Herald*, August 28, 1933.

8. *Washington Post*, July 21, 1933.

9. Ickes, *The First Thousand Days*, p. 72.

10. *Philadelphia Record*, July 3, 1933.

11. *Buffalo News*, June 27, 1933; Johnson, *Blue Eagle*, pp. 368–69.

12. Reminiscences of Frances Perkins, vol. 5, p. 485, COHC.

13. Ickes, *The First Thousand Days*, p. 51.

14. William D. Reeves, "PWA and Competitive Administration in the New Deal," *Journal of American History* 60 (September 1973): 363–72.

15. H. S. Johnson to H. C. Ickes, August 27, 1936, Ickes Papers.

16. H. C. Ickes to H. S. Johnson, August 28, 1936, Ickes Papers.

17. Tugwell, *Roosevelt's Revolution*, p. 235.

18. Reminiscences of Frances Perkins, vol. 5, p. 485, COHC.

19. H. S. Johnson to F. D. Roosevelt, August 20, 1933 (not sent), Johnson Papers.

20. SIRB Minutes, November 27, 1933.

21. Johnson, *Blue Eagle*, p. 369.

22. Schlesinger, *Coming of the New Deal*, pp. 127–28; Tugwell, *Roosevelt's Revolution*, p. 235.

23. Bellush, *The Failure of the NRA*, p. 35.

24. *New York Times*, December 23, 1933; Hawley, *The New Deal and Monopoly*, pp. 72–73.

25. Shapsmeier and Shapsmeier, *Henry A. Wallace of Iowa*, p. 176.

26. SIRB Minutes, June 26, 1933; NRA Release #25, Marshall Coles Files, RG #9, NA; *Washington Daily News*, June 30, 1933.

27. Reminiscences of Henry Wallace, p. 301, COHC.

28. Reminiscences of Marvin Jones, pp. 696–97, COHC.

29. Russell Lord, *The Wallaces of Iowa* (Boston: Houghton Mifflin, 1947), 394.

30. G. N. Peek to H. S. Johnson, July 17, 1933, Peek Papers; SIRB Minutes, July 19, 1933.

31. Clapper Diary, July 19, 1933, Clapper Papers.

32. G. N. Peek to H. S. Johnson, July 20, 1933, Peek Papers.

33. G. N. Peek to H. S. Johnson, July 26 and 31, 1933, Peek Papers.

34. G. N. Peek to H. S. Johnson, August 5, 1933, Peek Papers.

35. H. S. Johnson to G. N. Peek, August 2 and 7, 1933, Peek Papers.

36. H. S. Johnson to F. D. Roosevelt, August 23, 1933, Roosevelt Papers, OF 1; S. Early to F. D. Roosevelt, August 23, 1933, Roosevelt Papers, OF 466.

37. Reminiscences of Jerome Frank, p. 31, COHC.

38. Reminiscences of Gardner Jackson, pp. 519–20, COHC.

39. H. A. Wallace to P. Y. Anderson, October 14, 1933, Secretary of Agriculture Correspondence File, RG #16, NA.

40. Josephson, "The General—III," p. 24.

41. Hawley, *The New Deal and Monopoly*, p. 74; Schlesinger, *Coming of the New Deal*, pp. 55–56.

42. H. S. Johnson to M. McIntyre, November 17, 1933, Roosevelt Papers, OF 466.

43. H. S. Johnson to D. R. Richberg, December 26, 1933, Consolidated Files, RG #9, NA.

44. H. A. Wallace to H. S. Johnson, January 26, 1934, and H. S. Johnson to H. A. Wallace, February 3, 1934, both in Secretary of Agriculture Correspondence File, RG #16, NA.

45. H. S. Johnson to R. G. Tugwell and H. S. Johnson to J. Frank, January 9, 1934, both in Secretary of Agriculture Correspondence File, RG #16, NA.

46. Ernest K. Lindley, *The Roosevelt Revolution* (New York: Viking Press, 1933), 256.

47. H. S. Johnson to D. C. Roper, September 22, 1933, Roosevelt Papers, OF 466.

48. Fine, *The Automobile under the Blue Eagle*, p. 80.

49. *New York Times*, October 28, 1933.

50. *New York Times*, September 14 and November 25, 1933.

51. Allan Nevins and Frank Ernest Hill, *Decline and Rebirth, 1933–1962*, vol. 3 of *Ford* (New York: Charles Scribner's Sons, 1963), 22–23; Fine, *The Automobile under the Blue Eagle*, p. 81.

52. Fine, *The Automobile under the Blue Eagle*, p. 82.

53. *New York Times*, July 1, 1934.

54. Fine, *The Automobile under the Blue Eagle*, p. 82.

55. Ibid., p. 93.

56. Leverett S. Lyon *et al.*, *The National Recovery Administration: An Analysis and Appraisal* (Washington: Brookings Institution, 1935), 830.

57. Mitchell, "The Versatility of General Johnson," pp. 586–88.

58. *Washington Post*, February 28, 1934.

59. *New York Times*, September 8 and 10, 1933; SIRB Minutes, August 4, 1933.

60. SIRB Minutes, August 21, 1933.

61. Bellush, *The Failure of the NRA*, p. 55.

62. *New York Times*, April 21, 1934.

63. Hawley, *The New Deal and Monopoly*, pp. 66–67; Schlesinger, *Coming of the New Deal*, pp. 120–21. For the discontent with NRA in one state, see Ronald L. Heinemann, "Blue Eagle or Black Buzzard? The National Recovery Administration in Virginia," *Virginia Magazine of History and Biography* 89 (January 1981): 90–100.

64. Hawley, *The New Deal and Monopoly*, p. 64.

65. Johnson Speech, November 23, 1933, Marshall Coles Files, RG #9, NA.

66. Bellush, *The Failure of the NRA*, p. 60.

67. Romasco, *The Politics of Recovery*, pp. 195–99; Schlesinger, *Coming of the New Deal*, p. 121; Skocpol and Finegold, "State Capacity and Economic Intervention," pp. 266–68.

68. *New York Times*, November 2 and 3, 1933.

69. Hawley, *The New Deal and Monopoly*, p. 79; M. Sullivan to B. M. Baruch, January 1, 1934, Baruch Papers, GC.

70. *New York Times*, November 3, 1933.

71. Johnson Speeches, November 7 and 10, 1933, Marshall Coles Files, RG #9, NA; *New York Herald Tribune*, November 9, 1933; *Omaha World Herald*, November 9, 1933.

72. Richard Lowett and Maurine Beasley, eds., *One Third a Nation: Lorena Hickok Reports on the Great Depression* (Urbana: University of Illinois Press, 1981), 78, 117–18; Bellush, *The Failure of the NRA*, pp. 60–61; Josephson, "The General—III," p. 23.

CHAPTER 10

1. *Baltimore Sun*, June 26, 1933.

2. Roos, *NRA Economic Planning*, p. 249; Schlesinger, *Coming of the New Deal*, p. 124.

3. NRA Release #28, July 3, 1933, Marshall Coles Files, RG #9, NA.

4. Roos, *NRA Economic Planning*, pp. 86–87.

5. Hawley, *The New Deal and Monopoly*, p. 63.

6. SIRB Minutes, August 14, 1933.

7. Schlesinger, *Coming of the New Deal*, pp. 122–23.

8. H. B. Swope to B. M. Baruch, August 11, 1933, Baruch Papers, GC.

9. Roos, *NRA Economic Planning*, p. 356; Schlesinger, *Coming of the New Deal*, p. 123.

10. NRA Release #281, August 10, 1933, Marshall Coles Files, RG #9, NA.

11. SIRB Minutes, October 16, 1933.

12. Hawley, *The New Deal and Monopoly*, p. 58; Roos, *NRA Economic Planning*, pp. 246–50.

13. Roos, *NRA Economic Planning*, p. 341.

14. Lyon, *The National Recovery Administration*, p. 761.

15. NRA Release #72a, July 20, 1933, Marshall Coles Files, RG #9, NA.

16. Tugwell Diary, April 23, 1934, Tugwell Papers; Tugwell, *Roosevelt's Revolution*, pp. 233–45.

17. Hawley, *The New Deal and Monopoly*, pp. 75–76; Reminiscences of Frances Perkins, vol. 5, p. 173, COHC.

18. Josephson, "The General—II," p. 25.

19. SIRB Minutes, August 14, 1933; *Washington Herald*, August 15, 1933; H. B. Swope to B. M. Baruch, August 15, 1933, Baruch Papers, GC.

20. Malcolm Ross, *Death of a Yale Man* (New York: Farrar and Rinehart, 1939), 111.

21. *Washington Daily News*, January 3, 1934.

22. Bellush, *The Failure of the NRA*, pp. 65–66; Hawley, *The New Deal and Monopoly*, pp. 76–77.

23. Johnson Press Conference, December 17, 1933, Marshall Coles Files, RG #9, NA.

24. Galambos, *Competition and Cooperation*, pp. 248–49; Hawley, *The New Deal and Monopoly*, pp. 77–80.

25. Bellush, *The Failure of the NRA*, pp. 69–70; Roos, *NRA Economic Planning*, pp. 280–81; Hawley, *The New Deal and Monopoly*, pp. 85–86.

26. A. Cash Koeniger, "Carter Glass and the National Recovery Administration," *South Atlantic Quarterly* 74 (Summer 1975): 349–64.

27. Johnson Speech, November 13, 1933, Marshall Coles Files, RG #9, NA.

28. Johnson, *Blue Eagle*, p. 274.

29. *New York Herald Tribune*, June 27, 1933.

30. Feinman, *Twilight of Progressivism*, pp. 69–70.

31. Johnson Speech, January 18, 1934, Marshall Coles Files, RG #9, NA.

32. Quoted by Roos, *NRA Economic Planning*, p. 376.

33. *Washington Post*, January 21 and 23, 1934.

34. *St. Louis Globe Democrat*, February 2, 1934.

35. Hawley, *The New Deal and Monopoly*, p. 82.

36. *Philadelphia Record*, February 21, 1934.

37. *Washington Post*, February 28, 1934.

38. Hawley, *The New Deal and Monopoly*, p. 92.

39. *New York Herald Tribune*, March 3, 1934.

40. Perkins, *The Roosevelt I Knew*, pp. 247–48.

41. Reminiscences of James M. Landis, p. 40, COHC.

42. Hawley, *The New Deal and Monopoly*, pp. 93–94, 360–61; Moody, "The Steel Industry and the National Recovery Administration," pp. 278–80.

43. H. S. Johnson to F. D. Roosevelt, December 13, 1933, Roosevelt Papers, OF 466.

44. Hawley, *The New Deal and Monopoly*, p. 82.

45. Stephen J. Sniegoski, "The National Recovery Review Board" (M.A. thesis, University of Maryland, 1972), pp. 21, 49; Kevin Tierney, *Darrow: A Biography* (New York: Thomas Y. Crowell, 1979), 428–29.

46. Lowell B. Mason, "Darrow vs. Johnson," *North American Review*, December 1934, p. 525.

47. National Recovery Review Board, *First Report to the President of the United States, Special and Supplementary Report to the President*, Roosevelt Papers, OF 466.

48. *New York Times*, May 12, 1934.

49. H. S. Johnson to F. D. Roosevelt, May 15, 1934, Roosevelt Papers, OF 466.

50. Johnson, *Blue Eagle*, pp. 272–73.

51. Sniegoski, "The National Recovery Review Board," pp. 37–48.

52. Ibid., p. 55; Irving Stone, *Clarence Darrow: For the Defense* (Garden City, N.Y.: Doubleday and Company, 1941), 510.

53. Schlesinger, *Coming of the New Deal*, p. 135; Sniegowski, "The National Recovery Review Board," p. 67; Hawley, *The New Deal and Monopoly*, pp. 96–97.

54. Leon Henderson, "N.R.A.," June 27, 1934, Roosevelt Papers, OF 466; Report to General Hugh S. Johnson, July 1934, Berle Papers.

55. Moody, "The Steel Industry and the National Recovery Administration," p. 296.

56. Johnson, *Blue Eagle*, p. 279.

57. Moody, in "The Steel Industry and the National Recovery Administration," quotes Johnson (pp. 297–98); Reminiscences of James M. Landis, p. 207, COHC; Memorandum concerning phone call from H. S. Johnson to F. D. Roosevelt, May 18, [1934], Roosevelt Papers, OF 466.

58. Moody, "The Steel Industry and the National Recovery Administration," pp. 298–300.

59. Tugwell, *Roosevelt's Revolution*, p. 242.

60. Hawley, *The New Deal and Monopoly*, p. 61; NRA Release #4152, March 31, 1934, Marshall Coles Files, RG #9, NA.

61. *New York Times*, May 28, 1934.

62. Hawley, *The New Deal and Monopoly*, pp. 97–98; Lindley, *The Roosevelt Revolution*, pp. 159–60.

63. Hawley, *The New Deal and Monopoly*, pp. 98–100.

64. *New York Herald Tribune*, June 9, 1934.

CHAPTER 11

1. Schlesinger, *Coming of the New Deal*, p. 136.

2. Reminiscences of Frances Perkins, vol. 5, p. 206, COHC; SIRB Minutes, August 14, 1933.

3. Quoted in Reminiscences of Frances Perkins, vol. 5, pp. 206–8, COHC.

4. Ibid., vol. 5, pp. 41–49; the quotation from Johnson is from Schlesinger, *Coming of the New Deal*, p. 145.

5. C. L. Sulzberger, *Sit Down with John L. Lewis* (New York: Random House, 1938), 68–69; Reminiscences of Frances Perkins, vol. 5, pp. 498 and 501–2, COHC; Johnson, *Blue Eagle*, p. 340; Dubofsky and Van Tine, p. 187.

6. Jerry M. Cooper, *The Army and Civil Disorder: Federal Military Intervention in Labor Disputes, 1877–1900* (Westport, Conn.: Greenwood Press, 1980), 250–51.

7. Kennedy, *Over Here*, pp. 265–68.

8. Johnson, *Blue Eagle*, p. 317; Huthmacher, *Senator Robert F. Wagner*, p. 163.

9. *Wall Street Journal*, June 15, 1933.

10. Johnson Press Conference, June 20, 1933, and Johnson Speech, June 25, 1933, both in Marshall Coles Files, RG #9, NA.

11. NRA Release #34, July 7, 1933, Marshall Coles Files, RG #9, NA; Johnson, *Blue Eagle*, pp. 344–45.

12. SIRB Minutes, August 14, 1933; Vadney, *The Wayward Liberal*, p. 130.

13. Statement Concerning Section 7a of National Industrial Recovery Act, August 23, 1933, Consolidated Files, RG #9, NA.

14. Vadney, *The Wayward Liberal*, p. 131.

15. Johnson, *Blue Eagle*, pp. 293, 343, and 423.

16. Ibid., p. 311.

17. Reminiscences of Frances Perkins, vol. 5, pp. 235–36, COHC.

18. Valerie Jean Conner, *The National War Labor Board: Stability, Social Justice, and the Voluntary State in World War I* (Chapel Hill: University of North Carolina Press, 1983), 181–82.

19. Johnson, *Blue Eagle*, pp. 208–9, 312.

20. Perkins, *The Roosevelt I Knew*, p. 237.

21. Thomas E. Blantz, *A Priest in Public Service: Francis J. Haas and the New Deal* (Notre Dame, Ind.: University of Notre Dame Press, 1982), 90–91.

22. *New York Times*, October 11, 1933.

23. *Philadelphia Public Ledger*, December 3, 1933.

24. NRA Release #2126, December 7, 1933, Marshall Coles Files, RG #9, NA.

25. *New York Times*, November 23, 1933.

26. F. D. Roosevelt to H. S. Johnson, October 19, 1933, Roosevelt Papers, OF 407. Johnson is quoted by Fine, *The Automobile under the Blue Eagle*.

27. Fine, *The Automobile under the Blue Eagle*, p. 186.

28. Bellush, *The Failure of the NRA*, pp. 100–102; Schlesinger, *The Coming of the New Deal*, pp. 148–49.

29. Schlesinger, *The Coming of the New Deal*, p. 149; Roos, *NRA Economic Planning*, pp. 212–13.

30. Fine, *The Automobile under the Blue Eagle*, pp. 193–202; *Philadelphia Record*, March 13, 1934.

31. NRA Release #3125, February 4, 1934, Marshall Coles Files, RG #9, NA.

32. Bellush, *The Failure of the NRA*, p. 103; Vadney, *The Wayward Liberal*, pp. 133–34.

33. *New York Times*, March 8, 1934.

34. *Philadelphia Record*, February 27, 1934.

35. Johnson, *Blue Eagle*, pp. 311–13.

36. *New York Times*, March 16, 1934.

37. Norman Beasley, *Knudsen: A Biography* (New York: Whittlesy House, 1947), 148.

38. *New York Times*, March 16, 1934.

39. Reminiscences of Leo Wolman, pp. 233–24, COHC.

40. Fine, *The Automobile under the Blue Eagle*, pp. 218–26, 235–36; Bellush, *The Failure of the NRA*, pp. 104–6; Nevins and Hill, *Decline and Rebirth, 1933–1962*, pp. 43–45.

41. Johnson Press Conference, May 8, 1934, Marshall Coles Files, RG #9, NA; Bellush, *The Failure of the NRA*, p. 138; Fine, *The Automobile under the Blue Eagle*, p. 229.

42. Dubofsky and Van Tine, *John L. Lewis*, pp. 198–99.

43. James P. Johnson, *The Politics of Soft Coal: The Bituminous Coal Indus-*

try from World War I through the New Deal (Urbana: University of Illinois Press, 1979), 182–93.

44. Bellush, *The Failure of the NRA*, pp. 44, 127–28; Galambos, *Competition and Cooperation*, pp. 259–60.

45. Galambos, *Competition and Cooperation*, p. 258.

46. James A. Hodges, "The New Deal Labor Policy and the Southern Cotton Textile Industry, 1933–1941," (Ph.D. diss., Vanderbilt University, 1963), pp. 242–43.

47. *New York Times*, June 2, 1934; Galambos, *Competition and Cooperation*, pp. 259–60.

48. *New York Times*, June 2, 1934; Johnson, *Blue Eagle*, pp. 315–17.

49. Galambos, *Competition and Cooperation*, p. 260.

50. Moody, "The Steel Industry and the National Recovery Administration," pp. 249–51.

51. Johnson Speech, June 8, 1934, Marshall Coles Files, RG #9, NA.

52. *New York Times*, June 7, 1934.

53. Moody, "The Steel Industry and the National Recovery Administration." pp. 252–54.

54. Johnson Speech, June 8, 1934, Marshall Coles Files, RG #9, NA.

55. Moody, "The Steel Industry and the National Recovery Administration." pp. 253–63.

56. Johnson, *Blue Eagle*, p. 320.

57. Bellush, *The Failure of the NRA*, pp. 108–9; Blantz, *A Priest in Public Service*, p. 99.

58. Perkins, *The Roosevelt I Knew*, pp. 239–42; Reminiscences of Frances Perkins, vol. 5, pp. 511–16, COHC.

59. *New York Times*, April 10, 1934.

60. *Philadelphia Record*, April 10, 1934.

61. *New York Times*, April 18, 1934.

62. Johnson Press Conference, May 25, 1934, Marshall Coles Files, RG #9, NA.

63. Fine, *The Automobile under the Blue Eagle*, pp. 229–30.

Chapter 12

1. *New York Herald Tribune*, April 4, 1934.

2. *New York Herald Tribune*, June 1, 1934; "Hugh Johnson: NRA Chief after Year's Gigantic Labor," *Newsweek*, June 23, 1934, p. 15.

3. *Washington Post*, February 21, 1934.

4. Ickes, *The First Thousand Days*, pp. 147–48.

5. Reminiscences of Frances Perkins, vol. 5, pp. 515–25, COHC.

6. H. B. Swope to B. M. Baruch, August 11, 1933, Baruch Papers, GC.

7. Richberg, *My Hero*, p. 173; Morgenthau Diaries, August 8, 1934, Morgenthau Papers.

8. H. S. Johnson to NRA Staff, March 26, 1934, General Correspondence File, RG #40, NA.

9. Richberg, *My Hero*, p. 173; *New York Times*, April 10 and 13, 1934.

10. Reminiscences of Frances Perkins, vol. 5, pp. 528–29, COHC.

11. Hawley, *The New Deal and Monopoly*, p. 97.

12. Reminiscences of Frances Perkins, vol. 7, p. 63, COHC.

13. Gerber, *The Limits of Liberalism*, pp. 285–89; Vadney, *The Wayward Liberal*, pp. 120–21, 137; Johnson, *Blue Eagle*, pp. 242–43, 371, 374.

14. David E. Lilienthal, *The TVA Years, 1939–1945, Including a Selection of Journal Entries from the 1917–1939 Period*, vol. 1 of *The Journals of David E. Lilienthal* (New York: Harper and Row, 1964), 42, 92; Schlesinger, *Coming of the New Deal*, p. 154; Vadney, pp. 138–39; Johnson, *Blue Eagle*, pp. 332–33.

15. Reminiscences of Frances Perkins, vol. 5, p. 482, COHC.

16. F. Perkins to F. D. Roosevelt, March 14, 1934, Roosevelt Papers, OF 15.

17. Reminiscences of Ernest Gross, p. 277, COHC; Gerber, *The Limits of Liberalism*, pp. 285, 287–88.

18. B. M. Baruch to H. S. Johnson, November 1 and 4, 1933, Baruch Papers, GC, and Baruch to Johnson, February 8, 1934, Baruch Papers, SC; Schwarz, *The Speculator*, pp. 290–92.

19. B. M. Baruch to H. S. Johnson, February 8, 1934, Baruch Papers, SC; and B. M. Baruch to H. S. Johnson, May 21, 1934, Baruch Papers, GC.

20. H. S. Johnson to B. M. Baruch, February 12, 1934, Baruch Papers, GC.

21. Reminiscences of Frances Perkins, vol. 5, pp. 108–13, 543–47, COHC.

22. *Washington Post*, September 28, 1934.

23. *New York Times*, May 3, 1934.

24. *New York Times*, May 5, 1934.

25. *New York Times*, May 9, 1934.

26. Lilienthal, *Journals*, 1:99.

27. *Washington Post*, September 28, 1934.

28. Josephson, *Infidel in the Temple*, p. 273; *New York Times*, June 1, 1934.

29. F. Perkins to F. D. Roosevelt, June 18, 1934, Roosevelt Papers, OF 466; see also Bellush, *The Failure of the NRA*, p. 153.

30. Richberg, *My Hero*, p. 174.

31. D. R. Richberg to F. D. Roosevelt, June 26, 1934, Richberg Papers.

32. Outline of Program, June 26, 1934, Richberg Papers.

33. Comments on Draft of Hugh Johnson Letter to FDR by B. M. Baruch, June 25, 1934, Baruch Papers, SC; H. S. Johnson to F. D. Roosevelt, June 26, 1934, Roosevelt Papers, OF 466; Johnson, *Blue Eagle*, p. 375.

34. Ickes, *The First Thousand Days*, p. 173.

35. Reminiscences of Frances Perkins, vol. 5, pp. 549–56, COHC. Johnson was so angered by the talk of his taking a vacation that he wrote Robert Straus that "I don't want anybody suggesting vacations for me. This has reached the proportions of a conspiracy and finally was suggested by the President today" (H. S. Johnson to R. Straus, June 26, 1934, quoted in Martin, *Madam Secretary*, p. 534, n. 23).

36. F. D. Roosevelt to H. S. Johnson, July 2, 1934, Baruch Papers, SC.

37. *New York Times*, July 11, 1934.

38. Tugwell Diary, June 26, 1934, Tugwell Papers.

39. M. McIntyre to F. D. Roosevelt, July 9, 1934, and H. S. Johnson to F. D. Roosevelt, July 9, 1934, both in Roosevelt Papers, OF 1332; Bellush, *The Failure of the NRA*, pp. 122–23.

40. Johnson, *Blue Eagle*, pp. 321–22.

41. Schlesinger, *Coming of the New Deal*, p. 393.

42. Mike Quin, *The Big Strike* (New York: International Publishers, 1979),

154–55; Irving Bernstein, *Turbulent Years: A History of the American Worker, 1933–1941* (Boston: Houghton Mifflin Company, 1970), 291–92; Johnson, *Blue Eagle*, p. 322.

43. David W. Mabon, "The West Coast Waterfront and Sympathy Strikes of 1934," (Ph.D. diss., University of California, Berkeley, 1966), pp. 160–61; Quin, *The Big Strike*, p. 154.

44. *New York Herald Tribune*, July 18, 1934.

45. Charles P. Larrowe, *Harry Bridges: The Rise and Fall of Radical Labor in the U.S.* (New York: Lawrence Hill and Co., 1972), 86; H. S. Johnson to F. D. Roosevelt, July 19, 1934, Roosevelt Papers, OF 466.

46. Mabon, "The West Coast Waterfront and Sympathy Strikes of 1934," pp. 161–62.

47. Bernstein, *Turbulent Years*, p. 292; Martin, *Madam Secretary*, p. 322.

48. Quin, *The Big Strike*, p. 175.

49. Johnson to Roosevelt, July 19, 1934, Roosevelt Papers, OF 466; Bernstein, *Turbulent Years*, pp. 292–93; Johnson, *Blue Eagle*, pp. 324–25; Mabon, "The West Coast Waterfront and Sympathy Strikes of 1934," pp. 162–80; *New York Times*, July 22, 1934.

50. *Washington Herald*, July 21, 1934; *New York Times*, July 22, 1934.

51. "Crack Down on the General!," *New Republic*, August 1, 1934, pp. 304–5; *New York Times*, July 22, 1934.

52. H. B. Swope to B. M. Baruch, July 25, 1934, Baruch Papers, GC.

53. Martin, *Madam Secretary*, pp. 317–20; Richberg, *My Hero*, p. 180.

54. *San Francisco Chronicle*, July 21, 1934.

55. Johnson, *Blue Eagle*, pp. 326–27, 382.

56. Morgenthau Diaries, August 10, 1934, Morgenthau Papers.

57. F. D. Roosevelt to G. P. Nye, June 26, 1934, Roosevelt Papers, OF 466; "Union under Johnson," *Time*, July 2, 1934, p. 8; "General Johnson: Strikebreaker," *Nation*, July 4, 1934, p. 4; *New York Herald Tribune*, July 8, 1934; Reminiscences of Gardner Jackson, pp. 524–25, COHC; Johnson, *Blue Eagle*, pp. 329–30; Bellush, *The Failure of the NRA*, pp. 113–14.

58. Johnson, *Blue Eagle*, p. 331.

59. William P. Mangold, "On the Labor Front," *New Republic*, September 5, 1934, pp. 103–4; Johnson, *Blue Eagle*, pp. 331–32.

60. Johnson, *Blue Eagle*, p. 329.

61. L. K. Garrison to H. S. Johnson, August 17, 1934; the quotations are from H. S. Johnson to L. K. Garrison, August 18, 1934, Perkins Papers.

62. *New York Times*, August 23, 1934.

Chapter 13

1. Berle, *Navigating the Rapids, 1918–1971*, ed. Berle and Beal, p. 102.

2. Reminiscences of Frances Perkins, vol. 5, p. 557, COHC.

3. D. R. Richberg to M. McIntyre, August 16 and 18, 1933, Richberg Papers.

4. Tugwell, *In Search of Roosevelt*, p. 300.

5. Moley, *The First New Deal*, p. 8.

6. Johnson, *Blue Eagle*, pp. 385–86; "NRA: With Code Phase Over, New Deal Shake Up Aims at Compliance, Cooperation, and Performance," *Business Week*, August 25, 1934, p. 34.

7. H. S. Johnson to B. M. Baruch, August 19, 1934, Baruch Papers, GC.

8. Martin, *Madam Secretary*, p. 336.

9. Ibid., p. 337.

10. Johnson, *Blue Eagle*, pp. 387–88; Richberg, *My Hero*, p. 175; Martin, *Madam Secretary*, pp. 337–38; "NRA: New Reorganization Starts as President Roosevelt Confers, Richberg Smiles, Johnson Growls, and Public Waits," *Newsweek*, September 1, 1934, pp. 3–4; Morgenthau Diaries, August 20, 1934, Morgenthau Papers.

11. Johnson, *Blue Eagle*, p. 389.

12. H. S. Johnson to F. D. Roosevelt, August 20, 1934, Johnson Papers.

13. Johnson, *Blue Eagle*, p. 390; F. D. Roosevelt to H. S. Johnson, August 20, 1934, Johnson Papers.

14. Johnson, *Blue Eagle*, p. 390.

15. Roosevelt Press Conference, August 24, 1934, Roosevelt Papers.

16. Johnson, *Blue Eagle*, pp. 390–91; Schlesinger, *Coming of the New Deal*, p. 156.

17. D. R. Richberg to M. McIntyre, September 5, 1934, with attached memorandum, September 4, 1934, Roosevelt Papers, OF 466.

18. R. G. Tugwell to F. D. Roosevelt, September 7, 1934, Roosevelt Papers, OF 466; Sternsher, *Rexford Tugwell and the New Deal*, p. 163.

19. H. S. Johnson to F. D. Roosevelt, September 9, 1934, Roosevelt Papers, OF 466.

20. Bellush, *The Failure of the NRA*, pp. 128–31; Galambos, *Competition and Cooperation*, pp. 260–63.

21. S. Early to M. McIntyre, September 13, 1934, Roosevelt Papers, OF 466.

22. Johnson, *Blue Eagle*, p. 320.

23. *New York Times*, September 15, 1934.

24. Bellush, *The Failure of the NRA*, p. 134; Hodges, "The New Deal Labor Policy and the Southern Cotton Textile Industry," p. 289.

25. Leonard Baker, *Brandeis and Frankfurter: A Dual Biography* (New York: Harper and Row, 1984), 299, 312–13; Nelson L. Dawson, *Louis D. Brandeis, Felix Frankfurter, and the New Deal* (Hamden, Conn.: Archon Books, 1980), 65–66; Bruce Allen Murphy, *The Brandeis/Frankfurter Connection: The Secret Political Activities of Two Supreme Court Justices* (New York: Oxford University Press, 1982), 143–47; Lewis J. Paper, *Brandeis* (Englewood Cliffs, N.J.: Prentice-Hall, 1983), 347–49.

26. Hodges, "The New Deal Labor Policy and the Southern Cotton Textile Industry," p. 289.

27. F. Frankfurter to F. D. Roosevelt, September 30, 1934, in *Roosevelt and Frankfurter*, annotated by Freedman, p. 233.

28. Johnson, *Blue Eagle*, p. 319; F. Frankfurter to A. E. Cohn, October 30, 1935, in *Roosevelt and Frankfurter*, annotated by Freedman, pp. 288–91.

29. D. R. Richberg to M. McIntyre, September 15, 1934, Roosevelt Papers, OF 466.

30. *Washington Post*, September 28, 1934.

31. Drew Pearson and Robert S. Allen, "How the President Works," *Harper's Magazine*, June 1936, pp. 6–7; Richberg, *My Hero*, p. 176; Reminiscences of Charles E. Wyzanski, p. 248, COHC.

32. Johnson, *Blue Eagle*, pp. 396–97.

33. *New York Times*, October 2, 1934.

34. B. M. Baruch to F. D. Roosevelt, October 8, 1934, Roosevelt Papers, PPF 88.

35. John T. Flynn, "Other People's Money," *New Republic*, September 12, 1934, pp. 129–30.

36. Ickes, *The First Thousand Days*, p. 197.

37. F. Kent to B. M. Baruch, October 1, 1934, Baruch Papers, GC.

38. *Philadelphia Record*, September 30, 1934.

39. "The Blessing of a Soldier," *Commonweal*, October 12, 1934, pp. 543–44.

40. Hawley, *The New Deal and Monopoly*, p. 139.

41. Ibid., p. 136; McElvaine, *The Great Depression: America, 1929–1941*, p. 161.

42. For an example of this kind of evaluation, see Bellush, *The Failure of the NRA*.

43. Ellis W. Hawley, "Hugh Samuel Johnson," *Encyclopedia of American Biography*, ed. John A. Garraty (New York: Harper and Row, 1974), 589–90.

Chapter 14

1. *New York Times*, September 28, 1934; *Baltimore Sun*, November 27, 1934.

2. *New York Herald Tribune*, October 12, 1934; *Washington Times*, October 14 and 15, 1934; *Wall Street Journal*, September 30, 1934; "Johnson Hangs Shingle," *Business Week*, October 20, 1934, p. 1.

3. *Washington Post*, January 17, 1935.

4. *Washington Herald*, October 4, 1934; *Baltimore Sun*, March 3, 1935.

5. Jules Archer, *The Plot to Seize the White House* (New York: Hawthorne Books, 1973), lx–x, 24–25, 127, 156–57, 170, 177, 184, and 186–87. Also see Anthony C. Sutton, *Wall Street and FDR* (New Rochelle, N.Y.: Arlington House Publishers, 1975), 143–60; Geoffrey Smith, *To Save a Nation: American Counter-Subversives, the New Deal, and the Coming of World War II* (New York: Basic Books, 1973), 68; and *New York Times*, November 21, 1934.

6. Roosevelt Press Conference, December 12, 1934, Roosevelt Papers; F. M. Robinson to M. Boyle, May 16, 1935, and B. M. Baruch to R. E. Wagner, April 4, 1935, Baruch Papers, GC; Schwarz, *The Speculator*, pp. 338–39.

7. Baruch, *The Public Years*, pp. 249–51; *Baltimore Sun*, December 16 and 25, 1934.

8. Roosevelt Press Conference, March 6, 1935, Roosevelt Papers; *New York Times*, January 27, 1935; *Washington Daily News*, April 17, 1935.

9. *New York Times*, December 11, 1934.

10. H. S. Johnson to D. R. Richberg, December 21, 1934, and January 7, 1935, and D. R. Richberg to H. S. Johnson, December 23, 1934, all in Richberg Papers; Vadney, *The Wayward Liberal*, pp. 155–56.

11. S. Early to D. R. Richberg, January 1, 1935, Richberg Papers; F. Kent to B. M. Baruch, February 14, 1935, Baruch Papers, GC; *Philadelphia Record*, January 15, 1935.

12. John T. Flynn, "Other People's Money," *New Republic*, April 3, 1935, p. 212.

13. Frances R. Newman, interview June 14, 1965; *New York Times*, March 9, 1935.

14. Alan Brinkley, *Voices of Protest: Huey Long, Father Coughlin and the Great Depression* (New York: Alfred A. Knopf, 1982), 8–168.

15. Charles J. Tull, *Father Coughlin and the New Deal* (Syracuse, N.Y.: Syracuse University Press, 1965), 82–83, 91–92; Arthur M. Schlesinger, Jr., *The Politics of Upheaval*, vol. 3 of *The Age of Roosevelt* (Boston: Houghton Mifflin Company, 1966), 9–10, 242–44.

16. Brinkley, *Voices of Protest*, p. 291, n. 6; E. Balmer to L. Howe, February 20, 1935, Roosevelt Papers, OF 1332.

17. "Demagogues," *Newsweek*, March 16, 1935, p. 5.

18. B. M. Baruch to L. Colcord, n.d., Baruch Papers, GC.

19. Hugh S. Johnson, "Pied Papers," *Vital Speeches*, March 11, 1935, pp. 354–60.

20. Samples of letters and telegrams commenting on Johnson's speech can be found in the Roosevelt Papers, OF 1332. Also see *New York Times*, March 6, 1935.

21. Smith, *To Save a Nation*, p. 32; Tull, *Father Coughlin and the New Deal*, pp. 83–84; *New York Times*, March 6, 1935; Walter Lippman, *Interpretations, 1933–1935* (New York: Macmillan, 1936), 272–74.

22. Brinkley, *Voices of Protest*, p. 291, n. 7.

23. *Detroit News*, March 6, 1935.

24. Schlesinger, *Politics of Upheaval*, p. 9.

25. Ibid., p. 248; Brinkley, *Voices of Protest*, pp. 7, 209–15, and 245; Smith, *To Save a Nation*, pp. 33–34; Tull, *Father Coughlin and the New Deal*, pp. 86–87.

26. James T. Patterson, *Congressional Conservatism and the New Deal: The Growth of the Conservative Coalition in Congress, 1933–1939* (Lexington: University Press of Kentucky, 1967), 22–23.

27. *Evening Star*, Washington, D.C., March 24 and 29, 1935; *Baltimore Sun*, March 24, 1935.

28. *Baltimore Sun*, May 7, 1935.

29. *Baltimore Sun*, December 10, 1934; H. S. Johnson to M. LeHand, December 1, 1934, Roosevelt Papers, OF 1332; *Washington Post*, February 10, 1935.

30. *New York Times*, February 21, 1935; Schlesinger, *Politics of Upheaval*, pp. 276–77.

31. Martha H. Swain, *Pat Harrison: The New Deal Years* (Jackson: University of Mississippi Press, 1978), 92–93.

32. Senate Committee on Finance, *Investigation of the National Recovery Administration, Hearings*, 74th Cong., 1st sess., 1935, pp. 2404–506.

33. *New York Herald Tribune*, May 28, 1935; *Washington Post*, May 28, 1935.

34. *Philadelphia Record*, May 30, 1935.

35. F. Frankfurter to A. E. Cohn, October 30, 1935, in *Roosevelt and Frankfurter*, annotated by Freedman, pp. 288–91.

36. Moley, *After Seven Years*, p. 307; Roosevelt Press Conference, May 31, 1935, Roosevelt Papers; Schlesinger, *Politics of Upheaval*, pp. 287–90.

37. *Washington Post*, June 5, 1935; Johnson Speech, June 10, 1935, Baruch Papers, GC; H. S. Johnson to F. D. Roosevelt, April 13, 1937, Roosevelt Papers, PPF 702.

38. H. S. Johnson to F. D. Roosevelt, April 30, 1935, Roosevelt Papers, OF 1332.

39. H. S. Johnson to F. D. Roosevelt, May 21, 1935, and June 9, 1935, PPF 702; Roosevelt Press Conference, June 12, 1935, Roosevelt Papers, PC.

40. *New York Herald Tribune*, December 23, 1933; *Washington Herald*, December 23, 1933; H. S. Johnson to H. L. Hopkins, October 26, 1935, Hopkins Papers, p. 10. The Johnson communication constitutes Johnson's final report on his activities as WPA director for New York City and is hereafter cited as the Johnson Report.

41. Barbara Marilyn Blumberg, "The Works Progress Administration in New York City: A Case Study of the New Deal in Action" (Ph.D. diss., Columbia University, 1974), pp. 67–70; Searle F. Charles, *Minister of Relief: Harry Hopkins and the Depression* (Syracuse, N.Y.: Syracuse University Press, 1963), 154.

42. *Washington Post*, June 26, 1935; Johnson Speech, October 12, 1935, Hopkins Papers.

43. *New York Times*, July 6, 1935.

44. K [?] to M. McIntyre, July 30, 1935, Roosevelt Papers, OF 1332.

45. H. S. Johnson to F. D. Roosevelt, n.d., Roosevelt Papers, PPF 702.

46. Johnson Speech, October 12, 1935, Hopkins Papers.

47. H. S. Johnson to H. L. Hopkins, July 18, 1935, and H. L. Hopkins to H. S. Johnson, July 20, 1935, both in Hopkins Papers; Johnson Report, pp. 6–10; *New York Times*, July 31 and August 1, 1935.

48. Johnson Report, p. 3.

49. Ibid.; John D. Millett, *The Works Progress Administration in New York City* (Chicago: Public Administration Services, 1938), 34–35; Blumberg, "The Works Progress Administration in New York City," pp. 106–9.

50. Johnson Report, p. 4.

51. H. S. Johnson to W. H. Lange, August 29, 1935; Johnson Report, pp. 21–23.

52. Millett, *WPA in New York City*, p. 37.

53. Joseph C. Goulden, *Meany* (New York: Atheneum, 1972), 52–53.

54. Johnson Report, p. 11.

55. *New York Times*, July 3, 1935.

56. Goulden, *Meany*, pp. 52–53; Blumberg, "The Works Progress Administration in New York City," pp. 90–95; George Meany, interview with Ralph F. de Bedts, New York City, December 20, 1966.

57. Johnson Report, p. 11.

58. *New York Times*, August 6 and 8, 1935.

59. Goulden, *Meany*, pp. 55–56; *New York Times*, August 9, 1935.

60. *New York Times*, August 10, 1935; Johnson Report, p. 11.

61. Goulden, *Meany*, p. 58.

62. Ibid., p. 59; Millett, *WPA in New York City*, p. 43.

63. *New York Times*, September 21, 1935; Millett, *WPA in New York City*, p. 44; Johnson Report, p. 12.

64. Millett, *WPA in New York City*, pp. 39–40.

65. Ibid., p. 40.

66. Robert A. Caro, *The Power Broker: Robert Moses and the Fall of New York* (New York: Alfred A. Knopf, 1974), 501.

67. Johnson Report, pp. 25–27; *New York Times*, September 15–18, 1935.

68. H. S. Johnson to H. L. Hopkins, September 4 and 18, 1935, Hopkins Papers.

69. H. S. Johnson to F. D. Roosevelt, September 13, 1935, Roosevelt Papers, PPF 702.

70. *New York Times*, April 11, 1936, and March 23, 1938; *New York World-Telegram*, June 9, 1938.

71. Millett, *WPA in New York City*, p. 45; Blumberg, "The Works Progress Administration in New York City," pp. 110–12.

72. *New York World-Telegram*, September 22, 1935.

73. *New York World-Telegram*, October 29, 1935.

74. *New York Times*, May 7, 1935.

75. *New York Times*, October 29, 1935; *New York World-Telegram*, May 18, 1935.

76. *New York World-Telegram*, November 23, 1935; *New York Times*, September 23, 1935; *Washington Herald*, January 7, 1936.

77. H. S. Johnson to F. D. Roosevelt, September 27, 1935, Roosevelt Papers, PPF 702.

78. H. S. Johnson to M. LeHand, January 6, 1936, Roosevelt Papers, OF 1332.

CHAPTER 15

1. "Columnist to Columnist," *Time*, September 28, 1936, pp. 56–58; F. Kent to B. M. Baruch, March 22, 1935, Baruch Papers, GC.

2. Oliver Pilat, *Pegler: Angry Man of the Press* (Boston: Beacon Press, 1963), 139.

3. H. S. Johnson to M. Boyle, December 26, 1935, and F. M. Robinson to M. Boyle, June 12, 1936, both in Baruch Papers, GC.

4. Bernstein, *Turbulent Years*, pp. 608–10; *New York American*, March 12, 1937; Reminiscences of James B. Carey, pp. 40, 111–12, and Reminiscences of Julius Emspak, pp. 128–29, 133, both in COHC.

5. H. S. Johnson to M. Boyle, December 26, 1935, and December 20, 1939, both in Baruch Papers, GC; Kilbourne Johnston interview, August 28, 1965; Frances R. Newman interview, June 14, 1965.

6. *New York World-Telegram*, January 25, February 6 and 20, and September 11, 1936; H. S. Johnson to F. D. Roosevelt, April 29 and May 5, 1936, both in Roosevelt Papers, OF 1332.

7. G. N. Peek to H. S. Johnson, August 27, 1936, Peek Papers.

8. Johnson Speech, September 30, 1936, Peek Papers.

9. Harold L. Ickes, *The Inside Struggle, 1936–39*, vol. 2 of *The Secret Diary of Harold L. Ickes* (New York: Simon and Schuster, 1954), 7.

10. *New York World Telegram*, February 6, 1937; *New York Times*, February 8, 1937; F. D. Roosevelt to H. S. Johnson, February 9, 1937, in *F. D. R., His Personal Letters, 1928–1945*, ed. Elliott Roosevelt, 2 vols. (New York: Duell, Sloan and Pearce, 1950), 2:658.

11. Ickes, *The Inside Struggle*, pp. 168–69; Moley, *27 Masters of Politics*, p. 173.

12. *New York World-Telegram*, May 17, 1937.

13. *New York Times*, September 17, 1937.

14. H. S. Johnson to F. D. Roosevelt, February 9, 1937, F. D. Roosevelt to H. S. Johnson, February 16, 1937, H. J. Morgenthau, Jr., to H. S. Johnson, May 26,

1937, all in Roosevelt Papers, OF 401; S. A. Rice to M. McIntyre, August 28, 1937, Roosevelt Papers, OF 1332; Roosevelt Press Conference, November 17, 1936, Roosevelt Papers; Ickes, *The Inside Struggle*, p. 73.

15. H. S. Johnson, "The Third New Deal," *Vital Speeches*, July 1, 1937, pp. 564–67.

16. "Personnel," *Time*, May 17, 1937, p. 88; *New York World-Telegram*, January 29, 1937.

17. "Headache Man," *Time*, October 4, 1937, p. 32.

18. Fon W. Boardman, Jr., "Political Name Calling," *American Speech* 15 (December 1940): 353–56.

19. Ickes, *The Inside Struggle*, pp. 470, 474–75; Schwarz, *The Speculator*, p. 331; Roosevelt Press Conference, June 7, 1940, Roosevelt Papers.

20. *New York World-Telegram*, March 18, 1936.

21. *New York Times*, April 25, 1939.

22. *New York World-Telegram*, July 28, 1935, September 1 and December 30, 1936, and October 9, 1937; Senate Committee on Foreign Relations, *Neutrality, Peace Legislation, and Our Foreign Policy, Hearings*, 76th Cong., 1st sess., 1939, pp. 280–81.

23. Manfred Jonas, *Isolationism in America, 1935–1941* (Ithaca, N.Y.: Cornell University Press, 1966), 100–135.

24. *New York World-Telegram*, July 30, 1935, and September 28, 1940; Hugh S. Johnson, "Could Hitler Invade America?," *Reader's Digest*, December 1939, pp. 34–36.

25. *New York World-Telegram*, September 28 and October 25, 1940; Hugh S. Johnson, "Is Britain Fighting Our War?," in *We Testify*, ed. Nancy Schoonmaker and Doris F. Reid (New York: Smith and Durrell, 1941), pp. 94, 99–100; Hugh S. Johnson, *Hell-Bent for War* (Indianapolis: Bobbs-Merrill, 1941), 49; Johnson, "Could Hitler Invade America?," p. 34.

26. *New York World-Telegram*, January 7, 1939, February 3, July 6, and December 13, 1939; *New York Times*, September 28, 1939. The quotation is from the December 13 *World-Telegram*.

27. *New York Times*, February 23, 1938, and January 29, 1940; *New York World-Telegram*, February 21 and September 4, 1940. The quotation is from the January *Times*.

28. *New York Times*, November 22, 1939; *New York World-Telegram*, November 24, 1939; Ellsworth Barnard, *Wendell Willkie: Fighter for Freedom* (Marquette: Northern Michigan University Press, 1966), 148–49, 154; Herbert S. Parmet and Marie B. Hecht, *Never Again: A President Runs for a Third Term* (New York: Macmillan, 1968), 70–72.

29. *New York Times*, April 7, 1940.

30. Hugh S. Johnson, "I Am Not Nominating Him," *Saturday Evening Post*, June 22, 1940, pp. 9, 112–16.

31. C. Nelson Sparks, *One Man—Wendell Willkie* (New York: Rayner Publishing, 1943), 8–9.

32. *New York World-Telegram*, July 20, 1940.

33. H. S. Johnson to G. N. Peek, July 29, 1940, Peek Papers.

34. *New York Times*, August 13, 1940.

35. Field, *Bernand Baruch*, pp. 91–92; Hugh S. Johnson, "Anchors Away," *Saturday Evening Post*, October 15, 1940, pp. 14–15, 75; *New York World-*

Telegram, August 17, August 23, September 5, October 9, and October 21, 1940; *New York Times*, October 16 and November 1, 1940; B. M. Baruch to H. L. Ickes, October 3, 1940, Baruch Papers, GC.

36. Jonas, *Isolationism in America*, pp. 253–56.

37. *New York Times*, October 20, 1940; *New York World-Telegram*, November 2 and 4, 1940.

38. H. S. Johnson to F. D. Roosevelt, November 6, 1940, Roosevelt Papers, PPF 702.

39. H. S. Johnson to R. W. Howard, February 20, 1941, Baruch Papers, SC; "Moving Day for Columnists," *Time*, March 17, 1941, pp. 38–39.

40. H. S. Johnson to G. C. Marshall, March 28, 1941, Johnson Papers.

41. H. S. Johnson to F. D. Roosevelt, April 16, 1941, Roosevelt Papers, OF 1332.

42. W. H. Haislap to G. C. Marshall, April 19, 1941, Roosevelt Papers, OF 1332.

43. E. M. Watson to H. S. Johnson, April 28, 1941, Johnson Papers.

44. H. S. Johnson to E. M. Watson, April 29, 1941, Johnson Papers.

45. Johnson Press Release, April 30, 1941, Johnson Papers; *New York World-Telegram*, May 2, 1941.

46. *New York Times*, May 4, 1941; James Roosevelt, *My Parents: A Differing View* (Chicago: Playboy Press, 1976), 240–41; "The General Is Retired," *Time*, May 12, 1941, p. 14.

47. F. M. Robinson to J. Byrnes, January 28, 1942, and H. S. Johnson to S. Early, May 2, 1941, both in Johnson Papers.

48. F. M. Robinson to M. Boyle, November 27, 1941, Baruch Papers, GC.

49. F. D. Roosevelt to H. S. Johnson, December 24, 1941, and H. S. Johnson to F. D. Roosevelt, December 26, 1941, both in Roosevelt Papers, PPF 702; Kilbourne Johnston interview August 28, 1965.

50. *New York World-Telegram*, January 14, 1942.

51. *New York Times*, April 16, 1942; Death Certificate for Hugh Samuel Johnson, District of Columbia Health Department, Bureau of Vital Statistics.

52. *New York Times*, April 16, 1942; *Chicago Daily News*, April 16, 1942; B. M. Baruch to J. J. Pershing, April 20, 1942, Baruch Papers, GC.

BIBLIOGRAPHY

ARCHIVAL SOURCES

National Archives. Collection of Personal Papers. Record Group 200.

National Archives. Records of the Department of Agriculture. Record Group 16.

National Archives. Records of the Department of Commerce. Record Group 40.

National Archives. Records of the National Recovery Administration. Record Group 9.

National Archives. Records of the Office of the Adjutant General. Record Group 94.

National Archives. Records of the Office of the Chief of Staff. Record Group 165.

National Headquarters of the Selective Service System. Reference Library Files.

Washington National Records Center. Records of the Office of the Chief of Ordnance. Record Group 156.

Washington National Records Center. Records of the Office of the Provost Marshal. Record Group 163.

Washington National Records Center. Records of the Office of the Quartermaster General. Record Group 92.

Washington National Records Center. Records of the War Industries Board. Record Group 61.

MISCELLANEOUS RECORDS

District of Columbia. Health Department, Bureau of Vital Statistics. Death Certificate for Hugh Samuel Johnson.

Northwestern Oklahoma State University. Office of the Registrar. Record of Hugh M. [sic] Johnson.

United States Military Academy Library and Archives. Academic Record of Hugh Samuel Johnson, USMA 1903.

PAPERS OF PUBLIC PERSONS

Baker, Newton D. Library of Congress.
Baruch, Bernard M. Princeton University Library. Princeton, N.J.
Berle, Adolf. Franklin D. Roosevelt Library.
Clapper, Raymond. Library of Congress.
Crowder, Enoch H. Joint Collection, University of Missouri Western Historical Manuscript Collection and State Historical Society of Missouri Manuscripts. Columbia, Missouri.
Frankfurter, Felix. Library of Congress.
Goethals, George W. Library of Congress.
Harbord, James G. Library of Congress.
Hopkins, Harry L. Franklin D. Roosevelt Library.
Ickes, Harold L. Library of Congress.
Johnson, Hugh S. In possession of author.
March, Peyton C. Library of Congress.
Mills, Ogden L., Jr. Library of Congress.
Moley, Raymond C. Hoover Institution on War, Revolution and Peace. Stanford, Calif.
Morgenthau, Henry, Jr. Franklin D. Roosevelt Library.
Peek, George N. Joint Collection, University of Missouri Western Historical Manuscript Collection and State Historical Society of Missouri Manuscripts. Columbia, Missouri.
Perkins, Frances. Rare Book and Manuscript Library, Columbia University.
Pershing, John J. Library of Congress.
Richberg, Donald R. Library of Congress.
Roosevelt, Franklin D. Franklin D. Roosevelt Library.
Tugwell, Rexford G. Franklin D. Roosevelt Library.

INTERVIEWS, REMINISCENCES, AND STATEMENTS

Brown, Alvin. Interview with Ralph F. de Bedts. Washington, D.C., June 21, 1965.
Carey, James B. Reminiscences. COHC.
Davis, Chester C. Reminiscences. COHC.
Davis, William H. Reminiscences. COHC.
Dorr, Goldthwaite. Interview with Ralph F. de Bedts. New York City, N.Y., August 2, 1966.
Emspak, Julius. Reminiscences. COHC.
Epstein, Harold. Interview with Ralph F. de Bedts. New York City, N.Y., July 15, 1965.
Frank, Jerome N. Reminiscences. COHC.
Gross, Ernest. Reminiscences. COHC.
Handler, Milton. Reminiscences. COHC.

Jackson, Gardner. Reminiscences. COHC.

Johnson, General Hugh S. Statement. Baruch Papers.

Johnston, Kilbourne. Interview with Ralph F. de Bedts. Hamilton, Ohio, August 28, 1965.

Jones, Marvin. Reminiscences. COHC.

Landis, James M. Reminiscences. COHC.

Meany, George. Interview with Ralph F. de Bedts. New York City, N.Y., December 20, 1966.

Meyer, Eugene, Jr. Reminiscences. COHC.

Moley, Raymond C. Interview with Ralph F. de Bedts. New York City, N.Y., July 16, 1965.

Newman, Frances R. Interview with Ralph F. de Bedts. Winter Park, Fla., June 14, 1965.

Peek, George N. Statement. Baruch Papers.

Perkins, Frances. Reminiscences. COHC.

Pierce, General Palmer E. Statement. Baruch Papers.

Swope, Gerard. Reminiscences. COHC.

Wallace, Henry A. Reminiscences. COHC.

Warburg, James P. Reminiscences. COCC.

Wilson, M. L. Reminiscences. COHC.

Wolman, Leo. Reminiscences. COHC.

Wyzanski, Charles E. Reminiscences. COHC.

LECTURES BY HUGH S. JOHNSON

"Draft Problems." Delivered at the Army War College, December 22, 1924. U.S. Army Military History Research Collection, Carlisle Barracks, Penn.

"Feasible Peacetime Approaches to Industrial Mobilization." Lecture delivered at the Army Industrial College, February 2, 1940. Library of the Industrial College of the Armed Forces, Washington, D.C.

"Industrial and Man-Power Mobilization." Lecture delivered at the Army War College, December 1922. Baruch Papers.

"Selective Service." Lecture delivered at the Army War College, October 20, 1939. U.S. Army Military History Research Collection, Carlisle Barracks, Penn.

PUBLIC DOCUMENTS

Report of the Provost Marshal General, 1917. Washington, D.C.: Government Printing Office, 1918.

Second Report of the Provost Marshal General, 1918. Washington, D.C.: Government Printing Office, 1919.

U.S. Congress. House. Committee on Military Affairs. *Selective Service Act, Hearings.* 65th Cong., 1st sess., 1918.

U.S. Congress. House. Committee on Military Affairs. *Taking the Profits out of War. Hearings.* 74th Cong., 1st sess., 1935.

U.S. Congress. Senate. Committee on Finance. *Investigation of the National Recovery Administration. Hearings.* 74th Cong., 1st sess., 1935.

U.S. Congress. Senate. Committee on Foreign Relations. *Neutrality, Peace Legislation, and Our Foreign Policy. Hearings.* 76th Cong., 1st sess., 1939.

U.S. Congress. Senate. Committee on Military Affairs. *To Prevent Profiteering in Time of War. Hearings.* 75th Cong., 1st sess., 1937.

U.S. Congress. Senate. Special Committee to Investigate the Munitions Industry. *Final Report of the Chairman of the United States War Industries Board to the President of the United States, February, 1919.* Senate Committee Print 3, 74th Cong., 1st sess., 1935.

U.S. Congress. Senate. Special Committee to Investigate the Munitions Industry. *Minutes of the War Industries Board from August 1, 1917, to December 19, 1918.* Senate Committee Print 4, 74th Cong., 1st sess., 1935.

U.S. Congress. Senate Special Committee to Investigate the Munitions Industry. *Munitions Industry. Hearings.* 74th Cong., 1st sess., 1935.

War Department Annual Reports, 1919.

NEWSPAPERS

Baltimore Sun, 1933–1935.
Birmingham Post, 1933–1934.
Boston Post, 1933.
Brooklyn Eagle, 1933.
Buffalo News, 1933.
Charlotte (N.C.) *Observer,* 1933.
Chicago Daily News, 1942.
Detroit News, 1935.
Detroit Times, 1933.
Evening Star (Washington, D.C.), 1918–1935
Kansas City (Mo.) *Times,* 1933.
Moline (Ill.) *Dispatch,* 1951.
New York American, 1917–1937.
New York Herald Tribune, 1933–1935.
New York Times, 1917–1942.
New York World-Telegram, 1935–1942.
Omaha World Herald, 1933.
Philadelphia Public Ledger, 1933.
Philadelphia Record, 1933–1935.
Roanoke Times, 1941.
Rochester (N.Y.) *Democrat and Chronicle,* 1934.

St. Louis Globe Democrat, 1934.
San Francisco Chronicle, 1934.
Wall Street Journal, 1933–1934.
Washington Daily News, 1933–1935.
Washington Herald, 1933–1936.
Washington Post, 1933–1942.
Washington Times, 1934.

BOOKS

Abrahamson, James L. *America Arms for a New Century: The Making of a Great Military Power.* New York: Free Press, 1981.

Alinsky, Saul. *John L. Lewis: An Authorized Biography.* New York: Vintage Books, 1970.

Ambrose, Stephen F. *Duty, Honor, Country: A History of West Point.* Baltimore: Johns Hopkins University Press, 1966.

Archer, Jules. *The Plot to Seize the White House.* New York: Hawthorne Books, 1973.

Baker, Leonard. *Brandeis and Frankfurter: A Dual Biography.* New York: Harper and Row, 1984.

Baker, Ray Stannard, and William Dodd, eds. *The Public Papers of Woodrow Wilson,* 6 vols. New York: Harper and Brothers, 1925–1927.

Barnard, Ellsworth. *Wendell Willkie: Fighter for Freedom.* Marquette: Northern Michigan University Press, 1966.

Baruch, Bernard M. *American Industry in the War: A Report of the War Industries Board.* Edited by Richard H. Hippelheuser. New York: Prentice Hall, 1941.

———. *Baruch: The Public Years.* New York: Holt, Rinehart and Winston, 1960.

Beasley, Norman. *Knudsen: A Biography.* New York: Whittlesy House, 1947.

Beaver, Daniel R. *Newton D. Baker and the American War Effort, 1917–1919.* Lincoln: University of Nebraska Press, 1966.

Bellush, Bernard. *The Failure of the NRA.* New York: W. W. Norton and Company, 1975.

Berle, Beatrice Bishop, and Travis Beal Jacob, eds. *Navigating the Rapids, 1918–1971: From the Papers of Adolf A. Berle.* New York: Harcourt Brace Jovanovich, 1973.

Bernstein, Irving. *Turbulent Years: A History of the American Worker, 1933–1941.* Boston: Houghton Mifflin Company, 1970.

Blantz, Thomas E. *A Priest in Public Service: Francis J. Haas and the New Deal.* Notre Dame, Ind.: University of Notre Dame Press, 1982.

Blumenson, Martin, ed. *The Patton Papers, 1885–1940.* Boston: Houghton Mifflin Company, 1972.

Brinkley, Alan. *Voices of Protest: Huey Long, Father Coughlin, and the Great Depression*. New York: Alfred A. Knopf, 1982.

Brody, David. *Steelworkers in America: The Nonunion Era*. Cambridge: Harvard University Press, 1960.

Caro, Robert A. *The Power Broker: Robert Moses and the Fall of New York*. New York: Alfred A. Knopf, 1974.

Charles, Searle F. *Minister of Relief: Harry Hopkins and the Depression*. Syracuse: Syracuse University Press, 1963.

Clarkson, Grosvenor B. *Industrial America in the World War: The Strategy Behind the Line, 1917–1918*. Boston: Houghton Mifflin, 1923.

Coffman, Edward M. *The Hilt of the Sword: The Career of Peyton C. March*. Madison: University of Wisconsin Press, 1966.

————. *The War to End All Wars: The American Military Experience in World War I*. New York: Oxford University Press, 1968.

Coit, Margaret L. *Mister Baruch*. Boston: Houghton Mifflin, 1957.

Conner, Valerie Jean. *The National War Labor Board: Stability, Social Justice, and the Voluntary State in World War I*. Chapel Hill: University of North Carolina Press, 1983.

Cooper, Jerry M. *The Army and Civil Disorder: Federal Military Intervention in Labor Disputes, 1877–1900*. Westport, Conn.: Greenwood Press, 1980.

Creel, George. *Rebel at Large*. New York: G. P. Putnam's Sons, 1947.

Cuff, Robert D. *The War Industries Board: Business-Government Relations during World War I*. Baltimore: Johns Hopkins University Press, 1973.

Dawson, Nelson L. *Louis D. Brandeis, Felix Frankfurter, and the New Deal*. Hamden, Conn.: Archon Books, 1980.

Dickinson, John. *The Building of an Army: A Detailed Account of Legislation, Administration and Opinion in the United States, 1915–1920*. New York: Century Co., 1922.

Dubofsky, Melvyn, and Warren Van Tine. *John L. Lewis: A Biography*. New York: Quadrangle, 1977.

Equality for Agriculture. Moline: H. W. Harrington, 1922.

Feinman, Ronald L. *Twilight of Progressivism: The Western Republican Senators and the New Deal*. Baltimore: Johns Hopkins University Press, 1981.

Field, Carter. *Bernard Baruch: Park Bench Statesman*. New York: McGraw-Hill Book Company, 1944.

Fine, Sidney. *The Automobile under the Blue Eagle: Labor, Management and the Automobile Manufacturing Code*. Ann Arbor: University of Michigan Press, 1963.

Fite, Gilbert C. *George N. Peek and the Fight for Farm Parity*. Norman: University of Oklahoma Press, 1954.

Fleming, Thomas J. *West Point: The Men and Times of the United*

States Military Academy. New York: William Morrow and Company, 1969.

Freidel, Frank. *Franklin D. Roosevelt.* Vol. 3, *The Triumph.* Boston: Little, Brown and Company, 1956.

————. *Franklin D. Roosevelt.* Vol. 4, *Launching the New Deal.* Boston: Little, Brown and Company, 1973.

Galambos, Louis. *Competition and Cooperation: The Emergence of a National Trade Association.* Baltimore: Johns Hopkins University Press, 1966.

Gerber, Larry G. *The Limits of Liberalism: Josephus Daniels, Henry Stimson, Bernard Baruch, Donald Richberg, Felix Frankfurter and the Development of the Modern American Political Economy.* New York: New York University Press, 1983.

Goulden, Joseph C. *Meany.* New York: Atheneum, 1972.

Graham, Otis L. *Toward a Planned Society: From Roosevelt to Nixon.* New York: Oxford University Press, 1976.

Grant, James. *Bernard Baruch: The Adventures of a Wall Street Legend.* New York: Simon and Schuster, 1983.

Hammond, Paul Y. *Organizing for Defense: The American Military Establishment in the Twentieth Century.* Princeton, N.J.: Princeton University Press, 1961.

Hampton, H. Duane. *How the U.S. Cavalry Saved Our National Parks.* Bloomington: Indiana University Press, 1971.

Hawley, Ellis W. *The Great War and the Search for a Modern Order, A History of the American People and Their Institutions, 1917–1933.* New York: St. Martin's Press, 1979.

————. *The New Deal and the Problem of Monopoly: A Study in Economic Ambivalence.* Princeton, N.J.: Princeton University Press, 1966.

Hewes, James E., Jr. *From Root to McNamara: Army Reorganization, 1900–1963.* Washington, D.C.: Center of Military History, 1975.

Himmelberg, Robert F. *The Origins of the National Recovery Administration: Business, Government, and the Trade Association Issue, 1921–1933.* New York: Fordham University Press, 1976.

Holley, I. B., Jr. *General John M. Palmer, Citizen Soldiers, and the Army of a Democracy.* Westport, Conn.: Greenwood Press, 1982.

Huntington, Samuel P. *The Soldier and the State; The Theory and Practice of Civil-Military Relations.* Cambridge: Harvard University Press, 1957.

Huthmacher, J. Joseph. *Senator Robert F. Wagner and the Rise of Urban Liberalism.* New York: Atheneum, 1968.

Ickes, Harold L. *The Secret Diary of Harold L. Ickes.* Vol. 1, *The First Thousand Days, 1933–1936.* New York: Simon and Schuster, 1953.

————. *The Secret Diary of Harold L. Ickes.* Vol. 2, *The Inside Struggle, 1936–1939.* New York: Simon and Schuster, 1954.

James, D. Clayton. *The Years of MacArthur. 1880–1941.* Boston: Houghton Mifflin, 1970.

Johnson, Hugh S. *The Blue Eagle from Egg to Earth.* Garden City, N.Y.: Doubleday, Doran and Company, 1935.

———. *Hell-Bent for War.* Indianapolis: Bobbs-Merrill Company, 1941.

Johnson, James P. *The Politics of Soft Coal: The Bituminous Coal Industry from World War I through the New Deal.* Urbana: University of Illinois Press, 1979.

Jonas, Manfred. *Isolationism in America: 1935–1941.* Ithaca, N.Y.: Cornell University Press, 1966.

Josephson, Matthew. *Infidel in the Temple: A Memoir of the Nineteen-Thirties.* New York: Alfred A. Knopf, 1967.

Kahn, E. J., Jr. *The World of Swope.* New York: Simon and Schuster, 1965.

Kennedy, David M. *Over Here: The First World War and American Society.* New York: Oxford University Press, 1980.

Kreidberg, Marvin, and G. Merton Henry. *History of Military Mobilization in the United States Army, 1775–1945.* Washington, D.C.: Department of the Army, 1955.

Larrowe, Charles P. *Harry Bridges: The Rise and Fall of Radical Labor in the U.S.* New York: Lawrence Hill and Co., 1972.

Lilienthal, David D. *The Journals of David E. Lilienthal.* Vol. 1, *The TVA Years, 1939–1945, Including a Selection of Journal Entries from the 1917–1939 Period.* New York: Harper and Row, 1964.

Lindley, Ernest K. *The Roosevelt Revolution.* New York: Viking Press, 1933.

Lippmann, Walter. *Interpretations, 1933–1935.* New York: Macmillan, 1936.

Livermore, Seward W. *Politics Is Adjourned: Woodrow Wilson and the War Congress, 1916–1918.* Middletown, Conn.: Wesleyan University Press, 1966.

Lockmiller, David A. *Enoch H. Crowder: Soldier, Lawyer and Statesman.* Columbia: University of Missouri Press, 1955.

Lord, Russell. *The Wallaces of Iowa.* Boston: Houghton Mifflin Co., 1947.

Lowett, Richard, and Maurine Beasley, eds. *One Third a Nation: Lorena Hickok Reports on the Great Depression.* Urbana: University of Illinois Press, 1981.

Lyon, Leverett S., et al. *The National Recovery Administration: An Analysis and Appraisal.* Washington, D.C.: Brookings Institution, 1935.

McCoy, Donald R. *Calvin Coolidge: The Quiet President.* New York: Macmillan Company, 1967.

McElvaine, Robert S. *The Great Depression: America, 1929–1941.* New York: Times Books, 1984.

McReynolds, Edward C. *Oklahoma: A History of the Sooner State*. Norman: University of Oklahoma Press, 1964.

March, Peyton C. *The Nation at War*. Garden City, N.Y.: Doubleday, Doran and Co., 1932.

Martin, George. *Madam Secretary: Frances Perkins*. Boston: Houghton Mifflin Company, 1976.

Michelson, Charles. *The Ghost Talks*. New York: G. P. Putnam's Sons, 1944.

Millett, Allan R. *The General: Robert L. Bullard and Officership in the United States Army, 1881–1925*. Westport, Conn.: Greenwood Press, 1975.

Millett, John D. *The Works Progress Administration in New York City*. Chicago: Public Administration Services, 1938.

Moley, Raymond. *After Seven Years*. New York: Harper and Brothers, 1939.

———. *The First New Deal*. New York: Harcourt, Brace and World, 1966.

———. *27 Masters of Politics in a Personal Perspective*. New York: Funk and Wagnalls, 1949.

Murphy, Bruce Allen. *The Brandeis/Frankfurter Connection: The Secret Political Activities of Two Supreme Court Justices*. New York: Oxford University Press, 1982.

Nash, Gerald D. *United States Oil Policy, 1890–1964: Business and Government in Twentieth-Century America*. Pittsburgh: University of Pittsburgh Press, 1968.

Nelson, Otto L., Jr. *National Security and the General Staff*. Washington: Infantry Journal Press, 1946.

Nevins, Allan. *Herbert H. Lehman and His Era*. New York: Charles Scribner's Sons, 1963.

Nevins, Allan, and Frank Ernest Hill. *Ford*. Vol. 3, *Decline and Rebirth, 1933–1962*. New York: Charles Scribner's Sons, 1963.

Nordhauser, Norman E. *The Quest for Stability: Domestic Oil Regulation, 1917–1935*. New York: Garland Publishing, 1979.

Paper, Lewis J. *Brandeis*. Englewood Cliffs, N.J.: Prentice-Hall, 1983.

Parmet, Herbert S., and Marie B. Hecht. *Never Again: A President Runs for a Third Term*. New York: Macmillan, 1968.

Patterson, James T. *Congressional Conservatism and the New Deal: The Growth of the Conservative Coalition in Congress, 1933–1939*. Lexington: University Press of Kentucky, 1967.

Perkins, Frances. *The Roosevelt I Knew*. New York: Viking Press, 1946.

Perkins, Van L. *Crisis in Agriculture: The Agricultural Adjustment Administration and the New Deal*. Berkeley: University of California Press, 1969.

Pilat, Oliver. *Pegler: Angry Man of the Press*. Boston: Beacon Press, 1963.

Pusey, Merlo J. *Charles Evans Hughes.* 2 vols. New York: Macmillan, 1951.

Quin, Mike. *The Big Strike.* New York: International Publishers, 1979.

Richberg, Donald R. *My Hero: The Indiscreet Memoirs of an Eventful but Unheroic Life.* New York: G. P. Putnam's Sons, 1954.

Rollins, Alfred B., Jr. *Roosevelt and Howe.* New York: Alfred A. Knopf, 1962.

Romasco, Albert U. *The Politics of Recovery: Roosevelt's New Deal.* New York: Oxford University Press, 1983.

Roos, Charles Frederick. *NRA Economic Planning.* Bloomington, Ind.: Principia Press, 1937.

Roosevelt and Frankfurter: Their Correspondence, 1928–1945. Annotated by Max Freedman. Boston: Little, Brown and Company, 1967.

Roosevelt, Elliot, ed. *F.D.R., His Personal Letters: 1928–1945.* 2 vols. New York: Duell, Sloan and Pearce, 1950.

Roosevelt, James. *My Parents: A Differing View.* Chicago: Playboy Press, 1976.

Rosen, Eliot A. *Hoover, Roosevelt, and the Brains Trust: From Depression to New Deal.* New York: Columbia University Press, 1977.

Rosenman, Samuel I., ed. *The Public Papers and Addresses of Franklin D. Roosevelt.* 13 vols. New York: Random House, 1938–1950.

Ross, Malcolm. *Death of a Yale Man.* New York: Farrar and Rinehart, 1939.

Saloutos, Theodore. *The American Farmer and the New Deal.* Ames: Iowa State University Press, 1982.

Schlesinger, Arthur M., Jr. *The Age of Roosevelt.* Vol. 2, *The Coming of the New Deal.* Boston: Houghton Mifflin Company, 1958.

———. *The Age of Roosevelt.* Vol. 3, *The Politics of Upheaval.* Boston: Houghton Mifflin Company, 1966.

Schwarz, Jordan A. *The Interregnum of Despair: Hoover, Congress, and the Depression.* Urbana: University of Illinois Press, 1970.

———. *The Speculator: Bernard M. Baruch in Washington, 1917–1965.* Chapel Hill: University of North Carolina Press, 1981.

Shapsmeier, Edward L., and Frederick H. Shapsmeier. *Henry A. Wallace of Iowa: The Agrarian Years, 1910–1940.* Ames: Iowa State University Press, 1968.

Shideler, James H. *Farm Crisis: 1919–1923.* Berkeley: University of California Press, 1957.

Skowronek, Stephen. *Building a New American State: The Expansion of National Administrative Capacities, 1877–1920.* Cambridge: Cambridge University Press, 1982.

Smith, Geoffrey. *To Save a Nation: American Counter-Subversives, the New Deal, and the Coming of World War II.* New York: Basic Books, 1973.

Sparks, C. Nelson. *One Man—Wendell Willkie*. New York: Rayner Publishing Co., 1943.

Sternsher, Bernard. *Rexford Tugwell and the New Deal*. New Brunswick, N.J.: Rutgers University Press, 1964.

Stone, Irving. *Clarence Darrow: For the Defense*. Garden City, N.Y.: Doubleday and Company, 1941.

Sulzberger, C. L. *Sit Down with John L. Lewis*. New York: Random House, 1938.

Sutton, Anthony C. *Wall Street and FDR*. New Rochelle, N.Y.: Arlington House Publishers, 1975.

Swain, Martha A. *Pat Harrison: The New Deal Years*. Jackson: University of Mississippi Press, 1978.

Tierney, Kevin. *Darrow: A Biography*. New York: Thomas Y. Crowell, 1979.

Tuchman, Barbara. *Stilwell and the American Experience in China, 1911–1945*. New York: Macmillan, 1970.

Tugwell, Rexford G. *The Brains Trust*. New York: Viking Press, 1968.

———. *In Search of Roosevelt*. Cambridge: Harvard University Press, 1972.

———. *Roosevelt's Revolution: The First Year—A Personal Perspective*. New York: Macmillan, 1977.

Tull, Charles J. *Father Coughlin and the New Deal*. Syracuse: Syracuse University Press, 1965.

Urofsky, Melin I. *Big Steel and the Wilson Administration: A Study in Business-Government Relations*. Columbus: Ohio State University Press, 1969.

Vadney, Thomas E. *The Wayward Liberal: A Political Biography of Donald Richberg*. Lexington: University Press of Kentucky, 1970.

Wilson, Joan Hoff. *Herbert Hoover: Forgotten Progressive*. Boston: Little, Brown and Company, 1975.

Winters, Donald L. *Henry Cantwell Wallace as Secretary of Agriculture, 1921–1924*. Urbana: University of Illinois Press, 1970.

ARTICLES

Beaver, Daniel R. "George W. Goethals and the Problem of Military Supply." In *Some Pathways in Twentieth-Century History: Essays in Honor of Reginald Charles McGrane*, edited by Daniel R. Beaver. Detroit: Wayne State University Press, 1969.

———. "The Problem of Military Supply, 1890–1920." In *War, Business, and American Society: Historical Perspectives on the Military-Industrial Complex*, edited by Benjamin Franklin Cooling. Port Washington, N.Y.: Kennikat Press, 1977.

"Bernard Mannes Baruch." *Fortune*, October 1933, pp. 32–39, 103.

Blanchard, Margaret A. "Freedom of the Press and the Newspaper Code: June 1933–February 1934." *Journalism Quarterly* 54 (Spring 1977): 40–49.

"The Blessing of a Soldier." *Commonweal*, October 12, 1934, pp. 543–44.

Boardman, Fon W., Jr. "Political Name Calling." *American Speech* 15 (December 1940): 353–56.

Brand, Donald R. "Corporatism, the NRA, and the Oil Industry." *Political Science Quarterly* 98 (Spring 1983): 99–118.

Chambers, John Whiteclay III. "Conscripting for Collossus: The Progressive Era and the Origins of the Modern Military Draft in the United States in World War I." In *The Military in America: From the Colonial Era to the Present*, edited by Peter Karsten. New York: Free Press, 1980.

Chapman, B. B. "The Land Rush of 1893, As Seen at Kiowa." *Kansas Historical Quarterly* 31 (Spring 1963): 67–75.

"Columnist to Columnist." *Time*, September 28, 1936, pp. 56–58.

"Crack Down on the General!" *New Republic*, August 1, 1934, pp. 304–5.

Crawford, William H. "He Risked Disgrace to Speed the Draft." *New York Times Magazine*, June 9, 1918, pp. 4–6.

Cuff, Robert D. "Bernard Baruch: Symbol and Myth in Industrial Mobilization." *Business History Review* 43 (Summer 1969): 115–33.

"Demagogues." *Newsweek*, March 16, 1935, p. 6.

Fite, Gilbert C. "The Farmers' Dilemma, 1919–1929." In *Change and Continuity in Twentieth-Century America: The 1920s*, edited by John Braeman, Robert H. Bremner, and David Brody. Columbus: Ohio State University Press, 1968.

Flynn, John T. "Other People's Money." *New Republic*, September 12, 1934, pp. 129–30, and April 3, 1935, p. 212.

"The General Is Retired." *Time*, May 12, 1941, pp. 14.

"General Johnson: Strikebreaker." *Nation*, July 4, 1934, p. 4.

Hanson, Elisha. "Official Propaganda and the New Deal." *Annals of the American Academy of Political and Social Science* 179 (May 1935): 176–86.

Hawley, Ellis W. "Hugh Samuel Johnson." In *Encyclopedia of American Biography*, edited by John A. Garraty. New York: Harper and Row, 1974.

"Headache Man." *Time*, October 4, 1937, p. 32.

Heineman, Robert L. "Blue Eagle or Black Buzzard? The National Recovery Administration in Virginia." *Virginia Magazine of History and Biography* 89 (January 1981): 90–100.

Himmelberg, Robert F. "Business, Antitrust Policy, and the Industrial Board of the Department of Commerce, 1919." *Business History Review* 42 (Spring 1968): 1–23.

"Hugh Johnson: NRA Chief after Year's Gigantic Labor." *Newsweek*, June 23, 1934, p. 15.

"Hugh Samuel Johnson." *Assembly*, April 1943, pp. 10–12.

"Hugh Samuel Johnson." *Current Biography, 1940* (New York: H. W. Wilson Co., 1941).

"Johnson Hangs Shingle." *Business Week*, October 20, 1934, p. 1.

Johnson, Hugh S. "Anchors Away." *Saturday Evening Post*, October 15, 1940, pp. 14–15, 75.

———. "Could Hitler Invade America?" *Reader's Digest*, December 1939, pp. 34–36.

———. "Fallacies of 'The Universal Draft.'" *Army Ordnance* 10 (November–December 1929): 155–57.

———. "How Caldwell 'Made Good.'" *Appleton's Magazine*, December 1906, pp. 693–99.

———. "I Am Not Nominating Him!" *Saturday Evening Post*, June 22, 1940, pp. 9, 112–16.

———. "Is Britain Fighting Our War?" In *We Testify*, edited by Nancy Schoonmaker and Doris F. Reid. New York: Smith and Durrell, 1941.

———. "The Lamb Rampant." *Everybody's Magazine*, March 1908, pp. 291–301.

———. "Lascar." *Scribner's Magazine*, August 1907, pp. 173–83.

———. "The Mission of the Service Magazines." *Cavalry Journal* 19 (October 1908): 301–8.

———. "Pied Pipers." *Vital Speeches*, March 11, 1935, pp. 354–60.

———. "The Third New Deal." *Vital Speeches*, July 1, 1937, pp. 564–67.

Johnson, James P. "Drafting the NRA Code of Fair Competition for the Bituminous Coal Industry." *Journal of American History* 53 (December 1966): 521–41.

Josephson, Matthew. "The General." *New Yorker*, August 18, 1934, pp. 21–25, August 25, 1934, pp. 18, 23–28, and September 1, 1934, pp. 22–28.

Koeniger, Cash. "Carter Glass and the National Recovery Administration." *South Atlantic Quarterly* 74 (Summer 1975): 349–64.

Koistinen, Paul A. C. "The 'Industrial-Military Complex' in Historical Perspective: The Interwar Years." *Journal of American History* 56 (March 1970): 814–39.

———. "The 'Industrial-Military Complex' in Historical Perspective: World War I." *Business History Review* 41 (Winter 1967): 378–403.

Lear, Linda J. "Harold L. Ickes and the Oil Crisis of the First Hundred Days." *Mid-America* 63 (January 1981): 3–17.

Leuchtenberg, William E. "The New Deal and the Analogue of War." In *Change and Continuity in Twentieth-Century America*, edited by John Braeman, Robert H. Bremner, and Everett Walters. Columbus: Ohio State University Press, 1964.

Mangold, William P. "On the Labor Front." *New Republic*, September 5, 1934, pp. 103–14.

"Man of the Year." *Time*, January 1, 1934, pp. 8–9.

Mason, Lowell B. "Darrow vs. Johnson." *North American Review*, December 1934, pp. 524–32.

Milan, Joe B. "Opening of the Cherokee Outlet." *Chronicles of Oklahoma* 9 (September and December 1931): 268–86, 454–75, and 10 (March 1932): 115–37.

Mitchell, Jonathan. "The Versatility of General Johnson." *Harper's Magazine*, October 1934, pp. 585–96.

"Mixed Doubles." *Time*, September 10, 1934, p. 6.

"Moving Day for Columnists." *Time*, March 17, 1941, pp. 38–39.

Nash, Gerald D. "Experiments in Industrial Mobilization: WIB and NRA." *Mid-America* 45 (July 1963): 157–74.

"NRA: New Reorganization Starts as President Roosevelt Confers, Richberg Smiles, Johnson Grumbles, and Public Waits." *Newsweek*, September 1, 1934, pp. 3–4.

"NRA: With Code Phase Over, New Deal Shake Up Aims at Compliance, Cooperation, and Permanence." *Business Week*, August 25, 1934, p. 34.

Ohl, John Kennedy. "General Hugh S. Johnson and the War Industries Board." *Military Review* 55 (May 1975): 35–48.

———. "Hugh S. Johnson and the Draft, 1917–1918." *Prologue: The Journal of the National Archives* 8 (Summer 1976): 85–96.

———. "The Navy, the War Industries Board, and the Industrial Mobilization for War, 1917–1918." *Military Affairs* 40 (February 1976): 17–22.

———. "Tales Told By a New Dealer—General Hugh S. Johnson." *Montana: The Magazine of Western History* 25 (Autumn 1975): 66–77.

Pearson, Drew, and Robert S. Allen. "How the President Works." *Harper's Magazine*, June 1936, pp. 1–14.

"Personnel." *Time*, May 17, 1937, p. 88.

Reeves, William D. "PWA and Competitive Administration in the New Deal." *Journal of American History* 60 (September 1973): 363–72.

Robbins, William G. "The Great Experiment in Industrial Self-Government: The Lumber Industry and the National Recovery Administration." *Journal of Forest History* 25 (July 1981): 128–43.

Skocpol, Theda, and Kenneth Finegold. "State Capacity and Economic Intervention in the Early New Deal." *Political Science Quarterly* 97 (Summer 1982): 255–78.

"Union under Johnson." *Time*, July 2, 1934, p. 8.

DISSERTATIONS AND THESES

Blumberg, Barbara Marilyn. "The Works Progress Administration in New York City: A Case Study of the New Deal in Action." Ph.D. diss., Columbia University, 1974.

Hodges, James A. "The New Deal Labor Policy and the Southern Cotton Textile Industry, 1933–1941." Ph.D. diss., Vanderbilt University, 1963.

Mabon, David W. "The West Coast Waterfront and Sympathy Strikes of 1934." Ph.D. diss., University of California, Berkeley, 1966.

Moody, Jesse Carroll, Jr. "The Steel Industry and the National Recovery Administration: An Experiment in Industrial Self-Government." Ph.D. diss., University of Oklahoma, 1965.

Ohl, John Kennedy. "'Old Iron Pants': The Wartime Career of General Hugh S. Johnson, 1917–1918." Ph.D. diss., University of Cincinnati, 1971.

Sniegoski, Stephen J. "The National Recovery Review Board." M.A. thesis, University of Maryland, 1972.

Wolvin, Andrew Davis. "The 1933 Blue Eagle Campaign: A Study in Persuasion and Coercion." Ph.D. diss., Purdue University, 1968.

INDEX